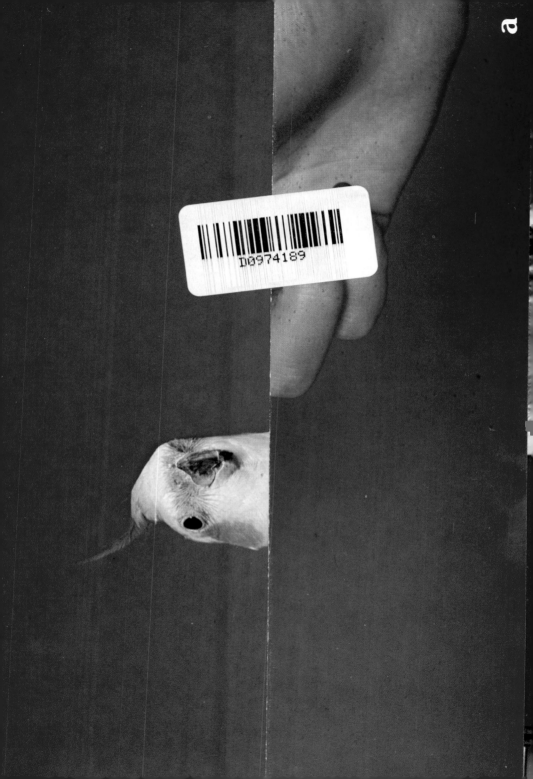

Cockatiels

W. A. Starika

Cover photographs: Normal male Cockatiel by Ralph Kaehler (front); Pied Cockatiels, courtesy of Vogelpark Walsrode (back).

Distributed in the UNITED STATES by T.F.H. Publications, Inc., 211 West Sylvania Avenue, Neptune City, NJ 07753; in CANADA by H & L Pet Supplies Inc., 27 Kingston Crescent, Kitchener, Ontario N2B 2T6; Rolf C. Hagen Ltd., 3225 Sartelon Street, Montreal 382 Quebec; in ENGLAND by T.F.H. Publications Limited, 4 Kier Park, Ascot, Berkshire SL5 7DS; in AUSTRALIA AND THE SOUTH PACIFIC by T.F.H. (Australia) Pty. Ltd., Box 149, Brookvale 2100 N.S.W., Australia; in NEW ZEALAND by Ross Haines & Son, Ltd., 18 Monmouth Street, Grey Lynn, Auckland 2 New Zealand; in SINGAPORE AND MALAYSIA by MPH Distributors (S) Pte., Ltd., 601 Sims Drive, # 03/07/21, Singapore 1438; in the PHILIPPINES by Bio-Research, 5 Lippay Street, San Lorenzo Village, Makati Rizal; in SOUTH AFRICA by Multipet Pty. Ltd., 30 Turners Avenue, Durban 4001. Published by T.F.H. Publications Inc., Ltd. the British Crown Colony of Hong Kong.

Contents

Posters: a—Finger-tame Normal male (photo by Vincent Serbin). **b**—Doors hinged at the bottom provide a landing platform (photo by Vincent Serbin). **c**—Nestlings, a little more than a week old (photo by Ralph Kaehler). **d**—Pearl Pied, Lutino, and Pied Cockatiels (photo by Louise Van der Meid). **e**—Young Cockatiels (photo by Louise Van der Meid). **f**—A companion in the home (photo by Nancy Richmond).

Illustrations: Herbert R. Axelrod, 59. Michael Gilroy, 24. Eliot Goldfinger, 20. H. Reinhard, courtesy of Vogelpark Walsrode, 17. Nancy Richmond, 18, 19, 22, 23, 57, 58, 62, 63. Vincent Serbin, 64. Louise Van der Meid, 60. R. A. Vowles, title page, 4, 13, 31, 36, 47, 67, 80.

With its long tail, the Cockatiel qualifies as a parakeet.

Cockatiel Characteristics

The Cockatiel is only one of the more than 8600 species of living birds listed in the current world check-lists. It belongs, though, to one of the most distinctive groups of birds, the parrots (order Psittaciformes, some 340 species). The birds belonging to this order are characterized by a feature everyone is familiar with: "a beak like a parrot." While other orders of birds also have bills (beaks) that could also be called hooked, the shape is not the same; it has happened that *hookbill* refers only to the species of the order Psittaciformes, the order of psittacine birds (from the Latin word *psittacus,* "a parrot"). The second main characteristic of all parrot species has to do with their feet: two toes point forward and two back, which is unlike most bird species, in which three are forward and one back. Again, however, this zygodactyl foot is not unique to psittacines; it is also found in woodpeckers and cuckoos, for example. But the combination of these two characteristics designates a parrot.

Within the order of parrots there are various groups. The macaws are perhaps the most visible parrots in the public eye, and not only because of the large size and bright colors of some macaw species. Amazon parrots are another group that is well known, probably because of the talking ability that is a specialty of this group. Through history the most famous parrot has been the Grey Parrot, especially because of its reputation as a talker.

At last we have come to a parrot that has the word *parrot* as part of its English name. Scientifically, it should be said, Scarlet Macaws and Blue-fronted Amazons, to name two species, are just as much parrots as the Grey Parrot, though the word is not part of the species's name.

If one had to pick the parrot that most people have been close to, in whatever sense, the choice would be easy: the most widely kept pet parrot of all is the Budgerigar. "He means the parakeet," you may be thinking. True enough, in many senses the Budgerigar is *the* parakeet, but in another sense, it is only one of many parrot species that qualify as parakeets. To qualify as a parakeet, a parrot species should have a comparatively long tail, as the Budgerigar does. Species with comparatively short tails are called parrots, as the Grey Parrot is. Tail length, then, is the characteristic according to which parrots might be called parrots or parakeets. The lovebirds, a popular parrot group

Cockatiel Characteristics

not mentioned so far, are appropriately described as small parrots.

Another group of psittacines, which may be called parrots on the basis of tail length, that have lately come more into the public eye (perhaps because of television) are the cockatoos. This group of some 28 species is certainly not remarkable because of their stubby tails, but have instead conspicuous feather crests as their most remarkable feature. These feather headdresses can be raised and lowered most expressively, the way dogs and cats use their tails.

Just as the parrots are one of the most distinctive groups of birds, among the psittacine species the Cockatiel is one of the most distinctive. In no other parrot species are the erectile crest and the long tail combined. On this basis, as well as other characteristics, most ornithologists place the Cockatiel in a group of its own. This is to say that just as there are many species of cockatoos or of macaws, differing from one another is size and coloration (the most usual differences), there might have been several species of cockatiels—but in the course of evolution that has not happened; there is only one species of cockatiel: the Cockatiel.

But many people are uncomfortable with a group containing only one member. It doesn't seem to be enough of a group; so the obvious question is, To which other parrots is the Cockatiel most closely related? Two possibilities have seemed the most obvious: the cockatoos and the broad-tailed parakeets, of which the rosella species are probably the best known. This is not the place to summarize the characteristics that were evaluated to decide the Cockatiel's affinities. Besides the obvious external features of crest and tail length, other anatomical characters and behavioral patterns have been compared, so that most recent researchers are prepared to conclude that the Cockatiel's closest relatives are the cockatoos.

That this relationship was noted long ago is evidenced by the name Cockatiel itself: it comes from a Portugese word meaning "little cockatoo."

It's a happy fact that throughout the English-speaking world the Cockatiel is coming to be known by a single name. Even the Australian check-lists now call this parrot species Cockatiel, instead of Quarrion. However, the Australian man-in-the-street is still likely to call the bird a Quarrion. Its scientific

Cockatiel Characteristics

name is *Nymphicus hollandicus,* "nymph of New Holland" (New Holland being an eighteenth-century name for Australia).

The Wild Cockatiel

In Austrialia today the Cockatiel is one of the most common wild parrot species. Though its range covers almost the entirety of the continent, flocks of Cockatiels—typically numbering about twenty—are found only in those locales that offer suitable food. These are grassy habitats, for Cockatiels are comparatively specialized feeders, relying principally on small grass seeds. Cockatiels have been observed feeding on fruits and nectar, as some other parrot species do, but adaptive evolution has made the Cockatiel a somewhat atypical parrot in that it feeds mostly on the ground. Observers have noted that Cockatiels are unable to hang on the grasses, as their neighbors the grass-finches do. Instead they walk along, picking seeds that have fallen to the ground. This food supply is controlled by the vagaries of weather. As in most semiarid regions, brief periods of localized rainfall are followed by longer periods of drought. Cockatiels thus are adapted to life in a harsh environment and survive on a restricted diet, in comparison to other parrot species. Perhaps this explains why captive Cockatiels often do surprisingly well in the spartan conditions in which they are sometimes kept.

In their native environment, Cockatiels are compelled to travel great distances for food. Like the human beings who must live off the land in such environments, Cockatiels must be nomadic. This results in a continuous genetic mixing, as flocks come into contact and merge for a time, and breed perhaps, then disintegrate again, as small parties break away as food becomes depleted. Hence the Cockatiel is a monotypic species; no nomadic group is isolated from another long enough for differences to arise. There are no subspecies of the Cockatiel.

Because the rainfall is so irregular, Cockatiels must be prepared to breed whenever the opportunity—sufficient food— presents itself. Study of their behavior indicates that the coming of the rain itself tells them that it is time, that there will *be* time, to breed.

Other field observations have

Cockatiel Characteristics

revealed interesting aspects of social life in the Cockatiel flock. The tightly knit flocks in which all the birds move in unison testify to the gregariousness of Cockatiels. After feeding, the flock will fly to a tree to rest and preen. Instead of spacing themselves out among the branches, they prefer, as often as possible, all to perch on a single branch. This often results in a good deal of squabbling, for Cockatiels like to be near one another, but not touching. Unlike some other parrot and some estrildid species, they do not "clump." With Cockatiels, preening one another is the principal form of social contact—in the physical sense (copulation aside).

In the course of obtaining these observations, it became evident that Cockatiels are quite shy when feeding on the ground and drinking, flying off at the slightest provocation. Perched in trees, however, they permit much closer approach and give an impression of tameness.

Tameness

The business of taming a Cockatiel becomes easier if you have some understanding of why it is that any animal becomes as tame as it does. This is to say that different animal species exhibit different degrees of tameness. To call the dog, rather than the cat, man's best friend is, among other things, an indication of the differences in tameness between these two animals. Similarly, just as we are able to recognize differences in tameness between dogs and cats—different mammal species—so do we notice varying degrees of tameness among avian species. You may have had some personal experience of this in wild birds. Many of us have seen American Crows, but few of us have had a close look. This crow knows to avoid people, since many people that have tried to get close to crows have done so in order to kill them. In contrast, few bird species have as as great a reputation for being confiding as the Black-capped Chickadee. At bird feeders, especially in winter, these Chickadees quickly become tame to the extent that they fly to one's open palm to take the bits of peanut offered. Probably this is the reason why the Black-capped Chickadee has been rated America's favorite bird. Many of these wild (in one sense) individuals are very nearly free-living pets.

These examples should make it clear that different species of

Cockatiel Characteristics

birds—and different individuals within species—react differently to the approach of people. Usually, birds let us move closer and closer and—then they fly away. The distance to which birds allow people to approach is more or less characteristic of a species; it is known as *fleeing distance.*

The behavior of the Black-capped Chickadee just described illustrates what is central in the mind of most people when they talk about a tame bird: that it is *hand-tame.* This is the kind of tameness that most pet owners hope for in their Cockatiel companion. On the other hand, the crow shows that bird species can quickly learn to recognize their enemies. There is every reason to suppose that the fleeing distance of this species was much less when white men first appeared on its continent.

The American Crow is the only bird species native to the United States that federal laws allow to be taken and kept as pets, without special permits—the law regards them as pests. But if you've ever had the acquaintance of a pet crow, you may have decided, as many crow keepers have, that it "doesn't make a very good pet." It may be that the first people who had the opportunity of keeping a Cockatiel made a similar assessment of that species. Is this somehow relevant to the fact that while Cockatiels have been held in captivity for a century and a half, they have become truly popular only recently?

Domestication

As a result of the ever-increasing popularity of Cockatiels among bird fanciers, the species is rapidly becoming domesticated. To provide a working definition of domestication, many researchers will call a species domesticated if it has been bred in captivity to the extent that different breeds have been developed. A moment's thought about cows, chickens, and dogs will provide enough illustrations of this. But notice that breeds are viewed as being different principally in body shape (physique), not in coloration. In the context of this definition of domestication, then, the fact that several color varieties of the Cockatiel now exist merely indicates that it is *becoming* domesticated. Of the bird species kept as pets, the Canary is the best example of a species that can be called domesticated in accordance with the definition above. The Norwich, the Border, the Gibber Italicus—all

Cockatiel Characteristics

illustrate the varying conformations among Canary breeds. At present, all captive-bred Cockatiels have much the same shape; however, selective breeding to show standards is producing larger birds, and we can expect that before long, differences in size and shape among Cockatiels will allow them to be classed as Budgies are now: exhibition Budgerigars and pet-quality Budgerigars. As you ponder this discussion of domestication, note that in the opinion of many people, pet-quality Budgerigars do indeed make better pets.

Of course, domestication also can simply mean that because animals are born in captivity, they are familiar with people. The importance of this to pet potential cannot be underestimated. If you do want to have a pet crow, it's best to try to obtain a nestling before its eyes are open and hand-rear it. Such a crow will never have seen another crow.

All the Cockatiels available in the United States and Europe today have been bred in captivity. In 1960, Australia prohibited the export of its native birds. Thus it will probably soon be true that all the Cockatiels alive outside Australia (except for a few smuggled-out birds) will be captive-bred. How

many wild-caught Cockatiels can there be still alive, enjoying their golden years?

That Cockatiels are captive-bred may no doubt partly explain why Cockatiels have the reputation of being easy to tame. Moreover, captive-bred Cockatiels that are also hand-reared become tame in the course of growing up. Like the hand-reared crow nestling, these Cockatiels become the tamest Cockatiels. What remains to be considered is why hand-reared Cockatiels and hand-reared crows turn out to be such different pets, why one makes a "better" pet than the other.

Cockatiels as Fliers

The first point that will be proposed is this: people find Cockatiels to be good pets because of those characteristics that distinguish them, and other parrot species as well, from other groups of birds. You'll recall that these are the beak and the feet. Like most other birds, parrots fly, of course, but it appears that no other birds climb as much as parrots. Focusing on feeding behavior, the activity most important to every animal, one can observe that crows fly from place to

Cockatiel Characteristics

place to feed, as do parrots or chickadees, for that matter. But at a feeding location, the crow, a ground feeder, will walk around until the food is exhausted. The chickadee typically feeds in trees: it flies around in the canopy of a tree, taking food here and there as it spots it. As a group, parrots too are mainly arboreal birds. Amazons and macaws, for example, fly from tree to tree to feed. But once in a tree, they search for food by climbing in the branches, not by flying from branch to branch. Amazons and macaws don't behave this way simply because of their size; even the smallest parrots—some of which are about the same size as a chickadee—feed by climbing about.

For climbing, parrots in effect have three prehensile feet: the third "foot" is the bill. If a parrot cannot step from one perch to another, its next choice is to grab hold with its bill and, if the perch proves stable, it brings first one foot, then the other, along.

This is a good time to deal briefly with the question of whether parrots like to fly. Answering this question no doubt demands a breadth of experience no one has. Suffice it to say that finch keepers are often impressed with the what seems to be the sheer exuberance of the little birds as they zip back and forth the length of the flight—what reason can they have for behaving this way? Budgerigars are pretty small as parrots go—do they impress their keepers similarly? You can pursue this line of thought yourself when you have the opportunity of observing the larger parrot species kept in flights in the zoos and bird parks.

To ask whether parrots like to fly is not the same as asking whether they need to fly. At least one eminent veterinarian whose chief life-long concern has been the care of pet birds is prepared to conclude that this need is not as great as one might imagine. No doubt he would shade his opinion if asked about this large psittacine species or that small one, but in the main, he feels, parrots are content to stay in their cages or on their stands or playgrounds and don't hanker after the skies. You'll recall that wild Cockatiels fly great distances in search of food. If this is an accurate formulation of what is actually happening, it's evident that Cockatiels fly out of necessity, not because they have, say, a need for exercise.

It's remarkable that the flight muscles of caged birds that never have the opportunity to fly

Cockatiel Characteristics

stay in condition so well. Maybe parrots instinctively know how to do isometrics. True enough, parrot keepers have noticed birds moved from a cage to a flight fly poorly at first and then gradually improve. In comparison, it's doubtful that a passerine bird given a comparable change of enclosure would at first fly as well as parrots do. One suspects that those who have had a long-time caged parrot accidently escape while outdoors will have some information to contribute to this topic.

Escaped parrots are once again "free as a bird." Is it not possible that the vaunted freedom of the birds is something that exists only in the minds of earth-bound, terrestrial mankind, something that testifies to the gulf between one class of animals and another? What of ours, one wonders, might the birds envy?

Cockatiels as Pets

To summarize the discussion thus far, parrots can be described as climbers that happen to fly. To pursue this line of reasoning, the chickadees may be said to be fliers that happen to hop, and crows fliers that happen to walk. Like crows,

Cockatiels feed principally on the ground; there are few field reports of them feeding in trees. While on the ground, they walk. In contrast, like the chickadee, on the ground the Canary hops. It's worth reflecting on these differences among bird species, for the insight they offer into the appeal of parrots as pets. Think about the experiences you've had with pet passerine birds. The passerines are the perching birds; Canaries and finches are the best known passerine pets. If a Canary isn't flying, it's usually perched somewhere. If it has to, it will hop to feed, but just as often it will fly. Flying, perching, and hopping constitute the entire repertoire of movement of a Canary. If you have a tame Canary, it may fly to you, perch on your finger, and hop along your arm. If it wants to get on your head, it will fly there. Compare this with the behavior of a pet Budgie. The Budgie too may fly to your hand, but once it's arrived, it's likely to proceed to walk and climb all over you. Budgies climb to their owners' shoulders, nibble at their ears, investigate jewelry, and may even venture to inspect pockets. Enough said—in behavior, a pet Budgie is clearly more amusing than a pet Canary. Isn't it the climbing that

Cockatiel Characteristics

makes the difference? Perhaps we find it easier to relate to psittacine birds more than to other birds because they move as we do (let's forget about chickens just now). To adduce another analogy, the most conspicuous climbing mammals are the primates—visitors to zoos spend more time before their cages, enjoying the acrobatics, than before those of other animals.

Such suggestions as these amount to mere attempts to analyze why, of all birds, parrots have proved to be the best companions for people. And for those persons who have the most need of companionship, psittacine birds rank high among the possible animal companions.

Cockatiels as Companions

We have been considering why Cockatiels make good pets. The reasons given point up the anatomical characteristics of psittacine birds. Anatomy, of course, also delimits some of behavior. But there are aspects of parrot behavior that appear unrelated to anatomy; to these we turn now to make a second proposition about parrots as pets: Cockatiels, and other parrots as well, make good companions because of an innate disposition, an

instinct, if you will.

It's not surprising that people interested in studying animals scientifically soon turned their attention to economic animals; after all, these creatures were readily at hand. Time spent observing rabbits in pens yielded more data than the same number of hours in the field did. This approach was used by Charles Darwin himself; indeed, the interesting questions raised by observing animals in captivity somewhat diverted his attention from species in the wild, resulting in a major treatise on domestication.

A hand-tame Cockatiel is a congenial companion.

13

Cockatiel Characteristics

Konrad Lorenz founded the study of animal behavior as a separate discipline (ethology). As he had always had a dog, it was natural for him to think about dogs as companions to people. In *Man Meets Dog*, Lorenz explains how wild canids live in packs and have a complex social organization. The ability wild dogs have to form social relationships with their conspecifics has persisted under domestication. Summarily put, a pet dog has a relationship with it owner that is like a relationship it would have to another dog in the pack.

Animal lovers who are attracted to furry animals very probably like at least some dog breeds. You may be such a person and, upon seeing a squirrel, may have thought that it might be fun to have a squirrel for a pet. If this thought has in fact crossed your mind, there's no need to say more about the fuzzy tail, the cuteness, and so forth. But if, as a prospective squirrel fancier, you sought out a book like this one, you might be surprised to find that it would discourage you from trying to keep a squirrel. "Impractical pets" they've been called. As it turns out, it's the relationships that prevail among squirrels that make them poor pets. Except during the relatively brief breeding periods (once or twice a year in some populations), adult gray squirrels are solitary, each living apart from the other. If you've noticed a group of squirrels inhabiting a hollow tree, this was a family group of a female and her still immature young. In short, once a squirrel is mature, it wants contact with another animal only to breed. A young squirrel, though, makes a sweet pet while it is young. It's a sad day when the hormones start to flow, and the squirrel's temperament changes.

At the risk of oversimplifying matters, let it be said that the social behavior of Cockatiels is more like that of dogs than of squirrels. Indeed, as a group, psittacine birds exhibit strong social needs. Most species exhibit life-long pair bonding. Naturally, they segrate in pairs in order to breed. Outside the breeding season, these psittacines form flocks, large in some species, small in others. The smallest flocks appear to be family groups, but even in large flocks the members of a pair tend to keep close by one another—while roosting, notably.

Thus Cockatiels and other parrots are disposed to have life-long companions. In the absence of a conspecific, a Cockatiel will attempt to form a bond with another creature. This chapter opened by

Cockatiel Characteristics

promising some understanding of why an animal species becomes tame to the extent that it does. This is not the place even to attempt to essay the origins of the Cockatiel's social relationships. But if your curiosity has been piqued, by all means look into the extensive ornithological literature on avian social behavior.

One purpose of our discussion has been to encourage the understanding that Cockatiels have pet potential for reasons other than the fact that people find them beautiful, or appealing, or amusing. You can choose which of the following formulations best sums up the situation: Cockatiels become good companions for people because they're impelled to—they need to—they want to.

One hopes too that the foregoing comments provide a perspective in which you will undertake the care of any Cockatiel you acquire and that you will be encouraged to form a bond of companionship with it.

You are probably aware that such a bond may not come to pass easily. To the extent that it may be true that all children are angels at birth, so one too might suppose that all Cockatiels have equal pet potential when they hatch. Unfortunately, there is a good deal of evidence to the contrary. To make another analogy between human beings and Cockatiels: just as we recognize other people as individuals, so do Cockatiels see their conspecifics as different from one another. This should be most evident to those of you who have bred birds; the fundamental rule to follow if you wish your birds to breed is this: Let them choose their mates. You don't need much experience with bird breeding to discover that some pairs you try to put together simply "don't like" one another. The breeder, of course, can't see any reason why this should be so, any more than a mother sometimes is unable to understand why her daughter prefers to marry a boyfriend other than the totally suitable candidate she has in mind. Since one Cockatiel is able to dislike another, isn't it possible that a Cockatiel may also be capable of disliking a person who purchases it, intending that it should become a pet?

If a parrot doesn't tame readily, it's labeled as a problem bird; if it persists in resisting the efforts to make it a tame bird, it's called a bronco. On what basis does a human being expect that another creature should become his companion?

Cockatiel Characteristics

As you know, there are other animal species more closely related to human beings than Cockatiels are. It seems to be the case that our ability to detect individual differences in other species diminishes the more distantly related they are to us. However, this phenomenon occurs even with our closer animal relatives. Until one has some acquaintance with a troop of chimpanzees for a period of time, differences in individuality (i.e., temperament or personality, if you will) are not apparent. For some bird keepers, therefore, discerning individual differences among the individuals of a species (apart from obvious marks) is one of the things that keeps the hobby interesting. From such observations it becomes clear that, as with people, some Cockatiels, say, stand out as individuals more than others. Not every bird of a species has "personality."

All the evidence indicates that the members of an animal species are all individuals, even though some species exhibit a greater capacity, generally, for individuality than others. This must be emphasized in an age of mass production. So far as things that can be bought go, the various pieces of a product are wonderfully uniform. Quality control has meant that one size-9 pair of shoes of a given design is almost indistinguishable from another. In a bygone age, when things were made by hand, the buyer would be inclined to scrutinize each available size-9 pair carefully. But today, we are in the habit of purchasing uniform items. When purchasing live animals, we must try to put aside this habit. Pet-shop personnel all have a collection of funny stories about people who walked in off the street and asked for, say a blue Budgie, without even looking at one, as though blue Budgies were no different from red jellybeans.

Photographs, pages 17—24: 17—Adult Normal male Cockatiel; the presence or absence of gray in the facial mask is the most obvious difference between Normal adult males and females. 18—The effect of the Pearl factor is evident on the wing coverts; the patch of white on the rump suggests the presence of Pied as well. 19—Normal male, showing the white wing patches; in this instance the wing trim involved shortening the primary feathers of both wings. 20—Hand-tame Lutino Cockatiel; in this specimen there is comparatively little yellow suffusion on the body. 22—Cockatiels for sale in a pet shop: Normals, Pieds, Pearls, and Lutinos (the other two birds are a Canary-winged Parakeet and a Red-crested Cardinal). 23—Pied Cockatiel with quite symmetrical markings. 24—Lutino Cockatiel; traces of barring can be seen on the tail feathers.

16

22

Selecting a Cockatiel

Once you decide that you want to own a Cockatiel, take your time about making a purchase. Pet Cockatiels often live ten to fifteen years; a few with very sturdy constitutions (or is superior care the cause?) live as long as twenty-five years. Nowadays many couples stay married for a shorter length of time; by analogy, perhaps you'll agree that a Cockatiel should not be purchased on impulse.

Taking your time should involve the following: Try to make your selection from a group of Cockatiels. If you're not an experienced purchaser, the range of differences in Cockatiels will be more apparent if you are able to look at a number of individuals in close proximity. Some time spent in the close study of a group will allow you to form some impressions about Cockatiels; these can be kept in mind, should you come upon only one Cockatiel for sale in some other location. If, after you're satisfied that you've looked enough Cockatiels over, you find one that seems ideal, don't go right ahead and buy it. Instead, look it over carefully, and then express your interest in the bird to the seller. Ask any questions you have in mind, including the price. At this juncture, the novice Cockatiel purchaser is well advised to ask if the seller will reserve the bird for a couple of days. It's wise to want to have a second look.

The purpose of this strategy, once again, is best illuminated by a human analogy: The two visits you make to look at a Cockatiel you're interested in may be thought of as your first and second dates. Everybody knows that on the second date any faults will begin to show.

Cockatiels and You

So far we haven't considered what you've been looking for. Depending on your own personality, you may be attracted to the more extroverted Cockatiels you see. If you're the quiet sort, perhaps a vivacious male will allow you some vicarious experience of what you don't yourself possess. Yet another quiet person might find a male Cockatiel too lively and vocal to be good company and so would prefer a calmer female instead. This is not say that all male Cockatiels are lively; certainly the activity shown by some young females would shame some of the males.

There's no reason not to look for the inklings of a relationship when you begin your shopping. The

Selecting a Cockatiel

Cockatiel that flees as far as possible as you approach probably should be given one more chance, but that's all. But perhaps another bird in the same enclosure will retire a little and then stand its ground and look you in the eye. The meaning of this body language should be obvious—what if another human being did the same? Such birds are called steady and are said to be good candidates for taming.

It's no doubt true that some Cockatiels are naturally more timid than others; this is simply a facet of individuality. Those who regularly hand-rear nestlings can detect differences in temperament already at this stage; in the brood there are likely to be one or two bold ones. But, as with all other organisms, life experience makes a difference with Cockatiels too. On one hand, close contact with people in the course of hand-rearing produces tameness; on the other, if the only close contact with humans a Cockatiel experiences is of another kind, the results can be very different. Now all Cockatiels are captive-bred, but if they are reared by their natural parents, it's entirely possible that the experience of some has been limited to seeing a keeper pass by daily—or even less frequently—to replenish food and water, and to

being caught up any number of times in the course of what may be a journey of many stages from the breeding enclosure to the cage in which you finally see it.

In this scenario, the only contact with people the Cockatiel has had that can be called close is being handled. This may be the reason why, in the course of taming a Cockatiel, people find that no sooner will a Cockatiel step up onto a finger but that it wants to scurry up the arm onto the shoulder. Since the bird is probably familiar with dowel perches, isn't a finger a similar thing? Why doesn't the bird want to linger there? The answer, it seems, is that a Cockatiel is likely more afraid of hands than it is of any other part, or even the whole, of a person. This is somewhat surprising, since we usually suppose birds fear us mostly because we are larger.

Need it be said that if you want a Cockatiel to be a pet, you should make every effort not to frighten it? As you know, if you move quickly, so will a bird—away, usually. Shy or frightened Cockatiels are therefore best approached with calm, slow movements. If a stranger rushes right up to a cage of birds, these birds will likely panic, and it will take some time for them to settle

Selecting a Cockatiel

down to normal again.

It's been said of dog and cat owners that they resemble their pets; so far, though, nothing similar seems to have been said of bird people. But you may have heard the phrase *bird sense*. Like a green thumb, it seems that some people have a feathered finger, while others do not. Seriously, though, when a bird keeper shows his birds to visitors—strangers to the birds—he quickly notices that some visitors frighten the birds inexplicably, while others do not. The phenomenon occurs with all the birds in his collection: the steady individuals just retire a distance and become watchful, while nervous birds flap or fly about so alarmingly that the keeper tugs the stranger away by the sleeve.

If, for you, keeping a Cockatiel is at this point still only an appealing idea, take some time to find out how birds react to you. Notice how they respond to you, as compared to other people. You may conclude that you are not suited to being a Cockatiel lover.

There is a grand lady of my acquaintance who acknowledges that her long life has been rich because it was dominated by a love for birds. Yet she has come to recognize—with sadness, one feels—that the birds

she has taken care of for so long prefer the company of a neighbor to hers.

In all this, however, one should distinguish between being a bird lover, having bird sense (which means having the knack for taking care of birds), and being a person who is liked by birds.

Signs of Health

One aspect of bird sense that most bird people seem to develop, and are not born with, is the ability to detect the onset of illness in a bird. This ability is developed by observing birds closely. Birds are adept at hiding their illnesses, so that very often when the sickness becomes evident, it is too late for treatment. All too frequently this characteristic of birds makes buying them a chancy business. To counter some of the risk the neophyte especially takes, it's appropriate to consider how to tell sick birds from well ones, in so far as this is possible.

Animals of the class Aves have a high metabolic rate. In the hand, a Zebra Finch is as warm as a freshly baked dinner roll. With the onset of illness, metabolism slows, and a bird has difficulty maintaining its body

Selecting a Cockatiel

temperature. To counteract this, it fluffs its feathers in order to keep warm. In contrast, during those periods when a healthy bird is active, the feathers are held sleeked against the body; the wings feathers lie outside the contour feathers, ready to move. As most birds are most active in the early morning, that is the best time to observe this. If, instead, the morning sunshine shows a bird still sleeping, wings and head hidden in among the fluffed body feathers, it's time to start worrying. This is not to say that perfectly healthy birds don't sometimes nap in the middle of the day. Not only birds native to southerly latitudes take siestas, one finds. When the heat of the day comes, bird watchers give up and go home or wait around until late afternoon, for they know that most of the birds around will be perched and resting, if not sleeping, during this period. Similarly, if you decide to visit pet shops during your early-afternoon lunch hour, you can expect that the birds will mostly be languid.

When some birds sleep, you'll notice, one foot is drawn up into the contour feathers. What is happening here? Is this a good sign or a bad sign? Mostly, it's a good sign. Since birds, if they're not flying, are on their feet, it's reasonable to suppose that now and then their feet need a rest. Some birds settle onto their perches so that the breastbone touches; this probably serves to rest the feet. Perching on just one foot and raising the other has the same purpose. Most bird keepers are glad to see their birds perched on one foot, because the ability to maintain balance while doing so is a sign of health. In contrast, sick birds often are weak enough that they are unable to balance on one foot; instead, they perch on both feet, which are wider apart than normal. However, there is still another reason why a bird may perch on a single foot: because the other foot has been injured. Because one-foot perching is ordinarily such a good sign, bird keepers sometimes fail to notice a sore foot, because the bird holds it out of sight.

Another point to take note of is the bird's respiration. The breathing of healthy birds is not very apparent. But difficult, labored, obvious breathing is a sign of respiratory illness.

The above are all signs of health or illness that can be noticed by merely looking at a Cockatiel. Another indicator of a bird's health is the condition of its plumage. The healthy bird will hold its feathers

Selecting a Cockatiel

close, as you know. But the feathers should also have a bright sheen. On birds in poorer condition, the plumage will be dull looking.

What about tattered feathers? Remember that feathers are replaced in the course of molting. With the next molt, broken tail feathers will grow in anew. If a Cockatiel you like otherwise shows feather damage, try to figure out for yourself what the cause was; then ask the seller why the bird looks as it does, and see if his explanation jibes with yours. Confinement during transport is a frequent cause of ragged wing and tail feathers. But patches in the body feathers may be a sign of illness.

Physical Examination

After you've looked your favored candidate over on more than one occasion, the next step is to ask the seller to catch-up the Cockatiel so that you and he can take a really close look at it. This is the time to spread the feathers and give the bird as thorough a physical examination as possible. The seller will no doubt be holding the bird, but you might as well start to get some hands-on experience right now. Feel for yourself to find out whether the breast is well fleshed (you can prepare yourself for this beforehand by pausing to look carefully at the poultry counter in the market sometime when you're there). The Cockatiel should be well-muscled; if it's not, it's best to proceed no further.

There should be no lumps among the feathers nor should there be any sores or signs of blood. Eyes should be bright and clear, with no evidence of tears on the surrounding feathers. See that the nostrils are open and that there's no sign of discharge. The vent should not be "pasted," that is, there should be no evidence of droppings adhering to the surrounding feathers. A healthy bird's evacuation is similar to a person's expectoration. Finally, check to see that the Cockatiel has all its toes and claws. In a pet Cockatiel, a missing toe means little; if the bird is to be a breeder, it's another story.

Throughout your examination of the Cockatiel, notice too how the Cockatiel is reacting to all this. Some Cockatiels will struggle violently, and their eyes may reveal fright. Others will show themselves to be steady, though uncomfortable. As you watch the seller handle the Cockatiel, you should be able to come to some conclusions as to how

Selecting a Cockatiel

tame the bird is already and whether you may have problems handling and taming the bird further yourself. If you feel you'd like to see just how tame the Cockatiel is, this is the time to ask the seller to demonstrate this. Now, some sellers will be adept at handling birds, while others will not—remember to take this into consideration. If the Cockatiel seems relatively tame and you'd like to try handling it yourself, don't be afraid to ask if you may do so.

What is left at this point is for you to make a decision. If you are confident about the Cockatiel you've just looked at, go ahead and buy it. But it's perfectly all right to say that you want to wait and think about it some more. Maybe the seller will be willing to set the Cockatiel aside until tomorrow. If this proves to be the case, when the Cockatiel is returned to its cage, notice how long it takes for its excitement to abate. How quickly does its respiration return to normal? Does the bird seem exhausted from the ordeal?

This extra day can turn out to be a great convenience. It will allow you time to set up your Cockatiel's cage and get the furnishings in place. It's prudent to have everything ready before you bring your Cockatiel home. Try to minimize the amount of time the Cockatiel must spend in transit. Most bird keepers, by the way, would suggest transporting a single Cockatiel in a cardboard carton just large enough for the bird. The darkness calms the bird, and the small space prevents it from damaging its plumage or injuring itself, should it become frightened. Transporting a bird in its cage offers none of these advantages.

Acclimation

When you arrive home with your new Cockatiel, acclimation should be your primary concern. *Acclimation* is a bird keeper's term; in practice it entails minimizing the stress birds will experience in being moved from place to place. Temperature is often one of the most significant factors involved in acclimation. In a relatively short period of time, a Grey Parrot captured in tropical Africa can find itself in a home in Maine. Certainly this represents a radical change of environment. The change in diet is also sometimes treated as a aspect of acclimation. Our parrot may have had the experience of perhaps five different diets by the time it is settled in Maine. The transition

Selecting a Cockatiel

from the wild state to captivity presents even greater acclimation problems in the case of other, more delicate or specialized bird species.

Since the Cockatiel you acquire will have been bred in captivity, its acclimation amounts only to taking a few precautions. Since birds in general are sensitive to temperature changes, notice the temperature at which the Cockatiel you've acquired has been kept.

If you are a resident of Maine, and you're reading this with the thought in mind that you may buy yourself a Cockatiel for Christmas, it may happen that there will be quite a difference between the temperature setting on the thermostat in the pet shop in the mall and the setting in your energy-conscious abode. It would be prudent to raise the temperature in your home to that of the pet shop for the first couple of days, and then gradually lower it. In acclimation, the rule is that everything is done *gradually.*

To prevent your new Cockatiel from becoming upset by a sudden change in diet, be sure to find out what it has been eating. Obtain a supply of the seed mix—if that's what it's been fed—and continue to feed it to your Cockatiel until you have good reason to do otherwise.

In this context, saving a few pennies is not a good reason.

Which Sex?

You are now on your way home with your Cockatiel—but what kind of Cockatiel have you chosen? Is it a male or a female? Is it a youngster or an adult? What color is it? Let's take the first question first.

If you have bought a Cockatiel for breeding, those considerations would have decided its sex. If you have acquired a Cockatiel that you hope

With proper accommodations, Cockatiels overwinter outdoors.

31

Selecting a Cockatiel

to keep singly as a pet, then its sex has to be decided on other bases. As mentioned previously, in general male Cockatiels are bolder than females. This can be a rule-of-thumb if you have specific ideas about what temperament you would like your Cockatiel companion to have. If companionability itself is the quality sought, then hens have the edge. Both males and females can become equally tame, one would have to say, but hens are likely to be more continuously affectionate.

If you hope that your Cockatiel will be a talker, then you will want to obtain a male. Males are more vocal than hens in their own language, so it follows that they will also be more inclined to mimic words. Of course, there are talking hens too and, as Cockatiels go, some hens develop quite extensive vocabularies. But the consensus of experienced opinion is still that you have the best chance of ending with a good talker if you acquire a male.

Age

There's an old saying, You can't teach an old dog new tricks. Sad, but these words do contain some truth. If you intend to teach your Cockatiel tricks, be sure to obtain a young bird. The same goes for talking. It is more difficult (though not impossible) for an adult human to learn a new language than it is for a child. Similarly, as a Cockatiel grows older, it appears to be less able to learn new words.

What about taming? The ease with which hand-rearing produces tame Cockatiels has already been mentioned. But the adaptability that the young possess lessens as time passes. Older, untamed Cockatiels have been tamed, of course, but those who have succeeded in doing so freely admit that the increased age of the bird made taming much more difficult and time consuming. It's probably true to say that older Cockatiels will never become as tame as those tamed while still young.

And tameness is closely allied with the companionship bond. You're aware by this time that Cockatiels are able to form such bonds with their owners. But the stage in Cockatiels' lives at which they are prepared to form bonds has not been talked about. Pair bonding occurs between Cockatiels at the time of sexual maturity, which occurs before they are a year old. From this datum, one may suppose that the search for a mate begins as early as around six months of age.

Selecting a Cockatiel

The implications for choosing a pet are clear: one should look for a Cockatiel less than six months old. One widely respected authority on taming and training parrots recommends that the Cockatiel be between ten and sixteen weeks of age.

Where does this leave the older, untamed Cockatiel we spoke of a bit ago? Since we have no case history before us, it's useless to speculate. Suffice it to say that among wild Cockatiels, if one of the pair is lost to predation or illness, the surviving member is likely to find a new mate. This happens as well in breeders' aviaries. A true account may illustrate what else may occur: The owner of an Orange-fronted Conure—let's call him Walt—one day "fell in love" with a young female Cockatiel he saw in a pet shop. By afternoon, Sweetie Pie was in her own cage across the room from Ton Ton, the conure. Time passed, and eventually the conure's noise became too much for Walt to bear. During this time, it seems fair to say—Walt being a busy, working person—there really hadn't been enough time for him to get either of the birds to be as tame as he might have liked. A new home was found for Ton Ton, and a male Cockatiel was brought in to be a mate for Sweetie Pie. They got along well enough, and once or twice Sweetie Pie surprised everyone by laying an egg on the floor of the cage, pretty much without warning. Buster was a lively fellow, who showed off to company by whistling the tune he had learned. He too was pretty tame, so it was a sad day when he fell ill and shortly died. He was only a few years old. Walt right away obtained a new young male and named him Jumper. Sweetie Pie, perhaps with the calm that comes with age, tolerated Jumper, but it was clear that she didn't find him very interesting. Yet, to the eyes of visitors and to Walt as well, Jumper was a dead-ringer for Buster in almost every way. One evening, reflecting on the several year's pleasure he'd by now had with Jumper and Sweetie Pie, Walt observed, "You know, she had a crush on the conure. She liked Buster too, but she really liked Ton Ton best."

The Responsible Pet Owner

This story also illustrates some of the avenues open to the Cockatiel owner when pet keeping runs into difficulties. That Walt acquired a mate for Sweetie Pie when he

Selecting a Cockatiel

realized that he wasn't able to devote to her the time that she needed is probably the most humane, responsible thing he could have done. The result, you'll notice, benefited all parties concerned. Apparently, Sweetie Pie was happy enough with Buster, and she doesn't really mind Jumper. And through the years Walt had had as much enjoyment from his Cockatiels as any pet owner has a right to. You prospective pet owners must understand that when you take delivery of your Cockatiel, you become *responsible* for the well-being of a living creature. Even a jailer is responsible for keeping his prisoners alive—this is no more than simple humanity.

Color Varieties

Sweetie Pie, Buster, and Jumper were all wild-color Cockatiels, but Walt could have chosen a differently colored Cockatiel. There's no need to write out detailed descriptions of these varieties, for they're adequately illustrated in the photographs in this book.

By a look through the photographs you can see that all of them are variations of the coloring found in the wild Cockatiel. In the wild, Cockatiels normally exhibit a particular coloration (although it is somewhat different between males and females). If the wild situation of the Cockatiel is taken as the norm, then it is totally appropriate to designate the wild-color birds as Normal. The Normal Cockatiel is predominantly gray, but white, yellow, and orange are also present. This is the full complement of colors that any Cockatiel can possess, to the best of our knowledge. Any possible variation can only redistribute the colors or take them away—leaving only white. We cannot expect that colors not present in the Normal Cockatiel will ever occur. There are only three pigments present in a Normal Cockatiel; a black, an orange, and a yellow. The white areas appear so because of an absence of pigment.

All the color varieties of Cockatiels have occured among birds in captivity and are the result of an inbreeding that has little likelihood of taking place among wild Cockatiels.

Color variations such as Cockatiels exhibit are spoken of as being the result of genetic mutations. As has happened in other bird species, the first mutation to appear was the Pied. The Pied (piebald) factor alters the disposition of the black pigment, so that the areas gray on a Normal Cockatiel are broken up by white. The orange and yellow markings are not predictably affected, though an increase in the extent of yellow often occurs. In this variety, then, one could say that the gray is pied by white. It is a characteristic of the Pied variety in all bird species that individuals of the variety exhibit considerable variation among themselves. Some are "heavily pied" by white, so that the gray areas are almost "clear" white. Almost-gray Pieds appeal to some people because they seem to represent the most complete expression of the mutation. At the other extreme, it's possible to find Pied males that have only a patch of white on the head to give away the fact that they are Pieds. To most eyes, however, a Pied Cockatiel is most attractive when the markings are symmetrical. On the show bench, a symmetrical Pied will receive a high score on that account.

That the Pied mutation occurred in 1949 in California, though Cockatiels have been bred in captivity since the nineteenth century, was probably the result of an increased interest in Cockatiel breeding in the United States. As one might expect, it appears (though the exact dates are lacking) that Cockatiels were first bred in their homeland, Australia. Outside Australia, Cockatiel breeding got underway around 1850. The occurrence of mutations is ultimately a matter of statistics: the more captive stock is inbred, the greater the likelihood that a new variety will crop up.

The second mutation to appear, the Cinnamon, occurred in New Zealand in 1950, time-wise hard on the heels of the first. However, it appears unlikely that the New Zealand Cinnamons are the ancestors of the Cinnamons extant today in the United States and Europe. So far as the history has been recorded, these Cinnamons derive from a separate appearance of the factor in Belgium in the late 1960s. At present, Cinnamons are not common, perhaps because they are not sufficiently unusual in appearance. Cinnamons are marked like Normals, and again it is the black pigment which is affected: the gray areas become a delicate light brown.

This mutation is another that can be expected; the same thing has happened to the melanin pigments (black) in Canaries, Zebra Finches, Budgerigars, and lovebirds, to name the most obvious examples. After

Selecting a Cockatiel

a moment's thought, you may object and say, "But Pied is a matter of markings, while Cinnamon is a matter of color—all that has happened is that the gray has been changed to a brown." True enough; you are right. For a color variety in which the markings—that is, the areas covered by a color—vary and the intensity of the color itself varies, consider the Lutino.

The Lutino factor in Cockatiels is interesting in that the extent of

---

In life history as well as in coloration, the Cockatiel and the Zebra Finch have many points in common.

yellow varies, as does the shade. Like the Pied Cockatiels, then, Lutino Cockatiels exhibit considerable variation in appearance. The situation is different with both Budgerigars and Peach-faced Lovebirds. In both of these species, the result of the Lutino factor is very uniform; in both species the Lutino variety is a bright yellow.

In a Lutino Cockatiel, the black pigment is completely absent, so there is no gray. What remains are the orange and yellow pigments. The orange is much the same from Lutino to Lutino, but since the intensity and extent of yellow varies, Lutinos range from birds that are almost entirely an off-white to those that are a butter yellow. The white Lutinos look different enough that they are often called "Albinos." The word *albino*, though, is reserved for a variety that would show a complete absence of all pigments. To call the whiter Cockatiels "Albinos" violates a well-established definition. The name of the variety is Lutino; if the Lutino you're talking about happens to be one of the whitish ones, to call it a "white Lutino" would be appropriate. Lutinos, which first occurred in Florida in 1958, were initially called "Moonbeam Cockatiels." Maybe it's sad that the more prosaic name

Selecting a Cockatiel

Lutino (though it's more self-explanatory to fanciers conversant with the jargon of color breeding) has come to supplant the much more poetic "Moonbeam." Which, one wonders, does more justice to the beauty of these birds?

The color variety that emerged in Germany almost ten years later is the one that seems to elicit the most expressions of pleasure when first seen. This variety is the Pearl. In effect, the Pearl factor is similar to the Pied in that it affects the disposition of the melanin pigment. As the feathers which are normally completely gray grow out, melanin deposition is interrupted, so that the fully grown feather has a band of white.

The best word to describe the overall visual effect is probably *scalloping*. If you look at the wings of a Pearl Cockatiel, you'll notice a resemblance to the pattern on the wings of a Budgerigar. In the Budgerigar, the scallops have been called *undulations* (thus one of the obsolete names of the Budgerigar is "Undulated Grass Parakeet").

The Pearl Cockatiel is similar to the Pied in another way: the extent of yellow is variable. As a result, some Pearl Cockatiels are yellow enough on the back to remind one of Opaline Budgerigars. That the lovely pearl markings of this variety belong to the hens must be noted. Pearl Cockatiel females retain their markings for life, but males are pearled only until the first molt, from which they emerge looking like Normals. All young Cockatiels start off looking like hens, so it's perfectly consistent that young Pearl cocks have pearl markings until they molt.

About the same time as the Pearl appeared, the 1960s, so did the Silver. Again the black melanin is affected, turned this time to a silvery gray. Since pigment is also reduced in the eye, the Silver factor is comparable to both the Lutino and the Cinnamon. In other bird species, a lightening of plumage melanins is talked about as *dilution*, so the Silver Cockatiel may be thought of as a dilute version of the Normal.

Another dilute variety appeared about a decade later; this is the Fallow. Fallow resembles Cinnamon in that black (gray) becomes brownish; generally, Fallows have a lighter brown shade than Cinnamons. As in the Silver, eye color is reddish. Unlike the Cinnamon, however, the extent of yellow is variable among Fallows.

If the last couple of color varieties have not sounded very interesting to

Selecting a Cockatiel

you, you are not alone. Both the Fallow and the Silver seem to have created little interest. As mutations go, both are difficult to develop because the effects of the operative genetic factors are subtle, and they are all too easy for even the most careful Cockatiel breeder to lose. That mutations have appeared and then have been lost has happened time and again in the course of color breeding in various bird species.

The most recent Cockatiel variety to appear, however, has caused every Cockatiel fancier to sit up and take notice. In this variety, named the White-faced, all the yellow and orange (carotenoid) pigments are absent (in Budgerigars this effect is responsible for the Blue series). These Cockatiels are simply gray and white. In its operation the White-faced factor can be compared to the Lutino: both result in the absence of one or the other of the two pigment classes. The Lutino inhibits the deposition of carotenoids, and the White-faced does the same to the melanin.

The establishment of the White-faced variety opens the way to a Cockatiel variety that hitherto has not existed, though the use of its name would lead one to believe it did—namely, the Albino. By collocating the Lutino factor and the White-faced factor, an Albino Cockatiel will result. The Albino, then, will be a *collocative* variety.

All the factors enumerated in this discussion are generally thought to be discrete from one another in their operation. (Some of them certainly are, and while others may not be so in fact, thus far it has proved expedient to treat them as though they were.) The best practical evidence that genetic factors are discrete comes from putting them together and producing an animal that exhibits the operation of both equally. The Albino Cockatiel does just that. The collocation of factors most commonly exploited by breeders involves Pied and some other suitable factor. If you consider each of the factors available to the Cockatiel breeder, it becomes clear that the collocative varieties most worth attempting are Pearl Pied and Cinnamon Pied. Of these two, only Pearl Pieds are often seen; Cinnamons are still too uncommon to be used to produce the Cinnamon and Pied collocation.

Of all the varieties mentioned, the prospective purchaser will find that only some are readily available. These are—besides the Normal, of course—Pieds, Lutinos, Pearls, and, less often, Pearl Pieds. The remaining varieties are still mainly birds for the serious breeder, if only because the prices they command immediately make one serious.

It almost goes without saying that all the varieties generally available are likely to be reliable breeders—they wouldn't be available otherwise. All the varieties receive equally high marks for pet potential. Variations in coloration have no bearing on how good a pet a Cockatiel will be.

Cockatiel Development

Although the management of breeding Cockatiels is outside the scope of this book, an outline of Cockatiel development is nevertheless pertinent. For a bird species that is comparatively long-lived, the Cockatiel matures quickly; no doubt this is best understood as an adaptation to its native environment, and wild characteristics persist under domestication, of course. We can suppose that in the wild the length of the courtship period may be quite variable; the same can be true in captivity, but observations suggest that one can expect three to four weeks of courtship before eggs are

laid. The clutch may consist of four to six eggs, produced at two-day intervals usually. Both the male and female participate in incubation, which may begin after the second egg. Correspondingly, the chicks hatch in the order in which the eggs were laid. Of course, various factors may cause alterations in any part of this timetable. For example, the incubation period for a Cockatiel egg is said to be eighteen days; this is essentially an average, and some chicks may hatch a day earlier or a day or two later.

The nestlings have closed eyes, are covered with yellow down, and are helpless. By about ten days of age, their eyes will be open, and feather shafts will be emerging from the skin. It takes about five weeks from hatching for the chicks to grow to the point that they are able to leave the nest. After fledging, the chicks continue to depend on their parents for food, for about three weeks. In sum, then, the breeding cycle from egg laying to independent young will take about eleven weeks.

At hatching the bill of a Cockatiel chick is a light color; it will darken at about three months of age (in those color varieties in which melanin deposition is affected, this may not occur). The molt from

Selecting a Cockatiel

juvenile to adult plumage also begins about this time. In Cockatiels this molt is protracted and takes several months; typically it is complete by ten months of age. Sexual maturity, the ultimate indicator of adulthood (in birds, at least), is attained shortly thereafter.

Distinguishing the Sexes

Since very likely you have a preference for a male Cockatiel instead of a female, or vice versa, the following gives the visual guidelines, both reliable and unreliable, for distinguishing the sexes.

Normal: Adults are different from one another (sexually dimorphic). Give a photo of a Normal adult pair a close look, and you will have no trouble telling the sexes apart. Young of both sexes resemble adult hens. Young males may have relatively brighter coloration on the face, compared to young hens.

Pearl: Young of both sexes resemble adult hens. Young males may have relatively brighter coloration on the face, compared to young hens. Adult males look like adult Normal males.

Pied, Cinnamon, Silver, Fallow, White-faced: The dimorphism of adults is like that of Normals, within the constraints of the coloration of the variety in question. Youngsters are alike.

Lutino: Adult hens have a dark yellowish spot on the underside of each of the flight feathers of the wings; these spots are absent from adult males. Youngsters are alike.

As you see, appearance offers little help if you are interested in knowing the sex of a young Cockatiel. Happily, sounds promise to be more reliable. Young males often give themselves away by their vocalizations. The larger the group you have to choose from, the greater the likelihood that the noisiest youngsters in the crowd will be the males. Of course, this may take a little time, but it's time well spent. Pick out a singer or two one day, then come back another day and wait around to see if the same birds are singing, making the characteristic Cockatiel whistling noises. In applying this test, note that silence doesn't give the same odds that a bird is a female; it could be a silent male.

c

Taming and Talking

This focus on young Cockatiels, as you know, has to do with the fact that youngsters have the greatest potential for taming, training, and forming a companionship bond. It's a simple truth that whether a Cockatiel becomes tame or not depends as much, if not more, on the trainer as the Cockatiel. Taming a Cockatiel should be seen as comparable to cultivating a friendship with another person. It's not an undertaking like baking chocolate-chip cookies. The Chinese have a saying, There's more than one way to boil rice. This can be applied to taming parrots. At the moment that Cockatiel and trainer meet for the first time, both carry the burdens of their previous experiences. The Cockatiel might be a bird that has already had several owners; the trainer might be the occupant of the "new home" to which such Cockatiels go. More often, the situation is brighter than this. But since every situation has its peculiarities and contingencies, in these few pages we must limit ourselves to a consideration of a few of the maxims of taming and training.

Since taming is the basis for a bond between the tamer and the Cockatiel, it is best if the pet owner does the taming himself. However, since it's true that once a Cockatiel is tame to one person, it extends its confidence to other people to a greater or lesser degree, employing a professional trainer, if that becomes necessary, is not to be rejected.

The Importance of Observation

Since confidence arises from familiarity, it follows that the tamer should spend as much time as possible with the Cockatiel. This doesn't mean that one must spend the entire day sitting beside the cage. Instead, during the first days, frequent short visits to the Cockatiel are in order. Just how frequent and how short the visits should be may depend on any number of factors; thus the maxim that should rule such questions is this: *Observe the Cockatiel.* For example, as soon as you notice that your presence makes it nervous, move away. Try to develop bird sense. Don't ask yourself how *you* would feel if *you* had just been transported into a new situation and were surrounded by strange animals; ask yourself instead, based on what you know about birds in general and Cockatiels in particular, how *a*

Taming and Talking

Cockatiel would feel if *it* had been transported, and so forth.

Cockatiels probably do have feelings, if by that one refers to those visceral impulsions that occur in humans and that science tells us originate in body chemistry. Observation of your Cockatiel will show you that it has moods. You may have already noted some of them while you were deciding that this was the Cockatiel you wanted to acquire. Perhaps people are able to exert more control over their moods than Cockatiels are; let's suppose so. Based on your assessment of your Cockatiel's mood at the moment, decide whether the time is ripe for a taming or a training session—or maybe this is the moment to simply offer a favorite food by hand and then go away. If the Cockatiel ignores your gift, don't be discouraged. Remember, you are the manipulator. You are in a position to be the protagonist of the friendship.

Intelligence

As friendship is a matter of the heart, intelligence is a matter of the mind. If the ability to learn is the criterion of intelligence, there's no gainsaying that Cockatiels are intelligent animals. Now, many an intelligent person has wished that he could somehow target his learning toward things he really needs to know; that doing so will become increasingly difficult seems to be the trend of human evolution. But a species's evolution need not take our course of ever-increasing adaptability; instead many bird species have developed toward specialization to the extent that, if they are placed in situations too foreign, they are mostly unable to learn to deal with them. Phrased differently, many are specialized to exploit only particular situations in their environment. The Gang-gang Cockatoo is very difficult to maintain in captivity because it is such a specialized feeder, for example. And it's difficult to breed some toucan species because their social behavior cannot be accommodated easily in enclosures. In the light of such comparisons as these, and in comparison to other bird species generally, Cockatiels have proved themselves to be quite adaptable to the circumstances of captivity and are therefore easy to take care of.

We know that people and animals learn less readily as they grow older, and those things which have been

42

Taming and Talking

learned and which experience has shown to be worth knowing become incorporated into habitual behaviors. However, it may be that the time of ease of learning is shorter in birds, relative to the whole length of life, than it is in humans and other animals. Those of you who hope to increase your understanding of what the world is like through the eyes of a bird will want to reflect further on this. Some of you, no doubt, will already have had the terms *imprinting* (from ethology) and *sensitive period* (from child psychology) come to mind.

Thus, to turn from theory to practice, you will probably discover if you keep Cockatiels that they are mostly slow to accept new foods. In comparison, omnivorous birds, like the crows we've spoken about, are quick to sample anything, if only once. Bird breeders, if asked, would probably agree that parrots can be slow to form pair bonds too. Likely they would soon introduce the matter of age into this discussion. Canary breeders, on the other hand, find that when cocks and hens are in breeding condition, it quickly becomes clear whether they going to "nick" or not. Canaries pair only for the breeding period, and often their romance does not last until the chicks are reared. But in respect to feeding habits, Canaries may be even more conservative than Cockatiels. Does it seem unreasonable that a monogamous bird species, like the Cockatiel, should be slow to form social bonds, is conservative in this respect? Thus the counsel that should apply here is: *Be persistent!*

Talking

If this maxim applies to taming and training, it applies doubly to talking. If parrot owners are at fault in their birds' failure to learn to talk, lack of persistence almost always is the cause, not the teaching method used. Akin to persistence is repetition: the first step in speech training is to persist in teaching only one short word by repeating it over and over again. Your Cockatiel would of course prefer not a person but another Cockatiel to talk to. Lacking that, if there is another bird in the house, it will likely end up talking to that one, and *like* it— unless the other bird mimics words! So, if a Cockatiel would be a second bird for any of you, please take note. Cockatiel vocalizations are mostly short, so you have no basis for expecting this species to say anything more than short phrases.

Taming and Talking

Males are all too adept at whistling, many people feel, so you may not want to encourage this by whistling antiphonally with your bird. Because a Cockatiel's voice is pitched high, it may imitate a woman's voice more quickly than a man's; a child may be the best teacher of all.

Most professional bird trainers employ food rewards in training, using the principles of behavioral psychology. In simplistic terms, this amounts to making a response (any movement you might make is considered a response) only to those behaviors you want the bird to continue. But if your Cockatiel behaves improperly, do nothing, or go away. Offering rewards will add impact to your responses. According to this strategy, for example, if your Cockatiel persists in making too much noise, shouting to it to quiet down is counter-productive in that you have made a response, which serves to reinforce the behavior.

It should be mentioned that Cockatiels can on occasion be quite loud, but this usually lasts for only a short while. Compared to Budgies and lovebirds, Cockatiels spend much less of the day vocalizing, at whatever volume. Most of the time they're silent.

The bird-behavior problem that behavioral psychology addresses best is biting. A parrot's most characteristic feature is often a curse to his keeper. The bill, powerful in relation to any parrot species's size, is employed primarily to obtain food often difficult to extract. Just as a parrot tests an unfamiliar nut to see if it contains something good to eat, so too will it test a perch with its beak to see whether it will support its weight. If you offer a parrot a finger, it may decide to test it too. While some tame parrots will, in the course of rough play, bite hard enough to cause pain or even injury, most parrot bites are delivered from fear. A Cockatiel's beak can easily break the skin, but that's about all. Even lesser bites are unpleasantly painful, however, especially if the site is the cuticle of one of your fingers.

If your Cockatiel bites you, try to make no response. Very likely, shouting "No!" will only frighten the bird further. Striking the bird is totally useless; there's no basis for supposing that a Cockatiel can come to understand that a blow is intended to show it that you're the boss. What other meaning could one intend the blow to convey? But, does one indeed want to be the boss?

Accommodations

You've heard that a man's home is his castle. Whether or not you're the boss in your home, your Cockatiel would like to be in its. This aspect of animal behavior is usually discussed in terms of the concept of territoriality, but this seems an unnecessarily technical way to point up the simple fact that your pet Cockatiel will come to regard its cage as its home. Some people believe that the old saw originally went, Home is where the heart*h* is.

The hearth means warmth, comfort, and, most importantly, food. Many pets let out of their cages return voluntarily when they're hungry. Feeding your Cockatiel only in its cage is a good way to foster this behavior. It's also possible that the Cockatiel finds its cage the most comfortable place in the room; some rooms are remarkably devoid of places for a bird to perch. Even though the cage in which you've installed your Cockatiel may be brand new, it's still familiar inasmuch as it very much resembles the other enclosures in which the Cockatiel has been kept. For an untame bird, a cage offers security. Even though those treacherous hands may enter now and then, they mostly keep away.

Pointing out that your Cockatiel's new cage is very like other places in which it's been housed implies that Cockatiel cages should all have similar characteristics. It would be difficult to specify a cage design that would be suitable only for Cockatiels but no other bird species; very likely it would be just fine for some other parrots as well. Accommodations for parrots are principally affected by a single behavior trait that characterizes all psittacines: all are chewers to a greater or lesser extent. The power of the hooked bill is useful to the birds in two main areas: feeding and breeding. Some foods that are accessible to no other birds will yield to a parrot's beak, and they employ their beaks to hollow out cavities for nesting.

As parrots go, Cockatiels are not notorious chewers, as are some of the conure or cockatoo species. Still, they do exhibit a need to chew. Apart from the business of hulling seeds, the bird keeper is likely to notice the effects of this activity first on the perches. From what's just been said, it should be no surprise that the nest box will be chewed and, perhaps, even chewable parts of the cage as well.

Because Cockatiels do chew, they are generally kept in all-wire cages. These may be the usual bird cages

Accommodations

with wire "bars" or cages constructed out of wire mesh of whatever size. The other major kind of bird cage is the box cage, which has wire on the front only; the top, bottom, sides, and back are solid. The solid portion is usually made of wood. Though Cockatiels are not usually kept in box cages, there's no reason that they shouldn't be. It's hard to imagine a situation so extreme that a Cockatiel would begin to chew on the smooth wood interior.

In selecting a cage for a singly kept pet Cockatiel, the most important point is that it not be too small. Any cage in which the Cockatiel can't move around without always brushing its feathers against the wires is too small. A rule of thumb says that a bird cage should be large enough for the bird to extend and flap its wings freely (some confined parrots will exercise by holding onto a perch and flapping their wings furiously). As a pet is expected to have some time outside the cage, a flight cage, one in which a Cockatiel could actually fly from perch to perch, is unnecessary.

Larger cages are always better, as they allow greater freedom of movement. If it should happen that your pet doesn't get to have the time outside its cage that it—or you—would like, the fact that the cage is larger will somewhat compensate for this. It may happen that in time you will want to get your Cockatiel a mate; with a larger cage already, you won't need to get another. In brief, a cage twenty inches square by about twenty-six inches high would be a good choice.

Cockatiels have bred in cages large enough to accommodate the pair of birds, with the nest box attached outside the cage. This is the arrangement probably used by most breeders of Cockatiels. Of course, these birds are also bred in flights, both in separated pairs and in colonies.

Among the many cages suitable for Cockatiels that are available in shops there is considerable variation in design. These variations are not so important in the perspective that all these cages will serve the purpose of confining a Cockatiel. Instead design should be assessed in terms of convenience, perhaps more for the Cockatiel keeper than the Cockatiel. For example, a flat wire roof is a place where another perch can be installed, making it possible for the Cockatiel to climb out and up its cage and perch on top. If the cage is large enough, this area can serve as a playground.

Accommodations

Doors should be large, particularly large enough to take the Cockatiel in and out easily and permit the necessary chores to be done easily. (Don't worry that a large door will make it easy for your Cockatiel to escape; remember, the most untame Cockatiel will regard the cage as its refuge. The difficulty you'll have will be getting it out.)

That most bird keepers prefer cages that have trays that slide out and can be removed is reflected in the design of most commercially available cages. This facilitates removing droppings and bits of food that might otherwise spoil. Having a tray makes it easy to do this daily. A deep tray offers more versatility than a shallow one. In older cage designs, the tray slid into the base of the cage, which was permanently attached to the wire part. An attractive feature of more modern cages is that the wire part can be detached from the pan (base). The pan, quite deep, is fitted with a tray. A cage of this design is much easier to clean, and it's also simple to store and transport, because the wire typically comes apart and can be folded flat.

Most bird cages for sale come with a couple of food cups that fit somewhere into the cage. Sometimes they are very serviceable, sometimes

not. As they're so various, it's difficult to say much about them. The saving factor is that all of them can be removed if necessary and replaced by feeding utensils better suited to your feeding program and the other furnishings of the cage.

Perches

Similarly, cages include a couple of perches, often hardwood dowels,

---

A Cockatiel's food consumption can be monitored by offering each kind of seed in a separate dish.

sometimes plastic. Most often it turns out that a couple more perches, perhaps of a different length, will be needed. The placement of perches should be done in relation to the food and water containers, the purpose being to keep both food and water as much as possible from being fouled with droppings. That this is important should be obvious.

Another consideration regarding perches is their diameter, or thickness. Bird keepers have found that if all the perches in a cage are the same diameter, foot problems can occur eventually, because the bird's grasp while resting is always the same. Thus a cage should always have perches of at least two different diameters, to allow the foot's grasp to be varied. A better approach is to use branches from trees or shrubs, as these will likely vary in thickness throughout. To determine the appropriate perch size for a bird, the rule is this: the perch should be large enough that the tips of the claws come into contact with the perch. If the claws overlap around the perch, it is too small. This optimum-thickness perch should be your guide in choosing perches. For example, if you are installing three perches in a cage, one should be the optimum size,

another slightly smaller and the third slightly larger.

As mentioned earlier, it's likely that a Cockatiel will chew its perches. Don't try to prevent this; instead, look at perches as things that will be worn out and will have to be replaced. If you're using dowel perches, install some that are soft wood, not hard. An attractive feature of branches is that the Cockatiel may divert itself by stripping the bark—willow branches serve nicely in this respect.

Cage Design

After you have had to give a cage a thorough cleaning a few times, you will undoubtedly decide that simplicity of design is the greatest virtue a cage can possess. A plain cage may not be as appealing visually, but remember that every ridge and corner will require a little more attention in cleaning than a flat surface will; every curlicue and twist of wire is another place where "dirt" can collect. Keep in mind that psittacine birds use their beaks as they climb around inside a cage; this means that saliva gets onto the wires. If this isn't cleaned frequently, certain spots of the cage will be covered with a tough film

Accommodations

that stands up amazingly well even to the newest household wonder cleaners. It's annoying to find that the cage will have to be soaked in water for a time.

Your Cockatiel sees its cage as its home, and it's not a bad idea that you look at it that way too. But this isn't to suggest that a bird needs a house. Wooden "bird houses" with gables and sloping roofs are fine designs as nest boxes for wild birds outdoors, but the only birds that should be kept under a gabled roof indoors are cuckoos, and they should be able to tell the time. It's true that bird cages don't fit in well with the usual home decor, but in the end everyone is happier if one resigns oneself to the fact that rooms are decorated for the comfort of people, and birds are not people. In a way, when you think about it, a bird is a pretty foreign object to have in a house; it seems to follow that a bird cage might as well be too.

The next factor in choosing a cage is quality of construction. As always, you can pretty much expect to get what you pay for, and in bird cages the differences in cost between comparable cages usually reflects differences in workmanship and quality of materials used. Look for heavier gauge wire and substantial

metal or plastic on the other parts of the cage. It not so much that your Cockatiel will damage the cage as time passes, but that a sturdier cage stands up better to the cleanings you'll be giving it.

Since Cockatiels like to move about by climbing, wire running horizontally acts like a ladder. Still, if you watch a Cockatiel in a cage that is vertically wired, you'll find that it doesn't have much trouble getting around. Thus it's difficult to assess how important this feature is, at least to the Cockatiel's ease of movement. Many Cockatiel-sized cages don't have horizontal wiring for whatever reason. Or you may find some that have horizontal wiring on two sides and vertical on the others. Usually the only argument given in favor of horizontal wiring is that it makes it easier for the parrot to climb about; in fact, there is a second reason: horizontal wiring makes it much easier to install perches at the optimum heights in the cage.

A good example of a cage that is totally unsuited to a Cockatiel but is very attractive to a wide spectrum of people is the bamboo cage. Imported from the Orient, these nicely made cages have all the appeal generated by the handiwork that goes into making them. By all

Accommodations

means, buy one for decoration; you can own one without putting a live bird inside it. At best, these bamboo cages are suited to the smaller finches, but in use, finch keepers find them a trial. It might be amusing, if a Cockatiel-sized bamboo cage could be found, to see just where and what a Cockatiel would decide to chew on—with such an expanse of opportunity, the Cockatiel might find it difficult to choose the first place to gnaw a hole.

Bird cages might be grouped into those that overall have a rectangular shape and those that are "round," in fact cylindrical. Most bird keepers hold the opinion that birds are happier in rectangular cages, but if asked, they would probably admit to knowing some instances of pet birds that were perfectly comfortable in cylindrical cages. For a time there was talk that "round" cages were the cause of a nervous illness, the so-called twisting disease. It was thought that the bird became mentally confused because it couldn't orientate itself in the circular space. Some people still hold this opinion, but without any compelling evidence to support it. It's often prudent to remember the adage, Where there's smoke, there's fire; but probably this is

one of the times it's best forgotten. However, the matter of rectangular vs. circular cages can be resolved from the point of view of the keeper, if not the bird. The fact is, it's easier to furnish a rectangular cage. It's easier to fit perches and to situate food and water containers appropriately. In practice, too, it usually turns out that rectangular cages fit better into the space chosen for them in the room.

Situating the Cage

This brings us to the situation of the cage in the home. The first point to consider is whether to choose a room that has a great deal of activity, such as a family room, or to place the cage instead in a quiet room, such as a bedroom. The answer in this instance is clear: pet Cockatiels enjoy company. A single bird will take an interest in what the people around it are doing. Pets left to spend most hours of the day alone in a son's bedroom while the boy is away at school very often are more forgotten prisoners than cared-for pets. But there can be too much of a good thing: if the Cockatiel belongs to a large family of which the several members come and go, to work or to school, at very

Accommodations

different hours, a room like the kitchen would not be the ideal choice for the cage. Birds do best on a regular schedule; they prefer to have fixed daytimes and nighttimes. Thus it's best not to situate the cage in a room with round-the-clock activity. So long as you follow these guidelines, it doesn't much matter what household function the room you choose to place the cage in has.

The room should have a good level of light in the daytime, however. Avoid keeping your Cockatiel in a dark room, as light stimulates activity in birds. Just remember not to take a good thing too far and place your Cockatiel in its cage in front of a sunny window. Birds are susceptible to becoming overheated from being too long in the sunlight, so it's prudent to be mindful of this.

The room must also be evaluated in terms of temperature and drafts. Pet Cockatiels are comfortable at temperatures people are comfortable at. If your kitchen, for example, often becomes too warm for you because of the cooking, it's probably not a good room for the Cockatiel's cage. At the other extreme, a room of the house that is allowed to go heatless at night during cold weather is not a good choice either. The best way to assess whether a Cockatiel—or any bird, for that matter—is being kept at an adequate temperature is to *observe* it. Like people and other animals when temperature is right, a Cockatiel will be active. If it is either too hot or too cold, activity declines. This is not to say that a Cockatiel must be housed so that the temperature never varies; such a situation is not ultimately ideal either. Outdoors in the wild, Cockatiels obviously are able to cope with the daily range of temperature variation and, more significantly, the range of seasonal variation. But it appears that animals kept indoors are less able, for whatever reason, to accommodate temperature changes. A human parallel might compare an accountant to a farmer. The captive bird is to the wild bird as an accountant is to a farmer.

Evaluating the temperature at which your Cockatiel is kept will be easier if you know how the bird will look if it is either too warm or too cold. Birds don't have sweat glands, so they are unable to cool their bodies as people do. Instead, they do as many as three things: the first is to sleek the plumage against the body, which lessens its insulating function. Second, a bird will open its beak so that heat is lost directly from the moist tissue of the mouth

Accommodations

and throat; probably more air is circulated in and out of the lungs and air sacs too. Third, the wings are held slightly away from the body; this permits ventilation of the undersides of the wings, which are the most sparsely feathered areas of a bird's body.

A chilled bird reverses these measures. The plumage is fluffed out to trap air between the feathers (those of you who own down winter-wear should know all about this). The wings are held close to the body, so that they are overlapped by the body feathers. Finally, the head is turned back and the bill tucked between the wings (not in fact "under the wing," as the popular expression would have it), so that the air breathed is that warmed in the feathers. In sum, if you find that your Cockatiel presents either of these pictures the whole of its waking hours, the temperature is either too warm or too cold.

Associated with temperature in deciding where to situate a Cockatiel's cage is the matter of drafts. The younger readers of this book will probably have some difficulty in accepting what follows, but the older of you will have a personal appreciation of how unpleasant sitting in a draft can be.

As people may catch colds from sitting in a draft, so apparently can birds, and it often happens that in birds the illness worsens. Maybe this is so because a person can move out of a draft, but a caged bird cannot. For birds, fresh air and ventilation is a good thing, but there's a point when ventilation becomes a draft. Check the site you've chosen for the cage, and make sure it isn't in a draft. Of course, this includes drafts caused by air conditioners.

Avoid, too, placing the cage near radiators, heaters, and heat outlets. The drying effect of heat can be damaging to a bird's plumage, though it should be said that this may be less of a problem with Cockatiels than with other species.

The last point that should be mentioned in this discussion of cage situation is the height of the cage. Many species, unless they're tame, instinctively seek security by perching above other creatures they fear. Earlier we mentioned how wild Cockatiels react to the approach of humans. Therefore, at least at first, it's desirable to place the bird's cage at eye level or above, so that if its occupant becomes frightened, it can seek safety in the highest, farthest corner of its cage.

Accommodations

Accessories

To cover, or not to cover; that is the question. The answer depends, in some cases, on the situation of the cage, for different purposes can be served by covering a bird's cage. Most bird species, including Cockatiels, are diurnal animals, which means they are naturally active in the daytime. Most of the owls, on the other hand, are active at night. For a Cockatiel, light encourages activity, whether it be feeding, chewing, playing, or vocalizing, but darkness means that it's time to sleep—just like chickens going to roost. Covering the cage, therefore, is a way of darkening the cage so that the Cockatiel can sleep. For example, if you have your Cockatiel in a room in which the TV is sometimes kept on late, covering the cage at the Cockatiel's usual bedtime hour will allow it to get some sleep, but a family member can continue to watch TV. Obviously, for this purpose the cage cover should be made of an opaque cloth (cloth is best because it can be washed). It should be obvious, then, that it's the darkness, not the cage cover itself, that encourages sleep.

An associated use of such a cage cover is to quiet down an overly active Cockatiel. A scenario might be this: Company arrives and joins the family in the living room, which happens to be the same room in which the Cockatiel is kept. The Cockatiel, of course, decides to participate in all the excitement and vocalizes at the top of its lungs. This will provide everyone with a few moments' amusement, but when conversation gets underway, the Cockatiel's noise will become annoying. Darkening the cage with the cover at this point will let the Cockatiel know that it's time to quiet down and maybe get some rest.

The remaining use for a cage cover also has to do with sleeping. Covering the cage traps the heat generated by the bird inside, so that it will stay warmer through the night. Whether you choose to use a cover for this purpose depends, of course, on the situation of your Cockatiel's cage. If the situation is less than optimal, you may decide that it would be desirable to cover the cage. This use demands a thick cloth.

Another question that every bird keeper must answer for himself, if never entirely to his satisfaction, is what to use to cover the floor of the cage. There are several possibilities, but paper and sand are the most common. Most people settle on

Accommodations

placing paper in the tray. If it's absorbent, the droppings dry quickly, which is desirable. Some bird owners like to put several sheets in the tray at a time; this makes it easy to remove only the soiled top sheet daily, or even more often if they are fastidious. Newspaper is certainly an inexpensive choice. Even if the Cockatiel chews the paper, there should be no problems because the inks used are not toxic. With newspaper, though, it's wise to let the paper age before putting it in the cage. After reading today's paper you may have sometimes noticed from your hands that the ink wasn't as dry as you might like. Similarly, newspaper ink can soil a Cockatiel's plumage.

A layer of sand in the tray similarly serves to absorb the moisture from droppings or bits of food that may end up there. Another product that does the same thing and is becoming more popular with bird keepers is ground corn cob. Widely used as a bedding for laboratory animals, corn cob is highly absorbent and is not harmful if eaten by the Cockatiel.

Though one of the food cups that is supplied with the cage can be used to hold water, most bird keepers before long come to prefer offering water in a font rather than in a cup or dish. The typical font depends on a vacuum to dispense water via a spout in its base. The font is attached to the outside of the cage with the spout projecting inside, between the wires. Because of the small open area presented by the spout, the water is fouled by food or droppings usually only because of the occupant's mischief. Most of these fonts are large enough to hold enough water to last a Cockatiel a few days; however, the font should be emptied and cleaned daily and refilled with fresh water.

Toys

If you have kept a Budgie, you may be expecting your pet Cockatiel also to take an interest in toys. Well, in general, it can be said that Cockatiels are physically less active than Budgies and therefore find toys less diverting. Probably the most successful Cockatiel toys are ladders, bells, and mirrors.

Most playgrounds incorporate a ladder into their design; if not, suitable ladders are readily available as a separate item, whether for use on a playground or in a cage.

The appeal of bells seems to be that they make noise. If you decide

Accommodations

to get one, be careful that the bell, clapper, chain, and clips are sturdy enough that the Cockatiel won't be able to pull it apart. It's important to avert the possibility that some part will be swallowed.

Before you decide to let your Cockatiel have a mirror, consider first why birds like mirrors. A Cockatiel or a Budgie is attracted to a mirror because there is another bird there; an attachment to the mirror is an instance of a bird's preference for another creature of its own kind. For this reason, some pet keepers have faulted mirrors for distracting the bird from becoming tame or from talking. It seems that they have a point. Alternatively, other pet owners feel that they themselves are unable to provide sufficient companionship for their pets; the bird in the looking glass improves a less-than-wonderful situation, they feel.

A number of objects that make fine Cockatiel toys can be found around the house and would otherwise simply be discarded. Let your Cockatiel chew them up or tear them apart before you throw them away. The most suitable objects are those made of wood or paper; plastic items should be assessed more cautiously. Small paper boxes or the tubes on which paper towels or tissue are rolled are the likeliest possibilities nowadays; maybe one could say that in the days when thread came on wooden spools, parrots had more fun.

Maybe the best reason to obtain a playground for a pet Cockatiel is that they seem to enjoy the time they spend on the playground. We can imagine that a tame bird is glad for a change of scene and that it appreciates the time it's permitted to spend in the same space with its owner. Moreover, the playground is the place a pet bird should be when it is let outside the cage. Once the Cockatiel becomes familiar with the playground it will tend to stay put there, rather than to wander about the room. Just as people have their favorite chairs, so would a Cockatiel settle on favorite perches if it were given the run of a whole room. You might be surprised (and probably dismayed) at the few spots the bird would regularly choose; even if the room has a lot of perching places— objects that would feel comfortable to its feet, such as drapery rods, —in time a very few sites would emerge as favorites. A playground, then, is attractive because it is a comfortable place, and familiar, for the dowels of the playground are just like the perches in its cage. In choosing a playground, the

Accommodations

thickness of the dowels is the most important feature to notice. Those made for Budgies, for example, will have much thinner dowels. The edge of the board into which the dowels are set is edged with strips of lattice. This is handy, because it keeps toys from rolling off. Since the floor of the playground is not usually covered with paper or sand, it's not important that the tray formed by the lattice be deep. It's easier just to wipe up after each time it's used.

Lighting

A final accessory that you should consider is a light for the cage. Many pet birds, evidence suggests, are not given an adequate level of light. Lack of exposure to sunlight may be subtly detrimental, because of the role ultraviolet radiation can play in nutrition. Many bird breeders have in recent years become enthusiastic about lights initially developed to enhance plant growth, which were soon taken up by aquarists, keepers of other sorts of animals, and aviculturists. Because accommodations for birds can be so various, it's difficult to assess exactly how much effect these lights can have. Is it the wide spectrum emitted—closer to sunlight, the proponents say, and wider than that produced by ordinary bulbs or tubes—that is beneficial, or is it the fact merely that the intensity is greater? Until the facts become known, the opinions of the users should not be dismissed. Thus far, such lights appear to have been little used with pet birds. Still, if you're not satisfied with the light level in the room where you have to keep your Cockatiel, this is something you can do about it. Besides, some of the lights make plumage look different than it does in ordinary light.

Photographs, pages 57—64: 57—Adult Pied female; note the gray on the face and the light beak. 58—The Lutino color variety has no gray in its plumage. 59—Adult Normal female; both the gray facial mask and beak of the Normal female are altered variously in the different color varieties. 60—A Lutino and two Pieds in a cage furnished with a suitable perch and a mineral block. 62—Once a Cockatiel is accustomed to perching on a hand-held dowel, often the next step in hand-taming is teaching it to step onto a finger. 63—Smooth plumage and an alert eye characterize a healthy bird; this Normal male holds his wings away from the body after a few moments' exertion flying around the room. 64—It's wise to allow pet Cockatiels the opportunity to become familiar with mirrors and windows.

Cockatiel Nutrition

Good color and shiny plumage, you'll recall, is not merely a matter of the light under which birds are viewed. Feather growth depends on nutrition. "You are what you eat," a nineteenth-century philosopher announced. With some bird species, eating reddish foods is necessary to maintain the reddish color of the plumage. Though Cockatiel coloration also depends on carotenoid pigments, don't bother to try to improve your Cockatiel's color by color feeding; it doesn't work. For this species, that we know.

Scientists would say that we have a detailed understanding of the nutritional requirements of only one avian species: domesticated chickens. Since we have good reason to believe that the dietary needs of Cockatiels may be similar—or at least more similar to those of a chicken than to those of a human being or a dog—poultry studies can be a point of departure. It's no surprise that chicken nutrition follows the same principles that apply to other animals—and what has become a guiding idea is the notion of a balanced diet. Balance in this context refers to the relative proportions of various nutrients, either in terms of classes (proteins, fats, carbohydrates) or, more finely,

the nutrients themselves (the various animo acids, lipids, vitamins, and so on). We are able to specify a poultry diet in fine terms, but with Cockatiels we are still not absolutely sure about the balance required between the classes. As we can't specify with certainty the relative proportions of carbohydrates, fats, and proteins needed by Cockatiels, neither in general nor individually, we have to rely on supposition (which has worked well in practice) that a varied diet has the best chance of being a balanced diet. Practically, then, Cockatiels should be fed as varied a diet as possible.

Allowing a Cockatiel to subsist on a seed mix—from which it may prefer to eat only some kinds of seeds, taking others only when the favorites are gone—is the epitome of a one-sided diet. From the perspective of current nutritional thinking, a seed mixture featuring sunflower seeds can be faulted as being too high in carbohydrates and fats and deficient in vitamins. On a diet of this kind a Cockatiel may do well enough for a time, but we suspect that its long-term effect will be to shorten the Cockatiel's life. (Those of you who have thought about human nutrition will recognize the parallels here.)

Cockatiel Nutrition

The Seed Mix

A mixture of dry seeds, then, should amount to only part of a Cockatiel's diet. There are only a few kinds of seeds that are usually included in most Cockatiel seed mixes, whether they are prepared commercially or mixed at home by Cockatiel keepers and breeders. These are sunflower seed, white millet, canary seed, and oat groats. Of course, other seeds could be included as well, and sometimes are; for example, hemp, teazle, safflower, peanuts, and buckwheat, to name a few. To discuss the merits of the various seeds could amount to a book in itself. If you have heard that there is a debate about the use of safflower vs. sunflower, you have heard rightly. The "old hands" reading this will nod knowingly at this point, and many of them will have already taken a position on this question. Those other readers, the novice Cockatiel keepers, will do well to begin by offering their Cockatiel the same, probably conventional mix that the Cockatiel they've acquired is used to. Their first task is to vary its diet beyond the seed mix; once that has been accomplished, and the Cockatiel is no longer exclusively a seed eater, then it will be time to reevaluate the seed mix that's been in use.

From the point of view of maintenance in captivity, Cockatiels have always been considered seed eaters. In the main, this view is accurate, since seeds are the principal constituent of a wild Cockatiel's diet. But *principal* does not mean *sole,* and seeing seeds in bins and boxes makes us forget that seed is ever anything but dry. Though Cockatiels in the wild feed on seeds found on the ground, it may be worth suggesting that seed on the ground is not necessarily there because it has fallen from ripeness. Another thought to ponder is whether the seeds wild Cockatiels consume are fresh—in this context, *fresh* could have more than one meaning.

Fruits and Vegetables

Keepers of captive Cockatiels today are quite vocal about the importance of fresh fruits and vegetables in Cockatiel nutrition. Though many Cockatiels will show themselves reluctant to eat foods other than the dry seeds that may be their favorites, green vegetables are the better sources of nutrients lacking in the seed mix, so these are the ones to emphasize. The

Cockatiel Nutrition

following greens are regularly available in the market: carrot top, the greener lettuces like chickory and romaine, spinach, and beet greens. Other desirable greens are readily available elsewhere: broccoli, dandelion and alfalfa. Of the non-green vegetables, corn on the cob will likely prove to be the favorite, but the root part of the carrot is another good choice.

Current bird-keeping prudence warns against using certain vegetables as bird food: avocado, egg plant, rhubarb, and parsley. The reasons for leaving these out of your Cockatiel's food dish range from folklore to scientific fact. Since so many other vegetables can be fed, there's no need to devote further discussion to these views here.

Our fruits generally are liked less. The ones to try first are apple and banana, then orange, grapefruit, and papaya.

Sprouted Seed

The produce sections of markets nowadays stock sprouted seeds, for they are in vogue as "health foods." That they are healthy to eat is undeniable, for humans and Cockatiels as well. You may find it convenient to purchase sprouts, but it's also easy to sprout them yourself. Sprouting some of the Cockatiel seed mix will serve another purpose as well: if most of the seeds sprout, this is a sign that the mix contains fresh, nutritious seeds.

It's not necessary to wait until the seeds have actually grown so large as sprouts; the seeds will take on a different nutritive value as soon as they begin to germinate. In the period between the time of germination and the point when the seed has been exhausted in producing the sprout, the relative preponderance of nutrients constantly changes. For example, as carbohydrates are converted in the

Dandelion is a green all too familiar to those who like a nice lawn.

Cockatiel Nutrition

course of germination, the percentage of carbohydrate declines relative to the protein, which remains constant; the result is that sprouted seeds contain a higher proportion of protein than do dry seeds.

In practice, sprouting a mixture of seeds provides the benefits of all the stages of this process because the different seeds develop at different rates. For example, at the end of, say, four days, some seeds in the mixture will have become good-sized sprouts, while others are no further along than germination. Besides sprouting the kinds of seeds fed dry to a Cockatiel, you can also sprout those which are not. In fact, sprouting is the ideal way to incorporate into the diet seeds a bird otherwise would ignore. Soybeans and mung beans, for example, are examples of seeds containing a high proportion of vegetable protein. At the moment, however, the use of soybeans is being questioned by some breeders who have always kept in the vanguard with respect to parrot nutrition.

The Protein Question

The mention of protein raises the question as to what proportion of a Cockatiel's diet should consist of protein. At present, this question cannot be answered as accurately as one might like. It's probably true that Cockatiel protein needs vary from individual to individual and also are different at different stages of an individual's life. This view derives more from our knowledge of the nutrition of humans and other animals than from any studies of the Cockatiel alone.

But we also know from research into the nutritonal needs of other animals that these needs vary according to the season of the year. This has to do with ambient temperature principally. A pet Cockatiel owned by someone who keeps his home a warm, cozy 78 F. throughout the winter will certainly have different nutritional requirements from the bird which finds that its owner has decided the furnace should go off during the night and that the temperature in the cage falls to 60 F.

Also, Cockatiels kept indoors throughout the year will probably experience less temperature change both daily and seasonally then those kept in an aviary outdoors; it stands to reason that the seasonal nutritional needs of the latter group will vary more than those of the former. Of course, how great the

Cockatiel Nutrition

variation is in these instances remains open to question, and this question has to be answered before one has a sound basis for altering Cockatiels' diets.

So once again, in the absence of answers derived from scientific fact, we rely on practical bird keeping. The consensus of opinion holds that Cockatiels' maintenance needs are adequately met by a diet of seed and vegetables. It appears to be unnecessary to offer a pet Cockatiel the high-protein animal foods that appear to be beneficial in the diets of other parrot species. For example, many keepers of amazon parrots occasionally feed their birds cooked meat. Still, if one does wish to include more nonvegetable protein in a Cockatiel diet, cheese may be the answer. At least some Cockatiels readily take to cheddar-type cheeses, perhaps because of color. You might try experimenting to discover which texture of cheddar proves most acceptable. Cheese of this sort also has a high fat content, which may or may not be desirable. Again, some Cockatiel keepers have noted that feeding such cheeses improves the appearance of the plumage; this is probably the result of the oil they contain. Other Cockatiel keepers prefer to offer a low-fat cheese; in this instance the

choice is cottage cheese. Although nutritional research projects dealing with Cockatiels are now in progress, their results so far tend to support what Cockatiel keepers have already long observed: Cockatiels can be maintained remarkably well on a diet that appears inadequate, and certainly would be for many other parrot species. This is completely consistent with what we know of the life of the Cockatiel in the wild: it is a species adapted to the vicissitudes of a comparatively harsh environment.

Special Diets

The word *maintenance* was introduced a few sentences ago. It's possible to distinguish between the nutrients required merely to maintain health in an animal and those needed for special situations. A person who enjoys running as an amateur provides a good analogy: most of the time his diet will be determined by what he does for a living; however, if he plans to run in a marathon, he will alter his diet considerably in the days prior to the race. With Cockatiels and other birds, it's mainly important to distinguish between two types of

Cockatiel Nutrition

diets: maintenance diets and breeding diets. (Canary keepers might wish to add molting diets, and veterinarians prescribe recuperative diets as well.) The conclusion of practical bird keeping is that the diet needed by breeding Cockatiels is little different from that required for maintenance.

Only some breeders advocate the use of egg food when Cockatiels are breeding and rearing young; others might suggest a bread or cake, perhaps soaked in milk. Depending on the exact formula used, these two "rearing foods" could be different nutritionally, notably in terms of protein content. Remember, though, that the use of these foods is supported in this way: "When I offer rearing foods, the chicks turn out to be sturdier and healthier." It's very possible that the value of these rearing foods is that they are soft foods. They don't have to be retained long by the parent birds after being eaten; in a short time—compared to dry seed, say—they are ready for regurgitation into the mouths of hungry chicks. In short, the use of a rearing food may allow parents to feed better. And if the virtue of a rearing food lies mostly in its texture, then other soft foods might be employed as well—sprouted seed, for example.

Dietary Supplements

With all this said, it's time to discuss dietary supplements. Since it's not easy to sharply distinguish dietary supplements from foods in all cases, it may be easiest to begin by mentioning the most common dietary supplement: a vitamin mixture. The vitamin mixture can serve as an example to illustrate the part supplements play in nutrition, avian or otherwise. Since the ingredients of a vitamin supplement (the various vitamins) are also found in foods, in theory such a supplement is necessary only if insufficient vitamins are obtained from the foods that make up the diet. Unfortunately, it's not at all a simple matter to tell whether this is happening.

At issue here are not clear-cut cases of vitamin deficiency, which produce symptoms dramatic enough for the owner to hurry to phone a veterinarian. Vitamin deficiency is something insidious usually, that develops slowly over a long period of time. Put simply, giving your Cockatiel a vitamin supplement can be seen as insurance against the possibility of a deficiency developing. Whether it actually will develop, of course, can't be foreseen. It may be that most cases

Cockatiel Nutrition

of vitamin deficiency originate as a constitutional metabolic defect in the bird and not in the diet offered by its keeper. But whatever the cause, the only solution involves a vitamin supplement in the diet or administered otherwise.

To sum up, a reasonable recommendation seems to be this: if your pet Cockatiel is eating the kind of varied diet advocated earlier in these pages, add a dietary supplement once a week. But if the Cockatiel eats a persistently one-sided diet, a small quantity of a vitamin mixture should ge given daily. To put this advice into perspective, it must be said that there have been Cockatiels that have lived long lives without ever coming near a vitamin supplement.

If you choose to offer a dietary supplement, it might as well be a complete as possible. This means that you should read the label. The range of available products is immense; some preparations contain fewer than a half-dozen vitamins; on others the list of vitamins, minerals, and amino acids seems endless. Each item listed may counter some possible deficiency.

Another choice you have involves how the supplement is offered; some supplements are powders, others oils, and still others are soluble in water. Those in powder form have the edge: they can be sprinkled on vegetables or other softer foods and will be consumed along with the food. But what if your Cockatiel wants only to eat sunflower seeds?— a water soluble vitamin is one answer. But with Cockatiels, which don't consume much water, this route is not ideal. Happily, the number of commercially available products for diet supplementation is legion. One of them consists of seeds coated with a supplement; some of this will certainly come off onto the bird's tongue as it hulls the seeds. Needless to say, a different product will offer the possibility of solving some other bird-feeding problem.

A word of caution about using dietary supplements: follow the dosage advised by the manufacturer, unless you have very sound reasons for doing otherwise. With the ready availability of so many avian diet supplements, veterinarians have noticed an increase in illness caused by overdosing, usually with vitamins. Most minerals are needed only in very small quantities (a trace), so consuming an excess of these elements can be toxic.

(Dietary supplements, by the way, should not be confused with *food additives*. Additives are put into a

Cockatiel Nutrition

food not to alter its nutritional value but for some other purpose: to make it keep better, have a longer shelf-life, look more appealing, and so forth.)

"New" Foods

Earlier in this chapter the importance of nutrient balance was mentioned. A little more discussion of this notion is germane by now. The possibility that your Cockatiel will refuse to eat a varied diet has already been hinted at. That the pet owner should persist in offering such a diet goes without saying. Use your ingenuity to figure out ways to get your conservative Cockatiel to eat what you think it should eat. Mixing the "new" foods in among the seeds is an obvious way to start. Another tack involves rationing: if your bird is hooked on sunflower, for example, offer only small quantities of it twice a day in a separate dish, while all the other foods are available to the bird continuously. It's unlikely that your Cockatiel will be so stubborn as to starve itself, but if you employ rationing, keep the possibility in mind. Eventually, most Cockatiel owners find, persistence will pay off; or they one day by chance offer

some food never tried before, and the Cockatiel gobbles it up immediately. Remember too that birds are copycats: if one bird sees another eating something, it's more willing to take a chance too.

This chapter has adopted a manipulative stance with regard to feeding, it should be pointed out. At least this is consistent with other aspects of pet keeping: caging, taming, and training. But, you may ask, wouldn't a Cockatiel be capable instinctively of satisfying its nutritional needs if it had the opportunity? No, the experienced bird keeper would answer, if only because it doesn't have the opportunity. As a species, the Cockatiel has adapted over centuries to a diet of certain items only. It's possible that if all these items, be they few or many, were available to a caged Cockatiel, it might be able to regulate its diet appropriately. Needless to say, none of the dietary items of the wild Cockatiel are ordinarily available to a captive Cockatiel. And, from what's been said, wouldn't it be necessary also to duplicate the cycles of seasons, climates, and temperatures the wild Cockatiel is adapted to? Domestication, we know, can alter the somatotype of a species; what can be the relationships that prevail

Cockatiel Nutrition

between diet, selective breeding, and the resulting breeds? Is this like asking which came first, the chicken or the egg?

Pelleted Diets

As the experiences of keeping pet parrots are summed, it has increasingly become evident that many of them do fail to regulate their diets when given free choice; instead, many of them settle on a favorite seed (usually sunflower) to the exclusion of all others. If a bird has free choice of however varied a diet, there is no way that the bird keeper can be sure that the nutrients in the diet are balanced. The only way to ensure a balanced diet is to eliminate free choice.

If you've kept other kinds of pets besides birds, you probably fed them with a commerically prepared diet, something that came out of a can or a bag. Each of these products has been formulated by animal nutritionists to provide a good diet for the animal species for which it was designed. It's probably true that the diets manufactured for some animals have received more nearly unanimous approval than those for others, but it's undeniable that rats, gerbils, hamsters, monkeys, dogs,

and cats generally do extremely well on such diets. For a long while, the only diets prepared for birds were pellets formulated for soft-billed birds, "mynah pellets." These too have been successful by and large, and have made maintenance of softbills much easier than it would be otherwise.

Thanks to the explosion of interest in keeping birds of all kinds, companies have developed pelleted diets for more kinds of birds: Canaries, finches, Budgerigars, parrots, lories, flamingos, ratites, waterfowl, and others. It must be said that these pellets are still relatively new products (some more so than others); while users have been enthusiastic, it can't yet be said that all have stood the test of time. But what advantages do they offer? The pellets are meant to be fed almost exclusively—manufacturers recommend that other foods be given only in small quantities and occasionally—so they amount to a complete diet. The ingredients also constitute a balanced diet, as far as the best current scientific research into avian nutrition allows. Thus the pellets can be said to represent state-of-the-art avian nutrition technology. Undeniably, using pellets is very convenient. In addition to a maintenance

Cockatiel Nutrition

formulation, companies offer "special needs" pellets. The frugal bird keeper will find pellets appealing because the whole thing is eaten and nothing is wasted. Fastidious pet owners will be happy that there are fewer seed hulls to clean up in and around the cage.

Some possible disadvantages of pellets also come to mind. It may be that a bird fed pellets will find this monotonous, and the lack of the diversion provided by conventional feeding will have to be compensated in other ways. It may happen that so much ease in pet maintenance will make the owner careless, so secure that everything is well with his bird's diet that he fails to give the animal the close daily scrutiny that may be is just as important under this regimen as it is in conventional feeding. Also, pet lovers may find that some of their enjoyment of a bird companion is lessened—shouldn't treat foods be foresworn as much as possible? "Polly want a pellet?"

Since a number of Cockatiel breeders now maintain their breeding pairs on pellets and wean youngsters to pellets, it's possible that you may find that a Cockatiel you're interested in buying is already eating pellets. If this is the case, there are obvious reasons for your continuing to feed the bird pellets. Perhaps by this point you've concluded that pellet feeding would fit in with your style of Cockatiel keeping, and you'll search for such a Cockatiel. Finally, if you already own a Cockatiel and you wish to try pellets, be aware that converting it to pellets may turn out not to be easy. Certainly it would be unwise to try to convert a Cockatiel from a conventional diet to pellets unless the bird is well acclimated, settled in its surroundings, and confiding with its owner. It would be dangerous to prematurely try to convert a "new" Cockatiel to pellets.

Food Treats

Once upon a time, crackers must have been the most common food treat for psittacines. We all learned as children what treats are; since treating a pet like a child is almost inescapable, the same guidelines you would use in giving treats to your child should be applied to your Cockatiel. Always evaluate treat foods nutritionally—this applies equally to commerical bird treats and "people foods." For both these classes, small quantities should be the rule. Remember that any food

Cockatiel Nutrition

item that a Cockatiel enjoys can be employed as a treat, or a reward, if that is what you wish. Professional parrot trainers reward their charges for performing tricks with ordinary sunflower seeds. Of the foods mentioned earlier in this chapter, cheese makes a good food treat.

Bird Sand

People who have been around chickens know that they spend a lot of time pecking on the ground. They pick up seed, of course, but they also ingest tiny pebbles, bits of rock of a size technically classified as sand. In the chicken's gizzard (ventriculus) this sand serves to grind up food. In this respect, Cockatiels resemble chickens; in the wild they too ingest sand. Pigeons exhibit an even greater need for sand than do chickens; once again it's clear that different bird species have different needs. It is evident that Cockatiels naturally require sand, so captive ones might as well have access to it at all times. But experience in Cockatiel keeping also shows that their need for it is not at all great, compared to chickens or pigeons. Maybe their digestive system is more efficient, but it's more likely that sand needs depend

on what it is exactly that's eaten. A pigeon, for example, swallows seeds without hulling them, so it must grind the hull as well as the kernel; on the other hand, the Cockatiel swallows only the kernel.

Recently some bird keepers have come to conclude that parrots do better in captivity if they are not allowed any sand at all. They suspect that sand may be the cause of digestive diseases in some instances. Their psittacine birds were apparently able to get along without it, they noticed, and many seemed to do even better than before. Perhaps it is the natural-vs.-unnatural aspect of this practice that has made it so controversial. At the time of this writing, it remains controversial, for too little time has elapsed for any long-term effects of withholding sand to have become apparent. But time alone will not supply the answer; it's unlikely that the matter can be resolved unless it is directly addressed by research projects. Perhaps the following suggestions will be helpful in the meantime.

The grinding action of sand in the gizzard depends on the fact that it is more or less indigestible. Some particles ingested are absolutely indigestible and are eventually passed through the digestive tract.

Cockatiel Nutrition

With particles such as these, size is important; it seems evident that different bird species prefer particles of different sizes. It would be nice now to specify what size of sand Cockatiels require, but this is not known (finding out would make a fine high-school science project). Practically, then, it is best to offer a Cockatiel one of the commercially available bird-sand (grit, gravel) mixtures that is composed of particles of various sizes. This way, the bird will be able to choose what suits it. Don't expect the Cockatiel to empty the cup; instead, to ensure that sand of a suitable size is available, fresh sand should be offered periodically; any that remains should be discarded. How often this should be done will, of course, depend on the individual Cockatiel. Once a week is probably a good rule. When you offer a fresh supply, watch your Cockatiel closely; if it hastens to the sand, this can be taken as a sign that the sand available has been inadequate.

Besides particle size, other characteristics may also be important; for example, it's been suggested that sharp edges on the particles may damage the lining of the digestive tract.

As mentioned above, the mineral particles ingested by birds are more or less indigestible. It's likely that the more digestible ones are broken down in time and thereby serve also as a source of minerals. The most significant of these minerals is probably calcium, necessary in the production of bones, feathers, and egg shells. For captive birds, digestible calcium is provided most obviously by cuttlebone and oyster shell. A commercially available mixture labeled "grit" very likely contains oyster shell and other digestible mineral compounds in addition to indigestible sand; a mineral block presents digestible minerals in another form.

All the commercially available mineral products for birds contain ingredients thought or known to be beneficial to the health of captive birds. Of course, the ingredients and their proportions vary from brand to brand, so choosing one in preference to another is a matter of reading the label.

The cuttlebone and the mineral block have another function in addition to the nutritional one: they are an opportunity for chewing, which "conditions" the beak.

In practice, then, three items can be recommended to ensure that a Cockatiel's mineral needs will be met: a cuttlebone, a mineral block, and a sand mixture.

Caring for a Cockatiel

Foresight may not be something that every human being possesses, but it is surely more characteristic of the human species than any other. Certainly one wouldn't fault a Cockatiel for a lack of it. Foresight entails imagining what may happen and then preparing to meet all the contingencies. The future is full of uncertainties, as we all know, and many of us are inclined to prepare for whatever may occur. Put more tersely, when we don't know, we try to ensure. This is practical wisdom that applies just as well to bird keeping, in which there seem to be as many unknowns as anywhere else. Thus many of the suggestions that follow amount to insurance against what only may happen in owning a Cockatiel. It's impossible to know, for example, how well any individual Cockatiel will do on a given diet, or what the likelihood of its meeting with an accident is. Many of you will certainly be interested in going beyond what is minimally necessary, to ensure health and to prevent accidents from occurring.

Hygiene

Much of the day-to-day care involved in Cockatiel keeping has to do with prevention. The importance of hygiene in the prevention of disease is a comparatively recent discovery in human history. Just as good nutrition is the way to prevent organic disease, good hygiene prevents infectious disease. If you own only one pet bird, it should have little opportunity to pick up an infectious disease since there are no other birds around. If the bird is free of infectious disease when you acquire it, it should remain so. Still, frequent cleanings make good sense. Illness from spoiled food, molds, and funguses can occur, so regular cleaning continues to be necessary.

A Cockatiel's personal hygiene entails bathing. Some Cockatiels are quite willing to bathe in water as so many other bird species do, but there are others that don't. For those that like a bath, a large flower-pot saucer makes a good tub. The others usually come to enjoy a shower provided by a plant mister, or some such sprayer. Many people prefer to bathe before bed, but this should not be allowed to birds. Be sure that your Cockatiel has its bath early enough for it to become completely dry before bedtime.

Caring for a Cockatiel

Preventing Illness

A major cause of illness in pet birds is poisoning. A pet Cockatiel out of its cage may chew on something that will prove toxic. Mainly for this reason, pets should not be allowed out of their cages unless someone is in the room to keep an eye on them. Some of the most apparently innocuous things can turn out to be poisonous. A friend of mine almost lost her pet Grey-cheeked Parakeet to poisoning; she suspects the marking-pen ink on some paper the Grey-cheek chewed. Also, some houseplants are poisonous. And, of course, foods offered your Cockatiel should always be washed thoroughly to be certain that any surface insecticides are removed.

A tame Cockatiel can be as curious as a child, and just as accident-prone. Many Cockatiels have met with accidents in the kitchen by climbing on the stove or drowning in a container of liquid. People can die from smoke inhalation, but birds are even more susceptible. The fumes from the nonstick coating of an overheated cooking utensil have caused the deaths of many birds. The list of dangers could go on, but we shall consider only one more: birds flying into windows or mirrors. This can easily occur if a bird is not familiar with these materials. Some Cockatiels are better able to cope with these than others, but even a Cockatiel that usually recognizes what a window is may go right on through if it's frightened enough.

Wing Trimming

Since birds that are able to fly appear to be more likely to meet with accidents, many pet owners choose to keep their bird's wings trimmed. *Wing trimming* is a phrase that novices may misunderstand. In wing trimming, all that is being cut is feathers; cutting into the flesh of the wing is something else, called pinioning. The feathers that are trimmed are those that enable the bird to fly. By shortening them, the bird's flying ability is hindered. As a greater number of feathers are shortened and more is cut off each, the bird progressively is rendered less able to fly.

Trimming wings is not difficult, but it is a procedure that people unused to handling birds probably should not undertake. If the bird is not tame, restraining it may prove difficult. There is a possibility that the Cockatiel may be injured or the

78

Caring for a Cockatiel

handler bitten. And, of course, it's always helpful to watch how something is done before attempting it yourself. In short, if you are a first-time Cockatiel owner and you want your Cockatiel to have a wing trim, have it done by an experienced person. Very likely, the person from whom you acquire your Cockatiel will be willing to do this; otherwise, take it to a veterinarian.

Among experienced bird keepers there are differences of opinion as to which style of wing trimming is best: whether to clip all the primaries or to leave a couple at the end of the wing intact; whether to clip all adjacent feathers or every other one; whether to strip the vanes; whether to trim both wings or only one. However, if someone suggests that the feathers be plucked, pay him absolutely no attention.

Preventing accidents is not the main reason for advocating wing trimming. Most people agree that it's helpful in taming a bird. It might be said that a wing trim puts a Cockatiel on an equal footing with the tamer. The Cockatiel no longer has the advantage of being able to fly away.

Like hair, feathers grow back, so wing trimming has to be done periodically. Many a pet owner has

been surprised one day when his hitherto flightless parrot launched itself into the air and flew.

Claw Clipping

The claws and the beak too may require clipping. When a Cockatiel gets old, it's not unusual that its beak will need attention occasionally. Youngsters and adult Cockatiels, in contrast, should be able to keep their beaks in condition without needing any help from you. If this is not the case, investigate to find out what's amiss. It's best to limit your work on the beak to what can be done with a diamond nail file; anything more should be left to a veterinarian.

The claws of wild Cockatiels are worn down as fast as they grow. Captive Cockatiels do not have as much contact with abrasive surfaces, and the claws of birds kept in cages especially tend to become overlong. For Cockatiels, a good tool is human toenail clippers, and there are other special scissors and clippers that will serve as well. Until you become experienced at this task, clip only a very little at a time, because the center of the claw has a blood supply, and you must avoid clipping the claw so short that

Caring for a Cockatiel

it bleeds. If that does happen, remember the first rule of first aid: Stop the bleeding.

First Aid

There is little the average pet owner can do to treat illness in birds, either accidents or diseases, so we will limit our discussion to first-aid measures. When a bird is ill it requires *gentle* handling. Even though this may seem obvious to you, this simple measure can mean the difference between life and death. The bird is already suffering stress from its illness; make every effort not to stress it further by hasty or unnecessary handling. Think before you act. With both accidents and diseases, your first thought should be to *keep the bird warm*. With an accident, it may be appropriate to immobilize the bird by wrapping it in a towel; this will also help to conserve body heat. If the bird is in its cage, a towel—the heavier the better—can be wrapped around the cage.

A phone call to your veterinarian should come next. You should not have to grab the Yellow Pages. A responsible parent will have a doctor's phone number close at hand; a responsible Cockatiel owner will have had the foresight to locate a veterinarian, preferably one experienced in avian medicine, at the same time that he acquired his Cockatiel. If it happens that the bird cannot be taken to the veterinarian immediately, continue to keep it warm as best you can. A heating pad, a heat lamp, or even an ordinary light bulb can be pressed into service. Try to keep the bird at a temperature between 85 and 90 F. Be careful not to overheat the bird.

Because bird illnesses so often become serious, and do so quickly, sick birds should be taken to veterinarians. Laymen have very little success in treating birds, because many diseases produce the same symptoms. Only veterinarians have the wherewithal to undertake accurate diagnosis and appropriate treatment.

f

The China Fallacy

The China Fallacy

How the U.S. Can Benefit from China's Rise and Avoid Another Cold War

DONALD GROSS

BLOOMSBURY

NEW YORK · LONDON · NEW DELHI · SYDNEY

Bloomsbury Academic

An imprint of Bloomsbury Publishing Plc

175 Fifth Avenue	50 Bedford Square
New York	London
NY 10010	WC1B 3DP
USA	UK

www.continuumbooks.com

Library of Congress Cataloging-in-Publication Data
A catalog record for this title is available from the Library of Congress

ISBN: PB: 978-1-4411-4789-9
HB: 978-1-4411-0083-2
PDF: 978-1-4411-3234-5
ePub: 978-1-4411-8746-8

Typeset by Fakenham Prepress Solutions, Fakenham, Norfolk NR21 8NN
Printed in the United States of America

In Memory Of
Gloria And Robert Gross

CONTENTS

CHAPTER ONE

Introduction: the unfulfilled promise of U.S.-China relations

Following the collapse of the Soviet empire in 1989, Americans began to worry deeply about another threat to the well-being of their country: the People's Republic of China. Though the United States became the world's only superpower at the end of the Cold War, strategists and analysts continued to search for dangers that might arise in the future. Among states that could potentially become big-power adversaries, China led the pack. Without doubt, the "China threat" today resonates deeply in the national political psyche, as Americans worry about China displacing the U.S. in Asia, taking U.S. manufacturing jobs, carrying out industrial espionage, modernizing its military forces, hacking into computers, and causing a multitude of other problems.

Not so long ago, Americans considered another country to be the United States' most dangerous adversary. During the Cold War, only the Soviet Union seemed to have the power and desire to unleash a devastating nuclear attack on cities and strategic targets across the U.S. Few seriously questioned the U.S.S.R. was masterminding an international communist conspiracy that threatened the "American way of life." Though anti-communist fears peaked during the McCarthy period of the early 1950s, the ideological struggle continued through the Cuban missile crisis, the Vietnam War, the era of *Glasnost*, the break-up of the Soviet Union and beyond.

While most Americans would admit that China does not possess the military prowess of Russia and is not actively seeking to export its ideological views around the world, many believe the U.S. should do all it can to prepare for an "inevitable" military conflict with China. They think it is only prudent to build up U.S. military bases and forces in the Pacific, in the face of China's continuing military modernization. They are inclined to support U.S. trade policies imposing tariffs, quotas and other protectionist measures on Chinese imports that enter the country "illegally." While they cannot help buying low-cost Chinese goods and enjoying low interest rates resulting from China's large holdings of U.S. Treasury securities, they condemn policies that led the American government to borrow billions of dollars from China. On a gut level, many people fear "cheap Chinese labor" will cause the decline of the United States economy and that U.S. industry will continue to suffer from China's "unfair trade practices." From a values standpoint, Americans feel most comfortable when their leaders strongly criticize China for violating human rights and restricting political freedoms. Most believe in their hearts that China's Communist Party still reverberates with the thoughts of Chairman Mao and that the Party is only willing to incrementally cede political controls through force or necessity.

With so many reasons to fear, despise and worry about China, Americans nevertheless cannot help admiring China's accomplishments and being intrigued with this emerging power. Many watched the opening and closing ceremonies for the 2008 Olympic Games and came away deeply impressed by the brilliant spectacle. Most cannot help but admire and be inspired by China's achievement of raising more than 400 million people out of poverty, virtually wiping out widespread illiteracy, developing a large middle class and creating a dynamic, consumer society. Many realized that China was a different place altogether from the impoverished, dispirited and totalitarian country they had heard about for years. Nevertheless, most Americans shook their heads knowingly when television commentators dutifully noted that Chinese authorities sharply limited demonstrations and dissent in Beijing during the Olympics. They could not help but feel sympathy for Tibetans whose protests were violently suppressed only weeks earlier by the Chinese military (just as most Americans felt compassion for blind dissident Chen Guangcheng, who sought refuge and protection at the U.S. Embassy in Beijing in late April 2012).

Looking back, the drumbeat of critical views about China among American academics, policy experts and journalists gathered strength during the Clinton administration and has continued to the present day. The "China threat" has many security, economic and political dimensions that experts frequently cite to justify their fears.

On security matters, some critics assert, as an article of faith, that China is bent on pushing the U.S. out of Asia and eventually dominating the world. These "China hawks" argue that China could move at any time to forcibly occupy Taiwan and reunify the island with the mainland. Such a successful attack on Taiwan, bolstered by explicit and implied military threats against other countries in East Asia, would enable China to dominate the region as a whole. China would then double down on its ultimate goal, this reasoning goes: replacing the United States as the world's only superpower. From the standpoint of the China hawks, a war between the United States and China is inevitable, since the U.S. stands in the way of China achieving its strategic objectives.

Regarding China's threat to U.S. jobs and economic growth, critics with strong protectionist views argue that the sharp increase in the United States trade deficit with China has had a devastating impact on American workers, causing the loss of nearly 2.8 million jobs between 2001 and 2010.[1] They claim that China has unfairly achieved its large bilateral trade surplus with the United States, which reached approximately $295 billion in 2011, because in their view, China couples its aggressive export strategy with measures to manipulate and artificially undervalue its currency, giving Chinese products an unfair advantage in foreign markets.[2]

While both China hawks and protectionists condemn China for its one-party communist regime, lack of democracy and poor human rights record, they largely accept the country's domestic political situation as an inalterable fact. Though they may hope for China's eventual transition to full democracy and high human rights standards, their primary concern is protecting the United States against the threat that China poses to America's security and economic well-being.

Shaping U.S. policy

In many respects, it is the views of the China hawks that have informed ongoing American security policy toward China over the last decade. During the George W. Bush administration, the U.S. initiated a major buildup of forces in the Pacific as part of what it officially termed to be "hedging" against a potential Chinese military threat. Under the rubric of preparing for the "contingency" of a war with China, U.S. hedging has effectively amounted to a containment strategy. Beyond significantly increasing the number of naval, air and land forces at U.S. bases in the Pacific, the buildup strengthened close-in naval intelligence gathering along China's coast as well as extensive air force surveillance and reconnaissance of the country as a whole. The Obama Administration hardened this policy through measures it announced in November 2011 that accelerate the strategic encirclement of China, including deploying U.S. marines to Australia's northern territory and adopting a new "Air Sea Battle Concept" to carry out long-range strikes deep inside China in the event of war.

Though the Bush administration, by encouraging market reform and promoting U.S. investment, pursued "engagement" with China on economic matters, it increasingly adopted restrictive trade measures such as imposing extensive import duties on Chinese products. Under pressure from protectionists in Congress, Bush officials moved to this more combative posture in their second term in the belief that China was benefiting unfairly from liberalized trade.[3] The Obama Administration supported and magnified this approach. Preeminently, U.S. policy relies on trade measures called "anti-dumping" actions that penalize Chinese companies for allegedly selling their products in the U.S. market at below the cost of production. The Obama Administration also imposed high punitive tariffs on some Chinese products and created a new "enforcement unit" to ramp up U.S. investigations of Chinese trade practices.

While critics often lament internal political conditions in China, they are far more focused on security and economic issues. The broad lack of interest in strengthening China's democracy and human rights practices had a definitive policy impact during the Bush administration and remains in place during the Obama Administration: aside from cataloging political abuses and shortcomings in an annual State Department report, addressing individual cases of concern and making periodic official statements that emphasize American political values, the U.S. government does little that will effectively promote democracy and human rights in China.[4]

The views of critics who deeply fear a "China threat" have unduly shaped U.S. government policy and anaesthetized Americans to its weaknesses. To many people, United States security policy toward China seems prudently designed to prepare for an uncertain future. Given widespread fear of the threat China might someday pose, many Americans see strengthening defenses in the Asia Pacific as a matter of common sense. On economic issues, many believe it is only fair for the U.S. government to protect American jobs and manufacturers against purportedly nefarious Chinese commercial practices. If this policy sometimes requires confronting China over trade issues, they are willing to live with the consequences. Finally, while most Americans broadly dislike China's authoritarian political system, they show little overall interest in adopting policies to help move it toward greater democracy and protection of human rights.

Shortcomings of U.S. policy toward China

The strong views of China hawks and protectionists cannot hide the fact that shortcomings in U.S. policy prevent the United States from achieving more optimal relations with China that could lead to far greater benefits for the American people.

Much of current U.S. security policy toward China derives from outdated Cold War views and is founded, in large part, on the unrealistic premise of maintaining U.S. military primacy in Asia for the indefinite future. If China hawks are correct in suggesting that a future war with China is "inevitable," it will be precisely because the policy they shaped creates a self-fulfilling prophecy. Such a costly and unnecessary military confrontation with China could lead to devastation on both sides.

On economic issues, greater protectionism against Chinese products is largely a defensive and narrow response to global economic trends that are causing a painful restructuring of the U.S. economy. Instead of increasing prosperity and allowing Americans to benefit from China's remarkable economic growth and development, protectionist policy is highly likely to cause continuing major friction on trade issues between the two countries.

In the political realm, where it is critical for the U.S. government to advance the core American values of support for democracy and human rights, current policy also falls short. Little in U.S. policy will lead directly, in the foreseeable future, to a more democratic China that observes universal human rights standards. This serious failing makes the soundest long-term basis for friendly United States relations with China—a commonality of political norms and values—all the more unattainable.

There is, however, no reason to despair. One of the greatest virtues of the American political system is its flexibility, its willingness to accept innovation in the face of failure, and its openness to new ideas. It is not foreordained that the United States and China must clash militarily and slide toward nuclear war. It is not written in stone that the long American tradition of promoting free trade must give way to endless protectionist policies toward China. And it is not inevitable that China's communist regime will forever suppress the democratic impulse among its own people.

The difficulty of moving beyond current policy

Despite the questionable premises underlying much of prevailing U.S. policy toward China, policymakers and commentators find it difficult to move beyond existing views. There are several reasons why this is so.

To begin with, current policy is complex. It stresses preparation for a security threat from China at the same time as it promotes U.S. business interests there. It protects uncompetitive American companies from the adverse effects of China's rapidly growing economy (unintentionally creating a nationalist backlash in Beijing) while largely ignoring China's domestic political system. The seemingly contradictory elements of U.S. policy—in the face of real uncertainty about the direction of China's military, economic and political development—mask the true dangers and weaknesses of the overall U.S. approach.

A second reason why policymakers and commentators find it difficult to move beyond existing China policy is that groups with vested interests have a stake in its various components. These groups attempt to mold public opinion by defining "acceptable" and "mainstream" views of China, which provide strong support for the existing policy framework. This is especially true of security policy, where hawks who believe in a coming military clash with China also argue that the U.S. should pursue a military buildup to prepare for it. Not surprisingly, the military services and defense contractors in the United States are important members of the political constituency that favors an aggressive security strategy toward China. The specter of a large and amorphous "China threat" has proved useful as a replacement for the "Soviet threat" to spur the Pentagon's acquisition of advanced weapons systems, especially at a time of overall defense budget cuts. Another group with a vested interest in a hard line security policy is the traditional "China lobby" (originally strong supporters of the anti-communist regime that led Taiwan after the Chinese revolution in 1949) which has concentrated in recent years on ensuring the U.S. supplies large quantities of high-quality weapons and military equipment to Taiwan to deter and defend against a possible Chinese attack.

Perhaps the overriding reason why many policymakers and commentators cannot easily move beyond existing views of China is that they do not sufficiently factor into their analysis the major security, political and economic benefits that the United States and its Asian allies could achieve through improved U.S.-China relations. Many commentators tend to emphasize worst-case scenarios and pessimistic assessments which are seen by the media as "sober-minded" and "realistic." It seems fruitless to these analysts to describe future benefits from a state of affairs that they believe will likely never come to pass. Influenced by the "tyranny of the status quo," policymakers and commentators often feel the best they can do is to propose incremental changes that could achieve small policy improvements over time.

U.S. politicians who attack Beijing for economic practices that lead to "shipping American jobs to China" also discourage policymakers and experts from highlighting the benefits of improved relations between the two countries. When these politicians exploit patriotic feelings and engage in demagogic "China bashing" to attract votes, they have a chilling effect on policy analysts. In this atmosphere, proposals that could significantly improve relations become vulnerable to political attacks as "appeasement," "un-American" or "weak on China." Conversely, highly questionable protectionist measures to help uncompetitive companies are seen as "tough" and "pro-American." The upshot is that the acceptable bounds of the policy debate on China are far narrower than they ought or need to be.

What to do

To rectify American security policy toward China, the United States needs to return to its traditional policy goal of preventing any foreign power from exercising regional dominance in the Asia Pacific. This policy served America well for over a century and underpinned broad U.S. resistance to Japanese aggression across the Pacific during World War II. The U.S. has never sought undisputed geopolitical primacy (or "hegemony" as some call it) in Asia; this position was thrust upon the United States by the surrender of Japan and the ensuing power vacuum in the region. Looking to the future, the U.S. needs to embrace the view that while it will not allow China to assert dominance in Asia, neither does America seek to maintain its own dominance in the region as a security objective either. Adopting this view will allow the United States to best realize peace and stability in East Asia for the indefinite future.

Regarding economic relations with China, the U.S. would be much better off explicitly taking the position that eliminating remaining trade barriers would unleash far greater trade and investment between the two countries, a result that would be in the best interests of the United States. Participating robustly in China's economic development, exporting extensively to the Chinese market, investing in China's manufacturing sector and infrastructure, and encouraging Chinese investment in the United States will significantly increase American prosperity. Protectionist sentiments should not be allowed to heavily influence U.S. economic policy toward China. The U.S. should instead encourage extensive American investment in China as well as billions of dollars of direct foreign investment in the United States by Chinese companies. Doing so will create a large number of American jobs, reduce production costs for U.S. companies and prices for American consumers, and spur the development of innovative products.

The best way for the United States to encourage greater democracy and human rights practices in China is to improve U.S.-China relations by resolving outstanding security issues, and in so doing protect Taiwan's democratic system for the long term. Friendly relations will sharply undercut the ability of China's Communist Party to justify internal repression on security grounds. The Party would lose what former Soviet dissident Natan Sharansky calls "its most dependable weapon in the struggle for unassailable domination—an external threat ... that can unify the people and justify draconian security measures at home."[5] With the "U.S. threat" gone, the regime would no longer be able to argue that internal dissent weakens China's ability to confront an attack by the United States. And in the absence of ongoing tension with the U.S. on security issues, Chinese people seeking democracy and human rights could far more openly express support for a multiparty system and indeed, the political practices followed in America, Taiwan and Hong Kong.

A new paradigm for U.S.-China relations

Achieving the major security, economic and political benefits of improved U.S.-China relations is not a small task. It will require a fundamental shift in U.S. policy and an effort by both countries to build the foundation for a "stable peace" by establishing a new paradigm for their relations. A stable peace between the United States and China would be characterized by coexistence and greater cooperation. It can be realized by pursuing rapprochement with China through a process of reciprocal restraint, where each country practices accommodation and expects reciprocal actions in return. The principles and goals to guide this process are best embodied in a Framework Agreement which would create a new diplomatic architecture between the two countries, strengthening stability and enhancing prosperity in the Asia Pacific for generations to come.

As the dominant country in the Asia Pacific, the United States now faces a crucial strategic choice: it can use its superior diplomatic, economic and political power to seek a stable peace with China by achieving a new paradigm for U.S.-China relations. Or, on the contrary, the U.S. can narrowly focus on protecting its domestic markets from Chinese business and building up its military presence in East Asia in the expectation of an inevitable armed conflict with China.

Former Secretary of State Henry Kissinger clearly sums up the risks of future conflict between the U.S. and China in his 2011 history and memoir, *On China*. Kissinger writes:

> I am aware of the realistic obstacles to the cooperative U.S.-China relationship I consider essential to global stability and peace. A cold war between the two countries would arrest progress for a generation on both sides of the Pacific. It would spread disputes into internal politics of every region at a time when global issues such as nuclear proliferation, the environment, energy security, and climate change impose global cooperation.[6]

To China hawks and protectionists who tend to approach the future fearfully, a U.S. policy toward China of the kind proposed here—based on reciprocal restraint and enlightened self-interest—may seem objectionable. But a policy which relies on American power to facilitate a long-lasting framework for peaceful and prosperous relations with China would best advance the interests of the great majority of Americans, now and in the future.

CHAPTER TWO

The real military balance

For more than a decade, the faction of U.S. policy analysts, journalists and academics known popularly as "China hawks" has fanned public fears of a coming war with China. They have called for the United States to safeguard its "primacy" as the world's only remaining superpower against a future "China threat."

In 1992, former Under Secretary of Defense Paul Wolfowitz postulated that the "number one objective of U.S. post-Cold War political and military strategy should be preventing the emergence of a rival superpower."[1] Wolfowitz's view turned America's traditional strategic approach to Asia on its head. For more than a century, the United States strived to prevent any other power from dominating the Asia Pacific, and on the basis of this widely accepted strategic doctrine, fought a war against Japan which sought to impose a "Greater East Asia Co-Prosperity Sphere" on the region. Under Wolfowitz's formulation, however, rather than deterring another power from exerting hegemony, the U.S. strategic goal would become maintaining American dominance for the indefinite future.

Time and again, history has shown that empires eventually decline and misguided attempts to preserve primacy often lead to unnecessary wars and conflicts. In the twenty-first century, an even greater flaw in the quest for primacy is that it does not bring real national security. Instead, it inspires other countries to modernize their armed forces, seek nuclear weapons and build stronger militaries to protect their sovereignty and independence. A policy of primacy also weakens America's ability to build critical alliances to meet transnational threats arising from terrorism, weapons proliferation, pandemic disease and energy insecurity. Overcoming these difficult international problems requires extensive cooperation and collaboration among governments more often than unilateral action. Cooperation arises through a process of relationship-building which places a premium on mutual equality and respect.[2]

Yet China hawks in the United States have embraced the premise of Wolfowitz's argument about U.S. primacy and taken a starkly negative view of China's strategic objectives. As a result of their influence, U.S. policy strives to prepare for a hypothetical threat from China that does not exist now and may well never exist in the future.

Historian and policy expert Michael Lind of the New America Foundation explains the profound significance of the new policy of primacy as a "radical departure" in the history of American foreign policy:

> American grand strategy since the emergence of the United States as a great power in the late nineteenth century has combined two objectives: preserving U.S. hegemony in North America, and preventing the hegemony of a hostile power in any of the three regions outside of North America with major industrial or energy resources—Europe, Asia, and the Middle East. In both world wars, U.S. leaders sought to prevent hegemony in other regions by means of great power cooperation in a multipolar world, not by means of solitary and exclusive U.S. global hegemony. Following the collapse of the Soviet Empire, American leaders broke with this tradition .... [I]n the 1990s and 2000s, U.S. leaders sought to convert the temporary hegemonic alliance system the United States had constructed during the Cold War into the basis of indefinite U.S. global hegemony .... [T]his plan for U.S. domination of every region ... represents a *radical departure* from America's previous policy of seeking to preserve rather than prevent a diversity of power in the world, while sharing the burdens of preserving the peace with other rich and militarily powerful states.[3]

China hawks who advocate American primacy often obscure the striking fact that China does not now pose a significant military threat to the United States. None of them offers proof that China will one day become a major military threat to the U.S., because such proof does not exist. Instead, they extrapolate a possible trajectory of developments by pointing to allegedly dangerous activities the Chinese regime has undertaken as well as to historical precedents. Their core argument is that the U.S. must be prepared to deal with worst-case scenarios which may come to pass if China's leadership shifts from its long-standing focus on economic development to a strategy of militarily dominating Asia and the world.

Here are several leading examples of these views:

> [China] is an unsatisfied and ambitious power whose goal is to dominate Asia, not by invading and occupying neighboring nations, but by being so much more powerful than they are that nothing will be allowed to happen in East Asia without China's at least tacit consent .... [China] has set goals for itself that are directly contrary to American interests,

the most important of those goals being to replace the United States as the preeminent power in Asia, to reduce American influence, to prevent Japan and the United States from creating a kind of 'contain China' front, and to extend its power into the South China and East China Seas so that it controls the region's essential sea-lanes. China aims at achieving a kind of hegemony. (Richard Bernstein and Ross H. Munro)[4]

China's hard-eyed communist rulers have set out on a coolly pragmatic course of strategic deception that masks their true goals: undermining the United States around the world and raising China to a position of dominant international political and military power. They seek to push the United States out of the vital Pacific region and achieve virtual Chinese hegemony in Asia .... The reason Americans should take the threat from China so seriously is that it puts at risk the very national existence of the United States. (Bill Gertz)[5]

China's quest for hegemony may take it through three phases:

Basic Hegemony: the recovery of Taiwan and the assertion of undisputed control over the South China Sea

Regional Hegemony: the extension of the Chinese Empire to the maximum extent of the Qing

Global hegemony: A worldwide contest with the U.S. to replace the current *Pax Americana* with a *Pax Sinica*. (Steven W. Mosher)[6]

No regime poses a greater threat to global security today than communist China. With the collapse of the Soviet Union, and the internal disarray of the Russian Federation, the People's Republic of China sees itself as the sole communist superpower in the world. (Edward Timperlake and William C. Triplett II)[7]

Views of China in international relations theory

The views of hawkish foreign policy analysts draw support from some theorists of international relations. Based on international relations theory that claims the ultimate aim of any state "is to be the hegemon—the only great power in the [international] system"—Professor John Mearsheimer of the University of Chicago argued in 2005 that "China cannot rise peacefully, and if it continues its dramatic economic growth over the next few decades, the United States and China are likely to engage in an intense security competition with considerable potential for war." Mearsheimer further stressed that since "it is too hard to project and sustain power around the globe ... the best outcome that a state can hope for is to dominate its own backyard." Consequently, China is "likely to try to push the United States out of Asia, much the way the United States pushed the European great powers out of the Western Hemisphere." The U.S. should react to China's probable attempt to dominate Asia, in Mearsheimer's view, by seeking to "contain China and ultimately weaken it to the point where it is no longer capable" of realizing this goal because the "United States does not tolerate peer competitors."[8]

Some international relations theorists analogize China to nineteenth century Germany or Japan in its current development trajectory, to argue that it is highly likely to challenge the status quo at some future time. Robert Kagan, Senior Fellow at the Brookings Institution, notes that

> rarely have rising powers risen without sparking a major war that reshaped the international system to reflect new realities of power .... Germany's rise after 1870, and Europe's reaction to it, eventually produced World War I .... The British tried containment, appeasement and even offers of alliance, but never fully comprehended Kaiser Wilhelm's need to challenge the British supremacy he both admired and envied. Japan's rise after 1868 produced two rounds of warfare—first with China and Russia at the turn of the century, and later with the United States and Britain in World War II.[9]

Mearsheimer and Kagan's thinking underlies the point of view many China hawks embrace—that the only "realistic" U.S. policy is one that prepares "for the worst."[10] Under this paradigm, significantly increasing U.S. military bases and forces in the Asia Pacific to heighten military preparedness, coupled with diplomatically balancing Japan and India against China, would enable the United States to successfully defeat China in a future conflict.

However, this perspective is seriously challenged by other scholars of international relations for failing to take into account unique factors in China's rise, including its acceptance of the U.S.-led international system, its limited security goals, its unwillingness to challenge the U.S. militarily, its focus on economic development, and its diplomatic approach of *winning acceptance* as a great power from other leading powers through peaceful means.[11] Former U.S. national security advisor Zbigniew Brzezinski points out that

> China is clearly assimilating into the international system. Its leadership appears to realize that attempting to dislodge the United States would be futile and that the cautious spread of Chinese influence is the surest path to global prominence .... [T]he Chinese leadership appears much more flexible and sophisticated than many previous aspirants to great power status.[12]

The postwar "international system" described by Professor Brzezinski is not comparable to the imperial system, often cited by China hawks, in which Germany and Japan attempted to become great powers. The current system is characterized by openness, relatively free markets and principles of nondiscrimination that have allowed China to rapidly develop its economy as well as to assert international leadership. As Professor John Ikenberry of Princeton University points out, "leading states, most of them advanced liberal democracies, do not always agree, but they are engaged in a continuous process of give-and-take over economics, politics, and security."[13] By cooperating with international partners in an age of acknowledged "globalization," China has acquired the ability to shape the policies and norms that govern global economic and security relations.

The postwar Western order, concludes Ikenberry, also "has a remarkable capacity to accommodate rising powers. New entrants into the system have ways of gaining status and authority and opportunities to play a role in governing the order."[14] Rather than seeking to overturn or displace the international order, China and other developing countries strive to obtain prestige and authority within this order.

U.S. "hedging" strategy toward China and its consequences

Based in large part on the views of China hawks, the U.S. government adopted a "hedging" strategy during the George W. Bush administration, so the United States would be prepared in the event China challenges its military dominance in the Asia Pacific. The Obama Administration has accelerated this approach. Although called "hedging," a term that conveys prudence and reasonableness, this strategy now amounts to the military containment of China. It assumes the worst-case scenarios of China attacking Taiwan or acting aggressively toward the U.S. or its allies in Asia—and aims to ensure an overwhelming American military victory in response to those actions.

In practice, hedging has several components. First of all, it entails conducting close reconnaissance and surveillance of China. The U.S. Navy regularly sends warships up and down China's coast, for the purposes of collecting maritime intelligence, reminding China of its relatively weak naval capabilities, and deterring any Chinese temptation to consider an attack on Taiwan. The U.S. Air Force similarly patrols China's periphery, testing the readiness of China's anti-aircraft defenses, while sending high-altitude planes for intelligence collection over sensitive military installations deep in China's interior. Together with imagery from spy satellites, Air

Force patrols enable the Pentagon to closely monitor Chinese military activities and, particularly, its missile deployments.

A second important aspect of the U.S. hedging strategy has been strengthening American forces in the Asia Pacific, especially on the island of Guam. Numerous U.S. strategic assets—particularly long-range bombers, aircraft carriers, and submarines—have been deployed to the region, even while the Pentagon engages in a major, multi-year construction project to build facilities that will house large new contingents of soldiers, sailors and marines.[15]

In the diplomatic arena, the Bush and Obama Administrations sought to bolster U.S. security relations with Japan largely for the purpose of containing China and preparing for a future military conflict. Washington and Tokyo have implemented agreements to ensure that U.S. forces can use Japan as a springboard for the defense of Taiwan in the event of a Chinese attack. U.S. and Japanese soldiers have exercised together and coordinated closely on military maneuvers in which Japan plays a vigorous supporting role in a potential U.S. armed response. More broadly, the U.S. has urged Japan to revise its constitution (imposed originally at American insistence) which currently restricts the activities of military forces to self-defense. With this legal change, Japanese forces would be able to range broadly through the Asia Pacific, assisting U.S. forces in the containment of China. Although China is not explicitly identified in official diplomatic communiqués as the driver for this U.S. policy, administration officials leave no doubt that their foremost concern is gaining greater Japanese help in countering China.

The Bush and Obama Administrations have also significantly improved U.S. security relations with India, which fought a border war with China in 1962. In careful negotiations over several years, the U.S. increased both the quality and quantity of sales to India of sophisticated weapons and technology with military applications, raising cooperation with India's military to a historically unprecedented level. Importantly, the U.S. has removed obstacles to extensive civilian nuclear cooperation between the two countries, eliminating sanctions imposed by the Clinton administration for India's test of a nuclear device in 1998.

The Obama Administration accelerates U.S. hedging strategy

In November 2011, the Obama Administration hardened the U.S. hedging policy against China in both word and deed. Secretary of State Hillary Clinton announced the shift in an article entitled "America's Pacific Century" that she published in the widely read journal *Foreign Policy*. Clinton argued that as the U.S. winds down its involvement in the wars in Iraq and Afghanistan, it should take a "strategic pivot" to Asia because "harnessing Asia's growth and dynamism is central to American economic and strategic interests." From a security standpoint, the U.S. would be "forging a broad-based military presence":

> The challenges of today's rapidly changing region ... require that the United States pursue a more geographically distributed, operationally resilient, and politically sustainable force posture. We are modernizing our basing arrangements with traditional allies [Japan and South Korea] in Northeast Asia ... while enhancing our presence in Southeast Asia and into the Indian Ocean .... [A] more broadly distributed military presence across the region ... will provide a more robust bulwark against threats or efforts to undermine regional peace and stability.[16]

President Obama and Secretary Clinton rolled out the administration's policy of accelerating the strategic encirclement of China during a week-long trip to Asia in early November 2011. Meeting with Australia's prime minister, Obama announced that 2,500 marines would be deployed to the country's northern territory for joint training and exercises as well as to give the U.S. Air Force increased access to bases close to the South China Sea. This agreement amounted to "the first long-term expansion of the American military's presence in the Pacific since the end of the Vietnam War."[17] In his speech to the Australian parliament, Obama emphasized that the U.S. would establish a newly enhanced presence across the region through additional measures to strengthen alliances with Japan and South Korea while bolstering military cooperation with Thailand, the Philippines, Indonesia, Malaysia, Singapore, and India.[18] Secretary Clinton flew to the Philippines where she dramatically stood on the deck of a U.S. guided missile cruiser anchored in Manila Bay, denounced China's use of "intimidation" tactics to bolster its territorial claims in the South China Sea, and proclaimed joint efforts to expand the U.S.-Philippine military alliance.[19]

In June 2012, the Obama administration moved decisively to implement its "strategic pivot" toward Asia. Secretary of Defense Leon Panetta announced the U.S. would deploy 60 percent of all naval forces to the Pacific by 2020— six aircraft carriers and a majority of the Navy's cruisers, submarines, destroyers and littoral combat ships. Panetta also sped up efforts to establish basing arrangements for U.S. forces in Vietnam, Thailand and the Philippines to "obtain a more extensive and persistent U.S. military presence" that would strengthen the strategic encirclement of China. The defense secretary expressed particularly great enthusiasm for a new U.S. presence at Vietnam's Cam Ranh Bay, saying that "Access for U.S. naval ships into this facility is a key component of [the U.S.-Vietnam] relationship and we see a tremendous potential here."[20] Panetta's remarks were especially striking since Vietnam is a communist country which bears responsibility for the deaths of nearly

60,000 American soldiers, sailors, airmen and marines during the Vietnam war, and has failed to account for approximately 1,700 MIAs.[21]

Perhaps the most profound indication of new U.S. efforts to confront the "China threat" came in an administration decision leaked to the *Washington Times* just as the President and Secretary of State left in November 2011 on the first leg of their Asia trip. For the first time, the Pentagon officially endorsed a new "Air Sea Battle Concept" (ASBC) that signaled a new "Cold War-style approach to China," according to an unnamed senior administration official.[22] The ASBC would create a new joint air-sea force designed to defeat China in the event of war. The elements of the ASBC strategy include: carrying out joint Navy, Marine Corps and Air Force "long-range penetrating strike operations" in mainland China; using Navy submarines to destroy Chinese air-defense systems to prepare the way for Air Force strikes; employing offensive mining by Air Force stealth and non-stealth bombers to support the Navy's anti-submarine warfare campaign; and launching joint Navy and Air Force cyber-attacks on Chinese forces.[23]

One retired Marine Corps officer, writing in the *Armed Forces Journal*, noted the "highly escalatory" nature of the ASBC strategy:

> Surely, given the nuclear weapons China possesses and its growing irregular warfare and economic assets, we should question very seriously any operational concept that requires extensive strikes on the Chinese mainland. A military confrontation with China would be the biggest national security challenge since World War II, yet [ASBC] advocates suggest it can be handled by just two of the four services. To the outside observer, this is astonishing; to the insider skeptic, it is absurd.[24]

While both President Obama and Secretary Clinton used diplomatic language to describe the new policy of accelerating military efforts to contain China, U.S. newspapers correctly characterized their approach. "Countering China, Obama Asserts U.S. a Pacific Power," read the headline of one story filed by Associated Press White House Correspondent Ben Feller.[25] In essence, the Obama Administration's "pivot" toward Asia amounted to endorsing and reinforcing the strategy articulated by Paul Wolfowitz in 1992—ensuring the continuation of U.S. primacy as the dominant power in the Asia Pacific for the indefinite future.

Australian strategist Hugh White, a former Australian senior defense official, was particularly blunt in assessing the significance of the administration's new policy, when he told the *New York Times*:

> [The] importance of last week's basing announcement [in northern Australia] lies in what it symbolizes about U.S. strategic aims in Asia .... America is determined to push back with all the instruments of American power against China's challenge and remain the

unquestionable leading power in Asia .... Many believe America has no choice because the only alternative to U.S. primacy is Chinese hegemony. But is that right? Does America need to dominate Asia in order to stop China dominating it? Or could America balance and limit China's power, while still allowing a rising China more space? Might there be a way to prevent Chinese hegemony and still avoid outright rivalry? We should start asking these questions now, because we are running out of time to answer them.[26]

American journalist and foreign policy expert Stephen Glain also offered a clear-eyed view:

Mr. Obama ... seems now to be embracing a militarized policy with regard to China, the sinew of which is a global network of military bases that has changed little since the peak of the Cold War. Far from reducing its profile in Asia, the Pentagon has been quietly ... building up forces on the United States territory of Guam, a far-reaching strategic enclave in the Pacific .... Washington justifies its Pacific buildup by citing China's increasingly menacing claims on the region's contested waterways. But there has been no serious American-led [diplomatic] effort to resolve such disputes .... Indeed, America's top diplomat has become the chief civilian advocate for military answers to diplomatic challenges.[27]

For his part, former National Security Council senior director for Asian Affairs Michael Green, now a professor at Georgetown University, noted the Obama Administration's abrupt change from its earlier view of China and suggested this shift was driven at least in part by domestic politics during a presidential election year:

In 2009, Obama's message for Asia emphasized a concert of power with Beijing based on mutual respect for each other's 'core interests,' 'strategic reassurance' and an elevated strategic and economic dialogue. The reality is that U.S. strategy toward China will by necessity be a mix of concert of power and balance of power—engaging and hedging. But this is better done quietly and consistently rather than swinging from one to the other. The political desire to score big points in domestic U.S. media may have blinded the White House to Theodore Roosevelt's famous maxim that the United States should 'speak softly and carry a big stick'.[28]

U.S. military clashes with China

Since the Bush administration, when the U.S. first adopted a hedging policy toward China, U.S. and Chinese military forces have clashed several times in the vicinity of the South China Sea. Each of these worrisome and, in some cases, little reported incidents arose from China's response to close-in surveillance and intelligence gathering by the U.S. Navy and Air Force. In April 2000, a Chinese interceptor jet collided with a U.S. Navy EP-3 surveillance aircraft near China's coast. The EP-3 then made an emergency landing on China's Hainan Island. The tense ten-day standoff that followed was ultimately resolved through China's return of the 24-member crew and a U.S. "expression of regret and sorrow" both for the death of the Chinese pilot and for entering Chinese air space without prior clearance. China treated the U.S. statement as an official apology but the U.S. indicated "we did not do anything wrong, and therefore it was not possible to apologize."[29]

In March 2009, Chinese vessels and aircraft harassed a U.S. Navy surveillance ship, the *Impeccable*, about 75 miles from Hainan Island, while it monitored submarine activity near a new base for Chinese nuclear submarines and advanced warships.[30] A Chinese Navy frigate crossed the *Impeccable*'s bow at close range and Chinese aircraft conducted 11 low-altitude flyovers. Five Chinese vessels subsequently shadowed the *Impeccable* and two of them came within 50 feet before the *Impeccable* left the area. Following the incident, the U.S. condemned the "unprofessional maneuvers by Chinese vessels" and formally protested that the ship was operating in international waters. China questioned the accuracy of the U.S. complaint and later claimed that the *Impeccable*'s activities constituted "preparation of the battlefield."

In March and May of 2009, a patrol vessel operated by the Chinese Bureau of Fisheries confronted another U.S. Navy surveillance ship, the *Victorious*, while it cruised approximately 120 miles off China's coast in the Yellow Sea. The U.S. vessel operated within China's 200 mile "exclusive economic zone" (EEZ), an area where China has the exclusive right to explore and use marine resources, including oil and gas deposits, under the Law of the Sea. The Chinese patrol boat illuminated the *Victorious* with high-powered spotlights and a Chinese maritime surveillance aircraft conducted 12 low-altitude fly bys before other Chinese vessels came within about 100 feet of the U.S. Navy ship in heavy fog, as it was leaving the area.

The clashes between U.S. and Chinese naval vessels since 2001 have two major causes. First, China regards the "Cold War-type surveillance operations" that the U.S. routinely conducts along the full length of China's Coast as "gravely threatening," according to Professor Lyle Goldstein of the U.S. Naval War College and former director of the China Maritime Studies Institute there.[31] Goldstein writes that "dangerous interactions between U.S. and Chinese aircraft and vessels have become the norm, and one life has already been lost, in the April 2001 surveillance-plane incident ...."[32]

China's increasing desire to protect its coasts and the maritime routes on which its economy heavily depends now "conflict with ever more aggressive and intrusive U.S. military intelligence probes," in the view of maritime policy expert Mark Valencia of the Nautilus Institute. Since extensive U.S. intelligence gathering is a critical part of the U.S. strategy for containing China, Valencia predicts that "it seems inevitable that the warships, submarines, and military aircraft of the two countries will increasingly encounter and possibly confront each other in and over the South and East China seas."[33] Lyle Goldstein rejects as "disingenuous" U.S. claims that China's opposition to U.S. military surveillance activities in the South China Sea threatens "freedom of navigation":

In fact, such U.S. surveillance activities all along China's coasts are excessive to the point of seriously disrupting the bilateral relationship and should thus be decreased, especially if linked to concrete progress on Chinese military transparency.

The intelligence benefits of the these activities (which could most likely be obtained by less provocative means) are not worth the political costs, which include aggravating Chinese nationalism to a high degree .... [These activities] remind Chinese on a regular basis of past humiliations related to 'gunboat diplomacy.' Bold decisions from Washington on this issue are now required.[34]

A second factor contributing to clashes between U.S. and Chinese military forces near China's coast is differing interpretations of the rights of states under the United Nations Convention on the Law of the Sea, which 161 countries and the European Community have thus far joined. Although the Law of the Sea established "exclusive economic zones" extending 200 miles off the shores of coastal states, China and the United States sharply dispute the rights of foreign states to carry out military activities within the EEZs. China argues that military activities conducted without consent that involve intelligence gathering, surveys and hydrography (mapping the ocean floor) are illegal because they show hostile intent and violate the Convention's core principle that EEZs shall be used for peaceful purposes. The United States, one of a handful of countries which signed but has not ratified the Law of the Sea, argues to the contrary that military activities of this kind are not "hostile" and therefore do not violate international law.

This unresolved dispute over legal requirements contributes to an atmosphere of uncertainty, confusion and ambiguity that allows potentially dangerous confrontations between U.S. and Chinese forces to continue. As China experts Michael Swaine of the Carnegie Endowment and M. Taylor Fravel of MIT point out:

While many outside observers regard China's physical challenges to U.S. or other foreign military surveillance activities within China's EEZ as a highly significant indication of increased assertiveness, from Beijing's perspective, such activities constitute a legitimate and understandable reaction to what is perceived as hostile behavior. Equally significant, China's more aggressive challenges in recent years were apparently prompted by increases in the tempo and intrusiveness of U.S. surveillance activities within China's EEZ in response to the ongoing modernization of China's naval forces. According to Chinese sources, Beijing repeatedly requested that Washington cease such increasing activities, apparently to no avail.[35]

One of the most disconcerting aspects of the ongoing friction between the U.S. and China over coastal surveillance and intelligence gathering is that the problem is highly likely to become worse because of rapid advances in technology. The U.S. is now far ahead in an arms race to develop a variety of maritime drones—crewless vessels and submarines—that promise to be more effective and less detectable surveillance "platforms" than those currently in use. Together with satellites, high-altitude reconnaissance aircraft like U-2s, ocean surveillance ships and aerial drones, the new unmanned surface vessels and unmanned underwater systems that are under development will increase the U.S. ability to sense and dominate what the Pentagon terms the "battlespace." Mark Valencia of the Nautilus Institute sums up the greater risk of confrontation that will arise as nations deploy the new technologies:

> The situation is presently beyond international control. Thus, continued intrusive probes are likely to generate frustration and resentment that may translate into the forcible halting of such 'intrusions' when and if detected. The scale and scope of maritime and airborne intelligence collection activities are likely to continue to expand rapidly in many countries, involving levels and sorts of activities quite unprecedented in peacetime. They will not only become more intensive; they will generally be more intrusive. Indeed, stepped up drone-missions may even be considered a prelude to impending warfare. They will generate tensions and more frequent crises; they will produce defensive reactions and escalatory dynamics; and they will lead to less stability in the most affected regions, especially in Asia.[36]

U.S. engagement with China on security issues

The U.S. has also pursued "engagement" with China on two major international security issues during the past 15 years: countering global terrorism and ending North Korea's nuclear weapons program.

Following the September 11, 2001 terrorist attacks, Chinese president Zhang Jemin made a critical decision to assist the United States despite a major deterioration in relations the previous spring, when Chinese Air Force jets forced down a U.S. patrol aircraft for allegedly penetrating China's air space. Beijing importantly supported the U.S. policy of confronting international terrorism based on its view that a U.S.-dominated international system provides the stability China needs to successfully develop its economy and achieve greater prosperity. China also believed that cooperation with the U.S. would be the best way of countering Muslim separatist movements in the country's western region. U.S. and Chinese cooperation against global terrorism continues to the present day and has involved major exchanges of intelligence information since 2001.

On North Korea, once the Bush administration took an internal decision to seriously pursue the Six Party talks tasked with ending Pyongyang's nuclear program, it realized that China had more ability to influence North Korea than any other country participating in the negotiations. Since 2005, the U.S. has relied heavily on China to apply diplomatic pressure on North Korea which remains deeply dependent on China to support its ailing economy. (China provides a large percentage of North Korea's oil, foodstuffs and other critical resources.) China has consequently brokered several breakthroughs in the sensitive negotiations seeking to eliminate North Korea's capability to produce nuclear weapons.

After North Korea tested a nuclear device in October 2006 and again in June 2009, China's active support for U.S.-sponsored resolutions and sanctions in the United Nations Security Council proved especially critical. Following the death of North Korean leader Kim Jong Il in December 2011, China moved quickly to ensure a smooth transition to his inexperienced 27-year-old son, Kim Jong-un.

As part of these stabilizing efforts, China used its influence to encourage North Korea to reach a new agreement with the United States on nuclear issues. In late February 2012, after meetings of North Korean, American and Chinese negotiators in Beijing, Pyongyang agreed to suspend its nuclear weapons tests, allow international inspectors at its nuclear complex, and adopt a moratorium on long-range missile tests.[37] The agreement soon broke down over Pyongyang's insistence on conducting a rocket test in violation of UN sanctions, leading China to join the United States and all other members of the Security Council in condemning the test. After the Security Council vote, U.S. Ambassador to the United Nations Susan Rice stressed that China "worked with us closely to craft this [UN] statement" which demonstrated that "the international community is united in sending a clear message to North Korea that such provocations are serious and totally unacceptable."[38]

The nature of the Chinese security threat

China hawks are hard-pressed to cite any evidence that China has a current *intention* to broadly challenge the United States and its existing dominance in Asia. That is because China's leaders, as early as 1996, achieved "rough consensus" on a national strategy which "aims to engineer China's rise to great power status within the constraints of a unipolar international system that the United States dominates," as Professor Avery Goldstein of the University of Pennsylvania observes. This strategy

> is designed to sustain the conditions necessary for continuing China's program of economic and military modernization as well as to minimize the risk that others, most importantly the peerless United States, will view the ongoing increase in China's capabilities as an unacceptably dangerous threat that must be parried or perhaps even forestalled.[39]

Similarly, Asia experts Michael Swaine and Ashley Tellis of the Carnegie Endowment call China's national strategy a

> pragmatic approach that emphasizes the primacy of internal economic growth and stability, the nurturing of amicable international relations, the relative restraint in the use of force combined with increasing efforts to create a more modern military and the continued search for asymmetric gains internationally.[40]

China's national strategy is reflected in its major security objectives: 1) maintaining a stable international environment that is conducive to economic development; 2) keeping stability on China's borders; 3) countering, co-opting and circumventing U.S. power on China's periphery in "non-confrontational ways"; 4) deterring and defending against an attack on Chinese territory; and 5) augmenting China's political, economic and diplomatic influence.[41] Broadly speaking, these security goals are conservative in nature, with the purpose of maintaining stability and protecting China's territorial integrity while the country pursues economic and social development. In an overall strategic sense, China seeks to prevent its encirclement by any foreign powers, as former Secretary of State Henry Kissinger describes:

> China's greatest strategic fear is that an outside power or powers will establish military deployments around China's periphery capable of encroaching on China's territory or meddling in its domestic institutions.

When China deemed that it faced such a threat in the past, it went to war rather than risk the outcome of what it saw as gathering trends—in Korea in 1950, against India in 1962, along the northern border with the Soviet Union in 1969, and against Vietnam in 1979.[42]

Comparison of Chinese and U.S. military capabilities

China hawks frequently argue that "realism" requires U.S. strategists to look past China's current intentions, no matter how benign they may be. Since intentions can change easily—with a friendly country becoming hostile all too quickly under various historical circumstances—they contend the United States should measure only the capabilities of potential adversaries in order to appreciate the threat China poses. A side-by-side comparison of such capabilities, however, reveals that the U.S. outclasses China by a large margin, in virtually every military category as well as the most critical technological capabilities of command, control, communications, computers, intelligence, surveillance and reconnaissance.

It is instructive to first consider relative nuclear weapons capabilities. In an extensive report on "Chinese Nuclear Forces and U.S. Nuclear War Planning," the Natural Resources Defense Council found that "the Chinese-U.S. nuclear relationship is dramatically disproportionate in favor of the United States and will remain so for the foreseeable future."[43] Below are critical points of comparison:

> The U.S. nuclear warhead stockpile totals approximately 5,000 while China possesses about 240 warheads.[44]

> The U.S. currently deploys 450 intercontinental ballistic missiles (ICBMs) and about 290 submarine-launched ballistic missiles (SLBMs) that can reach China, most of them equipped with multiple warheads. China has up to 65 ICBMs that are capable of hitting targets in the United States.[45]

> The U.S. Navy currently fields 12 Ohio-class nuclear-powered ballistic missile submarines (SSBNs) and the majority of them operate in the Pacific.[46] China is developing a new nuclear-powered ballistic missile submarine, but now has no credible sea-based nuclear capability. According to the Pentagon, its "program has faced repeated delays."[47]

> The U.S. has 94 long-range bombers for precision strikes—18 B-2 stealth bombers and 76 B-52H *stratofortress* bombers—that can deliver nuclear bombs or nuclear-tipped cruise missiles. The stealth bombers have the "unique ability to penetrate an enemy's most

sophisticated defenses and threaten its most valued, and heavily
defended, targets." The Obama Administration revived work on a
new long-range bomber "as part of the Pentagon's 'strategic pivot'
towards the Asia-Pacific region, whose long distances pose huge
problems for military planners .... The so-called 'Long-Range
Strike Bomber' is meant to be stealthy, capable of carrying nuclear
weapons and ... can be remotely flown without a pilot on board."
China, by contrast, has no stealth bombers and "may have a small
number of aircraft with a secondary nuclear capability, but they
would be severely tested by U.S. and allied air defense systems or in
air-to-air combat."[48]

Clearly, the United States has overwhelming nuclear superiority—both
in quantity and quality—with respect to China.[49] Moreover, at a future
time when the National Missile Defense program proves effective and is
fully deployed, the U.S. would acquire the capability to carry out a first-
strike nuclear attack against China with a relatively low probability that
China could successfully retaliate. The prospect that the U.S. will be able
to neutralize China's minimal nuclear deterrent force is driving Chinese
military planners either to build up the country's missile capability or to
install multiple independently targetable warheads (MIRVs) on their ICBM
force, as will be discussed in greater detail later in this chapter.

On the conventional side, U.S. power projection capabilities are similarly
far superior to those of China:

> The U.S. Navy operates 11 aircraft carriers, each equipped with
> more than 55 fighters and ground-attack aircraft.[50] China has refur-
> bished one *circa* 1984 aircraft carrier, purchased from Ukraine, that
> is only used for training purposes.

> The U.S. has a fleet of about 185 F-22 stealth fighter aircraft that
> "project air dominance, rapidly and at great distances ... before
> being detected."[51] According to the U.S. Air Force, the "F-22
> cannot be matched by any known or projected fighter aircraft."
> China fields no fighters with stealth capabilities that prevent
> detection by radar.[52]

> The U.S. Air Force operates 32 E-3 aircraft—airborne warning
> and control systems (AWACS)—that are considered the "premier
> air battle command and control aircraft in the world today."
> The AWACS "provide all-weather air surveillance and command,
> control, communications and intelligence for tactical and air defense
> forces." China has deployed four KJ-2000 airborne early warning
> aircraft that are inferior to the U.S. E-3s.[53]

Beyond this telling comparison of U.S. and Chinese forces, the U.S. currently spends far more than China on defense. The U.S. base defense budget for fiscal year 2012 was $530.5 billion with an additional $115.1 billion designated for the wars in Iraq and Afghanistan, bringing total defense spending to $645.6 billion.[54] China's defense budget for 2012, by contrast, was $106 billion, though many U.S. defense analysts believe that real defense spending is higher.[55] (In 2010, the Pentagon estimated that actual expenditures were approximately twice the amount in the official budget.[56]) Even using a number that takes into account the Pentagon's adjustment factor, the U.S. currently spends more than three times as much as China on defense.

The only area where Chinese military strength exceeds that of the United States is in numbers of troops, the least important measure of a country's modern military capabilities. China's total personnel amounts to approximately 2.25 million while that of the U.S. is about 1.47 million. Yet even in this area, when combined with NATO, the number of U.S. military personnel far exceeds that of China, totaling approximately 3.81 million.[57]

Professor Avery Goldstein assesses that "the range and sophistication of U.S. air and naval forces give it the clout not only to threaten China's core security interests but also to offset Beijing's ability to exert influence over continental and maritime developments in the region beyond the PRC's borders."[58] A team of experts at the Center for Strategic and International Studies (CSIS) and the Peterson Institute for International Economics in Washington further clarifies that despite China's military modernization efforts, "the United States may still ensure that the gap between the military capabilities of the United States and [China] remains wide and formidable, while providing a sense of balance and reassurance in Asia and beyond."[59] In their study, these experts laid out specific measures the U.S. could take to preserve its massive military superiority, including safeguarding critical assets for command, control, communications, computers, intelligence, surveillance and reconnaissance to ensure their survivability.[60]

China's military modernization

As the U.S. buildup in Asia moves forward, China's military modernization continues apace. China's leaders are attempting to modernize their armed forces just as they make determined efforts to achieve economic and social development. They see a modernized People's Liberation Army (PLA) as a critical aspect of China's comprehensive national power.

Modernizing the Chinese Navy

No aspect of China's military modernization rivets the attention of American analysts more than efforts to increase the power and capabilities of the country's navy. To understand China's rationale for modernizing its navy, the strategy China has adopted and the new weapons systems China is developing, it is exceptionally helpful to turn to two experts in the field: Professor Bernard Cole of the National War College, a 30-year Navy veteran and former commanding officer of Destroyer Squadron 35, whose work *The Great Wall at Sea* is a classic in the field; and Rear Admiral Michael McDevitt (USN, Ret.), Director of Strategy Studies at the Center for Naval Analyses, who served as commandant of the National War College and commanding officer of a U.S. Navy aircraft carrier battlegroup.

The broad economic rationale for China's naval modernization is well described by Professor Cole:

[The Navy's] value as an instrument of statecraft is linked directly to maintaining and defending China's maritime stakes: the concentration of the nation's economic enterprises in its coastal regions, its dependence on one of the world's largest fleets of merchant ships and the world's second-largest ship-building capacity, its massive seaport infrastructure, its dependence on riverine and coastal maritime commerce, and the increasing national dependence on offshore fisheries and other natural resources, especially oil and natural gas.[61]

China's economic growth depends in large part on international trade, "most of which is carried on containers loaded on ships. As a result, security on the high seas is becoming a growing preoccupation for China ...."[62]

Admiral McDevitt clarifies the broad security rationale for China's naval modernization efforts:

China's maritime approaches are replete with unresolved sovereignty issues and genuine vulnerabilities. Strategic vulnerability from the sea is not a new issue for China. Weakness along its long maritime frontier has been a problem for Beijing since at least 1842, when the Treaty of Nanking ended the first Opium War and ushered in the so-called Century of Humiliation. The repeated military and diplomatic humiliations and defeats that China suffered were inflicted by Western powers including Japan that came mainly from the sea.[63]

The narrower maritime security goals that have also driven China's naval modernization in recent years are two-fold: 1) achieving eventual reunification with the island of Taiwan while preventing Taiwan from declaring national independence; and 2) asserting China's claims in disputes over territory and seabed resources with various Southeast Asian countries in the South China Sea and with Japan in the East China Sea. Since the United States Navy currently exercises maritime dominance in this region and is prepared to intervene militarily if China uses force to reach its immediate security goals, it would be correct to say that China's fear of the U.S. Navy is an over-arching factor driving modernization of the Chinese Navy. In Cole's words, "Beijing sees the United States as the primary threat to its strategic interests. The United States is the world's most powerful naval power and is the dominant power" in the Western Pacific.[64]

To realize its maritime security goals, China has adopted an "anti-access" strategy, primarily directed against the American Navy. The principal piece of this strategy is "sea denial," best defined as "preventing an adversary from using a discrete maritime area for a discrete period of time." In the case of a conflict involving Taiwan, the South China Sea or East China Sea, China's navy would strive to prevent aircraft carrier battle groups of the U.S. Navy from successfully intervening. From China's perspective, an anti-access campaign is "inherently defensive," in Cole's view, since it is seen as a response to U.S. naval forces either operating near China's coast or closing in on the Chinese mainland.[65]

In pursuing an anti-access strategy to deal with strategic contingencies in its own "backyard"—as opposed to seeking a "blue water navy" for asserting broad dominance of the high seas—China's naval planners have sought specific capabilities that explain the kinds of new weapons systems that the country has either developed or acquired in the last 15 years. As McDevitt relates, a successful anti-access strategy requires: 1) an effective surveillance system that covers ocean approaches; 2) long-range aircraft to fire long-range anti-ship cruise missiles; and 3) a sufficiently large submarine force to attack vulnerable surface ships.[66] Currently, Chinese capabilities fall short in the first two areas—the navy's ocean surveillance system is weak and it has a shortage of land-based aircraft for attacking enemy warships. However, China's robust submarine force, coupled with a new anti-ship ballistic missile under development (sometimes called the "assassin's mace"), will give it new capabilities.

Between 1997 and 2007, China commissioned 38 new submarines. By 2020, Cole estimates that China will have approximately 50 modern attack submarines, four to six ballistic missile submarines, and approximately 70 modern ships that are capable of surface combat.[67] China is also pursuing the world's first anti-ship ballistic missile, whose main purpose would be to disable or destroy aircraft carriers while they are far from China's coast. The new missile, if successfully developed, would have a range of at least 1,000 miles and pose a serious threat.[68] Yet, as McDevitt notes, "without an effective open ocean surveillance system that can locate and then continuously track approaching warships, none of [China's new hardware capabilities] will be of great use. The ocean remains very large, and ships, even ones as large as an aircraft carrier, are very, very small compared to the vastness of the Pacific. Surveillance is the 'brain' needed to make anti-access a reality. It is also the central nervous system of an anti-access war fighting capability, and if it can be disrupted, the entire anti-access concept of operations can be degraded."[69]

Much has been made of China's plans to field its first aircraft carrier, which for many people, symbolizes the country's future maritime ambitions. In 1998, China bought the approximately 15-year-old Ukrainian carrier with the intention of transforming it into a floating casino. The navy instead retrofitted the vessel and claimed it is "only a platform for scientific research, experiments and training."[70] Viewing the threat posed by the new carrier, Pacific Forum CSIS President Ralph Cossa offers this assessment: "When the Chinese finally deploy an operational aircraft carrier—and there is a big distinction between sea trials and becoming fully operational (measured in years, not months)—the proper U.S. response should be to congratulate Beijing on finally achieving the status of the Soviet (or Ukrainian) Navy, circa 1984."[71]

From a U.S. standpoint, the most critical questions concern the overall significance of China's naval development program: does this modernization pose a major threat to the United States and its allies, and is the comparative strength of U.S. and allied naval forces in the region sufficient to prevent China from exercising maritime domination?

After extensive study, Cole concludes that "China's navy will continue to modernize at a moderate pace" for the foreseeable future in pursuing its strategy of becoming a regional force. China will not be able to rely on its navy to protect vital sea lanes over which the country imports critical oil and natural gas unless the navy is expanded and improved "dramatically." However, "there is no evidence of that occurring ... which means that China will have to continue its current diplomatic and economic policies to ensure a steady supply of energy resources." Since China depends on sea lanes running through the Indian Ocean and Malacca Strait for 75 percent of its energy imports, its maritime vulnerability will remain considerable.[72]

The modernized ships, submarines and aircraft now available to the Chinese Navy do not give it "the ability to dominate East or South Asian waters, certainly when measured against the U.S. Navy or even the Japanese Maritime Self-Defense Force or the Indian Navy," Cole maintains. Chinese naval planners "understand the U.S. Navy's overwhelming superiority and are seeking the capability to avoid or counter it without directly challenging its potentially dominant role in maritime Asia."[73] However, in McDevitt's view, if the Chinese Navy eventually fields a long-range anti-ship ballistic missile, this capability coupled with its robust submarine force could allow it to pose a future "operational challenge" to the U.S. Navy in the case of a regional contingency.[74]

While China modernizes its fleet to carry out an "anti-access" strategy in the Western Pacific, the United States is developing counter-measures that should prove effective against the Chinese Navy. As McDevitt points out:

> The history of twentieth and twenty-first century warfare reveals that countries are in a constant competition that revolves around introducing a new capability, which is eventually addressed by a counter-capability, which is eventually trumped once again by counter-counter-capability. If the [Chinese Navy] succeeds in fielding a credible anti-access strategy, it will almost certainly be addressed by the United States and its allies, otherwise America would not be a credible guarantor of the security of its friends and allies [in the region]. Because a successful [Chinese] anti-access capability would render the U.S. unable to protect its vital interests in East Asia, it is reasonable to expect that the United States will keep a close watch on improving [Chinese] capabilities in this area and not stand idly by .... The conclusion seems clear: Washington will do whatever it takes to make certain its capabilities in East Asia match or stay ahead of [China's] in this vital area.[75]

Nuclear weapons modernization

Despite the great disparity between China and the United States in numbers of nuclear warheads and missiles, China's nuclear modernization has been "gradual and measured," according to experts Evan Medeiros, now serving as Director of Asian Affairs at the National Security Council, and Professor M. Taylor Fravel of MIT. They believe "there is little evidence that China has plans to expand significantly the size of its nuclear arsenal."[76] Rather, China is focusing on updating its older systems from the 1960s and 1970s, and building a large enough arsenal to ensure it is capable of deterring a U.S. nuclear strike even after the United States fully deploys strategic missile defenses.

To understand China's nuclear modernization, it is worth recalling a basic principle of deterrence theory: Country A's nuclear force can deter Country B from a nuclear attack only so long as Country A is capable of withstanding that attack and effectively retaliating. Country A's ability to retaliate is known as its "second strike capability." If a situation arises where Country B can wipe out most of Country A's nuclear force with an overwhelming surprise attack, and Country B also has strategic defenses to protect against Country A's weak retaliation, then Country A effectively lacks the ability to deter a nuclear attack.

Under current circumstances, China is in the position of Country A. China fears that highly advanced American intelligence, surveillance and reconnaissance will enable the U.S. to initially identify China's nuclear forces and that American conventional missiles would then take out China's nuclear weapons with precise long-range strikes. Those few ICBMs that China could launch in retaliation would, in turn, be shot down by effective U.S. strategic defenses. In this situation, China would not possess a "second strike capability." The United States would be able to use conventional weapons to eliminate China's nuclear forces in a crisis without "going nuclear" and still leave China largely defenseless.[77]

Thus, a great part of China's nuclear modernization program in the last decade has been driven by "advances in U.S. military capabilities," particularly U.S. strategic defenses and U.S. conventional strike capabilities, as well as improved offensive nuclear forces. China has undertaken a comprehensive program to ensure its second-strike capability for deterring a U.S. nuclear attack by making its ICBMs more reliable, survivable and able to penetrate American defenses. Examples of these efforts include developing new classes of "road-mobile" ICBMs, which are more survivable against a U.S. first strike; planning to deploy up to five ballistic missile submarines (SSBNs), which are harder to detect than land-based missile forces; and researching a number of new technologies that could allow China's retaliatory force to defeat U.S. strategic defenses. Among these technologies are decoys, jamming devices, and possibly, multiple independently targeted re-entry vehicles (MIRVs).[78] According to the Pentagon's 2011 report to Congress on the Chinese military, "Beijing will likely continue to invest considerable resources to maintain a limited nuclear force ... to ensure the [People's Liberation Army] can deliver a damaging retaliatory second strike."[79]

China's modernization efforts remain consistent with the country's traditional view (dating back to Mao and Deng) that nuclear weapons have two limited purposes: preventing coercion by other nuclear states and deterring nuclear attack. By preserving a secure second-strike capability, their modernization program aims to maintain an adequate deterrent against nuclear attack. Medeiros and Fravel offer this overall assessment of China's nuclear program:

> To use the language of Hans Morgenthau, [a leading figure in the development of international relations theory], one might characterize China's emphasis on developing only a small, credible arsenal as a 'prudent' foreign policy. Chinese leaders have believed that nuclear weapons were basically unusable on the battlefield and that once mutual deterrence was achieved, a larger arsenal or arms racing would be costly, counterproductive, and ultimately self-defeating. Likewise, China's leaders have never equated the size of their arsenal with China's national power. Instead, to be seen as powerful and to deter attacks against it, China needs only a small number of nuclear weapons.[80]

Miscalculating and exaggerating China's military modernization

While sophisticated analysts recognize the overwhelming military advantage the United States retains in spite of China's modernization programs, China hawks frequently seize on any improvement in Beijing's capabilities, or even any military test, to justify their thesis that China poses a major threat to the United States. In fact, miscalculating and exaggerating Chinese power feeds mutual strategic mistrust between the two countries and could lead to the same kind of "action-reaction cycle" that existed between the United States and Soviet Union during the Cold War, as Professor David M. Lampton of Johns Hopkins University clearly describes:

> Exaggeration of China's current and medium-term power will feed threat perceptions and defensiveness in the United States, much as underestimating Chinese capacities could breed reckless attempts to push Beijing around or failures to anticipate strong-willed PRC behavior. Chinese underestimations of U.S. strengths could produce imprudent assertive postures .... [O]ne of the sources of mutual strategic distrust in the bilateral relationship is that Americans are unduly alarmed about U.S. weakness in the face of exaggerations concerning Chinese strengths ....

> Both Beijing's and Washington's security establishments view the actions of the other as important rationales for contingency and force structure planning decisions and for training scenarios. Each is a primary intelligence target of the other, and each is therefore attuned to the other's moves and decisions and what they may portend for the future .... Predictably, one sees the evolution of worst-case analysis and the development of an action-reaction cycle in which the "prudent" responses to the acquisition of capability by one side produce a "prudent" counter response. This cycle results in an open-ended upward spiral of challenge and response, producing greater insecurity at ever greater cost to both countries and bystanders.[81]

Professor Charles Glaser of George Washington University emphasizes that the danger of exaggerating China's security threat to the United States is "even greater in the nuclear realm":

> The Obama administration's 2010 Nuclear Posture Review holds that 'the United States and China's Asian neighbors remain concerned about China's current military modernization efforts, including its qualitative and quantitative modernization of its nuclear arsenal.' The NPR, however, does not identify just what danger China's military modernization poses. There is no prospect that any conceivable nuclear

modernization in the foreseeable future will enable China to destroy the bulk of U.S. nuclear forces and undermine the United States' ability to retaliate massively .... The United States can retain formidable deterrent capabilities even if China modernizes its arsenal and a competitive nuclear policy could well decrease U.S. security by signaling to China that the United States is hostile, thereby increasing Chinese insecurity and damaging U.S.-Chinese relations.[82]

China's threat to Taiwan

On the subject of Taiwan, the Chinese government is often paranoid and intemperate. The possibility that Taiwan's political status could become a flash point for confrontation magnifies the fearful views of China hawks in the United States.

For the great majority of Chinese people, Taiwan is a last vestige and symbol of China's exploitation and dismemberment by outside powers— during the so-called "century of humiliation" that began in the 1840s. Colonized by Japan in 1895, Taiwan is seen by mainland Chinese as an integral part of China and as a remnant of foreign conquest, as Ted Galen Carpenter, Senior Fellow for defense and foreign policy at the Cato Institute, describes:

> It is often difficult for Americans and other Westerners to comprehend the depth of Chinese determination to get Taiwan to "return to the motherland." But to many (and probably most) Chinese, Taiwan is the most potent remaining symbol of China's long period of weakness and dependence, which began in the early nineteenth century, and its shabby treatment at the hands of various colonial powers. For the Chinese, the inheritors of an ancient and proud culture, that treatment was profoundly humiliating and opened deep emotional wounds that have yet to heal fully. It was during the period of weakness that Britain wrested Hong Kong away from China's control; that Japan seized Taiwan (and later Manchuria); that czarist Russia amputated portions of Chinese territory along their border; and that France, Germany, and other countries established colonies or enclaves .... Taiwan is now the principal piece of traditional Chinese territory that has yet to be recovered. That fact alone makes Taiwan's status a potentially explosive issue.[83]

China's long-time policy of seeking the reunification of Taiwan with the mainland is so important that China's Communist Party leadership "would fall if it allowed Taiwan to become independent without putting up a fight," in the view of Professor Susan Shirk of the University of California.[84] Carnegie's Michael Swaine concurs that China "would almost certainly fight to avoid the loss of Taiwan if it concluded that no other alternative existed, even if its chances of prevailing in such a conflict were low."[85]

The status of Taiwan was perhaps the most critical issue in negotiations leading to the diplomatic recognition of China by the United States in December 1978. A few months later, Congress passed the "Taiwan Relations Act" which declared that any use of "non-peaceful means" to determine the status of Taiwan was "a threat to the peace and security of the Western Pacific area and of grave concern to the United States." The Act committed the U.S. to provide arms and weapons systems to Taiwan so it would possess "a sufficient self-defense capability."[86] In keeping with this promise, the U.S. continued to bolster Taiwan's defenses after establishing diplomatic ties with China, even though U.S. arms sales have been a major aggravating factor in U.S.-China relations. Since the passage of the Taiwan Relations Act, the United States has sold Taiwan major naval vessels, advanced fighters, state-of-the-art weapons systems and cutting-edge technologies to prepare its armed forces against a possible Chinese attack.

The Taiwan Relations Act stands today as what experts at CSIS and the Peterson Institute call a "quasi-formal defense commitment" by the United States to Taiwan.[87] It embodies a long-standing U.S. interest in protecting the security of an island where Nationalist Chinese soldiers fled in 1949 to escape the victorious Chinese communist army at the height of China's civil war. Now that Taiwan has become a thriving democracy—evolving from its harsh, authoritarian rule under General Chiang Kai-Shek and his Nationalist Party—the preservation of Taiwan's political system has become an equally important concern to the United States.

For many years, there has been an ever-present danger that the political dispute over Taiwan's legal status could escalate to a military confrontation between China and the United States. A conflict almost occurred in the 1995–6 period when China launched missiles near Taiwan to warn the island against declaring independence and the United States sent two aircraft carrier battle groups to protect Taiwan in the event of a direct attack.

Were Taiwan to declare formal independence, Susan Shirk assesses the factors that could lead to war this way:

> Taiwan is an issue that arouses intense nationalist emotions in China
> .... [And yet], China's military and political leaders know full well that the United States, while not legally bound to intervene, has committed morally and politically to help Taiwan defend itself. They also realize that China's booming economy would be the first casualty in any military conflict with Taiwan and the United States. Nevertheless, [the Chinese regime] would use force to avoid domestic humiliation if they believed their political survival depended on it.[88]

In recent years, China has backed up its verbal threats by continuing to build up forces near Taiwan. Its military measures include deploying approximately 1,000 to 1,200 short-range ballistic missiles opposite Taiwan; positioning large numbers of attack fighters near the island; increasing surface and submarine deployments within range of Taiwan; conducting frequent, often large-scale exercises around the island; and refusing to renounce the possible use of force against Taiwan.[89]

Most China hawks believe the U.S. should defend Taiwan at all costs, though a U.S. conflict with China over Taiwan could prove disastrous. Under current conditions, if China seeks to reunify Taiwan by force, the U.S. would likely feel compelled to respond, both to protect Taiwan and maintain the credibility of the U.S. security guarantee to Japan and South Korea. A dynamic where each side tries to avoid being seen as caving in to the other is likely to cause rapid escalation in a crisis. Two possible highly undesirable outcomes could occur. First, if there is no immediate victor or one side inflicts serious damage on the other's conventional forces, the conflict could escalate to a nuclear exchange, putting millions of Americans at risk. Second, by relying on the strategic advantages conferred through geographic proximity, China's military achievements could exceed currently low expectations, embarrass though not defeat the United States and undermine U.S. deterrence in the region.

Moreover, any war is likely to lead to extensive loss of life and destruction of infrastructure on Taiwan. Military analysts predict that a conflict with China could entail major air and missile attacks on Taiwan's population centers. In addition to severe losses of life and property, the damage to Taiwan's economy—which depends heavily on international trade, including large-scale investments in China—would be immense.

Tensions over the status of Taiwan most recently mounted in 2003 and 2004, when former President Chen Shui-bian took measures seeking independence for the island. Exchanges of harsh and threatening rhetoric culminated in an "Anti-Secession Law" enacted by China in 2004. The law gave several grounds on which China could use "non-peaceful means" against Taiwan, such as its "secession" through a declaration of independence. By authorizing force, instead of requiring it, the Chinese leadership assuaged strong nationalist public opinion "without tying Beijing's hands" and without actually compelling an attack on Taiwan.[90]

Since the election of President Ma Ying-jeou in 2008, Taiwan has adopted a pragmatic approach of seeking more stable cross-Strait ties as a means of furthering economic development.[91] Among the tension-reducing measures that Taiwan has implemented since Ma's inauguration are resumption of a quasi-official dialogue with China on cross-Strait relations, establishing more than 100 direct weekly flights to and from China, allowing direct shipping between numerous Chinese and Taiwanese seaports, promoting visits by Chinese tourists to Taiwan, and easing restrictions on Taiwanese investments in China as well as Chinese investments in Taiwan. In July 2010, the two sides concluded an Economic Cooperation Framework Agreement that will eliminate tariffs on more than 800 products and has already resulted in a 35 percent increase in Taiwan's exports to China over its initial year in force.

Taiwan's citizens showed their appreciation for the benefits of improved cross-Strait relations and a stronger economy brought about by Ma's pragmatic policies when they re-elected him to a second term in January 2012. As important, millions of people in Mainland China closely followed the political campaign in Taiwan through the internet and extensive coverage in national media. Professor Jacques deLisle of the University of Pennsylvania describes the broader political significance of this event:

> Through social media and other channels, the processes of Taiwan's electoral democracy, including the presidential debates, became unprecedentedly accessible to Mainland residents. The democratic practices on display were, by any fair measure, appealing: peaceful, open, civil and characterized by fairly high levels of public enthusiasm .... Surely, Taiwan's democracy is the most relevant and accessible example of democracy for [China]. It is also devastating to any argument that democracy is unsuited to culturally Chinese conditions. And there can be little doubt that the Taiwanese example in fact inspires and attracts many citizens on the Mainland.[92]

China's threat to cyber security

Along with military modernization and China's threat to Taiwan, hawks frequently cite cyber-espionage as a compelling reason to regard China as a potential or actual enemy of the United States. This issue reached a fever pitch in Fall 2011, when the *Washington Post* editorial page accused China of "waging a quiet, mostly invisible but massive cyberwar against the United States, aimed at stealing its most sensitive military and economic secrets and obtaining the ability to sabotage vital infrastructure."[93]

Deputy Secretary of Defense William J. Lynn began focusing on this issue well before the *Washington Post* portrayed China as U.S. Public Enemy #1 for its alleged cyber offensive, and took a more measured view. In September 2010, Lynn observed that

> many militaries are developing offensive capabilities in cyberspace and more than 100 foreign intelligence organizations are trying to break into U.S. networks .... Predicting cyber attacks is also proving difficult, especially since both state and non-state actors pose threats ... Thus, the

U.S. government must be modest about its ability to know where and how this threat might mature. [94]

Lynn's remarks reflect the reality that cyber attacks carried out by foreign hackers are normally routed through computer servers in countries far from where the attack originates. The first and foremost objective of every hacker is to disguise its identity. As Graham Webster, an expert at the East West Center writes, "if an attack appears to originate in Delaware, it could just as well have come from Denmark. Thus, with any individual incident, the identity of the adversary is unclear." [95] Moreover, "dozens of nations have developed industrial cyber-espionage programs, including American allies such as France and Israel. And because the People's Republic of China is such a massive entity, it is impossible to know how much Chinese hacking is done on explicit orders from the government." [96]

U.S. intelligence officials believe that approximately 20 groups affiliated with the People's Liberation Army and a few Chinese universities bear responsibility for most cyber attacks originating in China. [97] Much of the Chinese hacking can be "classified as government-sponsored or government-tolerated," in the view of Adam Segal, Senior Fellow at the Council of Foreign Relations. Segal argues that there are economic, political and security motivations behind these attacks. From an economic standpoint, China relies on industrial espionage to achieve greater innovation and "move up the value chain." Beijing also encourages "political hacking [of foreign websites] as a sort of release valve for frustrated citizens," to distract them from criticizing their own government. Cyber attacks further "help China send a message of deterrence: that a limited regional conflict might not stay that way. Chinese intrusions into U.S. power grids or other critical infrastructure, especially when evidence is left behind, act as a warning that the U.S. homeland may not be immune to attack in the case of a conflict over Taiwan or the South China Sea." [98]

It is not often recognized that China regards *itself* as a prime target for foreign hackers seeking both government secrets and high-value technologies from Chinese companies. Segal notes that China "suffered close to 500,000 [cyber attacks] in 2011, with nearly 15 percent of them appearing to come from computers in the United States." Chinese policymakers point out that the "more dependent the Chinese economy becomes on the internet, the more vulnerable China becomes" to foreign hackers and cyber-espionage. [99]

As of Fall 2011, thanks to the leadership of Deputy Secretary of Defense Lynn, the U.S. has a new and fully operational "Cyber Command" and a well-thought-out strategy for defending the United States against cyber attacks, no matter where they originate. Rather than targeting a single country, the Pentagon treats "cyberspace as an operational domain, like land, air, sea and outer space" and employs "active defenses to stop malicious code before it affects our networks." The Pentagon is also working with private industry to protect commercial industry and secure critical infrastructure.[100]

While it mobilizes public and private resources to mount an effective defense against foreign hackers, the Pentagon is preparing offensive measures so the United States can "respond to serious cyber attacks with an appropriate, proportional, and justified military response."[101] Adam Segal points out that "Chinese analysts are no doubt aware that Washington is planning offensive operations, and they probably believe that it is behind other attacks—in particular Stuxnet, the computer worm credited with slowing down Iran's uranium-enrichment program …. Last March [2011], the Obama Administration considered using cyber attacks to disable Libya's air defense systems but chose not to for various legal and strategic reasons."

On the diplomatic front, Segal believes it is a "pipe dream" to try to negotiate a worldwide, comprehensive cyber security treaty to help protect against cyber threats, as the British government has proposed. To address the cyber threat from China, he maintains that a broad bilateral diplomatic approach is necessary to complement defensive measures:

> Even as the U.S. government attempts to defend itself against Chinese hackers, it must also work directly with the Chinese government to try to solve the problem. It has taken some preliminary steps in this direction …. Yet these official bilateral discussions are not expansive enough. Diplomats should take their cues from the planned dialogue on cyberspace between the United States and Russia, which is to include discussions about how each side's military views the Internet and an effort to establish a hot line that could be used during a cybersecurity crisis. Washington and Beijing need to have a clear communications channel in case of emergency. To build trust over the longer term, the two sides should also discuss come common threats, such as the potential for terrorist attacks on power grids.[102]

An approach that attempts to build strategic trust with China on critical cyber-security issues is likely to be far more effective over time than taking unilateral counter-measures against "suspected" Chinese hackers (as the *Washington Post* recommended in December 2011) and heightening the risk of a new Cold War.

Chinese assertiveness

The vehemence of some commentators who call attention to China's cyber threat reflects the overall deterioration of security relations with China

during the Obama Administration. At the end of 2009, U.S. relations
with China began to spiral downwards in a diplomatic action-reaction
cycle similar to the dynamic involving military modernization. Over the
next three years, U.S. officials often criticized China for its surprising
"assertiveness" in dealing with a range of issues. The United States was
understandably no less "assertive" in its rhetoric and actions toward China.

The deterioration in relations began in December 2009 in Copenhagen
at the international summit meeting on climate change when China resisted
the demands of American and some European negotiators for an agreement
on monitoring compliance with the greenhouse-gas emission targets that
would limit global warming. After formally opposing the U.S. position, the
Chinese delegation sent a low-level official to meet with President Obama
in what the U.S. side took to be a deliberate diplomatic snub. As Helene
Cooper of the *New York Times* explained at the time, "The whole incident
left a bad taste in the mouths of many Obama Administration officials,
who believed China had deliberately set out to belittle Mr. Obama, and
who were determined to push back and reassert American authority."[103]
Since the U.S. and China later reached a compromise at the summit on a
monitoring agreement, it was apparently China's diplomatic *faux pas* that
cut deepest.

A little over a month after the Copenhagen meeting, the Obama
Administration announced an arms sale of more than $6 billion to Taiwan
that had been under consideration for some time. Cooper described the
sale as a "direct strike at the heart of the most sensitive diplomatic issue
between the two countries since America affirmed the 'one China' policy"
in the 1972 Shanghai Communiqué, which recognized that "Taiwan is a
part of China." She further noted the "arms package was doubly infuri-
ating to Beijing coming so soon after the Bush administration announced
a similar arms package for Taiwan in 2008, and right as tensions were
easing somewhat in Beijing and Taipei's own relations."[104] Predictably,
China reacted strongly, with one official proclaiming "We believe this
move endangers China's national security and harms China's peaceful
reunification efforts. It will harm China-U.S. relations and bring about a
serious and active impact on bilateral communication and cooperation."[105]
China then suspended its participation in military-to-military talks with
the United States and imposed sanctions on U.S. companies that supplied
weapons to Taiwan.

On the same day that the Obama Administration announced its
new Taiwan arms sales in late January 2010, Secretary of State Hillary
Clinton warned China it would face economic consequences and diplomatic isolation if it failed to support new U.S.-backed sanctions, under
consideration by the UN Security Council, that aimed to stop Iran from
developing nuclear weapons. As a major importer of Iranian crude oil,
China was the only permanent member of the Security Council unwilling

to support the sanctions. After considerable behind-the-scenes negotiations with the United States, China agreed to tougher sanctions against Iran in late March and also accepted an invitation to attend the April 2010 nuclear summit in Washington that focused on how to safeguard weapons-grade plutonium and uranium to prevent nuclear terrorism. Deputy Secretary of State James Steinberg reflected the improvement in U.S.-China relations, when he commented that "China understands that an Iran which is seeking to develop nuclear weapons is not in its interest and that there is a need for a clear international message to go with that."[106] With Chinese support, the UN Security Council approved "the toughest sanctions ever faced by the Iranian government, " in the words of President Obama, in early June 2010.[107]

The seeming truce between the U.S. and China publicly broke down in July when the United States announced it was sending an American aircraft carrier, the nuclear-powered *George Washington*, along with 20 other ships and submarines as well as 100 aircraft to conduct exercises off the coast of South Korea. The show of force was a warning to both China and North Korea, following the sinking of a South Korean Navy vessel, the *Cheonan*, a few months earlier. China refused to accept the findings of a South Korean investigation that found North Korea responsible for torpedoing the ship, causing the death of 46 sailors.

After the Pentagon indicated that some future exercises would occur in the Yellow Sea, not far from China's coast and within striking distance of Beijing, the deputy chief of the PLA's general staff, Ma Xiaotian, told reporters that China "strongly opposed" the exercises. Another senior Chinese military official stressed the Yellow Sea was "a gateway to China's capital region and a vital passage .... China will be aware of the security pressure from military exercises conducted by a country in an area that is so close to China's heartland."[108] When the carrier *George Washington* and its battle group subsequently conducted exercises in the Yellow Sea (after North Korea unleashed a deadly artillery barrage on a South Korean island), a Chinese newspaper termed the drill a U.S. effort to "capitalize on the [North and South Korean] military dispute" that "seriously provokes China and exposes the US' strategic plot to curb China." American defense officials dismissed the Chinese criticisms and claimed the U.S. fleet had full legal rights to operate in international waters.[109]

China's diplomatic "assertiveness" reached a high point in late July 2010 at the annual security forum of the Association of Southeast Asian Nations (ASEAN), following a controversial speech by Secretary Clinton. As reported by Mark Landler of the *New York Times*, "Opening a new source of potential friction with China, the Obama Administration said Friday that it would step into a tangled dispute between China and its smaller Asian neighbors over a string of strategically significant islands in the South China Sea." Foreign Minister Yang Jiechi reacted sharply to

Clinton's declaration that the U.S. had a "national interest" in freedom of navigation in the South China Sea and wanted to play a major role in settling competing territorial claims over islands rich with oil and natural gas deposits. Yang characterized the U.S. position as "in effect an attack on China" which has claimed a large portion of the South China Sea as its territory since 1947, prior to the communist revolution.[110]

As Chinese assertiveness toward the United States on sensitive national security issues has increased, American analysts have looked for underlying causes. Many agree that greater Chinese nationalism and the ability of the Chinese public to express their views through influential media have played a major role in hardening policymakers' views at the highest levels. As Professor Thomas Christensen of Princeton University explains:

> Popular nationalism, the growth in the number of media outlets through which Chinese citizens can express their views, and the increasing sensitivity of the government to public opinion in a period of instability have provided the space for attacks on the United States and by association, criticism of Beijing's U.S. policy as too soft …. Apparently gone are the days when Chinese elites could ignore these voices. The government currently seems more nervous about maintaining long-term regime legitimacy and social stability than at any time since the period just after the 1989 Tiananmen massacre.[111]

Another aggravating factor has been Chinese internet bloggers and some journalists who frequently criticize the United States and Wall Street bankers, in particular, for causing the global financial crisis. Citizens are proud that China emerged quickly from the recession and that its economy led the global recovery. Some nationalist commentators take their views to an extreme and proclaim irrationally that the financial crisis caused a fundamental shift in the global balance of power, accelerating China's rise and the decline of the United States. In the view of Professor Joseph Nye of Harvard's Kennedy School, nationalism has produced arrogance and over-confidence, leading to the growth of China's assertiveness.[112] Ralph Cossa, president of Pacific Forum CSIS writes that "some have viewed Beijing's harsh reaction[s] and stern warnings as a sign of increased Chinese self-confidence (read: arrogance). Others see it as insecurity from a regime fearful of instability. Both are probably right."[113] Denny Roy, Senior Fellow of the East-West Center, adds that public "anger over perceived affronts to China's national honor or encroachments on vital Chinese interests (hot buttons that territorial disputes invariably push) often quickly turns to criticism of the Chinese government for failing to defend the country's national interests."[114]

In the action-reaction cycle which has increasingly characterized U.S.-China relations, the Obama Administration has shown more willingness to threaten China than any previous U.S. administration since the historic U.S. opening to China in 1972. As Helene Cooper reported,

> Mr. Obama's decision to accelerate the deployment of an American aircraft carrier group to the Yellow Sea for joint exercises with South Korea was meant in part to drive home a message to Beijing. Aware that China doesn't like any kind of display of American military might in its backyard, Obama administration officials are hoping to change Beijing's cost-benefit analysis until it decides that restraining North Korea is a lesser evil than seeing more American sailors playing war games outside its door.[115]

Mark Landler and Sewall Chan of the *Times* shed further light on the all-important role of domestic politics in the calculations of the Obama Administration:

> Political factors at home have contributed to the administration's tougher posture. With the economy sputtering and unemployment high, Beijing has become an all-purpose target. In this [political] season, candidates in at least 30 races are demonizing China as a threat to American jobs.[116]

Influenced by both China hawks and protectionists, the U.S. government has played to public fears of China, with the aim of matching China's new assertiveness, also driven in large part by Chinese public opinion. The question then arises: will the action-reaction dynamic that increasingly characterizes U.S.-China relations lead to another Cold War?

CHAPTER THREE

Rapprochement and a stable peace

One genius of the American political system has always been its promise of innovation and renewal. Faced with adverse circumstances or seemingly insurmountable obstacles, political leaders have leveled with the American people about current difficulties or unrealistic national expectations. They have often found the courage and political support to strike out in new, more promising directions for the greater good of the country as a whole. One day after the surprise attack on Pearl Harbor in December 1941 that decimated America's Pacific fleet, President Franklin Roosevelt rallied the nation against the Empire of Japan.[1] In his last speech to the nation, President Dwight Eisenhower warned of the "unwarranted influence, whether sought or unsought, by the military-industrial complex" and called for Americans to carefully scrutinize the role of the defense industry.[2] In his inaugural address, President John F. Kennedy summoned the American people to face the challenges of the Cold War and work with America's adversaries to "explore the stars, conquer the deserts, eradicate disease, tap the ocean depths, and encourage the arts and commerce."[3]

This spirit of American courage, renewal, and optimism is found in the writings of an important group of political thinkers—exemplified by Professor Charles Kupchan of Georgetown University and Professor John Ikenberry of Princeton—whose foreign policy views deserve far greater recognition in the debate over the U.S. role in the world.[4] These scholars emphasize ways for the United States to exercise its overwhelming influence as the world's sole superpower through policies that promote reconciliation, cooperation and stable relations with countries that are regarded by more pessimistic analysts as current or future enemies. Their explanation of why and how the U.S. should seek a "stable peace" with potential adversaries offers a stark contrast to the hawkish advocates of maintaining perpetual U.S. primacy in the Asia Pacific and accelerating preparations for a war with China.

In a seminal 2004 essay, Kupchan and Ikenberry wrote:

> The scope of American primacy will wane as this century progresses; the ultimate objective should be to channel rising centers of strength into cooperative partnerships with the United States. Furthermore, strength elsewhere, even if it comes at the expense of America's relative power, need not come at the expense of its influence and security. If rising centers of power are integrated into a rule-based order, they promise to be net contributors to international stability.[5]

By achieving rapprochement with potential adversaries, the United States can best realize international stability. As Kupchan notes in his 2010 work, *How Enemies Become Friends*,

> rapprochement entails a standing down, a move away from armed rivalry to a relationship characterized by mutual expectations of peaceful coexistence. The parties in question no longer perceive each other as posing a geopolitical threat and come to see one another as benign polities.[6]

Former Secretary of State Henry Kissinger uses the term "co-evolution" to describe this political condition. As he explains in his 2011 memoir and history, *On China*:

> [Co-evolution] means that both countries pursue their domestic imperatives, cooperating where possible, and adjust their relations to minimize conflict. Neither side endorses all the aims of the other or presumes a total identity of interests, but both sides seek to identify and develop complementary interests.[7]

Rapprochement between two countries does not arise by chance, because of flowery rhetoric, or through random political gestures. It can only be achieved through the practice of "reciprocal restraint," in Kupchan's view, where "both parties readily practice accommodation and expect reciprocity; [and where] cautious testing gives way to a purposeful effort to dampen rivalry and advance reconciliation." Instead of employing "unfettered exercise of power ... states withhold their power and demonstrate benign intent through the exercise of restraint." Both countries engage in *strategic* restraint which is valuable precisely because it fosters and sustains a stable peace, a peace that "requires mutual reassurance and respect, not mutual suspicion and resentment."[8]

Skeptics may say that pursuing reciprocal restraint and mutual accommodation to achieve rapprochement with China sounds nice in theory but could never happen in the "real world," especially where the United States is clearly the dominant power. Kupchan and Ikenberry take issue with this very point when they underscore this is the most rational and foresightful means for the United States to ensure future stability in its own best interests. In Ikenberry's view, a state that "finds itself in a dominant global position faces a choice: it can use its power to bargain and coerce other states ... [or] knowing that its power position will someday decline," a dominant state can recognize it has "an interest in conserving its power" by seeking arrangements that "will preserve and extend its advantages into the future."[9] Kupchan agrees, but offers a slightly different emphasis:

When preponderant states withhold their power and influence, they willingly give up the full advantages of primacy and forego immediate opportunities to capitalize on material advantage. They instead invest in stability over the long term by inducing [other] states to enter into a bargain based on the practice of mutual accommodation.[10]

What Ikenberry, Kupchan and other analysts who share their views are saying has great practical significance for the United States, as we emerge from the deepest financial crisis since the Great Depression, face a massive federal budget deficit of nearly $1.1 *trillion* in 2012, bring to an end the wars in Iraq and Afghanistan, and have recently experienced the sharpest domestic political divisions in generations. A truly critical question is how the United States can overcome its domestic difficulties, prosper economically and exert leadership in a world that is being transformed by the rise of emerging market countries.

According to the U.S. National Intelligence Council, the center for strategic thinking in the United States "intelligence community" that brings together 17 intelligence agencies and organizations, by 2025 "the unprecedented shift in relative wealth and economic power roughly from West to East now under way will continue" and "the international system will be a global multipolar one." The United States "will remain the single most powerful country but will be less dominant" as China, India, Brazil, Russia and other emerging market economies exercise greater international influence. In particular, "China is poised to have more impact on the world over the next 20 years than any other country."[11]

In planning for this future world, the United States can continue its current course of building up military forces in Asia to preserve its primacy in preparation for an expected war with China. Or, it can choose to diplomatically resolve its security and economic conflicts with China in order to bring about a "stable peace" for the foreseeable future. China hawks tend to believe the U.S. can defy the same geopolitical gravity that has diminished the power of every great power in human history. The Greek,

Roman, Aztec, Spanish, French and British Empires, to cite a few examples, are no more. It is therefore an exercise in hubris and unrealistic thinking to argue that the U.S. should concentrate on reinforcing its primacy in Asia by increasing defense expenditures to support a strategy that will not make the United States more prosperous or secure.

The alternative is to adopt a more prudent approach of conserving American power and investing in stability for the long term by seeking rapprochement with China through the practice of reciprocal restraint and mutual accommodation. Rather than burdening the U.S. economy with excessive defense expenditures for the indefinite future and heightening the risk of an unnecessary and costly war, U.S. security objectives in the Asia Pacific would be more than adequately met, at far lower risk and expense, by reverting to the traditional doctrine that guided American foreign policy for a century—preventing any other country, be it imperial Japan, the Soviet Union or China, from dominating the Asia Pacific. Returning to this traditional view would put China on notice that while the U.S. will not tolerate Chinese efforts to assert regional control, neither will the U.S. seek to contain China from a security standpoint, as it does now.

The flaws in U.S. security strategy toward China

To better understand the need for adopting a new U.S. strategy toward China, it is important to examine the questionable assumptions under-lying current policy. Among these assumptions are the following: the U.S. must maintain its military dominance in Asia for the indefinite future to safeguard U.S. security interests; a strategy of building up U.S. forces in Asia is required to fight an "inevitable" war with China; the U.S. should be prepared to defend Taiwan at all costs; aggressive U.S. military measures are the best way of responding to Chinese "assertiveness"; China's military modernization indicates it will achieve military superiority in Asia and elsewhere; and China is deliberately and broadly undercutting U.S. security interests. Upon close analysis, these assumptions lack sufficient credibility.

Maintaining U.S. military dominance in Asia

China hawks embrace the premise that the only way the United States can adequately protect against the threat of a rising China is to dominate the Asia Pacific from a security standpoint. The U.S. held the leading military position in Asia at the end of World War II and, following the demise of the Soviet Union, is now clearly the preeminent power there. The U.S. asserts its dominance, in practice, by controlling sea lines of communication

(SLOCs), operating large bases across the region to counter urgent military contingencies, and by possessing military capabilities far superior to any other country.

Maintaining a strong U.S. deterrence posture coupled with greater security cooperation is more than sufficient to prevent China from denying access to critical sea lanes, pursuing military aggression, or unduly pressuring neighboring countries. By clearly communicating both the capability and the will to counter and defeat aggression, the U.S. would effectively persuade China and other countries not to seek regional dominance. By closely cooperating with China and other regional powers to meet common security threats, the U.S. would demonstrate that these countries have far more to gain by maintaining close relations with the United States than by undertaking military challenges to American power.

Conversely, a U.S. policy to dominate Asia for the foreseeable future stokes resentment and spurs nationalism in China. One unintended though pernicious effect of such a policy is to confirm a belief held by some leading Chinese strategists that the United States intends to contain China for the indefinite future. If China's future leaders believe the U.S. is unfairly blocking China's rise by attempting to carry out a strategy of encirclement, they are more likely to risk war with the United States than choose peaceful co-existence and cooperation.

The security strategy which best advances American interests in Asia is therefore to revert to the traditional U.S. posture of deterring any other country from dominating the region. Insistence by China hawks that the United States continues to exercise regional dominance is not only costly and risky; it is entirely unnecessary for achieving the core goals of America's Asia policy: regional stability, security and prosperity.

Hedging and the "inevitable" war with China

Despite its vast military superiority over China, the U.S. is now pursuing an aggressive "hedging" strategy to counter China's possible, future military capability. This strategy has two major elements: significantly building up U.S. military forces and bases in the Pacific while reinforcing alliances with neighboring countries—particularly Japan and India—to balance China. Although it may seem wise to strengthen U.S. military forces to deal with future uncertainty, seeking to contain China creates deep insecurity in that country, stimulating the growth and accelerated modernization of China's armed forces to prepare for an expected American attack—thus increasing the very threat the U.S. hopes to prevent.

Most China hawks acknowledge that China has no current intention to broadly confront the U.S. militarily in Asia. They know that Chinese leaders accept a status quo in which the U.S. dominates the region from a military standpoint. Instead of giving weight to China's largely benign stance, however, these American experts hype China's future, potential capabilities to obscure the fact that the U.S. now dwarfs China in critical military and technological fields. They downplay and largely ignore both China's currently benign intentions and its relatively weak capabilities when they call for ramping up preparations against a possible future threat.

The real danger in this line of thinking is that building up American military forces in Asia can easily create the self-fulfilling prophecy of a war with China. China infers that the U.S. is planning for a future military conflict which the U.S. also regards as "inevitable." Seeing a sustained American buildup, China accelerates, in turn, its own hedging efforts by expanding and modernizing its own forces to confront the "U.S. threat." Momentum toward conflict continues to build as part of an "action-reaction cycle," in the words of Professor David M. Lampton, which "results in an open-ended upward spiral of challenge and response, producing greater insecurity at ever greater cost to both countries and bystanders."[12]

There is, in fact, nothing inevitable about a future military attack by China against the United States or its allies. If far-sighted leaders in the two countries work hard to address common threats and adjust their national interests, China and the United States can improve their relations and achieve major mutual benefits.

Defending Taiwan

Most China hawks accept without question the assumption that the U.S. should be prepared to defend Taiwan at all costs. Once a brutal dictatorship run by General Chiang Kai-shek who fled the mainland during the 1949 Chinese revolution, Taiwan has now evolved into the vibrant democracy it is today.

For decades, the U.S. has sold arms to Taiwan to allow it to preserve a military standoff with China. Viewing the "Taiwan issue" through a Cold War lens, the U.S. has been reluctant to take sustained diplomatic initiatives to move the risky status quo towards true resolution and the long-term stability that would result from a settlement. This is so even though achieving a secure and democratic Taiwan without a costly military confrontation is a critical policy goal of the United States.

More than ever before, the U.S. today has a far greater interest in defusing a conflict over Taiwan to protect the island's democratic system than it does in fighting a war to ensure Taiwan's legal sovereignty. There is no longer any reason that U.S. military credibility in Asia should hang on America's ability to defeat China in an unwanted conflict over Taiwan. The United States should not accept a risky and dangerous status quo in the Taiwan Strait, when it could help negotiate a stable outcome that both protects the island's democracy and removes the "Taiwan issue" as a severe irritant in U.S.-China relations.

The current U.S. strategic posture also fails to adequately protect Taiwan's democratic political system and national security over the long term. Despite the improvement in cross-Strait relations under President Ma, Taiwan still lives today with the threat of war with China. As long as the military standoff continues, Taiwan's people face the possibility of a conflict they know will be increasingly difficult to win through armed combat. The path to security, long-term preservation of Taiwan's democracy, and economic prosperity is through a Framework Agreement between the U.S. and China that would markedly reduce the risk of war and preserve Taiwan's political autonomy, as will be discussed at length in Chapter Seven.

Responding to China's assertiveness

The Obama Administration's decision in November 2011 to accelerate strategic hedging and containment of China, as noted in the previous chapter, culminated a roughly two-year period when the U.S. encountered what it considered new Chinese "assertiveness." China exhibited this assertiveness mainly through strong public criticism of U.S. arms sales to Taiwan, strident opposition to U.S. military exercises off China's coast, and sharp reaction against a new U.S. diplomatic intervention, announced by Secretary Clinton, to play a major role in mediating competing territorial claims involving China in the South China Sea. Chinese patrol boats and oceanographic vessels operating in this region were also unusually active, from the standpoint of the United States and neighboring countries, in reinforcing China's legal claims to islands and waters believed to hold large oil and natural gas deposits. (A more detailed discussion of South China Sea issues follows later in this chapter.)

Analysis of events between 2009 and 2011 shows that while China was undoubtedly more assertive than in the past, the U.S. was no less assertive in reinforcing its strategic position in the region, culminating in new military deployments to the Asia Pacific announced in November 2011. On one occasion, June 28, 2010, the Obama Administration sent a particularly blunt message reminding China of its vulnerability to U.S. surprise attack, when three large Ohio-class ballistic-missile submarines (SSBNs) carrying altogether more than 450 long-range cruise missiles with nuclear warhead capability—among the most powerful vessels in the U.S. fleet—surfaced simultaneously without prior warning in Busan, South Korea, Subic Bay, the Philippines, and in Diego Garcia, a strategic Indian Ocean naval and air base.[13]

A major lesson to be drawn from these events is that in U.S.-China relations, "assertiveness" is not the distinctive characteristic of one side.

Both the U.S. and China have engaged in ongoing, multiple assertive activities toward each other and it is pointless to fix blame on one country. The truly worrisome possibility is that an action-reaction dynamic can easily become more acrimonious over time and lead to a diplomatic rupture or armed conflict between the two countries. Perhaps the best analogy is the metaphor of "apes on a treadmill" coined by Ambassador Paul Warnke to describe the nuclear arms race between the United States and Soviet Union. In a famous article with this title that appeared in *Foreign Policy* in 1975, Warnke called for a process of "reciprocal restraint" to curtail the buildup of nuclear weapons by both countries, conceptually the same approach that can lead to rapprochement and a stable peace between states.[14]

Responding to China's assertiveness with equal or greater U.S. assertiveness—which increases the ever-present risk of this action-reaction dynamic spinning out of control—is clearly not an optimal strategy for advancing U.S. interests in Asia. Far better for each side to take actions which stabilize their relations, sharply reduce regional tensions, and strengthen the likelihood of cooperation on many security, diplomatic and economic issues of common concern.

China's military modernization

Most books and articles warning against the "China threat" focus heavily on China's programs of military modernization. Yet they largely ignore the context in which this military activity occurs.

To review, these popular works generally fail to point out the massive advantage the United States holds over China in military weapons, equipment, technology and know-how. The U.S. maintains a stockpile exceeding 5,000 nuclear warheads while China possesses approximately 240 warheads. The U.S. operates 11 aircraft carriers worldwide, each with a complement of 55 fighters and ground-attack aircraft while China's only carrier, used for training purposes, is 30 years out of date. America's impressive cyber-warfare capabilities and extensive network of satellites establish superiority on any battlefield, because of the decisive U.S. lead in the technological revolution in military affairs. China's primitive satellites are no match for their U.S. counterparts.

Reports of new Chinese military acquisitions or military modernization efforts describe developing capabilities in which the U.S. already has overriding advantages. To date, the major weapon systems China has acquired or developed are inferior to comparable U.S. systems and are highly vulnerable to U.S. countermeasures. There is every reason to believe that America will retain and strengthen its military superiority across the board in the future, especially since the U.S. spends more than three times as much as China on defense and has a far stronger technological base.

This assessment is reflected in an important nonpartisan study by two Washington think-tanks, the Center for Strategic and International Studies and the Peterson Institute for International Economics. According to the study, "The trajectory of the current modernization program seems to be one that will *eventually result* in a PLA that can project force in the Asia Pacific region, beyond China's borders, has *incipient* expeditionary capabilities, *will get better* at sustaining operations along exterior lines of communications, and *will develop selective but effective* pockets of technological capacity."[15] It is not at all clear, the report points out, that China can achieve even these limited goals since a "host of systemic problems endemic to the PLA, challenges from within greater Chinese society, and wild card events could preclude [even] the massive defense establishment from achieving its objectives."[16]

Nightmare scenarios also often ignore the ability of the United States to influence, shape and limit China's military development programs so they pose far less of a potential security threat. As the Pentagon has indicated, China's leaders face a series of critical choices on the trajectory of their military modernization efforts and "the path forward is not predetermined."[17]

If U.S. relations with China improve and stabilize, the primary factor driving China's military modernization—fear of imminent U.S. attack—would no longer exist. China would no longer feel compelled to devote as large a portion of its budget as it does now to military preparedness. To the contrary, the pressing needs of economic development and a perceptibly lower sense of external danger would eliminate the necessity for any focused anti-U.S. buildup.

The strategic pressure to modernize China's small nuclear force to prevent it from being neutralized by U.S. missile defense systems, would, in turn, ease considerably. Improved relations would markedly increase the likelihood that the United States and China could reach nuclear and conventional arms control agreements of the kind the U.S. concluded with the Soviet Union during the Cold War.

In fact, drawing China into negotiations to reduce its nuclear arsenal has been an explicit objective of American policy ever since President Obama, at a September 2009 summit meeting of the UN Security Council on nuclear proliferation and disarmament, supported the goal of a world without nuclear weapons. Obama's announcement gave official approval to a critical arms reduction process originally proposed in January 2007 by former Secretaries of State George Shultz and Henry Kissinger, former Secretary of Defense William Perry and Senator Sam Nunn, who wrote in the *Wall Street Journal* that "Reassertion of the vision of a world free of nuclear weapons and practical measures toward achieving that goal would be, and would be perceived as, a bold initiative consistent with America's moral heritage."[18]

One of the key conditions for reducing nuclear arsenals is that "progress should have been made in addressing and resolving regional disputes that threaten to trigger military actions," as Ambassador James Goodby, a leading arms control expert now at Stanford University, subsequently stressed in an important May 2011 analysis. Goodby points out that

> One of the merits of making the elimination of nuclear weapons a truly international enterprise [as Shultz, Kissinger, Perry and Nunn proposed], is that it shines a spotlight on 'frozen conflicts,' disputes that have festered for so long that they have become accepted as inevitable [though they could, in a worst case scenario, lead to nuclear war].[19]

The U.S.-China dispute over Taiwan clearly fits Goodby's definition of a "frozen conflict," and the disputes with China over maritime rights in the South China and East China Seas could achieve that unfortunate status, if not effectively addressed in the near future.

Chinese efforts to undercut U.S. security interests

Aside from its military modernization efforts, hawks often argue that China is deliberately harming America's security interests through espionage against foreign countries, including the United States, as well as programs to acquire "dual use" technology with both commercial and military applications. The United States is second to none in carrying out aggressive espionage overseas, particularly in countries like China and Russia that the U.S. now monitors closely. It should not be surprising that China's intelligence services watch the U.S. to glean information about American intentions, military capabilities and technological developments. China's intelligence activities in the United States—like U.S. activities in China—are spurred by the deep distrust that today imbues U.S.-China relations. As long as this situation prevails, the U.S. must seek to counter Chinese espionage and root it out to the greatest extent possible. But the existence of Chinese intelligence activities in the United States is clearly *not* evidence of China's intention to go to war with the United States—any more than extensive U.S. espionage in China indicates the U.S. has firmly decided to confront China militarily.

The same logic applies to China's documented efforts to obtain "dual-use technology" which can be useful for modernizing its armed forces. Like the United States and close U.S. allies including France, Britain, Israel, Japan and South Korea, China seeks to raise its defense capabilities by striving to procure technologies from abroad that it does not or cannot develop at home. As long as the current state of U.S.-China relations prevails, it is incumbent on the U.S. government to prevent China from acquiring technologies that could possibly be used against the United States in a future military confrontation. But the fact that China (or any foreign government) has programs to acquire technology that could help strengthen its national defense is *not* proof it intends to attack the United States or is seeking the capability to do so.

Hawkish analysts largely ignore or minimize how China's close cooperation with the United States has helped to advance core American security interests. Two critical examples come to mind. In the aftermath of the September 11, 2001 terrorist attacks, as noted earlier, China took a major political decision to assist the U.S. in countering terrorism and strengthening regional and global stability. This extensive cooperation has continued to date. China helps the CIA and FBI penetrate international terrorist networks. It works alongside U.S. immigration and customs authorities in tracking and seizing terrorist suspects as well as dangerous weapons and technologies. It aids U.S. Treasury officials in disrupting secret transfers of funds intended to finance terrorist activities.

Significantly, China has worked closely with the United States to halt North Korea's nuclear program in order to prevent the proliferation of nuclear weapons, materials, technologies and expertise to terrorists and rogue states. Since 2003, China has chaired the Six Party Talks on North Korean nuclear issues, a multilateral framework designed by the United States to constrain and end Pyongyang's nuclear efforts. Though these talks have not yet achieved their objective—largely due to North Korean intransigence— U.S. policymakers have long realized that China holds more diplomatic leverage over North Korea than any other country. The U.S.-Chinese effort to denuclearize the Korean peninsula is an example of common security interests that could bring greater security cooperation in the future.

Other flash points for military confrontation and the opportunity for peaceful settlement

Though the Spratly, Paracel and Senkaku Islands are not familiar names to most Americans, competing claims to these rocks and archipelagos in East Asia could give rise to an armed conflict with China that draws in the United States. In the last few years, various nations have asserted their rights to these islands and surrounding maritime areas of the South China and East China Seas, which are rich in oil, gas and fishing grounds. Hostile encounters have occurred among fishing boats, patrol vessels and oil exploration ships conducting seismic surveys, as each country tests the limits of its claims.

In the South China Sea, noteworthy friction took place in June 2010, when Vietnam claimed that China harassed one of its seismic survey vessels, severing the research cable it was trailing behind. In response, Vietnam conducted nine hours of live-fire naval exercises off its central coast, actions that mimicked China's own earlier naval exercises in the region. The June 2010 clash followed incidents where maritime patrols of China's Fisheries Administration seized a number of Vietnamese fishing boats for illicitly fishing in Chinese waters. On earlier occasions, China claimed its fishermen had been "detained and shot at" by vessels of other states.[20]

Such hostile encounters have increased in recent years in the South China Sea as five countries—Brunei, Malaysia, China, the Philippines, Taiwan and Vietnam—seek to solidify their respective territorial claims. At stake are exploration rights for a huge known deposit of approximately 61 billion barrels of oil and gas, plus a nearly equivalent estimated amount that is still undiscovered.[21] Moreover, the area contains significant fish stocks which are critical to the economies of surrounding countries.

China's modern claim to large areas of the South China Sea, as noted earlier, dates from 1947, prior to the communist revolution, and it bolsters this claim by arguing that various island groups have been considered Chinese territory for more than 2,000 years. Vietnam, on the other hand, asserts it exercised control of the islands in the region since the 1600s, and they are therefore Vietnamese territory.[22]

While China has offered to conduct bilateral negotiations to settle various claims, Vietnam in particular has pushed hard to internationalize the issue out of fear that China would have too much bargaining power in "one on one" negotiations. Secretary of State Clinton's July 2010 assertion of a U.S. "national interest" in the South China Sea, together with her emphasis on the need for a "multilateral" solution, significantly strengthened the negotiating leverage of Vietnam and other Southeast Asian countries vis-à-vis China. One analyst put it well when he observed that "a multilateral solution would pit China against a group of nations bargaining collectively and considerably weaken China's position. Given the underlying geopolitical factors, China is particularly reluctant to accept outside intervention."[23]

In the East China Sea, conflict between China and Japan focuses on competing claims to the uninhabited land and surrounding waters of the Senkaku/Diaoyu Islands. (The territory is known as Senkaku to Japan and Diaoyu to China.) The islands are located nearly 200 miles west of Okinawa and about 200 miles east of China's mainland, to the northeast of Taiwan. Between 1945 and 1972, when the United States administered the islands as part of its trusteeship of the Ryukyu Island chain, the U.S. military used the Senkaku/Diaoyu as a firing range. Only after a United Nations survey found in 1968 that large-scale petroleum deposits might exist in the area, did either China or Japan think seriously of contesting their ownership. China claims the territory based, in part, on documents and maps originating with the fifteenth-century Ming dynasty. Japan dates its claim back to the Treaty of Shimonoseki which ended the

Sino-Japanese War in 1895 and enabled Japan to formally annex the islands.[24]

The Senkaku/Diaoyu have been the site of two significant clashes between Japan and China in recent years. In December 2008, two ships of China's "Oceanic Administration" entered the 12-mile limit surrounding the islands which Japan regards as "off limits" to foreign vessels. Japanese patrol boats ordered the Chinese ships to leave and when they refused, the vessels of the two countries played a game of "chicken" for about nine hours, threatening to crash into each other, before the Chinese ships left the area.[25] In September 2010, a Chinese fishing trawler, whose captain was apparently intoxicated, attempted to ram a Japanese patrol boat in the vicinity of the Senkaku/Diaoyu. Japan took the unprecedented step of detaining the captain, and China responded by cutting diplomatic communications, detaining several Japanese citizens, and suspending exports of "rare earths," critical minerals utilized by Japanese industries. After several days of increasing tension and heated rhetoric, Japan freed the Chinese captain without trial and sent him home to a hero's welcome.[26]

Both incidents occurred in spite of a Japan-China "political agreement" for joint development of the islands concluded in June 2008. Because the two countries made no progress in achieving follow-on measures for energy exploration in the area, the 2008 agreement was never implemented, the conflict continued to fester and development of the energy fields remains limited. The possibility that a local confrontation between Japan and China over the islands could escalate to a conflict between the United States and China multiplied exponentially in September 2010, when Secretary Clinton indicated to Japanese Foreign Minister Seiji Maehara that the Senkakus are covered by Article 5 of the Japan-U.S. security treaty which authorizes the U.S. to come to Japan's defense in the case of armed attack "in the territories under the administration of Japan."[27] Ironically, Clinton committed the U.S. to protecting Japan's interests in the Senkakus against Chinese attack, even while continuing the long-standing official American policy of neutrality over which country actually holds sovereignty to the islands.

Tensions over the Senkaku/Diaoyu and the inability of the two countries to settle their territorial dispute have been played out against the background of China's increased naval activities in the East China Sea during the last several years. As Richard Bush, director of the Center for Northeast Asian Policy Studies at Brookings, notes, "China seeks to establish a strategic buffer in the waters east of its coast."[28] For this reason, the Chinese Navy has made its presence felt and expanded its areas of operations to international waters that are uncomfortably close to both undisputed and claimed Japanese territory. In October 2008, four vessels of the Chinese Navy passed through the Tsugaru Strait in international waters between the main Japanese islands of Hokkaido and Honshu, then circumnavigated Japan. One month later, Chinese Navy ships patrolled close to the coast of Okinawa, Japan's southernmost prefecture. Unlike these two cases, the great majority of incidents have entailed Chinese naval operations near the Senkaku/Diaoyu in territory disputed by the two countries. In late 2004, China sent a submarine through the Ishigaki Strait and in January 2005, Chinese destroyers reportedly traveled through the contested oil and gas fields. More recently, in 2010, a Chinese helicopter participating in naval exercises buzzed a Japanese Navy ship. In March 2011, a similar incident occurred, giving rise to a formal protest by Japan.[29]

Risks of conflict involving the United States

In the *South China Sea*, the most serious risk of armed conflict between the United States and China stems more from China's desire to limit close-in intelligence gathering by the U.S. Navy and Air Force than from its territorial disputes with Southeast Asian countries. As described in Chapter Two, serious clashes took place in March and May of 2009, when Chinese vessels physically challenged the operations of U.S. Navy surveillance ships seeking information about China's military deployments. Nevertheless, if a major clash over competing land claims in the South China Sea occurs in the future between China and an American ally like the Philippines, the United States might feel compelled to intervene by sending in the Seventh Fleet, if only to uphold U.S. military credibility in an area that Secretary Clinton proclaimed to be a U.S. "national interest."

Although China strongly criticized Clinton's declaration in July 2010 as "in effect an attack on China," Beijing has historically taken a largely cooperative approach to settling territorial disputes.[30] Professor M. Taylor Fravel of MIT has concluded on the basis of extensive research and analysis that

> China has been more likely to compromise in its territorial conflicts and less likely to use force than many policy analysts assert, theories of international relations predict, or scholars of China expect. China has not become more aggressive in pursuit of many of its claims as it has accumulated economic and military power over the past two decades. Instead, it has compromised frequently and, in some cases, substantially.[31]

Fravel acknowledges, however, that the dispute over the Senakaku/Diaoyu in the *East China Sea* is an exception to this general principle and "can easily spark a crisis between China and Japan."[32]

Richard Bush of Brookings also underscores the danger of conflict in the East China Sea because "Chinese and Japanese naval vessels and aircraft are operating closer and closer to each other in geographic space that each regards as strategically significant." In Bush's view, there is a "danger that strategic mistrust, military operations and points of friction might lead to a clash."[33] Bush lays out a tragic worst-case scenario where "even if objective interests dictate a mutual retreat from the brink, [China and Japan] might be unable to do so." Among the reasons this situation could arise are the ambiguous "rules of engagement" employed by the Japanese Coast Guard; the possibility that commanders on both sides might have "discretion to act independently in the heat of the moment"; Japan's "significantly more advanced naval capabilities [which] would, if employed, almost certainly cause the destruction of [Chinese Navy] units, with significant loss of life"; the distorted picture of an incident national leaders would likely receive from local commanders, leading to miscalculation; and the fact that "leaders may lose control and regard some outcomes, especially the appearance of capitulation, as worse than a growing conflict."[34]

The series of hypothetical events sketched out by Bush has acquired an even more frightening dimension following the Obama Administration's decision in September 2010 that a military clash near the Senkaku/Diaoyu would be covered by the Japan-U.S. Security Treaty. If Chinese vessels violate purported Japanese sovereignty over the islands and Japan responds with military force, the U.S. would be under immense pressure to come to Japan's assistance, even though the United States does not regard the Senkaku/Diaoyu as Japanese territory. Needless to say, a clash of this kind, just like a confrontation over Taiwan, could spin out of control and escalate to a broader war between the U.S. and China.

Interim measures

Because of the seemingly insurmountable difficulty of resolving territorial disputes in the South China and East China seas, government officials and policy experts have instead concentrated on interim measures the affected countries can take to lessen the chance of conflict. In July 2011, the foreign ministers of China and Southeast Asian countries reached consensus on the need to adopt a "code of conduct" that would serve as a "conflict avoidance and management mechanism" in the South China Sea. The new code would effectively implement a 2002 "Declaration on Conduct" for the region that had proved unenforceable and incapable of preventing clashes over competing territorial claims. Among the measures that negotiators will consider putting formally into effect are telephone hotlines to allow rapid exchange of information between defense ministries during crises; advance notification of military exercises as a means of lowering tensions; cooperation on combating piracy as well as conducting search and rescue training; a possible "incidents at sea agreement" to establish "rules of the road" at sea to prevent dangerous behaviors; and increased transparency about each signatory's regional military facilities and deployments so as to enhance trust and lower tension.[35] In the view of maritime expert Mark Valencia at the Nautilus Institute, it is also critical for the countries negotiating a Code of Conduct to commit to two major principles: "exercising self-restraint" by avoiding activities that could complicate or escalate existing territorial disputes; and devising practical, provisional arrangements "to manage and share the resources" in disputed areas.[36] It is not at all clear, of course, whether countries will truly observe the measures that make up the final "code of conduct" or even if they do, whether the code by itself could effectively prevent conflict when the underlying issues in dispute—competing claims to islands, fishing grounds and undersea petroleum deposits—remain fundamentally unresolved.

Richard Bush of Brookings has described in considerable detail a plan for "confidence-building measures" that Japan and China could adopt to lower the risk of military conflict in the *East China Sea*. These measures would disable the major potential "trigger" for a crisis—the worrisome "operational interaction" between vessels and aircraft of the two countries in the vicinity of the Senkaku/Diaoyu Islands. To regulate the conduct of these military forces that operate "in the same geographic space," Bush recommends establishing "rules of interaction and robust communications procedures to maintain a degree of separation." He believes these rules might include "direct communications links, codes of conduct, communications measures for dangerous incidents and explicit rules of engagement." The rules would place a "'safety' on the trigger of an unnecessary conflict"—and could be contained in a "maritime liaison mechanism" between defense ministries as well as in an "incidents at sea" accord. An incidents at sea agreement (INCSEA), modeled on the arrangement observed by the U.S. and Soviet Union, "could encourage restraint on both sides and give pilots and ship captains reasons to eschew risky behavior."[37]

Resolving the underlying conflicts

As vital as interim measures are to reducing the risk of armed conflict in the South and East China Seas, these measures originate from a pessimistic assessment of the chances for actual resolution of the disputes. One group of experts at the National Bureau of Asian Research describes the difficulties of the current situation in bureaucratic language that masks a sense of despair:

> While the immediate resolution of the maritime jurisdictional disputes should be the top priority for states in the region, the seemingly intractable nature of key aspects of these disputes and their complexity, coupled with historical and geopolitical factors, strongly suggest that enduring

resolution of the disputes is not likely to occur in the near to medium term. Given the importance of these areas, it is imperative that states agree on ways to mitigate tensions and move forward on cooperative activities and confidence-building measures in the absence of resolution. The status quo is simply unsustainable, holds the likelihood for future conflict [and] forestalls opportunities to access urgently needed resources .... To avoid a dire outcome, there are several mechanisms that could be useful for states to implement in the absence of final resolution.[38]

The overriding reason that the maritime disputes are intractable, complex and seemingly incapable of resolution, of course, is that they are closely tied to the rise of China. The all or nothing issue of sovereignty over the contested islands—whether China or another country controls specific territories—impedes a practical, mutually beneficial resolution. Until the United States and China address the deeper security issues that divide them, a final settlement of maritime claims in the South China and East China Seas, will elude the affected states.

This judgment strongly suggests that the way forward to achieving a stable peace in East Asia is through measures of reciprocal restraint contained in a new Framework Agreement between the United States and China, as will be outlined in Chapter Seven. Such an agreement would help resolve the fundamental security, economic and political disputes between the two countries, enunciating principles and measures for resolution that could be implemented over time in a step by step fashion.

Professor Lyle Goldstein, of the U.S. Naval War College, cogently makes the case for creating a new foundation for U.S.-China relations leading to ongoing peace and stability between the two countries:

> With an economy that may well be the largest in the world within 10–20 years, China cannot be treated as a hostile, revisionist power. The consequences for international security of doing so are unacceptably large: at best a new Cold War, at worst, military conflict on a par with the worst carnage of the twentieth century. Thus, there is an immediate imperative to 'reset' the US-China security relationship, adopting a systematic and genuinely strategic approach to pursuing peace and stability in the twenty-first century.[39]

A new Framework Agreement between the U.S. and China would have particular utility for resolving maritime disputes in the South and East China Seas for several reasons. First, it would entail a U.S. and China agreement in principle to establishing new coastal buffer zones. Every country has a legitimate need and desire for a strategic buffer along its coasts, which provides early warning and protection against attack from the sea or air. The United States is second to none in regarding naval or air activity by a foreign country near the U.S. coast as a potential threat that needs to be closely monitored and, if necessary, neutralized before it becomes an imminent security threat. However, the famous "12-mile limit" which marks where national waters end and international waters begin is not helpful in defining an appropriate security zone because it technically permits extensive military activities—including exercises and intelligence collection—close to China's coast. From the U.S. standpoint, the 200-mile "Exclusive Economic Zone" (EEZ) of coastal states, created under the 1982 UN Convention on the Law of the Sea, applies explicitly to the exploration and use of marine resources. The U.S. does not currently accept the EEZ's applicability to military activities, and more broadly, has never ratified the UN Convention.

If the U.S. recognizes a strategic buffer along China's coast and China accepts a strategic buffer along the coast of Japan, the sense of security against maritime threats in both China and Japan would increase considerably. China would become far more willing to resolve and accept decisions by an international judicial body on territorial issues in the South and East China Seas. Japan would become much more agreeable to resolving the dispute over sovereignty of the Senkaku/Diaoyu Islands and exploitation of nearby petroleum deposits. A deeper sense of security, founded on recognition of coastal buffer zones, would allow each country to contemplate true rapprochement, as expressed by Prime Minister Yasuo Fukuda during his state visit to China in 2007:

> [T]he time has come for the nations of Japan and China each to examine squarely the political and economic importance of the other and discuss how we can cooperate in order to resolve the various issues facing our region and international society .... I believe that it is possible for us to become creative partners who together can forge a bright future for Asia and the globe. By undertaking creative efforts jointly between Japan and China, we can build a relationship in which we receive the trust of nations all around the globe. From this perspective, it gives rise to great hopes, does it not? We should not try to find fault with each other but rather work together towards common objectives, hand in hand, for the benefit of the globe. What I hope for deeply is that Japan and China can be true friends of this sort.[40]

A Framework Agreement would also result in considerably scaling back coastal intelligence-collection activities which, in and of themselves, can trigger a military conflict. Mark Valencia of the Nautilus Institute notes that intelligence collection typically involves the

> active 'tickling' of China's defenses to provoke and observe a response, interference with shore-to-ship and submarine communications,

'preparation of the battlefield' under the false pretense of carrying out marine scientific research, and tracking China's new nuclear submarines for potential targeting as they enter and exit their base.

Valencia adds that

few countries would tolerate such provocative activities by a potential enemy without responding in some fashion .... [T]hese are not passive intelligence collection operations commonly undertaken and usually tolerated by most states, but intrusive and controversial practices ....[41]

A third key component of a Framework Agreement would be China's consent to submit its maritime disputes in the South and East China Seas to an independent judicial body established for this very purpose by the 1982 Convention on the Law of the Sea. Known as the "International Tribunal for the Law of the Sea," this international court possesses great expertise in investigating, analyzing and settling maritime conflicts. Detailed questions involving ownership of land and adjacent bodies of water as well as rights to underground and undersea resources are preeminently legal issues. Such issues are best decided in a court of law by judges skilled in examining technical maritime and property disputes, not by diplomats engaged in multilateral negotiations. If the parties prefer to avoid the risk of an adverse judicial decision, they could also pursue settlement negotiations directly between themselves, in the context of this legal proceeding.

Security benefits of sharply improved relations with China

Realizing the benefits to American security of improved relations with China will require a fundamental shift in American and Chinese policies. A shift of this kind is, in fact, possible, based on an agreement that could be reached on critical issues in dispute between the two countries, and implemented over time.

In the remaining portion of this chapter, it is valuable to consider the various security benefits that would accrue to the United States from such an agreement (while leaving a discussion of the economic benefits to the next chapter). After all, why should the U.S. engage in a considerable amount of diplomatic heavy lifting to enhance relations with China if the rewards are skimpy and the U.S. could conceivably weaken its position in Asia?

Overview

The foremost near-term security benefit to the United States of developing improved relations with China is that it would dramatically reduce the chance of a military conflict between the two countries. Such a conflict could escalate to a nuclear exchange and threaten the lives of millions of Americans.

Avoiding a military confrontation with China would also eliminate the danger that better than expected performance by Chinese military forces, during a crisis, would undermine the credibility of the U.S. security guarantees to Japan and South Korea. Preserving the current standing of the United States in East Asia would allow the United States to recalibrate deployments and shape the most sustainable security role in the region for the foreseeable future.

Following a major reduction in the "U.S. threat," China can be expected to sharply decrease the scope, scale and tempo of its modernization programs as well as the portion of the national defense budget devoted to modernization. China's leaders would no longer perceive an urgent need to develop the capability to counter an expected U.S. attack in the immediate future. The U.S. would be in a far better position to shape the direction of China's future military programs.

Improved relations with China would protect Taiwan's democratic political system and national security for the long term. Instead of negotiating under the threat of missile attack and invasion, Taiwan could deal with China in a stable security environment following the elimination, reduction and redeployment of Chinese missiles, aircraft and other forces currently threatening the island. Taipei could then either seek to settle sensitive political issues with Beijing concerning national reconciliation or maintain its current status of *de facto* independence.

Finally, in an era of improved U.S.-China relations, the United States could benefit from China's capabilities to meet transnational security challenges of concern to the United States as well as America's allies and friends in East Asia. These challenges include preventing the proliferation of nuclear weapons and materials, ending terrorism, ensuring energy security, assuring the safety of maritime commerce and severely restricting the trafficking of arms, narcotics and people. Bilateral U.S.-China cooperation within existing and new regional security structures in East Asia would significantly strengthen multilateral approaches to transnational problems. Instead of developing and deploying forces to meet a potential "U.S. threat," China could work alongside the United States in maintaining regional security and stability.

Taiwan

The issue that could most easily trigger a U.S.-China military confrontation is the status of Taiwan, as noted previously. Despite U.S. efforts to restrain separatist rhetoric by Taiwan and to warn China against threatening the island, a crisis could occur at almost any time. China or Taiwan's leadership might exploit the issue of Taiwan's legal status for *domestic* political reasons. For example, China could take threatening military steps either to reinforce its nationalist credentials or show opposition to Taipei's "separatism." This would almost surely lead to a wave of sympathy in the United States for Taiwan, and create strong political pressure for the U.S. president to move military assets near the island. Unlike the spring 1996 crisis, China might decide *not* to back down and instead seek to prove its mettle as a major regional power. One often mentioned scenario is that China could use its short-range missiles facing Taiwan to destroy key military targets, overwhelm missile defense capabilities and severely disrupt the island's economy—effectively forcing Taiwan's capitulation before the U.S. can intervene.[42] Alternatively, China might use new "asymmetric" capabilities that allow its weaker military to exploit the vulnerabilities of a stronger U.S.-led military force. It might attempt to sink an American aircraft carrier, without confronting the larger body of U.S. forces, for example, and then seek a cease-fire.

Instead of allowing the risk of a military conflict between China and Taiwan to persist over time, the United States would benefit greatly from fostering reconciliation between these two potential adversaries. Peaceful settlement of outstanding security disputes would remove the Taiwan issue as a possible source of crisis in U.S.-China relations and prevent it from escalating to a full-blown war. It would also allow the U.S. to further a long-sought diplomatic goal—a secure and democratic Taiwan.

Shaping China's military development

Improved relations with China would allow the U.S. to more easily shape the direction of China's military modernization programs and future security strategy. If the U.S. is perceived as a friend, rather than a potential rival, China is much less likely to invest in long-term military modernization efforts designed to threaten or defeat U.S. forces in a future confrontation. A lowered sense of hostility would discredit the rationale for conducting a focused anti-U.S. buildup, especially since China has so many other pressing material needs.[43]

Improved relations would also be conducive to reaching strategic arms control agreements that have eluded the two countries since they first established diplomatic ties in 1978. The United States would benefit significantly from restrictions on the number and capabilities of China's nuclear forces, even though its nuclear weapons only constitute a so-called "minimal deterrent." China has been deeply reluctant to enter into serious strategic arms control negotiations with the U.S. because of the small size of its own forces relative to the nuclear capabilities of the United States. In the context of improved relations, China as well as the U.S. would be much more amenable to arrangements establishing nuclear "strategic stability" between the two sides. A U.S.-China dialogue on the uses and purposes of nuclear weapons, ballistic missiles and missile defense could lead to an arms control regime that considerably lowers the risk of nuclear war.[44]

Improved relations with China would, moreover, allow the U.S. to shape China's overall security strategy by accelerating China's integration into the international community. Rather than attempting to limit China's role in the international system, in security, political or economic arenas, as it sometimes does now, the U.S. would consistently strive to "link [China's] systems to those of the rest of the world."[45] Douglas Paal, vice president at the Carnegie Endowment, points out that a more active role in the international system, consistent with China's "great power status," would effectively "[deter] China from seeking to obtain its goals through the use of force."[46]

Michael Swaine of the Carnegie Endowment concurs that China's deep involvement in the international system through multilateral organizations can limit its military modernization and thus temper any latent desire for aggressive military activity:

> Many Japanese—as many other Asians—hope that China's growing military capabilities can be constrained or blunted by successfully integrating Beijing into the multilateral international and regional security systems. Most Japanese appear to believe this effort has a good chance of succeeding as long as China is not isolated or contained.[47]

Indeed, fully integrating China into the international system cannot occur under a scenario of containment or isolation. On the other hand, improved relations with the United States would encourage China to continue to view Asian multilateral organizations in a positive light. The regional and global influence China derives from organizations where it plays a leading role will help deter it from relying on military force to achieve its security and foreign policy objectives.

Avoiding military competition with China will confer another major benefit on the United States that is not often sufficiently appreciated. The U.S. would no longer require the extensive military deployments in the Asia Pacific that it now maintains. Scaled-down U.S. forces could focus more exclusively on the North Korean threat while reinforcing the defenses of American allies—South Korea and Japan. The U.S. could devote the savings of defense budget dollars, equipment and personnel to other areas of pressing national need in security, economic and social arenas.

Security cooperation

A further result of improved U.S.-China relations would be greater security cooperation between the two countries, especially in Asia. From a practical standpoint, this would allow the United States to leverage Chinese capabilities to meet various transnational security threats to a far greater extent than the U.S. does now. As Asia expert Jonathan Pollack at Brookings points out, both countries seek to prevent proliferation of nuclear weapons and technologies, ensure energy security, assure the safety of maritime commerce and counter international terrorism.[48] Improved U.S.-China relations will expand significantly the areas of common concern and further the prospects for cooperation on security and other important issues. Professor David M. Lampton of Johns Hopkins University argues that "the United States' strategic task with respect to U.S.-China relations" is

> to work together with China and other partners to maintain a stable major power equilibrium in the region; to work in concert with the region and China to maintain and develop the security and human infrastructure necessary for economic and human development; and to address the transnational issues that are the existential challenges of this century—food, energy, climate, proliferation, resource availability (not least of which is water), and sustainable economic growth.[49]

The kinds of mutually beneficial security cooperation that would result from improved U.S.-China relations include the following:

> *Carrying out broad bilateral discussions on regional security*
>
> Through bilateral discussions, the U.S. and China could focus on how, in cooperation with other countries, they can prevent instability arising from terrorism, proliferation of weapons and other transnational threats. Quite conceivably, the U.S. and China could agree on common and complementary measures to leverage their respective strengths and security relationships to achieve agreed-upon goals.

> *Conducting much more effective military-to-military consultations*
>
> So long as China positions missiles and other forces in the vicinity of Taiwan and the U.S. prepares for an armed conflict with China, military-to-military discussion among likely future adversaries can be no more than limited and symbolic. Yet, in a new period of improved relations, each side's military organizations would be far more open to discussing ways to de-conflict

operations, cooperate to meet common security threats, and avoid any accidental confrontations.

Professor Lyle Goldstein identifies a number of specific initiatives in this area based on "the principle that China and the United States must work toward security cooperation as a vital foundation for peace in the twenty-first century and beyond." He believes

> a systematic approach that actually institutionalizes the habit of military cooperation is required at all levels and, in particular, at the junior-officer and staff levels. In the maritime domain specifically, cooperation, already initiated in some cases, should be accelerated in six major areas: confidence-building and crisis management; search and rescue; disaster relief; environmental stewardship; regional maritime security; and sea-lane security.[50]

Developing a "commonly held vision" for regional security[51]

A shared U.S.-China vision for regional security would serve to align U.S. and Chinese interests to the maximum extent possible, and facilitate cooperation on specific regional initiatives. As Bates Gill, director of the Stockholm International Peace Institute, observes, a common vision of this kind could "lead to closer cooperation between China and the U.S. alliance system in the region."[52] It could engender much improved Japan-China and Korea-China relations as well, along with far greater reliance on multilateral organizations to further regional security. A U.S.-led alliance structure that served as a bulwark against Soviet and Chinese aggression during the Cold War would likely no longer be necessary under changed strategic circumstances—where China cooperates closely with the United States, is committed to a common vision, and implements agreed practices which strengthen regional stability.[53]

Cooperating to peacefully transform "pariah" and "failed states"

Chinese diplomacy has too often been an obstacle hindering U.S. efforts to counter and transform failed states which oppress their own people. China has traditionally supported a hands-off attitude toward governments that severely infringe human rights, citing the principle that no sovereign state has the right, under international law, to interfere in the "internal affairs" of another sovereign state. A notable example of this view is China's decision, in early February 2012, to join with Russia in vetoing a UN Resolution aimed to forcing Syrian President Bashar al-Assad to yield power.

In recent years, scholars have found that "China has been quietly overhauling its policies toward 'pariah states'." Increasingly, China has sought to be perceived as more closely aligned on this issue with other major powers, including the United States and European Union, to demonstrate it is upholding its responsibilities to the international community.[54] Commenting on the development of this policy, Stephanie Kleine-Ahlbrandt of the International Crisis Group and Andrew Small of the German Marshall Fund write:

> China has moved from outright obstructionism and a defensive insistence on solidarity with the developing world to an attempt to balance its material needs with its acknowledged responsibilities as a major power. And so, when Washington and its allies formulate the policies toward pariah states, they should assume that China, although in some respects an obstacle, is now also a critical partner.[55]

Following a U.S.-China Framework Agreement, we can anticipate that Beijing's policy toward pariah states will evolve more strongly toward the views held by the United States and European Union. Resolution of major security disputes with the U.S. would strengthen China's support for the international system and for the norms of human rights and democracy that underlie it.

Locking in China's peaceful rise policy

To achieve its foremost national goal of economic development, China has, in recent years, adopted what it calls a "peaceful rise" policy and muted the criticisms of the United States that it frequently offered up prior to the mid-1990s. For more than a decade, China has often portrayed itself as a responsible partner of the United States and other Western countries in meeting common security and economic threats.

Some American scholars believe that China's peaceful rise policy signals a strategic shift towards a friendly relationship with the United States. Others argue that China's new benign policy represents a mere tactical change based on China's desire to avoid antagonizing the U.S. while it builds up its economy and modernizes its military forces.[56]

Regardless of whether China's proclaimed goal of "peaceful rise" represents a strategic or tactical shift, the United States would be wise to lock in this policy by resolving underlying disputes with China on security issues and, as will be discussed in the next chapter, by seeking new arrangements for free, fair and balanced trade between the two countries. These U.S. actions would effectively eliminate the possibility that a beleaguered

Communist Party might seek to mobilize Chinese nationalist feelings against the United States. They would also greatly strengthen the domestic forces in China that are bravely seeking more democracy, respect for human rights, and an end to one-party rule.

CHAPTER FOUR

China's economic juggernaut

As China's economy has boomed over the past decade—with rates of annual growth frequently exceeding 9 percent—many Americans have become increasingly concerned about the large American trade deficit with China, the loss of U.S. manufacturing jobs, the "artificial" level of China's currency, and other pressing economic issues. Some worry about China's economy dominating the United States in the future, even though the U.S. economy is now more than twice as large in GDP and almost six times larger in per capita income.[1] Critics often argue that while China is able to freely sell myriad products into the open U.S. market and unscrupulously undercut American producers, it restricts access to its own market and unfairly subsidizes Chinese manufacturers.

China's market reforms

To achieve unprecedented economic growth, with an enormous expansion of output, employment, productivity, exports and income, China has ironically followed the broad policy advice of the U.S. government for more than 30 years.[2] Beginning in 1978, Chinese leader Deng Xiaoping instituted reforms that substituted market forces for central planning, eliminated state-owned enterprises (SOEs), allowed factory owners and farmers to keep the profits they made, and rapidly increased both foreign trade and foreign investment. Deng established numerous Special Economic Zones to implement these market-driven policies along the Southeast coast of China, and by the mid-1980s began significantly cutting tariffs and reducing import barriers.[3] The U.S. advised China on the principles that intellectually underpinned Deng's economic reform measures. These included much greater reliance on market forces, encouraging manufacturers to compete on the world market, and welcoming foreign investments of capital, technology and know-how.

As a result of these reforms, continued by Deng's successors, China's economy increased seven-fold between 1980 and 2004. China has now become the second-largest economy in the world, with growth averaging more than 9 percent annually for the last 30 years. The income of ordinary Chinese workers has increased by a factor of seven. To put this achievement in historical perspective, China's growth rate exceeded the growth rate in the U.S., Japan and major European countries during the same period by five times or more. In human terms, China's growth has brought approximately 400 million people out of poverty.[4] As economist Jeffrey Sachs of Columbia University puts it, "China is the most successful development story in world history."[5]

The significance of China's growth and opening to world trade is captured in this insightful assessment by economist and journalist Fareed Zakaria:

> China is the world's largest producer of coal, steel, and cement. It is the largest cell phone market in the world .... At the height of the industrial revolution, Britain was called 'the workshop of the world.' That title belongs to China today. It manufactures two-thirds of the world's photocopiers, microwave ovens, DVD players, and shoes .... China has also pursued a distinctly open trade and investment policy. [Unlike Japan and South Korea, which followed] an export-led strategy that kept the domestic market and society closed, ... China opened itself up to the world. (It did this partly because it had no choice, since it lacked the domestic savings of Japan or South Korea.)[6]

Beginning in the mid-1980s, China sought membership in the World Trade Organization (WTO), the premier international economic organization that develops and enforces rules of the global market economy. Joining the WTO was viewed in China as allowing the country to "reclaim a place on the world stage that it ... lost in the last two centuries."[7] From a practical policy standpoint, WTO membership promised both to accelerate China's economic reforms and lock in those reforms to prevent them from being overturned by opposing domestic political factions. The WTO would mandate greater economic openness through lower tariffs, lower barriers to international competition, and greater transparency in both economic policy and regulatory decision-making.[8] Moreover, the WTO's pro-competition policies would help ensure that China did not follow the Korean and Japanese models of favoring big-business groups (i.e. *chaebol* and *kereitsu*) and that Chinese companies would rely far less in the future on the government.

In reaching final agreement on WTO membership with the United States in 2001, approximately 15 years after initially seeking WTO entry, China opened its doors widely to U.S. agriculture as well as manufactured products and services. In the view of Calman J. Cohen, President of the Emergency Committee for American Trade:

> China's accession to the World Trade Organization in 2001 represented the culmination of years of effort to encourage China's commitment to the basic rules of the global trading system. Without a doubt, substantial progress has been achieved in integrating China into the global trading system through the WTO. China's accession was on terms that were generally at a much higher level than for any other acceding country and efforts were made to address key issues that were particular to China, such as the role of state-trading enterprises.[9]

In its agreement to join the WTO, China cut tariffs from 31 percent to 17.5 percent for U.S. priority agricultural products (such as beef, poultry and pork) and from 24.6 percent to 7.1 percent on U.S. priority industrial products (including computers, telecom equipment and semiconductors); ended broad systemic barriers to U.S. exports, including quotas and licensing restrictions; eliminated export subsidies; and phased in new trading and distribution rights for U.S. manufacturers and agricultural exporters. China also gave new or improved access to U.S. companies, especially in the financial, consulting and telecom sectors; and permitted foreign securities companies to acquire minority stakes in Chinese joint ventures.

Since China joined the WTO in 2001, it has taken a number of additional steps to effectively implement its commitments. Among these measures are making further significant tariff reductions, eliminating hundreds of non-tariff barriers, reforming distribution rights in 2005 so foreign companies can distribute their products in China, liberalizing the regulatory requirements for foreign insurance companies, and expanding market access for foreign service providers.[10]

America's economic engagement with China

American banks, manufacturers, traders and investors of all kinds have long been eager to participate in China's economic rise. Their interests underlie the U.S. policy of economic engagement with China. Today, China is America's second-largest trading partner for merchandise and third-largest export market. (Only Canada and Mexico are larger.) China is also the largest source of imports into the United States. America is China's second largest trading partner (after the European Union) and its largest single-country export market.[11]

During the early years of the U.S. opening to China in the Carter and Reagan administrations—long before U.S.-China economic relations reached their current high level—the United States urged China, as noted earlier, to undertake market reforms, reduce government controls over the economy, rapidly expand the private sector, and allow major increases in foreign investment. The Clinton and George W. Bush administrations continued this approach, and persuaded China to cut tariffs, investment regulations and trade restrictions in order to join the WTO. As expected, the U.S. policy of economic engagement created major opportunities for American companies, which benefited from China's adherence to a set of international rules that engendered confidence and stability.

In several critical respects, however, the policy of U.S. engagement with China on trade and investment ran into increasing political resistance during the second Bush term. Members of Congress with protectionist leanings increasingly felt that unfair Chinese trade practices were to blame for factory closings and American job losses. They believed the trade deficit with China showed that the United States had gone too far in opening its markets to Chinese goods. They criticized Chinese companies for illegally "dumping" Chinese products in the U.S. and claimed that by failing to allow its currency, the Renminbi (RMB), to fluctuate freely, China acquired an unfair trade advantage. Even though China's economic advantage came in large part from forces of "globalization"—allowing U.S. manufacturers to much more easily out-source production to countries with lower costs (including India and various Southeast Asian nations as well as China)—China bore the brunt of political blame in the United States. In response to domestic criticism, the Bush administration in early 2006 proclaimed a "New Phase of Greater Accountability and Enforcement" in trade relations with China.[12] The new policy called for a major crackdown on Chinese goods entering the U.S. market and for imposing more stringent tariffs on products allegedly being sold at "less than fair value." Congress and the Bush administration also relied more heavily on national security laws (enforced by the Commission on Foreign Investment in the United States) to put up barriers to Chinese investment in sensitive industrial sectors, such as the energy industry.

By the end of the Bush administration's second term, the traditional U.S. engagement policy of encouraging greater American trade and investment with China—which helped to balance the far more suspicious U.S. view of China's military development—had come under serious challenge. Lobbying groups and associations representing major American business interests still strongly advocated continued economic engagement with China because it was so profitable. Yet political opinion had shifted toward greater protectionism and was reflected in harsher U.S. government enforcement of trade laws against China.

Coming into office with strong support from labor unions, President Obama continued the Bush policy of resisting "excessive" Chinese penetration of the U.S. market. In September 2009, the administration imposed a 35 percent tariff on Chinese-made tires, following a complaint filed by the United Steelworkers union. China responded angrily and threatened to impose its own tariffs on imports of American auto products and chicken meat. Observers with long experience in international trade worried that the U.S. decision and Chinese counter-measures could be the opening shots in a trade war. Some economists pointed out that the U.S. tariffs would merely boost U.S. imports of tires from Poland and Mexico, while providing little help to American workers.[13] Diplomats on both sides worked hard to defuse the controversy and were able to effectively lower tension on trade issues at a late October 2009 meeting of the U.S.-China Joint Commission on Commerce and Trade.

In October 2010, approximately a year after imposing the tariff on Chinese tires, the Obama Administration bowed to election year pressure in announcing it would investigate Chinese government subsidies for makers of wind and solar energy products, advanced batteries and energy efficient vehicles. This investigation came shortly after the U.S. House of Representatives in August condemned China's practice of allegedly undervaluing its currency to achieve a competitive trade advantage. (An artificially low RMB would allow China to sell its export products at prices that significantly undercut U.S. and other foreign competitors.) David Chen of the *New York Times* aptly attributed both measures to the anxiety of Americans about the country's economic decline, in the midst of the worst economic downturn since the Great Depression.[14] The *Times* reported that as early as spring, 2010, "national Democrats, including the House speaker, Nancy Pelosi, began to encourage candidates to highlight the [China] issue after reviewing internal polling that suggested voters strongly favored eliminating tax breaks to companies that do business with China."[15] The resulting ad campaigns, totaling tens of millions of dollars, effectively made China the scapegoat for voters' greatest concerns: the continuation of the recession and the lack of jobs. Even the Senate Majority Leader, Harry Reid, was not immune. His re-election campaign ran television ads that "wove pictures of Chinese factory workers with criticism that [Sharron Angle, Reid's opponent] was a 'foreign worker's best friend' for supporting corporate tax breaks that led to [job] outsourcing to China and India."[16]

The Obama Administration's protectionist measures toward China came at a time when China's growth engine was continuing to lead the global economy out of its prolonged recession. In 2008, as the global financial crisis took hold, the Chinese government implemented a massive $586 billion stimulus package and loosened the requirements for bank lending. Much of the Chinese stimulus funds were directed to capital-intensive infrastructure projects, construction and export manufacturing. The downside effect was to elevate the importance in China of "state-owned enterprises" over private sector entrepreneurs and cause serious market inefficiencies in the allocation of capital. Moreover, the stimulus policy spawned new regulations that favored domestic Chinese companies over foreign companies in order to promote "indigenous innovation." From a U.S. standpoint, these new regulations were discriminatory because they favored Chinese technology over foreign technology, especially in the very large government procurement market. They gave rise to considerable efforts by the American business community and government to eliminate the new rules.

More broadly, American officials and experts argued that China's recovery on the basis of its government's stimulus package was "unsustainable" since it relied so heavily on fixed infrastructure investment, state-subsidized loans and exports. U.S. officials maintained that these measures would unleash rampant inflation, create price "bubbles" and spur significant government debt. Consequently, they called for China to "rebalance" its economy toward much higher consumption and away from unnecessary production.[17]

Treasury Secretary Timothy Geithner cogently described the U.S. stance on rebalancing when he said in early 2011 that

> We want to encourage China to move definitively away from the export driven growth model of the last few decades to a growth model driven by domestic consumption. The Chinese leadership recognizes that China is now too large relative to the world economy for it to continue to rely on foreign demand to grow. And the government has adopted a comprehensive program of reforms to rebalance the economy and shift growth to domestic demand .... This transition will take time, but it is already having a major impact on the shape of Chinese growth, and providing increased opportunities for American companies. Domestic demand is contributing more to growth, and as a consequence, U.S. exports to China are growing more rapidly, and U.S. companies in China are seeing more opportunities.[18]

In October 2011, the protectionist impulse in Congress toward China emerged stronger than ever when a bipartisan Senate majority called for the government to impose high punitive tariffs on Chinese imports if it found China was manipulating the value of its currency to obtain an unfair trade advantage. Although China had allowed its currency to appreciate by approximately 7 percent over the prior year, critics argued that by intervening in currency markets, China kept the value of the RMB artificially low. This, in turn, allowed Chinese exporters of manufactured goods to undercut competitors in the United States. Jennifer Steinhauer, a journalist at the *New York Times*, noted the concern that if the Senate measure became law, it could spark a trade war with China, and explained the vote as follows: "[M]any members, especially those from manufacturing states, want to be seen as doing something about [China's] trade advantage, yet the White House and some leaders in both parties think it is far too risky to actually pull the trigger on a solution."[19] Cornell University Economics Professor Eswar Prasad commented that

> [A] lurking concern is that this bill will not help the U.S. economy significantly and could instead hurt job growth if China retaliates aggressively and trade tensions compound economic uncertainty, setting back an already fragile recovery. I suspect both parties are a little concerned about supporting such legislation if it backfires.[20]

Economists at the ING financial group estimated that if the Senate-approved tariffs were actually applied to Chinese imports, they could increase U.S. inflation by one percent and cost consumers $100 billion. "Retaliatory threats from China could also hit U.S. treasuries and destabilize global equity markets," the ING economists pointed out, "hitting confidence at a vulnerable time for the global economy."[21]

Approximately one week after the Senate adopted protectionist legislation condemning China's currency policy, Congress demonstrated that bipartisan support for free trade agreements is still possible to achieve in the United States. Congress approved FTAs with Korea, Colombia and Panama, sharply reducing the tariffs and non-tariff barriers impeding trade with those countries. Proponents of the FTAs, including the Obama Administration, argued they would increase overseas sales of American products, generate new U.S. jobs, reduce prices for American consumers, attract investments to U.S. manufacturing and generally spur U.S. economic growth. Not surprisingly, protectionist opponents of the FTAs warned that the trade deals would harm the U.S. economy by damaging the nation's industrial base and causing devastating job losses. Intrinsic to the successful approval of the free trade agreements was a revised program of "trade adjustment assistance" which provided compensation and retraining to workers who lost their jobs to foreign competition because of the FTAs. The benefits program received especially strong support from Democrats who regarded it as a critical underpinning of their vote in favor of the free trade agreements. Yet, despite passage of the trade adjustment assistance measure, many Democrats still voted against the FTAs.

Following legislative victories for the agreements with Korea, Colombia and Panama—which had the strong support of the U.S. Chamber of Commerce and other leading American business groups—the Obama Administration moved decisively in early November 2011 to declare its support for a new regional free trade bloc in the Asia Pacific. At a summit meeting of the Asia-Pacific Economic Cooperation forum (APEC) in Hawaii, President Obama announced that the U.S. would seek to finalize a regional trade agreement known as the Trans-Pacific Partnership (TPP) in 2012 with 11 other countries—Australia, New Zealand, Malaysia, Brunei,

Singapore, Vietnam, Chile, Peru, Japan, Mexico and Canada. In expressing his support for a new Asian trade bloc which would be realized through American leadership, the president spoke enthusiastically about the benefits it offered:

> The TPP will boost our economies, lowering trade barriers to trade and investment, increasing exports, and creating more jobs for our people, which is my number-one priority. Along with our trade agreements with South Korea, Panama and Colombia, the TPP will also help achieve my goal of doubling U.S. exports, which support millions of jobs .... [T]he TPP has the potential to be a model not only for the Asia Pacific but for future trade agreements. It addresses a whole range of issues not covered by past agreements, including market regulations and how we can make them more compatible, creating opportunities for small and medium-sized businesses in the growing global marketplace. It will include high standards to protect workers' rights and the environment.[22]

The administration's support for the TPP carried a blunt message for China, the largest economy in East Asia: rather than reduce protectionist measures against China's objectionable trade policies, the U.S. would take the unprecedented step of seeking to exclude China—for the foreseeable future—from a regional trade bloc that America dominated. By attempting to isolate China, the Obama Administration presumably hoped to strengthen the economic ties of other Asian countries to the United States and undercut China's relations with those same countries. In the view of Kenneth Lieberthal, director of the John L. Thornton China Center, and Jonathan Pollack, Senior Fellow, of the Brookings Institution, "the U.S. focus on developing a TPP that may well exclude China is an indication of the level of concern in Washington about China's future role in the region."[23]

After announcing the goal of completing TPP negotiations during 2012, both President Obama and his senior economic advisor Michael Froman strongly criticized China's economic policies. Obama called for China to "play by the rules" and said the U.S. would not do business with a country that is "gaming the system"—comments aimed at China's practice of unfairly holding down the value of its currency. Froman told journalists that Obama warned China's President Hu in a private meeting during APEC that the American business community is "growing increasingly impatient and frustrated with the state of change in China economic policy and the evolution of the U.S.-China economic relationship." Froman added that the U.S. would not invite China to join the TPP negotiations because "TPP is not something that one gets invited to. It's something that one aspires to."[24] Froman's comments reflected the U.S. Administration's view that China was not ready to meet the "high standards that are required of a TPP partner." The TPP, he pointed out, would be an "agreement that goes beyond the standard comprehensive free trade agreement" and deal with largely domestic issues like the role of state-owned enterprises, government procurement and state subsidies.[25]

In retrospect, it seems clear that the Obama Administration's moves to embrace the benefits of free trade through several country-specific FTAs and a new Trans-Pacific Partnership did not change its protectionist policies toward China and, in fact, reinforced them. The administration used its TPP initiative to punish and isolate China by seeking to exclude it from a future regional free trade zone that would embrace its neighboring countries in East Asia and its major trading partners. David Pilling of the *Financial Times* captured the likely impact of this strategy when he wrote that "China is now at the very centre of an Asian supply chain that is itself at the heart of the global manufacturing industry .... If the TPP smacks of 'an anyone-but-China club,' it is likely to be highly divisive in a region where Beijing is becoming more dominant, politically as well as economically."[26]

Threats posed by the Chinese economy

Though China has adopted U.S.-supported economic reforms and decisive market-opening measures, many Americans believe China's economic growth threatens the United States. Concern begins with two major factors—the large, growing bilateral trade deficit with China and the perceived loss of U.S. jobs to China. Public anxiety is magnified by China's undervalued currency, large holdings of U.S. treasury securities, failure to adequately enforce intellectual property rights (IPR), low regulatory standards for products that could harm American consumers, and "indigenous innovation" policy which undercuts the competitiveness of U.S. companies in China.

At the outset, it is important to make several general observations. First of all, while international trade brings innovation and greater efficiency, it can often cause painful dislocations. Structural shifts in the U.S. economy that produce a benefit for the economy as a whole can nevertheless cause real harm to businesses and workers in some sectors. Yet the overall result of such shifts is a "continuing and increasing positive boost to U.S. output, productivity, employment and real wages."[27] Rather than protecting certain industries from international competition, the far better approach is for the government to help businesses and workers alike move to more competitive areas.[28] For workers, government can provide critical training, assistance and job opportunities. For businesses, government can offer carefully targeted tax incentives and assistance in developing innovative products and services.

A second broad point is that the United States cannot expect to simultaneously grow its economy and oppose economic growth and development
in China.[29] The economies of the two countries are closely and inter-
dependently linked. If the U.S. attempts to hinder China's economic growth
through "buy American" laws, excessive U.S. tariffs on foreign goods, and
other nationalistic measures, this would inevitably damage the American
economy. Possible adverse effects would include increasing product prices
for U.S. consumers, raising U.S. interest rates that would make it harder for
Americans to borrow to buy a home or finance a business, and weakening
prospects for U.S. economic growth. In a globalized economy, nationalistic
efforts to restrain a foreign economy—out of resentment, fear or patriotic
impulses – have a boomerang effect.

We always need to bear in mind the role of protectionist policies in
causing the Great Depression, as Professor Barry Eichengreen of the
University of California and Douglas Irwin at Dartmouth, ably described
in 2009:

> While many aspects of the Great Depression continue to be debated,
> there is all-but-universal agreement that the adoption of restrictive
> trade policies was destructive and counterproductive and that similarly
> succumbing to protectionism in our current slump should be avoided at
> all cost .... [G]overnments erected tariff and nontariff barriers to trade
> in a desperate effort to direct spending to merchandise produced at home
> rather than abroad. But with other governments responding in kind, the
> distribution of demand across countries remained unchanged at the end
> of this round of global tariff hikes. The main effect was to destroy trade
> .... Recrimination over beggar-thy-neighbor trade policies made it more
> difficult to agree on other measures to halt the slump.[30]

Lastly, it is crucial to remember that a policy of expanding economic
relations through increased trade and investment has been intrinsic to
U.S. efforts to engage China over the last 30 years. As Thomas Lum and
Dick Nanto, two experts at the Congressional Research Service, recently
put it, "[T]he rationale behind engagement is that working with China
through economic [and other] interchanges helps the United States to
achieve important national security goals [including] fostering global
economic growth [and] prosperity for all Americans." America's trade
policy towards China "benefits both sides and allows for a more efficient
allocation of available resources; ... affords a rare opportunity for U.S.
businesses to become part of a huge and rapidly expanding market;
[requires China] to comply with international trading rules and spurs the
development of market forces; ... [creates] centers of power outside the
Chinese Communist Party, and [fosters] economic and social pressures for
democracy."[31]

The trade deficit

Critics with protectionist views often call attention to the large and rising trade deficit with China. In 2005, China exported $202 billion more to the United States than the U.S. exported to China. At the time, this was the largest trade deficit ever recorded by the U.S. with another country. In 2007, the trade deficit grew to $233 billion, and in 2011, it rose even further to $295 billion. For some Americans, the trade deficit symbolizes the inherent unfairness and inequality in the U.S.-China economic relationship. China is profiting far more from access to the American market, they believe, than U.S. companies and workers benefit from sales of American products and U.S. investments in China.

Critics inevitably fail to point out that the increase in America's trade deficit with China has occurred largely because other Asian economies have shifted their manufacturing and assembly operations to China. As expert Kenneth Lieberthal at Brookings puts it, since 2000, "[W]e have seen the emergence of an integrated East Asian manufacturing system in which China now imports parts and components from Japan, South Korea, Taiwan, Hong Kong and Singapore, then assembles the final products in China and ultimately exports those products to the U.S. and European Union.[32] As a result, the U.S. trade deficit with Japan, South Korea, Taiwan, Hong Kong and Singapore has plummeted. These countries now substantially export to the United States *through China,* rather than directly, as they did before 2000." As China's portion of the U.S. trade deficit has increased due to this shift, the portion of the trade deficit from trade with the rest of East Asia has significantly declined.[33] In fact, overall, the amount of the U.S. trade deficit attributable to East Asia, including China, has dropped from 75 percent to 49 percent during the last ten years.[34]

Since China is the destination of choice for *assembling* materials and components that are shipped there from other countries (including the United States), it is credited with the full value of the products which are exported to the U.S. In reality, the Chinese assembly operation only adds about half the value of these products.[35] In some cases, the value added in China to a product designated by the U.S. as "Chinese" is much smaller. A vivid example of the kind of statistical distortion that can occur is the case of a Barbie doll made in China which costs about $20 in the U.S. although China only receives about 35 cents of that amount. Nevertheless, the full cost of the doll is attributed by U.S. trade data to China. Just as importantly, almost 60 percent of Chinese exports to the U.S. are actually produced by *non-Chinese companies* operating in China. Many of these companies are American.[36]

Loss of U.S. manufacturing jobs and
rise in the export of U.S. services

Beyond the trade deficit, critics often blame China for the loss of U.S. manufacturing jobs. Numerous American companies have closed down their domestic operations because they could not compete with imports from overseas; in many cases, these same companies successfully later reopened their factories in China, India or countries in Southeast Asia.

Yet it is essential to recognize that trade deficits with China are not, in fact, a major cause of the loss of U.S. manufacturing jobs. These jobs have declined for decades, reflecting productivity gains which require fewer workers to make the same product. This long-term trend started well before China became a powerhouse in the world economy, when U.S. companies shifted toward services and higher-end, capital-intensive manufacturing from lower-end manufacturing. As a result, the share of U.S. employment attributable to the manufacturing sector declined from approximately 21 percent in 1979 to approximately 10 percent in 2004.[37] In any case, despite the political sensitivity around the topic, the number of U.S. manufacturing jobs that have moved overseas is, in fact, relatively small. Of the 15 million Americans laid off annually, only about two percent have lost their jobs due to so-called "off-shoring."[38]

Aside from U.S. manufacturers, American service providers—including banks and financial institutions, law firms, insurance companies, computer and healthcare companies—are playing a major role in China's development and generating thousands of new jobs in the United States to support their overseas operations. The United States currently has a trade surplus with China in the services area and this surplus stands to grow considerably over time. Once current regulatory barriers are removed, the U.S. surplus in services trade with China is expected to rise from $15.6 billion in 2009 to approximately $60 billion by 2015.[39]

Consider this observation by Alan Wheatley, the global economics correspondent for *Reuters*, who points out how the literal reporting of trade data can easily distort their true meaning: "For every Apple iPad sold in the United States, the U.S. trade deficit with China increases by about $275. Yet by far the most value embedded in the device accrues to Apple and sustains thousands of well-paid design, software, management and marketing jobs in the United States. By contrast, the value captured in China by the laborers who assemble Apple's products is a mere $10 or so, according to researchers led by Kenneth Kraemer of the University of California, Irvine, who crunched the data. Viewed through this prism, offshore manufacturing of electronic products like the iPad is a solution, not a problem, for the United States ...."[40]

So it is misleading at best to blame the trade deficit with China for the extensive loss of American jobs. The deficit—which measures the amount by which U.S. imports from China exceed U.S. exports—does not take into account the long-term shift away from lower-end manufacturing in the U.S. which has actually led to the major job losses. Nor does it reflect the fact that America's trade deficit with other Asian countries has decreased while the deficit with China has grown, following the relocation of manufacturing and assembly operations to China. The trade deficit numbers fail to measure the many U.S. jobs generated by the overseas investments of American companies. Moreover, the United States can expect to acquire a trade surplus with China in the future as China transitions to a more services-based economy, where U.S. banks, financial institutions, computer and healthcare companies play a major role.

The question of China's currency

China is often accused of unfairly and deliberately undervaluing its currency to achieve advantages in international trade.[41] When the currency value of the Renminbi (RMB) is relatively low against the dollar, it makes Chinese exports cheaper and contributes to China's trade surplus, which in turn strengthens that country's economic growth.

Many mainstream American economists believe it would be beneficial for China to allow market forces to fully determine the value of its currency against the dollar and other foreign currencies. They argue that unless China does so, the country "will find it ever harder to prevent speculative capital inflows from undermining its pursuit of independent monetary policy."[42]

With the goal of letting the market determine the RMB's exchange rate, China adopted a policy of currency reform in 2005, which has proved partially successful. By January 2009, the RMB had appreciated by approximately 25 percent against the dollar, including an adjustment for inflation. In June 2010, China further loosened the RMB's strict "peg" to the dollar to allow market forces greater influence on the currency's value. The Chinese currency appreciated by about another 7 percent as of Fall 2011. And in mid-April 2012, China took measures to allow additional appreciation, leading Treasury Secretary Geithner to comment that "the cumulative effect of what China has done on the exchange rate side ... is very significant and very promising."[43]

While RMB appreciation is in the best interests of China and the United States, so that the currency reflects actual market value, it is worthwhile keeping in mind that revaluation of the RMB will not have a significant impact on the U.S. trade deficit with China. Although American exporters would be able to offer products at lower prices to Chinese consumers (and thus increase their "market share"), the sheer number of these exported U.S. products is now relatively low in comparison to products imported from China.[44] So the overall dollar adjustment in the trade deficit is likely to be small. As Daniel Ikenson, Associate Director for Trade Policy Studies at the Cato Institute, observes:

> Recent evidence suggests that RMB appreciation will not reduce the U.S. trade deficit and undermines the common political argument for compelling China to revalue. Between July 2005 and July 2008, the RMB appreciated by 21 percent against the dollar .... During that same period, the U.S. trade deficit with China increased from $202 to $268 billion. [45]

Moreover, as currency revaluation occurs, Chinese exporters to the United States will do everything in their power to protect their market share. They will cut profits and reduce their costs as much as possible, striving to resist the complete loss of sales. In this sense, as well, RMB revaluation is not likely to assist the U.S. in overcoming its China trade deficit.[46] On the other side of the trade equation, U.S. companies that export to China do not regard the RMB-dollar exchange rate as an obstacle. In fact, these U.S. exports have grown by approximately 640 percent from 2000 to 2011.[47]

Many U.S. economic analysts believe that pressure *within China* from Chinese consumers will lead the government in the future to allow the RMB to appreciate to its full market value against the dollar. Consumers will demand more "buying power" to purchase imported goods. The influence of these consumers will be considerable since their annual disposable income is expected to increase from approximately $2.2 billion in 2008 to $9.6 billion in 2020. At that point, China's estimated population of 1.4 billion people "will make up a significant portion in the world's consumer market."[48] In the words of the National Intelligence Council's 2020 project, "rapidly rising income levels for a growing middle class will combine to mean a huge consumption explosion, which is already evident."[49]

No doubt it will be beneficial for U.S.-China economic relations if China's currency is allowed to appreciate to reflect its actual market value. The U.S. should strongly encourage China to move in this direction, which will assist in "leveling the playing field" among Chinese and American companies in international trade. A market-driven exchange rate would strengthen international competition for the good of all.

Blowing the RMB issue out of proportion, however, or allowing a distorted view of the trade deficit to generate public outrage will neither solve the problem of the U.S. trade deficit with China, nor induce China to take necessary measures that lead to currency revaluation. A real danger is that becoming fixated on issues such as China's alleged "manipulation" of its currency diverts American attention from more important developments in China that could have a much greater impact on the U.S. and global economies.

Moreover, the politicization of the currency issue which led the U.S. Senate in October 2011 to call for imposing high punitive tariffs on Chinese imports after a finding of currency manipulation, carries high risks, as economist Robert J. Samuelson has cogently pointed out:

No one should relish threatening China with a 25 percent tariff. It would be illegal under existing WTO rules; to save the postwar trading system, we'd have to attack it. This would risk an all-out trade war just when the world economy is already tottering. There's no guarantee that China would respond as hoped. Initially, it might retaliate. Cooperation on other issues would collapse. Prices of Chinese exports (consumer electronics, shoes) that we barely make would probably rise. Other countries might adopt protective measures. All this is dangerous stuff. [50]

China's holdings of U.S. treasury securities

China is the largest holder of foreign exchange reserves in the world, totaling about $3.3 trillion as of April 2012.[51] Nearly $1.2 trillion of these reserves have been invested in U.S. Treasury securities—which are widely considered among the safest investments worldwide.[52] It is undisputed that China's holdings of U.S. bonds have kept down U.S. interest rates, including mortgage rates, for a number of years and enabled the United States to finance its current budget deficit.

Critics of China's policy sometimes express fears that its American investments create a security vulnerability for the United States. They worry, in particular, that China could suddenly and perniciously sell most or all of its U.S. dollar holdings, thereby triggering a rapid increase in U.S. interest rates as well as inflation. This action could, in turn, harm a still fragile recovery from the global financial crisis.

Many leading U.S. experts, however believe that China is highly unlikely to intentionally harm the U.S. economy in this way.[53] China has continuously strived to portray itself as a strong supporter of global economic growth and stability. When China stood firm on not devaluing its currency at the request of Western governments during the 1997–8 Asia financial crisis, it slowed the rising panic and enhanced its international stature.[54] "Dumping" dollars or even generating a rumor that it might do so, would subject China to severe international criticism and damage its worldwide reputation.

More importantly from a purely economic standpoint, a sale of dollars, or rumors of a planned sale, would likely cause serious financial losses to China. It would be impossible for the Chinese government to quickly sell its large amount of accumulated dollar reserves, held in the form of U.S. Treasury bonds. Initiating a major sale would sharply drive down the prices of those bonds and cause sizeable self-inflicted losses. Given the sharp criticism of financial authorities by Chinese citizens in the past for incurring losses from currency sales, China's government would be exceptionally reluctant to face such public anger a second time.[55]

Another scenario recounted by Fareed Zakaria is that "if China began to divest [its holdings of U. S. Treasury securities] ..., it would trigger panic selling of the dollar. That would in turn hurt the U.S. economy, which is China's number one export market (not a good idea if you are the Beijing government trying to keep workers occupied in factories across China)." The reality, Zakaria points out, is that

> China is trapped into a cycle of buying our T-bonds. No matter what any ratings agency says, no other bond market is as big or as safe. So ignore all those theories about China doing America a huge favor. The reality is, they have nowhere else to go. We're probably doing them a favor.[56]

Intellectual property rights and consumer product safety

Two other recurring sources of conflict in U.S.-China economic relations are China's weak legal protection of intellectual property rights (IPR) and its poor regulatory system for ensuring product safety. Both issues give rise to considerable concern in the United States.

Among U.S. *manufacturers and exporters* to China, counterfeiting of American-made products as well as infringements of U.S. patents, copyrights and trademarks are critical issues.[57] U.S. industry's global fight to protect its products treats China as "a key battleground." The amount of financial losses from Chinese counterfeiting, internet piracy, and other thefts of intellectual property in 2009 alone was estimated by the International Trade Commission to be approximately $48 billion.[58]

China's weak regulatory regime for agricultural and manufactured products is also of great concern to American *consumers*. U.S. government agencies have issued many warnings, recalls and curbs on the import of suspect Chinese products, including tainted food and unsafe toys and tires. In one case, the Food and Drug Administration (FDA) recalled numerous Chinese-made pet foods that led to widespread illness and deaths of U.S. pets. In another instance, the FDA warned against toothpaste imported from China that contained poisonous chemicals. For its part, the National Highway Traffic Safety Administration ordered recalls of up to 450,000 defective Chinese-made tires. And the Consumer Product Safety Commission recalled millions of Chinese toys because of excessively high lead levels, loose magnets, toxic chemicals and burn hazards.[59]

In the case of both rampant IPR violations and unsafe Chinese exports, the root cause is similar: despite increasing efforts by China's central government to prevent these practices, enforcement at the provincial and local levels is sporadic.[60] The profits available to counterfeiters and illicit product manufacturers give them the means to bribe and conspire with local officials to thwart central government enforcement. Local officials then acquire a stake in criminal enterprises, and subvert the regulatory practices designed to protect intellectual property as well as consumer health and safety.

To address the issue, China's central government announced in fall 2010 a "Program for Special Campaign on Combating IPR Infringement and Manufacture and Sales of Counterfeiting and Shoddy Commodities." The U.S. Trade Representative evaluated this program in 2011 as having "positive outcomes" but the business community understandably believes that "further measures and actions are needed to ensure China develops an IP sector that provides U.S. innovators those protections and opportunities essential to cultivating a strong IP industry."[61]

In subsequent meetings with United States Commerce Secretary John Bryson in late 2011, the U.S. and China announced their joint efforts on improving cooperation against IPR infringement and other trade law violations. According to the Office of the U.S. Trade Representative, China agreed to a new nationwide mechanism, under high-level leadership, to "crack down on IPR infringement."[62] It remains to be seen how effective the new mechanism will be.

Until local governments in China act in much greater concert with the central government to stem IPR and product safety violations, the problems clearly will persist.[63] The U.S. needs to press China hard on these issues, but the ultimate solution will entail making systemic domestic changes in China. Professor Richard Baum of UCLA identifies the "fiscal starvation of local governments" by China's central government as the primary cause of IPR and regulatory violations. Until this "starvation" ends and local officials no longer find it in their interest to be willing partners in crime with unscrupulous manufacturers offering bribes and kickbacks, the problem will remain. It is also apparent that building a true national consensus in China on addressing IPR and product safety violations is essential. Without a consensus that includes local officials in broad "interest coalitions," enforcement of tough regulatory standards is likely to remain only partially effective.

Indigenous innovation

Next to "currency manipulation," the Chinese trade policy that has most incensed the American business community and U.S. government in recent years, is a practice known as "indigenous innovation." In its domestic stimulus package during the global financial crisis, China put new regulations into effect that strongly favored local firms. The regulations included: strict written standards that gave an advantage to domestic companies; patent laws that could force foreign companies to transfer key technologies and trade secrets to the Chinese government; and "anti-monopoly" rules that could block access by foreign companies to important industrial sectors such as energy and telecommunications. On top of the new regulations, China's government offered tax incentives and subsidies to Chinese companies to develop businesses in targeted high-tech sectors while discriminating against foreign companies in awards of lucrative procurement contracts. One astute journalist pointed out that "provincial and municipal governments across China have issued lists" of numerous products these governments are legally permitted to purchase. "Hardly any [lists] include goods made by foreign companies, even if they're produced in China."[64]

In early 2010, a coalition of the United States Chamber of Commerce, the Business Software alliance and a number of other major trade associations denounced "systematic efforts by China to develop policies that build their domestic enterprises at the expense of U.S. firms." The coalition called for the administration to pay "urgent attention to policy developments in China that pose an immediate danger to U.S. companies."[65] Pressure from the business community proved effective in achieving U.S.-China agreements in January and May 2011 on ending the practice of using government procurement to favor local Chinese companies. But the slow implementation of China's pledges was criticized by newly appointed U.S. ambassador to China and former Commerce Secretary Gary Locke, shortly after his arrival in Beijing. In his September 2011 inaugural speech on economic issues, Locke declared that

> China's current business environment is causing growing frustrations among foreign business and government leaders, including my colleagues in Washington .... [I have] identified what I [believe] to be the single largest barrier to improved U.S.-China cooperation: a lack of openness in many areas of Chinese society—including many areas of the Chinese economy.[66]

Locke went on to criticize practices where the government "effectively shuts out foreign competition altogether" and called for reforms that would create "a more open investment environment."

When Commerce Secretary John Bryson met Chinese officials in late November 2011, China took a reassuring approach. According to Bryson, China pledged a "fair and level playing field" for U.S. and all foreign suppliers who were competing for government contracts to develop clean energy and other emerging technologies. Foreign companies would also be eligible to receive Chinese government subsidies to support R&D on those technologies on the same basis as local companies. This new Chinese pledge covered "high-end equipment manufacturing, energy-saving and environmental technologies, information technology, alternative energy and advanced materials," as reported by the Office of the U.S. Trade Representative. In monetary terms, a great deal was at stake in these negotiations, since China announced plans to invest $1.7 trillion in all these sectors over the next five years.[67]

By the end of 2011, U.S. pressure on China to keep its market open, treat foreign companies fairly and end the practice of favoring local firms in government procurement appeared to pay off. After a nearly two-year effort by American trade officials, China agreed to roll back its policy of giving preference to "indigenous innovation" by local companies. The jury is still out, of course, on whether Beijing fully implements its promises. Regular follow-up by U.S. officials is surely warranted.

The collaborative, win-win approach taken by Ambassador to China Gary Locke, in his current post and his former position as U.S. Commerce Secretary, has been instrumental in achieving the policy changes long sought by both the American business community and U.S. government. His strategy to eliminate discriminatory government procurement regulations and accelerate greater reliance on free market principles is well reflected in the following remarks taken from his September 2011 inaugural speech:

We [in the United States] welcome a strong, prosperous and successful China that plays a greater role in world affairs because it's good for the people of China and the United States; it's good for the global economy; and it's critical to creating jobs in America ....

Creating more jobs for Americans is the foremost priority of the Obama administration. And given our economic interdependence, more jobs in America and a stronger American economy are also in the economic interest of the Chinese people .... Achieving these goals require a thriving China and a closer commercial relationship between our countries ....

America understands that China's modernization and evolution towards a more market-oriented economy is a process that will take time. But it's necessary to accelerate these efforts if China is to expand opportunity for its people and to meet the goals of its five-year plan, and to strengthen the global economy. When the United States speaks of openness, what we really mean is we want China to be open to letting the talents of its own people flourish. And open to competition, which fosters excellence. China's own recent history proves that when it opens itself, there is nothing its people cannot accomplish. A more open China will lead to a more prosperous and stable China. That's good for China, the United States and, indeed, the entire world.[68]

Ambassador Locke's collaborative approach to opening the China market stands in stark contrast to protectionist measures for punishing the Chinese government and Chinese companies that members of Congress and other Obama administration officials often advocate. The protectionist strand of U.S. economic policy normally singles out China and has almost triggered a trade war between the two countries on more than one occasion.

Benefits to the United States of close U.S.-China economic relations

Before considering the broad benefits to the United States of close economic relations with China, it is worthwhile to step back and appreciate the contribution that China's growth makes to the world economy. China expert James Kynge describes the country's role this way:

> From a global perspective, China's emergence is of enormous economic benefit. The value created by the release of 400 million people from poverty, the migration of more than 120 million from farms where they perhaps raised chickens to factories where they churn out electronics, the quantum leap in educational standards for tens of millions of children, the construction of a First World infrastructure, the growth of forty cities with populations of over one million, the commercialization of housing, and the vaulting progress up the technology ladder have helped unleash one of the greatest surges in prosperity in history. The prime beneficiary has been China itself, but the mobilization of wealth on such a scale is necessarily, in aggregate terms, lifting the fortunes of the planet.[69]

In the United States today, consumers benefit from low-priced Chinese products, producers rely heavily on Chinese inputs for American-made goods, many U.S. companies with factories in China run highly profitable operations, and American exporters have experienced unprecedented growth in sales of their products and services to China, generating numerous American jobs.

Some indicators of the potential economic benefits to the United States of future trade and investment with China are the following:

> From 2000 to 2011, the amount of exports to China, including Hong Kong, from the United States increased by approximately 640 percent, from about $16 billion to $104 billion.[70] During this period, American exports to China grew seven times faster than U.S. exports to all countries in the world other than Canada and Mexico.

The bilateral U.S. trade surplus in services with China stands to increase from $5.4 billion in 2007 to $60 billion by 2015, if current trade barriers are eliminated. This would create up to 240,000 new jobs in the U.S. services sector.[71]

At the future time when China consumes American products and services at the same rate as Japan did in 2010, the U.S. will be exporting approximately $632 billion in goods and services to China. This would represent about ten times the amount of goods and services that the U.S. exported to China in 2010.[72]

The U.S. is China's largest single-country trading partner and China is the third largest export market of the United States, after Canada and Mexico.

U.S. companies have invested approximately $50 billion in China. China has invested approximately $1.2 trillion in U.S. government treasury bonds and notes.[73]

This data underscores that China's market and growing economic capacity offer significant opportunities, in the future, for U.S. technology, capital, products and know-how. China is already the largest growth market for U.S. goods and services in the world. The United States is in an excellent position to further leverage China's economic development and strengths as a way of propelling the growth of the American economy over coming decades.

Treasury Secretary Geithner sums up the current and potential benefits from U.S. economic relations with China this way:

China needs the United States, but the United States also benefits very substantially from our rapidly expanding economic relationship with China. The benefits of this relationship are hard to capture in any one statistic, but remember this .... Our exports to China are growing at twice the rate of our exports to the rest of the world. These exports are supporting hundreds of thousands of jobs across the nation in all sectors—from high technology to soybeans, aircraft to autos and forklifts to financial services. We have a great deal invested in each other's success.[74]

The Emergency Committee on American trade emphasizes the same point: "As China continues to develop and grow its economy, it will be one of the most important world markets for decades to come, providing significant economic opportunities to U.S. farmers, manufacturers, service providers and their workers."[75]

While China has made unprecedented historical strides as the fastest growing world economy since 1978, it still has immense economic and social needs. Large amounts of U.S. technology and capital can profitably be invested to help Chinese people escape poverty, reduce severe environmental pollution, address major social problems, and achieve a standard of living on par with the United States, Japan and Western European countries. Economic benefits to the U.S. would come in the form of sharply increased profits for U.S. exporters and manufacturers, large numbers of high-quality American jobs generated by trade with China, major infusions of Chinese capital into U.S. companies, and a surplus for the United States in services trade with China.

The United States economy will also benefit from China's accelerated growth by harnessing the country's talents, resources and economic dynamism. Chinese scientists, engineers, technical experts and entrepreneurs offer a large pool of talent and expertise which U.S. firms can tap through cooperative and joint business projects. These Chinese human resources would help propel American industry to compete more effectively across a number of industrial sectors in the global economy. China also offers considerable natural resources, including oil, coal, natural gas, and metals, that can meet the needs of U.S. industry in the future.

Foreign direct investment in the United States

As China develops further, Chinese companies and entrepreneurs will make significant investments in the United States. With improved U.S.-China economic relations, Chinese capital would flow into the U.S. at an unprecedented rate for investment in new plants and infrastructure that will greatly strengthen the American economy. This, in turn, will create new jobs, more technological innovation, and new products that raise the U.S. standard of living. Over time, the balance of trade could also shift far more toward the United States, as China's economy matures and demand increases for high-value American goods and services.

According to a May 2011 report of the Asia Society and Woodrow Wilson Center for International Scholars, the "takeoff" for large-scale Chinese investment into the U.S. has already started:

> Chinese direct investment in the United States is soaring, both in value and number of deals. Businesses from China have established operations and created jobs in at least 35 of the 50 U.S. states and across dozens of industries in both manufacturing and services. Official data tend to obscure the exciting reality that the United States is open to Chinese investment and that that investment is, in fact, arriving in increasingly larger amounts—more than $5 billion in 2010 alone. The actual number of jobs that Chinese investors have created likely exceeds 10,000—many times the official estimate.[76]

The accumulated value of the investments between 2003 and 2010 is approximately $12 billion.

The foreign direct investment (FDI) from China has mainly involved new "greenfield" projects in sophisticated fields, including health care, aerospace, renewable energy, biotechnology, processed food and communications equipment. This investment is likely to grow exponentially across a wide range of U.S. industries. In the next decade, experts forecast that Chinese companies will invest $1 trillion to $2 trillion around the world and the U.S share of that amount will grow considerably.[77] By 2015, China will likely become a "net exporter" of foreign direct investment—sending more FDI overseas than what foreigners are investing in China.[78]

There are several major reasons why Chinese companies are now seeking to invest and expand their operations overseas.[79] A primary driver of FDI is the desire to secure natural resources, especially oil and key commodities. Acquiring stakes in overseas companies allows China to hedge against supply risks, enter profitable overseas markets, and strengthen bargaining power. Secondly, Chinese companies increasingly encounter competition from lower-cost manufacturers and face various trade barriers. FDI enables these companies to out-compete their rivals and "jump over" the tariff and non-tariff barriers placed at countries' borders. Third, Chinese companies are well aware they lag behind many American, Japanese and European firms in the quality of their products and the efficiency of their operations. FDI enables them to acquire prestigious international brands and valuable technologies while also developing their skills in marketing, distribution and innovation. In a macroeconomic sense, Chinese companies increasingly recognize that future growth in manufacturing will be less driven by expanding the scale of production than by providing high value-added services and utilizing superior technologies. Internationalizing their operations and pursuing global business strategies through foreign direct investment ensures that Chinese manufacturing will remain competitive and economically viable.

From the standpoint of the American public, of course, direct investment by Chinese companies generates widespread concern about a foreign "takeover" of U.S. industry—much like the fears many people held about investments by Japanese companies in the mid-1980s. The Japanese example is particularly instructive, since Japanese companies and their U.S. affiliates went on to invest hundreds of billions of dollars in the United States and have created jobs for approximately 700,000 Americans.[80] So it is important to outline both the potential benefits and risks of Chinese investment, while considering whether the United States has sufficient means of controlling the risks.

The greatest benefit from Chinese FDI is likely to be "in-sourcing"— bringing good jobs back to America that previously migrated overseas during the earlier years of "globalization" when U.S. companies sought to manufacture more cheaply in China, India, Vietnam, and other developing countries. Today, virtually every state and major city across the country seeks to attract foreign investment for this very reason.

FDI from China also promotes competition in the marketplace, reducing production costs for American companies and prices for American consumers, enhancing consumer welfare and spurring the development of more innovative products. Direct investment encourages research and development (R&D), improving the quality of products and strengthening the business practices of American industry as a whole.[81] A good example of positive spillover from R&D can be found in Japan's investments in the U.S. auto sector:

[Japanese] carmakers trained local workers, and their interactions with customers, suppliers, dealers, and researchers introduced new manufacturing concepts and organizational knowledge such as just-in-time inventory management and other practices. In addition, Japanese multinationals constantly increased their spending on technology development. Today, they spend around $5 billion each year for R&D in the United States.[82]

Most direct investments from China do not require U.S. government review for potential harm to national security by the organization that screens foreign FDI—the Committee on Foreign Investment in the United States (CFIUS), which includes the attorney general as well as the secretaries of treasury, homeland security, defense, state, energy and commerce. CFIUS screening focuses on national security threats that arise from any foreign investments with the potential to facilitate espionage or sabotage by a foreign power; allow access to sensitive technology and know-how; give a foreign company control over the production of critical defense-related products; or provide a foreign country with control of "strategic assets" such as telecommunication networks, oil pipelines or ports.[83] While the long-established policy and procedures for screening foreign direct investment are fundamentally sound, it is critical to preserve, protect and strengthen this screening system and remedy any regulatory weaknesses, as the recent expert report by the Asia Society and Woodrow Wilson Center suggests: "We should continue to screen out *all* deals with specific negative national security implications" and "handle *more general concerns* about the behavior of firms from China under U.S. domestic law once they have sunk their dollars into the United States and have something to lose".[84]

Most important is the report's bottom line:

After reviewing the ways in which FDI from China is capable of affecting the United States economically and in national security terms ... we conclude that China's impact on the United States will be highly beneficial economically, and that the downsides can be managed under existing U.S. investment doctrine and policy. The traditional policy of welcoming the economic benefits and competition from foreign direct investment remains sound in the case of China.[85]

Protectionism and national security criteria

As American companies lost market share to Chinese imports and the United States trade deficit with China mounted over the last decade, the American government often responded by imposing protectionist measures. Congress also sought to aggressively block Chinese companies from acquiring U.S. companies in some commercial fields based on their potential harm to national security.

It is fair to say that while U.S. hawks fear the danger China poses to American security, protectionists worry deeply that China's economic rise will harm the U.S. economy. As noted earlier, protectionists stress that the large U.S.-China trade deficit—reflecting the greater value of Chinese exports to the U.S. than U.S. exports to China—has caused major job losses, allegedly amounting to 2.8 million jobs between 2001 and 2010, according to a September 2011 report of the Economic Policy Institute.[86]

Behind much of the criticism of China's trade surplus is the fear that this economic powerhouse could dominate the United States in the future. China has averaged more than 9 percent economic growth, annually, for the last 30 years. This growth was more than five times the growth rate in the U.S., Japan and major European countries during the same period. Even in the midst of the global financial crisis, China's growth exceeded 8 percent in 2009, and was a major factor in preventing a global depression. In 2010, China became the world's second largest economy, surpassing Japan.

Looking back, China-bashing sentiment in the Congress has put pressure on the administration to wage a protectionist battle against Chinese imports and investments in the United States. Shortly after taking office in 2009, as discussed previously, the Obama Administration responded to a complaint of the United Steelworkers union and imposed a stiff 35-percent tariff on Chinese-made tires. In fall 2010, the House of Representatives voted overwhelmingly to threaten tariffs on a wide range of Chinese products exported to the U.S.; shortly thereafter, the U.S. Trade Representative launched an investigation of Chinese government subsidies to that country's clean energy industry. A year later, under pressure from the U.S. solar industry, the Commerce Department opened an investigation into alleged Chinese "dumping" of solar panels into the U.S. at prices lower than the cost of manufacturing. The solar investigation occurred at the same time as the Obama Administration came under fire for giving more than $16 billion in guaranteed loans to Solyndra and other American clean-energy companies to subsidize new lower-risk power plants owned by major U.S. conglomerates, utilities and investment banking firms. In October 2011, a bipartisan Senate majority demanded that the administration impose punitive tariffs on a variety of Chinese imports because of China's alleged currency manipulation. And during May 2012, the Obama administration imposed stiff tariffs of 31 percent on solar panels and up to 26 percent on wind-energy towers imported from China in what the *Associated Press* called "the latest strike[s] in an escalating trade war over clean energy."[87]

In response to each protectionist measure, China reacted sharply and threatened to retaliate against imported U.S. products. In a series of official statements, Beijing accused Washington of seriously violating international regulations and "escalating trade protectionism."[88] Each time an exchange of heated rhetoric took place, U.S. trade experts worried publicly that the protectionist measures could trigger a trade war between the two countries which could spin out of control and harm the U.S. recovery from the global financial crisis.

During the Obama Administration, Congressional protectionists have also continued their practice of blocking Chinese investments in U.S. companies. Their most common tactic has been to politicize the issue by stirring up widespread fear of potential harm to national security. In 2009, unions and policymakers brought political pressure against a Chinese wind-power manufacturer to stop a U.S. investment. In 2010, a coalition that included American steel industry groups and members of Congress successfully opposed an investment by China's Anshan Iron & Steel Group in a new Mississippi steel mill.[89] The most notorious example of protectionists in Congress politicizing a commercial investment involved the attempt in 2005 by the China National Offshore Oil Corporation (CNOOC) to acquire Union Oil Company of California (UNOCAL). Although UNOCAL supplied less than 1 percent of U.S. oil and gas needs—and CNOOC promised to keep all of UNOCAL's production within the United States—Congress declared by a lopsided 398 to 15 margin that CNOOC's planned acquisition would "threaten to impair the national security of the U.S."[90]

Administration support for free trade agreements

Alongside their strong protectionist efforts to punish China for perceived unfair trade practices, both Congress and the Obama Administration have demonstrated new-found interest in concluding free trade agreements and expanding U.S. exports, as noted earlier. Within days of passing high punitive tariffs against China in October 2011, the Senate approved three bilateral FTAs—with Korea, Panama and Colombia—that lowered tariffs, eliminated non-tariff barriers and put in place new procedures to promote international trade in the countries' mutual best interests. The measures followed the initiative announced by President Obama in early 2010 to double U.S. exports as a means of helping to create two million new jobs and overcome the devastating effects of the global financial crisis. In arguing for approval of these FTAs, proponents in Congress and the administration underscored the proven value of previous U.S. trade agreements in promoting U.S. exports. Especially impressive was the fact that between 2001 and 2008, U.S. exports to the 17 trading partners where free trade agreements were in force increased 63 percent. Free trade proponents cited other persuasive benchmark data including the near tripling of U.S. goods exports to Mexico and Canada between 1993 and 2008, following passage of the North American Free Trade Agreement (NAFTA); and the 350 percent jump in U.S. goods exports to Chile between 2003 and 2008 after the U.S.-Chile FTA became law.[91]

A Trans-Pacific Partnership that excludes China

The "schizophrenic" political mind-set of promoting free trade, particularly in the Asia Pacific, while protecting the U.S. market by penalizing China reached a new high point in November 2011, when President Obama gave a major push to the Trans-Pacific Partnership (TPP) agreement while effectively excluding China from the negotiations. In his speech to an APEC summit meeting in Hawaii, as discussed previously, Obama stressed the potential of the TPP to create a new Asian regional trade bloc to boost trade and investment among the member countries. The TPP's promise of ramping up U.S. exports and creating U.S. jobs caught the imagination of the American business community, as a December 2011 statement of the U.S. Chamber of Commerce to Congress makes clear:

A comprehensive, ambitious, and enforceable market-opening TPP has the potential to create an explosion of trade and new American jobs and would demonstrate continued U.S. leadership across the [Asian] region. It is an exciting vision which, on the right terms, can be an economic shot in the arm for the United States and for our friends and allies in the region. It can send a clear, unmistakable message that America's leadership in the Pacific is here to stay .... [At stake is] our best hopes for escaping high unemployment, massive deficits and exploding entitlements.[92]

Despite the general benefits that free trade agreements confer on the United States, a U.S. policy of taking protectionist and punitive measures against China while promoting free trade with other Asian and non-Asian countries is deeply misguided. Protectionist measures against China harm both the U.S. and global economies. If the U.S. succeeds in erecting trade barriers to Chinese imports, Chinese demand for U.S. and other foreign products will inevitably slow down. The resulting contraction and lower growth rate of China's economy hurts several critical groups—U.S. manufacturers that export to China, U.S. companies with investments and operations in China, and ultimately U.S. consumers who have to pay higher prices for less-than-competitive products. A decline in the Chinese economy, triggered in part by protectionist measures, translates into a longer recovery from the global financial crisis and slower economic growth in the United States.

It is important to remember, as policy experts Mona Sutphen and Nina Hachigian point out, that "benefits to the United States from emerging great economies [like China] are large, broad and lasting. [They include] cheaper goods, more profits, lower inflation, more innovation, and greater overall economic growth." By contrast, "protectionist measures send resources to old, unproductive industries that cannot compete and drain them from those that can."[93]

Moreover, various measures to punish China that find support in the Congress would be violations of America's own commitments to the World Trade Organization.[94] House and Senate legislation that blocks certain Chinese products from entering the U.S. or imposes punitive tariffs on Chinese goods because of the country's undervalued currency would quickly bring challenges at the WTO and sanctions against the United States for non-compliance with its legal obligations. This would undercut, in turn, the U.S. policy of promoting China's respect for inter-national economic rules that the United States helped establish in the first place.

In a worst case, raising U.S. trade barriers to block imports from China could trigger a trade war, with retaliatory measures on both sides quickly escalating the conflict. A resulting sharp slowdown to the U.S. and Chinese economies could easily spill over to the global economy. This scenario is a dire prospect at a time that the world is still growing out of the worst economic crisis since the Great Depression and since 2011, facing a new sovereign debt crisis in Europe.

Flaws in the administration's approach

It is surely essential for the United States to exert leadership in Asia by promoting greater trade and investment and by preventing any other group of countries from creating an exclusive trading area that excludes American companies and entrepreneurs. But adopting a strategy of excluding the second largest economy in the world from a trading bloc that the U.S. dominates, as the Obama Administration did in November 2011, is shortsighted and potentially dangerous. From a security standpoint, it is well to recall the wise words of former U.S. Secretary of State Cordell Hull who offered this insight in his memoirs after observing two world wars:

> I saw that you could not separate the idea of commerce from the idea of war and peace. You could not have serious war anywhere in the world and expect commerce to go on as before. And I saw that wars were often caused by economic rivalry conducted unfairly. I thereupon came to believe that if we could increase commercial exchanges among nations over lowered trade and tariff barriers and remove international obstacles to trade, we would go a long way toward eliminating war itself.[95]

The danger of excluding a country from a regional trade area which its neighbors and leading trading partners have all joined goes well beyond angering a few Chinese companies or policymakers. History demonstrates that open trade and the free pursuit of international commerce reduce the chance of conflicts between states. Countries that have a stake in an open and fair trading system most often stay committed to the stability and peace that normal commerce entails. For this reason, the long-standing U.S. policy of integrating China into the international economic community has always had a national security objective as well as an economic purpose. Helping China reap significant benefits from membership in trade organizations like the WTO and providing access to the U.S. market has been perhaps the most important way of ensuring China's support for the international system as a whole. Conversely, a policy that seeks to stymie the development of China's trade and overseas investment conveys another clear message: international trade can be transformed into a "mercantilist zero-sum game" that the U.S. intends to win.[96]

The Obama Administration's effort to exclude China from TPP negotiations is also baffling because it simultaneously welcomed Vietnam and Malaysia to full participation in discussions about becoming members of the new Asia trading bloc. An administration official contended that China was not ready to meet the TPP's "high standards" and goal of addressing "a whole range of [new] issues not covered by past [trade] agreements" including regulatory barriers, the role of state-owned enterprises and government subsidies favoring specific companies. Yet the administration deemed Vietnam qualified to discuss these important issues even though it is a communist country which relies heavily on state subsidies and state-owned enterprises—not to mention that it bears responsibility for the deaths of nearly 60,000 American military personnel and failed to account for approximately 1,700 MIAs during the Vietnam War, as noted earlier.[97] The administration also invited Malaysia to participate although its government heavily guides the country's economic development through regular "five year plans" while subsidizing selected products and controlling prices. (Moreover, Malaysia's former prime minister strongly opposed America's "War on Terror" because it "terrorized" innocent people, and he demanded the criminal trial of former President George W. Bush for attacking Iraq. In late November 2011, a Malaysian tribunal found both Bush and former British Prime Minister Tony Blair guilty of war crimes).[98]

The schizophrenic mind-set that welcomes free trade with many countries but advocates barring Chinese companies from investing in the United States is another clear example of objectionable protectionism against China. All too often, members of Congress, unions and China hawks have politicized proposed Chinese investments, calling them threats to American security. The accusations frequently reflect the vested interests of U.S. companies seeking to avoid competition, along with excessive fears that have little basis in reality. Yet the allegations still have a sharply negative impact: the Chinese company often abandons its planned investment long before a legal review on security grounds appears necessary or occurs. As Derek Scissors, an expert at the Heritage Foundation points out, the politicization of Chinese FDI is "nothing short of outrageous." The "legitimate and prudent restrictions" that the U.S. government imposes on FDI through the CFIUS process, he argues, "should not be permitted to morph into knee-jerk reactions that harm American interests."[99] The mixed message currently sent to potential Chinese investors in the United States does little to prevent politicization of proposed Chinese investments and often encourages it:

> The president makes high-minded statements about openness, but senior officials often express misgivings about doing business with Chinese firms. Critically, attitudes among congressional leaders range from skeptical to hostile, often leading to proposals to exclude Chinese interests. Business leaders endorse job-creating Chinese investment in the United States, but only when reciprocal concessions from China are available .... Sowing such confusion is not in the U.S. interest.[100]

Resolving economic disputes with China

The United States is far more likely to resolve problems in its economic relations with China through engagement and adherence to principles of open trade than through confrontation, protectionism and retaliatory trade measures. Serious disputes with China involving the value of its currency against the dollar, inadequate protection for intellectual property, new regulations to ensure consumer health and safety, and especially China's remaining barriers to trade and investment, should continue to be addressed in an expanded and reinvigorated Strategic and Economic Dialogue (S&ED), the channel for high-level discussion initiated by President Bush and President Hu Jintao in 2006 and expanded by President Obama in 2009.

Up to now, this high-level dialogue has achieved only "limited concrete successes" and is best considered "a valuable yet still limited exercise that has not realized its full potential," as Michael Swaine, Senior Fellow of the Carnegie Endowment, indicates.[101] A channel for diplomatic dialogue helps break down bureaucratic barriers in both governments, encourages conflict resolution and empowers officials seeking "win-win" negotiating outcomes. But it cannot overcome the effects of a U.S. policy that takes protectionist positions toward China and too often regards that country as an economic adversary.

No doubt the best way for American workers and companies to benefit from China's future growth is for the U.S. to significantly expand exports of products and services to China, invest heavily in China's economic development, and welcome extensive Chinese investment in the United States. To achieve these goals, which will result from fair and open trade, the U.S. needs to act boldly to eliminate tariffs and non-tariff barriers that now impede trade with China as well as negotiate measures to protect and promote investments in both countries. On a regional basis, the United States should welcome China's participation in a Trans-Pacific Partnership that will create a free trade area in the Asia Pacific. On a bilateral level, the U.S. should seek a free trade agreement with China that goes even further than the regional agreement in reducing trade barriers between the two countries.

As a member of the Trans-Pacific Partnership, China would be able to improve its trading relationships with a number of countries in the region. In negotiating its membership in this organization, China would therefore have major incentives to eliminate tariff and regulatory barriers, adopt new rules to facilitate trade and investment, provide a level playing field for foreign companies, sharply reduce the role of state-owned enterprises, agree to non-discriminatory and transparent rules for government procurement, and strengthen dispute-resolution procedures for foreign companies.

In a bilateral free trade agreement, the U.S. could achieve even deeper agreements to liberalize trade with China, open the Chinese market further to American firms, create "behind the border" transparency as a means of strengthening trust, and establish de-politicized and reciprocal investment access to allow far greater U.S. investment in China and Chinese investment in the United States. It is worth recalling that negotiating bilateral FTAs can take years and can sometimes encounter serious obstacles involving specific economic sectors in each country. On occasion, negotiators have agreed to "partial liberalization" of particular sectors or to exempt a sector entirely from a trade agreement. This was the case in the 2011 Korea-U.S. Free Trade Agreement where Korea's rice growers were fully exempted from the agreement although the FTA significantly opened other agricultural markets in Korea to U.S. firms.

By contrast, seeking to exclude China from a Trans-Pacific Partnership or rejecting discussions of a new bilateral free trade agreement are dysfunctional ways of dealing with China's rise as an economic power. They weaken the ability of the United States to benefit from China's economic growth. They feed suspicions that the U.S. wants to deny China the benefits of international trade and cross-border investment. They add unnecessarily to security tensions between the two countries.

Including China in a new regional trading bloc and achieving a free trade agreement with China would have an even broader impact than ensuring the United States benefits from China's economic growth over the long term. The detailed discussions of trade and investment issues leading to these agreements will deepen trust, significantly improve understanding of the other country's economic goals and challenges, and bring about steady (though sometimes slow) progress in overcoming obstacles to freer and more open trade. In the largest sense, these discussions will help integrate China into the international system.

The latter goal is perhaps most important from a macro-level perspective. As Professor John Ikenberry of Princeton University writes,

> [T]he United States cannot thwart China's rise, but it can help ensure that China's power is exercised within the rules and institutions that the United States and its partners have crafted over the last century, rules and institutions that can protect the interests of all states in the more crowded world of the future.[102]

It is especially critical for China to "be treated as a rule-maker and not simply as a rule-taker" by participating "in the norm-drafting process" in regional and bilateral trade agreements.[103] By adopting this approach, the United States will be much more successful in persuading China to uphold the international economic system for which the U.S. served as principal architect during the postwar period.

CHAPTER FIVE

Democracy and human rights

To achieve its current level of economic development, the Chinese Communist Party has been forced to grant a higher degree of personal freedom than ever before. But the country remains an authoritarian state run by a single political party that still tightly limits the space for dissent. China represses and arrests the leaders of demonstrations and political movements when it is unable to co-opt or discredit them. And the government is unwilling to brook any fundamental challenge to its authority despite the major societal changes it has engineered.

The status of human rights and democracy in China bears directly on the nature of U.S.-China relations. Across the American political spectrum, China's one-party regime inspires deep skepticism and some outright hostility. Even while the U.S. government seeks economic engagement and promotes U.S.-China trade and investment, American leaders know there is a political "red line" they cannot cross. Many Americans will not tolerate "too close" relations with China as long as it harshly represses religious and minority groups, practices torture, jails leaders of democracy and environmental movements, and restricts freedom of speech.

The converse is also true. If China were to uphold human rights and embrace widespread democracy, the American public would be far more receptive to a much closer U.S.-China relationship just as it has been to improving relations with India, which characterizes itself as the "world's largest democracy." On this point, it is valuable to keep in mind the critical insight of Professor Edward Steinfeld of MIT that China has achieved its great transformation to a world economic powerhouse by "playing our game":

[We] as Americans and citizens of the West ... face a situation [with respect to China] that we could have only dreamed about thirty years ago. China societally ... has chosen to develop by tying itself to us and trying to become like us. While neither blindly imitative nor insensitive to its own sovereignty, China has in remarkable ways exposed itself – indeed, tied itself – to a variety of external influences, particularly ones emanating from our own system. The country has in essence linked its domestic transformation process – its destiny – to a global system that we designed and that we dominate. In the process, China has increasingly absorbed – and even embraced as its own – values, practices, and aspirations that have in their origins our own.[1]

China's internal political conditions

Before assessing the current state of democracy and human rights in China, it is worthwhile to view China's domestic political situation from the standpoint of the Chinese government. The country's leaders are deeply concerned about political instability, as University of California China expert Susan Shirk writes:

> Chinese leaders are haunted by the fear that their days in power are numbered. They watched with foreboding as communist governments in the Soviet Union and Eastern Europe collapsed almost overnight beginning in 1989, the same year in which massive prodemocracy protests in Beijing's Tiananmen Square and more than one hundred other cities nearly toppled communist rule in China .... The worst nightmare of China's leaders is a national protest movement of discontented groups— unemployed workers, hard-pressed farmers, and students united against the regime by the shared fervor of nationalism. Chinese history gives them good reason to worry. The two previous dynasties fell to nationalist revolutionary movements. Mass movements that accused leaders of failing to defend the nation against foreign aggression brought down the Qing Dynasty in 1911 and the Republic of China in 1949.[2]

Political instability derives in large part from an imbalance between "institutional capacities" and growing public demands on the Chinese government for more income equality, better health services, improved education and environmental cleanup, in Professor David M. Lampton's view:

> Beijing is trying desperately to build new institutions and strengthen old ones .... Where institutions and resources do not exist to address issues, and the population is no longer willing to suffer in quiet resignation, there is repression from both local officials and central authorities, as well as continued efforts on the part of the aggrieved to organize to advance their interests.[3]

The number of "social disturbances" and "mass incidents" protesting inequalities or injustices in China has been quite large in recent years—approximately 180,000 in 2010 alone. Many of these demonstrations stemmed from land expropriations by corrupt local officials.[4] Underlying the protests was the deep-seated resentment and frustration of hundreds of millions of people—especially peasants, migrant workers and pensioners—who have been left out of China's modernization and have not shared in the country's growing wealth.[5]

The Communist Party has adopted two approaches to reinforce its political legitimacy while repressing its opponents. China's leaders consistently emphasize their ability to produce high economic growth which creates new jobs and national wealth. If China's economic growth were to fall below an annual rate of 7 percent, by one measure, the resulting dislocations and unemployment could lead to unrest that would threaten the Party's hold on power.[6]

Equally important, China's leaders rely on nationalism to build political support. Nationalism substitutes for communist ideals, which no longer appear credible or inspire popular enthusiasm. The Communist Party portrays itself as the only political body capable of advancing the country's national interests, both regionally and globally.

To strengthen their political legitimacy and prevent instability, China's leaders have implemented a series of specific policy measures that figure heavily in any assessment of the state of democracy and human rights in China.[7] They include:

Enlarging the scope of individual freedom

> The Party no longer imposes draconian controls over the lives of individuals as it did in the past. People are free to pursue personal goals, set up new businesses and express themselves in art, film and other cultural fields so long as they stay away from sensitive political issues.

Repressing potential opponents of the regime

> Chinese authorities regularly arrest the ringleaders of demonstrations and "mass incidents." They try to prevent discontented groups and individuals from contacting each other through the internet or by other means of communication. They have moved particularly harshly against religious groups such as the Falun Gong and national minorities such as the Tibetans.

Co-opting other potential opponents and recruiting them as Party members

> In 2002, the Communist Party made an official decision to recruit business people and "technical classes" who benefit from China's

growing economy. By co-opting entrepreneurs and technical experts, the Party aims to prevent a new capitalist class from emerging that could challenge its authority.

Adopting social measures to ameliorate existing social inequalities

China's leaders publicly support measures to reduce the country's social inequalities and funnel resources to people in need. They have committed the government to establishing an effective social security system, providing adequate medical care, addressing environmental problems and improving education.

Blaming local officials and supporting protestors

High-ranking Communist Party officials frequently identify publicly with the protests of peasants and impoverished workers; they do this by shifting blame to local and provincial officials for failing to address the inequalities and poor conditions that gave rise to the protests in the first place.

By employing these measures, China's Communist Party seeks to maintain social stability and its hold on power. It is uncertain, however, whether the Party will succeed over the long-term in resolving the underlying social problems that accompany rapid economic development. Combining coercion, relaxed social controls and policies that address serious social ills may work for a period of time. But unless China develops the institutional capacity to drastically reduce social inequality, rural poverty, environmental pollution, dilapidated medical infrastructure and other poor social conditions, a political crisis could well occur.

China's latest Five-Year Plan, released in March 2011, places a high priority on improving social welfare through increases in disposable income, expanded insurance coverage, more affordable housing, better healthcare, conservation of energy, environmental cleanup and new educational opportunities.[8] Moreover, China's leaders publicly emphasize the importance of both economic and political reform for addressing major social tensions caused by income inequality and corruption. In a March 2012 speech to China's parliament, the National People's Congress, Premier Wen Jiabao declared it was an "urgent task" to reform "the leadership system of the party and government .... Without successful political reform, it is impossible for China to fully institute economic reform and the gains we have made in these areas may be lost."[9] Without effective reform, Wen warned, "historical tragedies such as the Cultural Revolution may happen again in China."

Despite the acknowledged need for reform, it is not at all clear that "forces of democracy" would emerge to replace China's authoritarian regime in the event of major social instability. China's Party leadership is likely to employ severe internal repression, incite nationalism, blame foreign interference for the country's social breakdown and possibly take aggressive international actions to avoid being swept from power.

A China that is experiencing internal chaos would have very damaging spillover effects on the world economy. The pressure of a destabilized social system could incite nationalist forces calling for a military confrontation with the United States over Taiwan. Consequently, Western powers, and especially the United States, have a stake in upholding China's social stability even while they support more democracy and more meaningful human rights practices in the country.

Indicators of progress

Because the progress of human rights and democracy in China is, to some extent, in the eyes of the beholder, it is valuable to summarize both the negative and positive factual indicators. Human rights advocates tend to see the glass as more than "half-empty," pointing to the rights violations that currently occur and the improvements that need to be made. More optimistic observers tend to note the progress of democracy and human rights that has taken place. They see the glass as approaching half-full and point to signs that the regime is opening up to international political norms.

Negative indicators:

China regularly detains and sometimes imposes heavy sentences on people it believes are advocating improvements in human rights.[10] This includes journalists, lawyers, internet activists and members of religious groups not approved by the state. The government hardened its repression of human rights advocates in the period prior to the 17th Party Congress at the end of 2007 and before the summer Olympic Games in 2008. In February 2011, following calls by activists for a "Jasmine Revolution" inspired by the Arab Spring, authorities began the harshest crackdown in recent years. They put more than a hundred dissidents under house arrest, detained prominent human rights lawyers and carried out secret "disappearances" of democracy advocates.

According to the State Department's annual report on human rights, "[A] negative trend in key areas of [China's] human rights record continued [in 2010], as the government took additional steps to rein in civil society, particularly organizations and individuals involved in rights advocacy and public interest issues, and increased attempts to limit freedom of speech and to control the press, the Internet, and Internet access. Efforts to silence political activists and public interest lawyers were stepped up, and increasingly the government resorted to extralegal measures including enforced disappearance, 'soft detention,' and strict house arrest, including house arrest of family members, to prevent the public voicing of independent opinions. Public interest law firms that took on sensitive cases also continued to face harassment, disbarment of legal staff, and closure."[11]

China has made much of the legal avenues it provides citizens to present their grievances to authorities in Beijing. However, human rights groups report that many petitioners who seek redress from official seizures of land, or other arbitrary government actions are frequently subjected to detention and periods of "re-education" under the so-called "Reeducation through Labor System." Moreover, lawyers who handle human rights cases involving corruption, forced relocations or harmful environmental activities are harassed, threatened, and subjected to major procedural sanctions.

With respect to expanding democracy, China initiated direct elections at the village level in 1988. Elections now take place in approximately 700,000 villages throughout China and about 75 percent of China's population participates. But on the question of whether the efforts of China's leaders will likely lead to greater democracy in the future, Professor Barry Naughton of the University of California comments: "China's authoritarian rulers … have adapted to sweeping social changes that many expect to ultimately lead to democratization. Yet as of now, there is nothing in the Communist Party's political practice that portends a smooth transition toward deeper democratization or even suggests movement in this direction."[12]

Even though the Communist Party has allowed the extensive growth of non-governmental organizations (NGOs), it is uncertain whether this "civic mobilization" will lead to more democracy, so long as China's leaders retain their authoritarian values and attitudes.[13] This is especially true since the Party continues to repress the religious and ethnic groups it fears could organize significant opposition to its monopoly rule. In 1999, the government of President Jiang Zemin began to use torture, illegal imprisonment, forced labor and psychiatric abuses to persecute the 70 to 100 million Chinese who adhered to the spiritual group known as "Falun Gong." Since 2008, China has taken increasingly harsh measures against Tibetans protesting Chinese rule, periodically closing certain regions of Tibet to foreigners and engaging in a series of violent crackdowns.

Despite the massive growth of television, radio and the internet in China, the government utilizes a variety of techniques to assert control. Measures include weekly faxes notifying the media of current restrictions on coverage; computer messaging to journalists describing issues unsuitable for stories; mandatory submission of articles to government officials for approval; blocking of controversial websites; and forced firing of journalists and media figures who exceed acceptable limits.[14]

Positive indicators:

China's economic development has raised hundreds of millions of people out of poverty. This newly acquired material well-being has strengthened their so-called "economic and social rights" including freedom from hunger, access to a safe and secure home, safe working conditions, education and access to medical care. Unless people can meet their basic material needs, it is difficult for them to expand or exercise political rights.

Political freedom in China is considerably greater than in the past (though progress here is admittedly measured against a history of absolute totalitarian rule under Mao). The government and Communist Party no longer force citizens to participate in political activities or explicitly embrace certain ideological beliefs.[15] Students are no longer indoctrinated with "Mao Tse Tung Thought." Media often report on government failures or shortcomings, though journalists express their views within defined limits.

Legal reform in China has proceeded apace since the beginning of the Deng Xiao Ping era in 1979. Legal provisions that are contrary to core human rights principles have now been removed. People can no longer be charged with committing "counter-revolutionary crimes" that have vague and purely political content. A presumption of innocence has been established along with due process protections. In the last 20 years, China has enacted 245 new laws, 1,000 new administrative regulations and 7,000 new provincial laws. The number of lawyers has more than tripled since the early 1990s.[16]

Increasing numbers of NGOs have been established in fields ranging from the environment and public health to consumer rights and the protection of "vulnerable" members of the population, including women, children, disabled people and migrants. According to one estimate, the number of Chinese NGOs has now reached approximately three million. The existence of these non-governmental groups makes it more difficult for the authoritarian regime to impose strict controls on Chinese people.[17]

Rapidly increasing television, radio and social media in China have severely limited the regime's ability to restrict the flow of information, even though the government polices the internet. According to recent data, China has approximately 2,700 television and radio stations and a total number of mobile phones exceeding 700 million. More than 380 million Chinese use the internet, the largest number for a single country in the world.[18]

There is more tolerance in China for religion in general (with the important exceptions noted above). Millions of Chinese people attend state-approved religious churches or participate in Protestant and Catholic "house churches" that thrive, in spite of crackdowns, in the underground.

Assessment of progress

China has made real progress on expanding both human rights and democracy in the last 30 years. Nevertheless, this progress has taken place in the context of a still repressive, authoritarian political system. China's leaders do not hesitate to arrest and abuse individuals and members of groups they regard as potential threats to the Party's power. Their rationale for allowing greater individual freedom and expression of controversial ideas in the media is to encourage economic growth in a largely free market economy, and to provide a safety valve for relieving social pressure during a period of intense economic and social modernization. The most critical question, then, is whether the social changes that have previously taken place and are continuing to occur in China are likely to foster the emergence of a real democracy and the broad recognition of human rights in the future.

Growth of the middle class

From a sociological perspective, a high level of per capita GDP in a country often correlates with political liberalization and the breakdown of authoritarian regimes. Henry Rowen, professor emeritus of Stanford University, goes so far as to predict that China's current rate of economic growth will lead to its transformation into a democracy by 2015.[19]

The predominant theoretical view in the United States has been that the growth of a middle class in developing countries will inevitably give rise to democracy over time. Progressively better educated middle-class citizens who lack the privileges of the elite will demand political rights and legal protections to safeguard their newly won economic and social gains. Barrington Moore, the famous American political sociologist, sums up the theory (which actually has its origins with Aristotle) in a short phrase: "no bourgeoisie, no democracy."[20]

In the case of China, however, it is not clear that the large and growing middle class, now approximately 800 million people, will push forward and demand democratic freedoms. Rather than taking risks to achieve rapid political liberalization by publicly confronting and criticizing the authorities, a large majority of middle-class Chinese citizens—like China's leaders—seem to fear the spread of instability. They feel a significant stake in the continuing growth of China's economy and want to ensure that they and their children will receive its benefits. With relatively small assets and power, they carry a sense of vulnerability and often appear risk-averse.

Even though the thriving middle class in China may not inevitably or any time soon demand major political changes, their views and interests impose limits on the Communist Party's ability to unilaterally enact authoritarian measures. In effect, the growing and increasingly powerful middle class makes it more difficult for the Communist Party to take away the social, economic and political freedoms that the middle class has thus far acquired.

Equally significant is the fact that the Party itself has been progressively influenced by middle-class values and goals. Most Party members are well-educated professionals and engineers. Many have obtained post-graduate degrees overseas and remain heavily focused on career advancement. This represents a major change from the past when the Party was dominated by workers and peasants whose loyalty to communist dogma was considered far more important than their professional qualifications.

Inner-party democracy

In assessing the future transformation of China's political system, it is also important to note the emergence of "inner-Party democracy"—or "bipartisanship" within the Communist Party—as Cheng Li, Senior Fellow of the Brookings Institution, terms it. In Li's view, there is genuine competition between two factions of "fifth generation" political leaders who came of age during China's "Cultural Revolution" from 1966 to 1975 and are now assuming power. Members of these two factions—the "elitist" and "populist" coalitions—suffered severely from chaotic political conditions created by the Cultural Revolution during the 1960s and early 1970s. In many cases, they were "sent down" to rural areas where they experienced great hardship. The elitist coalition tends to represent the interests of China's "coastal regions, including the new economic sectors, entrepreneurs, the emerging middle class and foreign-educated returnees." By contrast, the populist coalition largely represents the interests of "the inland regions ... more traditional economic sectors and less-privileged social groups such as farmers and migrant workers." The common lifetime experience of the leaders of both factions enables them to effectively negotiate with each other and reach compromise agreements—essential characteristics of a democratic political system.[21]

Li believes that "inner-Party democracy" in China may lead in ten or fifteen years to an actual bipartisan political system, with the Communist Party formally splitting into two groups with different factional interests. This would be a momentous political change away from a single Communist Party that monopolizes political power and bans either a competing Party or an independent judiciary. Nevertheless, the process of reaching this formally bipartisan system could well be incremental, so that the split occurs nonviolently, as a culmination of legitimate factional politics. Observers will watch closely for political changes following China's leadership transition in the spring of 2013. As a result of the transition, the principal officials responsible for political, economic and military affairs as well as foreign policy will all be "newcomers" to the Party's 25-member Politburo and its powerful nine-member Standing Committee.[22]

The Bo Xilai crisis

The political scandal that erupted in February 2012 and led to the detention of Bo Xilai, former party chief of Chongqing as well as a member of the Politburo of the Communist Party, shocked the Chinese public and created a legitimacy crisis for China's government. Looking to the future, the incident could either undermine Party rule or accelerate progress toward greater democracy.

As of April 2012, the Party removed Bo, a rising political star, from the Politburo and accused him of "serious disciplinary violations" for allowing corruption and graft to occur in Chongqing, where he previously led anti-corruption campaigns.[23] The Party also held him responsible for wire-tapping other senior officials and obstructing justice in the investigation of his wife, who was accused of orchestrating the murder of a British businessman and former family friend after a business dispute. As a "neo-Maoist" who repressed legal professionals, popularized songs from the Cultural Revolution and showed anti-market tendencies, Bo was regarded as a major political threat by liberal intellectuals, the Chinese legal community and many businesspeople.

In April 2012, Premier Wen Jiabao reaffirmed the intention of China's government to hold high-level officials like Bo accountable for corruption and declared that corruption investigations should be open to public inspection. Wen identified corruption as a profound danger to the continuing rule of the Communist Party, saying that "If [this issue] is not handled properly, the nature of the regime may change, and its rule may end. It is an extremely difficult and important challenge we are facing right now." Wen adopted a particularly harsh tone in asserting that "China is a socialist country ruled by law, and the dignity and authority of the law cannot be trampled .... There is no special citizen before the law. It does not allow any special party members to override the law within the party."[24]

Close observers of China's elite in the United States saw two different possible outcomes from the Bo Xilai scandal. In the view of some analysts, the incident highlighted high-level misconduct among China's elite and cast serious doubt on their qualifications to rule the country. Professor Joseph Fewsmith of Boston University argued that "this [scandal] could have a deep and delegitimizing impact on China, not now, but in the long run .... This has got to be shocking to the people of China. I think the Party has lost a lot of credibility."

Another school of thought, exemplified by Cheng Li, maintained that the Bo case created "an opportunity to reach a new consensus and seriously pursue political reforms [in China]." The crisis laid bare major flaws in China's political system, including "the danger of allowing a demagogue like Bo to emerge, as well as the nepotism and corruption within the system." Li contended that "China has removed a major danger and avoided the worst scenario, which would have been taking the country down a Maoist, ultranationalist path." As importantly, the incident created an opportunity to realize several "profound transformations," including significant legal reforms to strengthen the rule of law, "bolder intra-party elections" to achieve greater democracy, and effective measures to "open up the official media."[25]

Internet and mass communications

As noted earlier, the use of the internet and cell phones has exploded in China over the last ten years, making it difficult for the government to control the flow of information. While censors try to shape and, in some cases, block communication on sensitive political and social issues, their efforts are often fragmented and incomplete. Sophisticated media consumers increasingly sabotage the electronic walls and barriers that government officials put in place. The sheer volume of internet messages and cell phone conversations makes it practically impossible for authorities to completely prevent discussions on topics they consider subversive.

The main political significance of the "Information Age" for China is that it erodes the authority of the Communist Party. Party leaders fear that citizens who can conduct private conversations on sensitive political issues will become increasingly contemptuous of government authority, acquire greater capability to organize as a political opposition and collectively develop strategies for circumventing rules and regulations they believe are undemocratic.

This is not to say that the revolution in communications brought about by new technology will ineluctably lead to the overthrow of the Communist Party. The Party may still be capable of strongly repressing the content of communications on the internet, in the mass media and on cell phones. However, it could alternatively decide to allow greater openness in communications, with the accompanying political pluralism that such a decision entails. Over the next ten years, the Party could increasingly accept an information-rich society which is vibrant, contentious and "noisy," as UCLA's Richard Baum puts it.[26]

Development of civil society

Closely related to the expansion of the internet in China is the growth of civil society, particularly the large number of NGOs which citizens organize to advance their social and economic interests.[27] The internet energizes and supports civil society by "offering new possibilities for citizen participation."

The growth of NGOs is a major positive indicator for the future of democracy in China, since these groups empower citizens to pursue civic activities outside the state. With some degree of legal and practical autonomy, non-governmental organizations effectively create constituencies with the capability to assert demands on political authorities and foreign companies. One good example is the persistent efforts of a coalition of Chinese environmental groups called Green Choice Initiative to hold Apple responsible for pollution and workers' rights abuses at the factories of its suppliers in China.[28] Following the release of widely publicized reports on dangerous working conditions that exposed employees to poisonous industrial chemicals, Apple agreed in February 2012 to audit conditions at plants in China where iPhones, iPads and other Apple products are manufactured.

The existence of independent Chinese NGOs, with enough funding and management savvy to sustain themselves, could eventually lay a sufficient foundation for a pluralist and democratic political system—where government responds far more extensively to public demands instead of unilaterally imposing its will on the general population. However, as Sharon Hom, executive director of Human Rights in China, notes, the dramatic growth of new civic organizations should not obscure the actual obstacles that NGOs face.[29] These obstacles include vague and confusing legal designations for different kinds of organizations; regulations that impose burdensome registration and sponsorship requirements; restrictions on the ability of NGOs to raise funds and acquire an adequate financial basis; and a requirement that some "independent" NGOs set up internal Communist Party organizations or face dissolution.

Charter 08

China's transformation to a democratic polity that upholds human rights cannot be imposed from the outside; it must come from within. Yet when groups of disparate Chinese citizens joined together in 1989 and called for greater democracy, a fearful Communist Party refused to give up monopoly control and repressed their movement. Most leaders of pro-democracy organizations at the time of the Tiananmen uprising were either killed, imprisoned, or exiled. Others went underground or voluntarily left the country for abroad. While Chinese citizens have acquired greater individual freedom since 1989 and though there are positive trends including the growth of the middle class, spread of the internet, and emergence of inner-Party democracy, the Communist Party appears to remain firmly in control.

The best recent evidence that democracy and human rights can take hold in China in the future is found in a democratic movement, which made its presence known in December 2008. At that time, approximately 300 people—intellectuals, activists, academics and ordinary citizens—endorsed a document called "Charter 08" which called for China to recognize "basic human values" and end its authoritarian system of government. Charter 08 was modeled on "Charter 77," a political manifesto that ultimately led to the "velvet revolution" in Czechoslovakia and the demise of its communist government. Like the Czech document, Charter 08 looks toward a process of engagement and dialogue with leaders of China's Communist Party about the political direction of the country. Since its release, thousands of people have joined as additional signatories.

The foreword to Charter 08's statement of "fundamental principles" is sharply critical of China's political system:

> The Chinese people, who have endured human rights disasters and uncountable struggles ... include many who see clearly that freedom, equality, and human rights are universal values of humankind and

that democracy and constitutional government are the fundamental framework for protecting these values. By departing from these values, the Chinese government's approach to 'modernization' has proven disastrous. It has stripped people of their rights, destroyed their dignity, and corrupted normal human intercourse. So we ask: Where is China headed in the twenty-first century? Will it continue with 'modernization' under authoritarian rule, or will it embrace universal human values, join the mainstream of civilized nations, and build a democratic system? There can be no avoiding these questions.[30]

Among the "basic universal values" endorsed by the signers of Charter 08 are freedom, human rights, equality, democracy and constitutional rule. The document offers specific recommendations on "national governance, citizens' rights, and social development" including a new constitution supplanting the power of the Communist Party, separation of powers, legislative democracy, an independent judiciary, guarantees of human rights, a comprehensive system of democratic elections, and freedom of expression.

The publication of Charter 08 has extinguished any doubt that a leading and diverse group in China currently seeks greater democracy and human rights. The document crystallizes, in a Chinese historical context, universal values and political arrangements which are embraced in Asian countries like Japan, South Korea and Taiwan as well as in Hong Kong. That these citizens would confront China's Communist Party with a blunt and powerful statement of their aspirations is a testament to the depth of their convictions and personal courage.

Not surprisingly, the Chinese government reacted intolerantly to the public release of Charter 08.[31] Police initially detained the two people they identified as ringleaders of the movement, writer Liu Xiaobo and activist Zhang Zuhua, and according to human rights groups, harassed and interrogated about a hundred other signers. Authorities also shut down or blocked websites that carried the text of Charter 08, though initially it was communicated widely over the web. In December 2009, a court handed down an 11-year prison term to Mr. Liu for alleged political subversion.

Shortly thereafter, at the annual session of the National People's Congress in March 2009, the parliamentary chairman, Wu Bangguo, delivered a "lengthy tirade against Western-style democracy."[32] He told the delegates to the Congress that "leadership by the Party can only be strengthened and in no way weakened," especially during the current financial crisis. Wu's strident views no doubt revealed the Communist Party leadership's deep concern about the new movement for democracy that gathered around Charter 08.

These views again came to the surface in Fall 2010 when China reacted angrily to the news that Liu Xiaobo had been awarded the Nobel Peace Prize. The foreign ministry called the decision a "desecration" of the Peace

Prize and said it "shows disrespect for China's judicial system" because Liu was a "criminal" under Chinese law. Over a period of several weeks, China conducted a vilification campaign against Liu and pressed European governments unsuccessfully to boycott the award ceremony.[33]

Another notable example of China's increased pressure on human rights activists occurred in spring 2011, during the "Jasmine Revolution" crackdown noted earlier, when authorities arrested dissident artist Ai Weiwei and accused him of "economic crimes." After nearly three months in detention, Ai was allowed to leave the country to take up a teaching post in Germany, but the government subsequently sent a harsh message by hitting him in November 2011 with a punitive $2.4 million bill for alleged tax evasion.[34]

U.S. policy toward democracy and human rights

The emergence in late 2008 of the Charter 08 movement, seeking constitutional democracy and human rights, is truly propitious. It holds out the possibility that democracy may emerge from *within* China and end the Party's monopoly on political power. However, Chinese authorities regularly take repressive measures against individual dissidents, such as Liu Xiaobo, Chen Guangcheng and Ai Weiwei as well as religious groups like the Falun Gong or Tibetans seeking a degree of political autonomy.

Several critical questions therefore arise. What is the significance of the development of democracy and human rights in China for U.S.-China relations? Has U.S. policy, to date, been successful in promoting democracy and human rights practices in China? And what can the United States do in order to more effectively support and promote political reform?

The significance of China's internal political reforms for U.S.-China relations

Reform of China's political system has the greatest importance to the Chinese people who have "endured human rights disasters and uncountable struggles," in the words of Charter 08. But Chinese political reform is also extremely significant for U.S. policymakers and has a direct impact on the content, quality and tone of U.S.-China relations.

The ongoing existence of China's single-party authoritarian regime sharply limits how far U.S. political leaders can go in cooperating with China because the American public takes a dim view of China's repression of religious organizations, ethnic groups and political dissidents. However, a transformation of China's one-party state would bring a long-lasting improvement to U.S.-China relations precisely because the American public would take a far more positive view of China's government.

Nowadays, American policymakers hold a firmly rooted belief that diplomatic relations between the United States and democratic countries are much stronger than relations between the U.S. and authoritarian regimes on either the political right or the left. The George W. Bush administration invoked this rationale to justify upgrading relations between the United States and India, the "world's largest democracy." Similarly, U.S.-Russian relations warmed after the fall of the Soviet Union, only to regress into periodic acrimony when President Vladimir Putin shut down opposition parties and intimidated politicians who objected to his policies during his first term in office, from 2000 to 2008. During the Cold War, by contrast, the U.S. often concluded security agreements with right-wing regimes, especially in Latin America and Asia, as a means of fending off communist subversion tied to Moscow or Beijing.

So it is fair to say that a common commitment to democratic principles and human rights practices is the soundest basis for long-term friendly relations between the United States and China. Transformation of China's political system would effectively dissolve opposition in the Congress and the American public to across-the-board cooperation with China. A "commonality of values" would foster the same quality of relations that are now possible with a democratic South Korea and Japan, despite a history of Korean authoritarianism and Japanese aggression during World War II.

Ironically, many China hawks who highlight the multi-front threat China poses to long-term American interests accept its political system as a given. They stress U.S. vigilance in countering China's military modernization but pay little attention to how the United States can best foster greater democracy and human rights practices in China. On the left, protectionists passionately condemn China's allegedly unfair trade practices and seek to protect U.S. jobs. Like the hawks, they are largely indifferent to domestic political conditions in China. As a consequence, the soundest long-term basis for amicable relations between the two countries—greater congruence of political norms and values—has received far less attention in the U.S. than it deserves.

The benefit to the United States of a democratic China that upholds human rights goes beyond pure adherence to common political values. As the distinguished British journalist Will Hutton notes, it is in the "Western interest" to replace communism in China with constitutional government, the rule of law, freedom of expression, an independent judiciary and a multiparty political system because only these "Enlightenment institutions" can save China from the "myriad of dysfunctions and internal contradictions" it currently faces. Without adopting fundamental political reforms, China could experience a "convulsion," Hutton believes—a period of major instability and internal conflict—that would be devastating to both the U.S. and world economies. Thus, it is in the strong self-interest of the United States and other western countries to help China make the "difficult transition from peasant poverty to modernity" and achieve a "well-functioning economy and society"—a transition that is only possible through fundamental political reform.[35]

Shortcomings and weaknesses in U.S. policy

Ever since Mao Tse Tung's communist forces took power in 1949, the United States government has regarded China's one-party authoritarian regime as highly objectionable. But this broad U.S. antipathy has often been pushed to the side in the formulation of American security and diplomatic policy. President Richard Nixon and Secretary of State Henry Kissinger engineered the famous American "opening to China" in 1972 after observing rising tensions between China and the Soviet Union—which nearly culminated in a Soviet nuclear strike on China. Washington forged a new strategic relationship with Beijing as a means of gaining leverage over the Soviet Union. This partnership for mutual advantage between former enemies proved useful in weakening the Soviet Union and helped lead to its ultimate demise in the late 1980s.

Although one of the central themes of President Jimmy Carter's foreign policy was strengthening human rights around the world, his administration negotiated formal diplomatic relations between the U.S. and communist China in 1978. While Carter's policy, like Nixon's, was primarily driven by security strategy, he also aimed to improve economic relations between the two countries. In late 1979, the Carter administration extended Most Favored Nation (MFN) status to China, which allowed it to export goods to the United States at the same relatively low tariff rates available to America's closest trading partners. Congress renewed MFN for China on an annual basis for the next ten years, without much opposition, largely to support the security relationship.

After the Communist Party suppressed China's democracy movement and massacred demonstrators in 1989 at Tiananmen Square, the political atmosphere in the Congress swung back to the view that American foreign policy should explicitly seek to achieve moral ends, especially in advancing human rights and democracy.[36] Congressional critics introduced legislation to curtail MFN and condition it on China reaching certain political benchmarks. President George H. W. Bush twice vetoed this legislation on the ground that "comprehensive engagement" was the best means of achieving political reform in China over the long term.

When President Bill Clinton came into office in 1993, his administration initially held the view that U.S.-China trade policy and China's access to the U.S. market, in particular, should be conditioned on progress toward improving human rights. Clinton strongly criticized President Bush during the presidential campaign for appeasing the "butchers of Beijing" and not demanding that China's leaders institute political reform. Less than two years into his administration, however, Clinton changed course, due in large part to the influence of then Deputy National Security Advisor Samuel R. Berger. Clinton strongly supported annual renewals of MFN status for China and embraced the view that the United States should encourage China to enact deeper market reforms as a condition for gaining entry to the World Trade Organization. He believed that if China liberalized its economic practices—by replacing the authoritarian direction of the economy with the market principles of a rule-based international system— this would engender a gradual flowering of democracy and human rights. The rise of the country's middle class would also favor broader political reform as China became more prosperous. Near the end of his second term, President Clinton led the effort to grant China "permanent normal trade relations" which would end the need for China to obtain approval of MFN status on a yearly basis.

In retrospect, U.S. policy has likely had a positive impact on internal political conditions in China. The U.S. economic engagement with China, which began in the late 1970s as a way of assisting American business has coincided with an improvement in human rights and a limited spread of democracy. China's market reforms and economic expansion have instigated a loosening of internal Party controls, greater rule of law and limited growth of democracy while giving ordinary people a new capability to seek redress of grievances from the government.

Professor Jacques deLisle of the University of Pennsylvania puts it this way:

> Overall progress in Chinese human rights has marked the post-Mao Reform Era, and has coincided with the American policy of engagement that accompanied normalization of U.S.-PRC relations in 1979. The post-Tiananmen improvement ... in human rights conditions corresponds to [the] deepening and expansion of U.S. engagement during the Clinton and George W. Bush presidencies .... Correlation, of course, is not causation. Many of the factors that have contributed to human rights gains are not products of U.S. policy. U.S. policy has only sometimes— and often only indirectly—affected them.[37]

Clearly, U.S. policy has not been effective in preventing China's authoritarian regime from repressing political dissidents, journalists, ethnic minorities and religious groups. China's leaders frequently employ these measures as part of an overall strategy for maintaining social stability, as noted earlier.

With the advent of the Obama Administration, the U.S. initially took a weaker approach to democracy and human rights in China. When Secretary of State Hillary Clinton visited Beijing on her maiden diplomatic trip during late February 2009, she explicitly stated that "pressing on [human rights] issues cannot interfere with the global economic crisis, global climate change crises and the security crises."[38] She sent a strong signal that human rights and democracy issues would take a back seat to addressing economic, environmental and security matters with China.

However, when President Obama met with the Dalai Lama a year later, in mid-February 2010, he effectively returned to the approach of clearly stating the importance that the U.S. attaches to human rights and democracy in China. The White House issued a statement affirming "strong support for the preservation of Tibet's unique religious, cultural and linguistic identity and the protection of human rights for Tibetans." As Douglas Paal of the Carnegie Endowment noted at the time, Obama followed the practice initiated by President George H. W. Bush in 1990 of showing support for the Dalai Lama "as a revered religious leader [while] not challenging the sovereignty of China over Tibet."[39]

Former U.S. Ambassador to China Jon Huntsman underscored the Obama Administration's recalibrated policy on human rights when he strongly protested, in April 2011, China's crackdown on democracy activists, including Liu Xiabo and Ai Weiwei. In his final address as ambassador, Huntsman stressed that "the United States will never stop supporting human rights because we believe in the fundamental struggle for human dignity and justice wherever it may occur."[40]

A U.S. State Department team, with assistance from China expert Jerome A. Cohen of the Council on Foreign Relations, gave new substance in May 2012 to the American policy of addressing individual human rights cases by negotiating an agreement that freed blind dissident Chen Guangcheng from house arrest and enabled him to travel with his family to the United States for study. After Chen sought refuge at the U.S. Embassy in Beijing, the case gathered considerable news media attention in the United States and threatened to severely strain U.S.-China relations if it could not be resolved diplomatically.

Towards a more effective U.S. policy for advancing democracy and human rights

During the Clinton era, as well as the ensuing administration of President George W. Bush, U.S. policymakers correctly believed that an excessively strong human rights policy relying on threats of sanctions against the Chinese government would be counterproductive.[41] They argued that "heavy-handed efforts to push democratization [would] look to the Chinese like a form of containment designed to keep China weak." China's leaders would play on resentment of American interference in China's domestic affairs and incite a nationalist reaction against U.S. policy.

It is no doubt true that if the United States were to adopt a heavy-handed approach and attempt unilaterally to punish China for human rights violations, a major deterioration in U.S.-China relations would occur. China would claim the U.S. is interfering in its internal political affairs and violating the country's sovereignty. This claim would almost certainly trigger a nationalist reaction within China.

In truth, there is not much danger of the U.S. adopting such an approach since policymakers are well aware that the use of sanctions and broad public denunciations of China's political system could backfire. Proponents of engagement have been so effective in pointing out the likely Chinese reaction that they have, perhaps unintentionally, also discredited the value of pursuing a stronger, U.S. policy on human rights that does *not* involve sanctions.

To reinvigorate human rights policy toward China, the U.S. should more effectively support domestic forces seeking a gradual transformation of China's political system. Providing this support in a way that does not open the U.S. to charges of illicitly "interfering in China's domestic affairs" is essential.

The optimal way for the United States to support political reform is to significantly improve security relations with China. It is not well recognized in the U.S. that China uses contentious security issues—the conflict over Taiwan, in particular—to publicly justify and provide legitimacy for repressing groups and individuals seeking domestic political reform. Whenever agitation for democracy or human rights occurs, China frequently cites the danger of instability that would allow foreign countries to exploit the country's weakness and internal divisions. (Such rhetoric resonates deeply with the Chinese public because of the "century of humiliation" when imperial foreign powers dominated the country.) The broad perception of the United States as a looming security threat bolsters the government's arguments that it must impose strict political controls to prevent harm to the nation as a whole.

Former Soviet dissident Natan Sharansky, who was punished with nine years in prisons and labor camps for his work as a human rights activist, explains that the 2010 Nobel Peace Prize awarded to Liu Xiabo is "a reminder that in an authoritarian state, the voice of the people is to be found not in the frenzied public claims of the regime, but among … unnoticed dissidents." In an important commentary on Liu's fate, Sharansky observes that "the regime worked desperately to ensure silence at home. Chinese media and major websites carried no reports about the first Nobel Prize ever awarded to a Chinese national."

[These actions demonstrated that] to survive, an authoritarian state must dominate the public discourse and spend vast energies policing what is said and by whom. Yet, despite its best efforts, time always works against the oppressor .... As its popularity shrinks, the regime must employ ever greater levels of dissimulation to maintain power, thus further eroding its support among the people .... *Trapped in this cycle, the regime deploys its most dependable weapon in the struggle for unassailable dominion—an external threat ... that can unify the people and justify draconian security measures at home.* This is the reason that tension between nations is so inextricably tied to oppression and instability within a nation.[42]

As Sharansky's analysis and testimony makes clear, the ability of Chinese leaders to cite the increasing external threat to China's security from the United States and its allies strengthens the legitimacy and power of the communist regime. If the U.S. were successfully to resolve its outstanding security issues with China, especially the dispute concerning Taiwan, this would significantly enhance the prospects for domestic political reform. In a climate of friendly and normal relations, China's leaders could no longer persuasively justify the necessity of either one-party rule or repressing dissent to bolster national defense against exploitative foreign powers.

The U.S. can greatly advance democracy and human rights in China, therefore, by resolving and overcoming the major security issues that now divide the two countries. With a less threatening external environment, Chinese dissidents (such the proponents of Charter 08) could more easily seek internal political reforms, including the formation of competing political parties. If the U.S. were no longer widely perceived as seeking to contain China, Chinese dissidents favoring reform could draw greater legitimacy from the U.S. democratic political system. They could freely cite the American (as well as Japanese and South Korean) constitution as the model for a new Chinese equivalent that enshrines human rights protections, federalism, separation of powers, an independent judiciary and other principles of democratic governance. Rather than being treated as a security threat and adversary seeking to prevent China's emergence as a world power, the United States could instead be regarded as a living example of the liberal political system that is possible in China.

Improved security relations between the U.S. and China would also open China to democratic influences from Hong Kong and Taiwan. Following a partial or complete resolution of the Taiwan issue, Chinese leaders, as well as democracy and human rights advocates, would be far more welcoming of Taiwan's political practices than they were previously. With a precipitous drop in the perceived "foreign threat," China would likely look to Taiwan as a model for new political practices that are appropriate for China as a whole. This is especially true because Taiwan developed its thriving democracy through internal political reform, which was accepted by the once-authoritarian Nationalist Party.

These multiple factors underscore the conclusion that current U.S. security policy—which regards China as a "strategic competitor" and likely future adversary—greatly hinders the ability of the United States to achieve one of its central political objectives regarding China: engendering democracy and human rights as a means of transforming the Communist Party's monopoly rule. Conversely, adopting a new U.S. policy that improves security relations with China would significantly strengthen the hands of Chinese reformers who seek to create a democratic state and uphold human rights.

The U.S. can also support Chinese advocates of human rights and democracy by negotiating agreement on political principles and international norms to guide future U.S.-China relations. An agreement modeled on the Helsinki Final Act of 1975, which advanced dissident movements in Russia and Eastern Europe, would formally commit China to unrestricted dissemination of information, respect for human rights and fundamental freedoms, free exchange of peoples, and open borders. Like the Helsinki Act, a U.S.-China agreement on political principles would allow Chinese dissident groups to hold their government accountable for human rights violations. It would become a "rallying point," in the words of former Secretary of State Henry Kissinger, for reformers seeking to free their country from one-party domination.[43]

Obtaining Beijing's adherence to the Helsinki principles, in the political section of a new U.S.-China Framework Agreement, would be feasible for two major reasons. The Helsinki principles would form an intrinsic part of the bargain to obtain a new security relationship with the United States. China would very much like to see a sharp reduction in the close-in U.S. military reconnaissance of its territory, through which the United States maintains day-to-day pressure and reminds China of its relative weakness. For years, China has also sought to significantly scale down or end U.S. arms sales to Taiwan. In the context of a Framework Agreement that achieves these national security goals, China can be expected to endorse political principles modeled on the Helsinki Final Act, in addition to making significant military concessions of its own. While aware of the historical impact of the Helsinki principles in Russia and Eastern Europe, China's leaders would reason, just as other communist governments which were signatories to the Act did, that their internal security forces would remain capable of quashing dissent and maintaining domestic stability.

Second, the Helsinki Final Act sets forth critical tenets of international relations that the Chinese government holds dear, as did the Soviet Union in 1975. Among the most important principles, from China's standpoint, are sovereign equality, territorial integrity of states and non-intervention in internal affairs. Beijing regards mutual sovereign equality as a critical component of China's relations with Western countries that once considered China and its people politically and racially inferior. Confirmation of China's territorial integrity, as embodied in the "one China" policy, is the foundation of U.S.-China diplomatic relations, dating from the beginning of informal ties between the two governments in 1972.[44] The principle against "non-intervention" in the internal affairs of other states is frequently invoked by China whenever a foreign government criticizes the country for an objectionable policy or negotiating position.

In an overall sense, the political provisions of a Framework Agreement, as will be described in Chapter Seven, would help advance the cause of human rights and democracy in China. Like the principles embodied in the Helsinki Final Act, they would serve to empower the country's courageous dissidents, enabling them to more vigorously counter human rights violations and more effectively affirm the value of democracy to the Chinese people.

CHAPTER SIX

The "soft power" of China's foreign policy

From the 1950s until the mid-1990s, Chinese foreign policy regarded the international system as essentially "multipolar," with the U.S. as but one among several major power centers. China also *advocated* a multipolar system in the belief that balancing the world's superpowers was in its best interests. Doing so strengthened China's ability to play a leadership role in a "non-aligned bloc" of "Third World" developing countries that could offset the power of the United States (and Soviet Union prior to 1989) on critical regional and global issues.

In embracing a "New Security Concept" in 1996, however, China adopted a fundamentally different view. Based on a new consensus of the country's leaders, China for the first time accepted what it considered the new reality after the fall of the Soviet Union: "unipolarity" of the international system—in which the United States served as the system's essential pillar. Intrinsic to this outlook was the unstated premise that China could benefit from working within the U.S.-dominated unipolar system by acquiring the stability, security and political space necessary for domestic economic development and modernization.

In 2003, after implementing the New Security Concept by cultivating good economic and security relations with various countries, China went a step further. It announced a "peaceful rise" policy to allay mounting concern that a "rising China," with economic growth exceeding 9 percent annually, posed a security threat in the Asian region and beyond. A linchpin of the peaceful rise policy was a determined effort to build close and cooperative relations with the United States.

Through its peaceful rise policy, China sought to distinguish itself from other rising powers, particularly post-Bismarckian Germany and Imperial Japan which "violently plundered resources and pursued hegemony" because they believed the international system was skewed in favor of other countries.[1] China's policy initiative was a response, in part, to foreign critics who claimed these historical cases were proof that a rising China would also lead to war. Far from allaying their concerns, however, the peaceful rise policy engendered further skepticism. Critics argued that China's benign posture merely served to buy time while it modernized its armed forces and rose into the first rank of world powers. China hawks highlighted the success of China's aggressive efforts to improve regional and global trade relations in the period after 2000, and suggested that its rapid increase in "soft power" posed a serious threat to U.S. interests.

China's "New Security Concept"

The "New Security Concept" that China's leaders adopted in 1996 aimed to replace zero-sum notions of power politics and international security with a "win-win" approach that would allow all countries to benefit. The essential principles of this new concept were cooperation, peaceful coexistence, mutually beneficial economic relations and settlement of international disputes without resort to force. China contrasted its new approach with strategies of *realpolitik* and traditional military alliances which it argued the United States and other countries still pursued. Chinese scholars argued that China's rise would help other countries, rather than harm or threaten them. Countries would benefit, in particular, from the large domestic Chinese market and the demands of China's growing economy for overseas resources, products and services. Explaining the new approach in 2005, a leading expert at the Chinese Academy of Social Sciences, Wu Baiyi, pointed out:

> What China pursues now is a security of sustained development .... [The] nature of its security policy, therefore, is accommodative, rather than confrontational. Compared to past policies, the current concept signifies two major changes.... For the first time, economic security is treated as equally important with those of 'high politics.' Second, it focuses more on the interrelationship between external and internal security challenges.[2]

The principles and rhetoric of the "New Security Concept" amounted to what China expert Avery Goldstein of the University of Pennsylvania calls a new "*de facto* grand strategy" for guiding China's international activities:

> The grand strategy aims to engineer China's rise to great power status within the constraints of a unipolar international system that the United States dominates. It is designed to sustain the conditions necessary for

continuing China's program of economic and military modernization as well as to minimize the risk that others, most importantly the peerless United States, will view the ongoing increase in China's capabilities as an unacceptably dangerous threat that must be parried or perhaps even forestalled.[3]

The critical means for implementing this new *de facto* grand strategy were two-fold: diplomacy to establish new international partnerships with leading countries and policies to heighten the perception of China as a "responsible member" of the international community.

In the past, especially during periods of friction with the United States, China often reiterated its belief in a multipolar world, where developing countries could band together to fend off and protect themselves from a dominant U.S. and other "First World" developed countries. Now China accepted current reality and aligned itself with the existing structure of the international system, led by the United States, in the belief that the system's stability would ensure the peaceful environment that China needed to modernize, accelerate its economic growth and address severe internal social problems.

China's foreign policy goals

After their adoption of the New Security Concept, China's leaders focused on achieving a series of specific foreign policy goals:

Securing a stable and relatively benign environment on China's periphery and in the international system to permit rapid economic modernization

> With its emphasis on developing the economy and addressing difficult social issues, China urgently sought to reduce any possibility of military confrontation along its frontier or in the larger East Asia region. China saw peace and stability for the foreseeable future as the necessary foundation to sustain economic growth. Professor David M. Lampton of Johns Hopkins University eloquently describes this core purpose of the country's foreign policy as creating a "cocoon protecting domestic economic and social development ... [where] the principal features of the domestic strategy are increased use of markets and material incentives; modernization of science, technology, education, and management; use of the international economic system to provide skills, capital, information, competition for domestic firms, and export markets; and a growing

domestic consumption class that provides stability and can drive internal growth, investment, and innovation so that China is not as export dependent as the earlier modernizing Asian tiger economies and Japan."[4]

Fostering economic exchanges and mutually beneficial economic agreements with other countries to strengthen economic development

To raise its living standards, reduce economic and social inequality and reinforce the legitimacy of its communist leadership, China required overseas natural resources, foreign capital, technology and know-how as well as extensive international markets for the country's manufactured goods. These economic requirements impelled it to conclude trade and investment agreements within East Asia as well as in Africa, Latin America, Southeast Asia and the Middle East. Economic requirements also imposed the need to reduce trade barriers and maintain stability in China's leading export market, the United States.

Increasing China's regional and international influence

For decades following the 1949 revolution, China saw itself as a relative outsider in international affairs and supported the non-aligned movement of developing countries opposed to super-power dominance in the international system, as noted earlier. In formulating the New Security Concept, China's leaders recognized the importance of increasing their country's global influence, stature and prestige. They believed China could achieve this goal by becoming widely recognized as a responsible member of the existing system.

Pressuring Taiwan and reducing its international standing

Within the New Security Concept, China continued its determined effort to strengthen its claims to Taiwan as part of "one China." It used growing economic clout to pressure other countries to end diplomatic and trade relations with Taiwan, even as it carried out negotiations with Taiwan to reduce tensions, as well as mitigate or resolve specific cross-Strait issues. In negotiating trade deals with developing countries, China often insisted that a potential trade partner cut all ties with the Taiwan regime.

Allaying fears that a rising China poses a threat to other countries

Through active bilateral and multilateral diplomacy, which emphasized both greater economic exchanges and security cooperation, China sought to portray itself as a force for peace, prosperity and stability. China specifically strived to lower tensions with the

United States to make it less likely that the U.S. and its allies would pursue a containment policy. In an overall sense, China tried to minimize the danger that a threatening international environment could emerge, as it modernized economically and built national power.[5]

China's "peaceful rise" policy

In the view of Elizabeth Economy, Director for Asia Studies at the Council on Foreign Relations, the emergence of China's peaceful rise policy was a "dramatic shift" that signified the "transition from a foreign policy that had been predicated on China as a developing country consumed with issues of domestic concern to one that declared China's potential as a regional and global power."[6] Senior Communist Party advisor Zheng Bijian explained the nature of China's peaceful rise, in a noteworthy *Foreign Affairs* article in 2005, where he laid out several strategies the country had adopted to avoid the wars and conflicts historically attributed to rising powers. These strategies included: 1) "forg[ing] a new path of industrialization" based on economic efficiency, relatively low consumption of natural resources and "optimal allocation of human resources"; 2) relying on international cooperation as the primary tool of economic development to avoid "the path of Germany leading up to World War I or those of Germany and Japan leading up to World War II"; and 3) "strengthening its democratic institutions and the rule of law and trying to build a stable society based on [China's] spiritual civilization." Zheng forecast that it would take China until 2050 to become a "modernized, medium-level developed country" and that it would face major challenges to get there.[7]

The foremost goal of China's peaceful rise policy was to acknowledge the country's great power ambitions while reassuring its neighbors and the United States, in particular, that China's development would bestow economic benefits and not pose a threat. Zheng emphasized these conclusions at the end of his piece:

> China is not the only power that seeks a peaceful rise. China's economic integration into East Asia has contributed to the shaping of an East Asian community that may rise in peace as a whole. And it would not be in China's interest to exclude the United States from the process. In fact, Beijing wants Washington to play a positive role in the region's security as well as [in its] economic affairs.[8]

In an overall sense, China's peaceful rise policy sought to improve the country's image by relying exclusively on its "soft power" rather than the "hard power" of military force. Soft power, as Professor Joseph Nye of Harvard University points out,

> rests on the ability to shape the preferences of others .... [It] is the ability to get what you want through attraction rather than coercion or payments. It arises from the attractiveness of a country's culture, political ideals, and policies. When our policies are seen as legitimate in the eyes of others, our soft power is enhanced. America has long had a great deal of soft power.[9]

Soft power has important economic and diplomatic components such as development assistance, humanitarian aid, cultural and educational programs, mutually beneficial or concessionary international trade agreements and major foreign investments. China has actively utilized all these measures since the early 2000s, as it improved diplomatic relations in key regions, established new high-level political and economic dialogues, proposed and implemented innovative trade measures, concluded lucrative investment agreements and promoted cultural exchanges.

Economic rationales for foreign investment

From an economic standpoint, China's overseas investment is motivated by four major factors. Most important, China is striving to secure access to raw materials and sources of energy to support its economic development. In 2008, it became the third largest global importer of oil, exceeded only by the U.S. and Japan.

A second motivation for foreign investment is acquiring new technology, brand recognition and business expertise. By entering into mergers and acquisitions with overseas companies, Chinese firms can move more quickly up the "technology ladder," becoming suppliers and exporters of high-value capital goods rather than low-end manufactured products.

Chinese firms have also decided to expand overseas because the domestic Chinese market, in some sectors, has become saturated. Firms believe they can obtain a "first mover advantage" in foreign markets that will increase their overall profitability.

Finally, Chinese companies have sought to overcome the trade barriers to their exported products—created by tariffs, quotas and other protectionist measures—through overseas investment. They have sometimes focused on building or acquiring factories in countries that face relatively low trade barriers for sales into the European and American markets. For example, at one time a Chinese television manufacturer bought a German television brand and carried out production in Europe to avoid European quotas on Chinese television imports, according to a report of the U.S.-China Economic and Security Review Commission.[10]

For these various reasons, China's foreign investment increased annually from about $12 billion in 2005 to more than $72 billion in 2011, totaling approximately $314 billion from 2005 to 2011. To put these figures in perspective, the U.S. in 2010 alone invested about $329 billion overseas in direct investment.[11] While China's increasing rate of foreign investment is impressive, the total amount is modest in comparison with the United States.

The allocation of China's overseas investment by region reveals that Latin America has proven most attractive, followed by Sub-Saharan Africa. Data compiled and updated in January 2012 by The Heritage Foundation show the following total investments for the 2005 to 2011 period[12]:

Latin America – $73.2 billion
Sub-Saharan Africa – $67.3 billion
Southeast Asia – $59 billion
West Asia (including Russia, Iran and Kazakhstan) – $55.8 billion
Europe—$52.1 billion
U.S. and Canada – $49.3 billion
Middle East – $44.1 billion
Australia – $42.5 billion.

Bilateral initiatives

To improve its bilateral relationships with emerging economies and developing countries—particularly in Latin America, Southeast Asia and Africa—China has established special economic pacts, developed cultural ties and agreed to broad principles of cooperation. Among these are so-called Friendship and Cooperative Partnership Agreements, Friendship Associations, Free Trade Agreements, and Strategic Partnerships. China has also opened more than two hundred "Confucius Institutes" for teaching Chinese language and culture in countries around the world.

A critical element of China's foreign investment policy is requiring governments that receive aid, grants and loans to enter into contracts with designated Chinese companies for projects to construct railroads, pipelines, pipelines and stadiums. This so-called "tied aid" (in the sense of obligating recipient countries to purchase Chinese goods and services) helps promote China's exports and increase the country's earnings of foreign exchange. Aid of this kind "has been a feature of European, American, and Japanese assistance to poor nations for decades," as the *Financial Times* points out. While developed countries within the Organization for Economic

Cooperation and Development have made progress in formally reducing this requirement, it persists in practice with "most contracts still [going] to donor countries' own firms," according to Professor Deborah Brautigam of American University.[13]

Latin America

To strengthen economic and diplomatic relations in Latin America since 2000, China signed strategic partnership agreements with Argentina, Mexico and Venezuela and entered into cooperative agreements with Columbia, Cuba, Bolivia, Chile, Ecuador, Jamaica, Costa Rica, and Peru. About 10 percent of China's foreign aid goes to Latin America. Though far less than the amount China gives to Africa or Asia, this aid has supported disaster relief and "concessional loans" (which have below-market interest rates and long grace periods for repayment) as well as assistance for education and housing, hospital construction and infra-structure development.

In 2005, China signed a Free Trade Agreement (FTA) with Chile. In 2007, China and Venezuela created a $6 billion joint development fund to finance energy and infrastructure development as well as social projects. In 2011, China finalized an FTA with Costa Rica, enabling Costa Rica to increase exports of coffee, beef and pork while allowing China to enlarge exports of textiles, leather, electric appliances and chemical products.

The three leading state-owned Chinese energy companies continue to pursue investments in Ecuador, Brazil, Bolivia, Peru, Colombia, Argentina and Cuba. Among the prominent deals to date are investments of $32 billion in Venezuela and $1 billion in Ecuador to obtain access to oil resources, agreements with Argentina for natural gas, wheat and soy, and a $4.35 billion investment in Argentina to renovate three freight rail lines that will carry agricultural products to ports for export to China.

During 2010 and 2011, Chinese firms focused heavily on Latin America, particularly Brazil, to increase access to mineral resources.[14] In 2010, Chinese firms invested more than $15 billion in the region, becoming the third largest foreign investor following the United States and the Netherlands. More than 90 percent of this amount was invested in extractive industries.

Experts at the Peterson Institute for International Economics in Washington recently assessed the impact of China's economic activity in Latin America this way:

Our research has found that Chinese investment in Latin America predominantly expands and makes more competitive the global resource base. Chinese investors tend to be more willing to take on new frontier projects that others pass up. This good news could turn to bad news, however, if Chinese companies, traditionally guided by a principle of nonintervention, are not held to high standards of corporate behavior. International standards have become more stringent over the past decade in terms of labor and environmental practices, transparency and control of corruption, and community outreach and support.[15]

Southeast Asia

In the last few years, China has significantly increased its trade and investment with the ten nations in Southeast Asia that form the Association of Southeast Asian Nations (ASEAN). These countries include Malaysia, the Philippines, Thailand, Singapore, Indonesia, Myanmar, Vietnam, Brunei, Cambodia and Laos. Trade between China and ASEAN grew by an average of 30 percent annually between 2001 and 2008. China has also signed a Free Trade Agreement with ASEAN, which created the third-largest free trade area in the world when it came fully into effect in 2010.[16] (Only the European Union and North American Free Trade Area are larger.) The Free Trade Agreement laid out progressive steps for reducing or ending tariffs on up to seven thousand items.

China has sought to develop close ties with ASEAN countries on various energy projects. Examples include Chinese firms investing $343 million in a gas processing plant and oil refinery in Malaysia; a joint research agreement between China and Singapore on biofuels; planned investment of billions of dollars in Indonesia's energy sector; and a production-sharing agreement between a Chinese state-owned energy corporation and the National Petroleum Authority of Cambodia for exploration of oil and natural gas.[17]

Africa

China laid out its current political-economic goals for relations with African countries in a document dating from early 2006.[18] Termed "China's African Policy," the white paper called for inaugurating "a new type of strategic partnership with Africa." The new policy would increase trade, either through duty-free treatment for exports, bilateral free trade agreements, or export credits for Chinese infrastructure investment. It recommended implementing a full range of measures to protect and encourage foreign investment, including dispute settlement mechanisms, joint business promotion and bans on double taxation. It also promised strong Chinese support to strengthen Africa's economic development while calling for debt relief and extensive cooperation in science and technology, cultural exchange and environmental issues.

Between 2001 and 2006, China's *imports* from Africa, mostly of raw commodities such as iron ore, oil, timber, cotton and diamonds, rose by about 600 percent, from $4.8 billion to $28.8 billion. China's *exports* to Africa increased from $4.42 billion to $19.04 billion, a 331 percent rise. Chinese investments in Africa have focused on the energy industry as well as infrastructure construction, such as railways, roads, dams and electric power generation complexes. The size of investment projects that China has pursued in these areas ranges from tens of millions to billions of dollars. By 2008, China's annual trade with Africa totaled about $107 billion, while U.S. trade with Africa was worth approximately $142 billion. In 2010, China-Africa trade reached approximately $127 billion.[19]

China has also rapidly increased its official development assistance (ODA) and trade finance for African countries.[20] This aid typically includes interest-free loans on a government-to-government basis, concessional low-interest loans and various types of outright grants. In the view of development experts, China's aid has characteristics of both traditional ODA and for-profit financing. The result is that some aid supports broad social and humanitarian projects such as hospitals, schools and low-cost housing while other aid is directed to more commercially oriented infrastructure projects. During the period 2009 to 2010, China gave more loans than the World Bank to poor countries, particularly in Africa.

Multilateral initiatives

To accelerate economic development, expand international influence and allay fears of its rise as a great power, China has become far more active in regional multilateral diplomacy. This policy represents a remarkable break from the period prior to 2000, when Chinese diplomats often expressed skepticism about multilateral involvements and saw existing regional organizations as instruments for restraining China's rise. China's activities to advance regional multilateralism have effectively enhanced the country's influence in a non-threatening way, in line with its peaceful rise policy. As Professor Susan Shirk of the University of California points out, China's approach echoes the strategy the United States followed in the period after World War II:

American leaders chose to bind their hands by creating international institutions like the United Nations. They anticipated correctly that if the United States agreed to abide by the rules of international organizations, it would make other countries more comfortable with American power. China is seeking to head off hostile reactions to its growing might in Asia by using much the same approach ....[21]

By integrating itself into organizations that strengthen regional cooperation through consensus decision-making, China has anticipated concerns about its potential dominance.[22] Working within these organizations has helped establish mutually beneficial relations with other member states with the goal of preventing possible conflicts from arising.

Latin America

China has taken several important multilateral initiatives in Latin America. In 2001, it joined the East Asia-Latin American Cooperation Forum, an organization established to enhance cooperation on science, technology, education and culture. In May 2004, it became a formal permanent observer in the Organization of American States, the region's leading multilateral body. In January 2009, China joined the Inter-American Development Bank, giving China's ambassador to the United States at that time, Zhou Wenzhong, an occasion to emphasize that China would promote "cooperation in trade financing and infrastructure construction and other areas of mutual concern so as to carry forward poverty reduction and socioeconomic development in Latin America and the Caribbean."[23] On a broader diplomatic level, China for the first time participated in a UN peacekeeping force in the western hemisphere in 2004, when it contributed 125 military personnel to the United Nations Stabilization Mission in Haiti.

Southeast Asia

In the security realm as well as through the China-ASEAN Free Trade Agreement that came fully into effect in 2010, China has pursued a number of important initiatives with ASEAN and its affiliated organization, the ASEAN Regional Forum. A measure of China's focus on this region is apparent in the vision of an Asian community it set forth at meetings with ASEAN and other Asian countries in 2004 and 2005.

At a November 2004 summit that brought together ASEAN, China, Japan and South Korea, Chinese Premier Wen Jiabao proposed a long-term process of strengthening cooperation and economic integration.[24] Wen argued that the ASEAN economic community could be extended through bilateral free trade agreements to include China, Japan and South Korea, based on a "win-win" approach as well as "openness, transparency and inclusiveness." To prevent future Asian financial crises of the kind that afflicted the region in 1997 and 1998, Wen stressed that cooperation on risk prevention and crisis management should occur alongside an expanded security dialogue and joint efforts to resolve transnational problems. He suggested that this long-term process would culminate in an "East Asian Community."

At the China-ASEAN summit in October 2006, Wen expanded on four key elements of China's regional policy in a speech entitled "Join Hands to Create a Better Future for China-ASEAN Relations."[25] First, each country should see the other as a cooperative partner and regard the other country's development as an opportunity, rather than a threat. Second, relations should be based on equality and mutual trust with the goal of building consensus by seeking common ground and putting aside differences. Third, "win-win" cooperation should infuse all country-to-country relations. And fourth, broad popular support for cooperation to reduce poverty, narrow the gap with more developed countries, accelerate economic growth, and achieve a better life should be the actual foundation for improving relations in the region.

Security cooperation between China and ASEAN reached a high point in July 2011, when these countries achieved consensus on the need to adopt a "code of conduct" for the South China Sea to prevent clashes over competing territorial claims in the South China Sea, as noted in Chapter Three.

Africa

China has also made a determined effort to expand economic cooperation and political ties with Africa on a multilateral level.[26] In October 2000, it helped form the Forum on China-Africa Cooperation at a summit in Beijing with the leaders of 45 African countries. At the November 2006 summit of this organization, China announced eight new initiatives to strengthen its "strategic partnership" with African nations that have subsequently been implemented: 1) significantly increasing economic and humanitarian assistance to Africa; 2) providing billions in preferential loans and buyers' credits to poor African countries; 3) creating a China-Africa development fund worth up to $5 billion to spur Chinese investment; 4) canceling prior interest-free loans to poor African governments; 5) providing greater duty-free treatment to exports of poor countries; 6) creating between three and five economic cooperation zones in Africa; 7) giving extensive training to Africans in agricultural technology while expanding scholarships for African students; and 8) building up to 30 hospitals, 100 rural schools and health centers for treating malaria.

At the November 2006 summit of the Forum on China-Africa Cooperation, Chinese leaders also signed 14 investment agreements for a variety of development projects totaling approximately $2 billion. These deals included cooperation on developing energy and resources, building highways, and advancing technology in the communications, finance, insurance and metallurgy sectors.

Beyond its partnerships with African countries through the Forum,

China has become a major contributor to the region's development banks. In 2007, it began capitalizing a new China Development Bank with $1 billion to encourage private investment in African infrastructure, manufacturing, agriculture and natural resources. China's Export-Import Bank pledged to support various African projects between 2007 and 2009 with $20 billion in financing. China also entered into cooperative agreements with the West, East and Southern African Development Banks.

On a broader diplomatic basis, China has accelerated its exchanges with the African Union, the premier international organization promoting socio-economic development and political integration of Africa and has gone so far as to finance construction of a new headquarters for the Union. China has also financially supported peacekeeping forces of the African Union in the Darfur region of Sudan and in Somalia.

Perhaps most significantly, China has come to increasingly rely on energy imports from a number of countries in Africa to sustain its economic growth.[27] As of 2012, about one-third of China's imported oil, 1.5 million barrels per day, comes from Africa, mainly Nigeria, Sudan, Angola, the Republic of the Congo, and Equatorial Guinea. The International Energy Agency estimates that by 2020 China will become the largest net importer of oil in the world, with its imports climbing from almost five million barrels per day in 2011 to about 13 million by 2035.

Central Asia

One of the most important multilateral initiatives that China has taken in recent years was founding the Shanghai Cooperation Organization (SCO) with the membership of China, Russia, Tajikistan, Kazakhstan, Kyrgyzstan and Uzbekistan. Though formally established in 2001, the organization emerged from treaties first signed by this group of states in April 1996 and April 1997 to confirm and demilitarize the borders between China and the former Soviet Union. Since then, the SCO has focused heavily on promoting counter-terrorism and cross-border security cooperation among its members. It set up an anti-terrorism coordinating center and conducted a series of joint military exercises, including a notable one in 2005 between China and Russia.

The SCO extended its mission to the field of economic cooperation, beginning in 2003. Delegates to the organization's annual summit considered how and when to negotiate free trade agreements and reduce nontariff barriers among member states.[28] China subsequently offered nearly $1 billion in export credits to Kyrgyzstan, Tajikistan and Uzbekistan while entering into agreements to build energy pipelines and rail links in member countries. The SCO now emphasizes the importance of "economic progress" as the "cornerstone of stability and security of the Central Asian region."

China's support of pariah states

In pursuing its foreign policy toward developing countries, China has sometimes reached diplomatic and economic pacts with oppressive regimes. The driving motivation for these agreements—with Myanmar, Iran, North Korea, Sudan and Zimbabwe among others—is economic. China urgently needs resources, especially energy, to support its development, and has been willing to overlook the harsh character of certain "Third World" governments to satisfy its industrial requirements.

Guided by the principle of non-interference in other states' internal affairs, China has pursued what is often characterized in the West as a "no strings attached" economic diplomacy. When the United States, European governments or global institutions like the World Bank negotiate development agreements, they often attach conditions on observing human rights and ensuring good governance as well as upholding labor and environmental standards. China, by contrast, does not impose these requirements on its foreign partners who contract to sell natural resources. China often justifies this approach as consistent with its "win-win" strategy towards developing countries: contracts focus only on issues where agreement is easy and feasible, while more difficult subjects are postponed to the future. The experience of one African leader, President Abdoulaye Wade of Senegal, captures this approach and the advantages it provides to Chinese negotiators:

> I have found that a contract that would take five years to discuss, negotiate and sign with the World Bank takes three months when we have dealt with Chinese authorities. I am a firm believer in good governance and the rule of law. But when bureaucracy and senseless red tape impede our ability to act—and when poverty persists while international functionaries drag their feet—African leaders have an obligation to opt for swifter solutions.[29]

Beijing persistently sought during the last ten years to expand its economic relations with Iran, which was, of course, subject to severe U.S. and United Nations sanctions for pursuing a suspected nuclear weapons program. China-Iran trade goes both ways: Iran is a major energy supplier and in 2004, signed a 30-year agreement worth $70 billion to provide oil and natural gas to China.[30] At the same time, China sells Iran textiles, light industrial goods and heavy machinery. It is heavily involved in Iranian infrastructure development, including construction of power plants, shipbuilding facilities, and facilities to support Iran's energy production. As a result of these strong economic ties, China has resisted harsh sanctions or military action against Iran, though it did agree, under U.S. pressure in the spring of 2010, to support some UN sanctions. Subsequently, in March 2012, China joined with the other permanent members of the UN Security Council in a joint statement urging Iran to give international inspectors full access to suspected nuclear weapon development sites.[31] One month later, following Chinese cutbacks in purchases of Iranian oil and greater involvement in multilateral negotiations with Iran, a senior U.S. official commented, "One of the key elements in making [sanctions against Iran] work is unity among the major powers. The Chinese have been very good partners in this regard."[32]

China also maintained close ties with the military junta in Myanmar, which was long the object of international criticism and UN sanctions for violating human rights until it began indicating a willingness to undertake political reform in the Fall of 2011. China has invested heavily in Myanmar's natural resources, including gas, timber and precious stones, while giving financial support for the construction of new infrastructure, including hydroelectric power plants. One of China's strategic economic goals in Myanmar has been to help develop China's poverty-ridden southwestern provinces of Sichuan and Yunnan by utilizing Myanmar's ports and new transportation links. China is now constructing a pipeline from the western part of Myanmar to Sichuan and Yunnan. The pipeline would allow energy supplies to be transported from the Middle East without having to pass through the Malacca Strait, the narrow waterway connecting the Indian and Pacific Oceans, a strategic choke-point that could be closed down by foreign navies during any military conflict.

Tensions between Myanmar and China nevertheless surfaced in late September 2011, when Myanmar's president suspended construction of a $3.6 billion Chinese-backed hydroelectric dam in the northern part of the country.[33] The project was deeply unpopular among thousands of people who lived in villages that would have to be moved to make way for the dam. China contributed approximately $10 billion in foreign direct investment to Myanmar in the 2010 to 2011 period, but many people in the country remain suspicious of the Chinese presence.

Although the international community strongly condemned Sudan for committing genocide against the ethnic minority in its province of Darfur, China has maintained a major presence in Sudan's energy industry. It purchased large shareholdings in Sudanese oil companies and helped finance the construction of pipelines and infrastructure for oil production and refining. In 2007, the China National Petroleum Company reached a production-sharing agreement to develop a major Sudanese offshore oil block.[34] China also agreed to a $1.15 billion contract to connect the country's capital, Khartoum, with its largest port, Port Sudan.

China's long-time relationship with Zimbabwe has also opened it up to severe international criticism.[35] For years, Zimbabwe's mineral resources have been of great interest to China, which has, in turn, provided Zimbabwe with significant economic assistance. To ensure access to Zimbabwe's natural resources, China has supplied technical expertise and low-cost financial support, while engaging in large-scale development projects. It has helped construct hospitals, factories, stadiums and infrastructure facilities. Zimbabwe has become a major purchaser of Chinese-produced military hardware such as tanks and fighter planes.

Criticism of China's use of "soft power"

During the late 1990s, the United States often criticized China for its unwillingness to join regional multilateral organizations and accept greater responsibility for security and economic arrangements. Chinese diplomats regularly countered that China did not feel "comfortable" expanding multi-lateral involvements; and that as a developing country itself, with limited resources, China could not do much to assist other states.

China's hesitancy about multilateral organizations derived in large part from a suspicion of American intentions. Chinese leaders feared that the U.S. was attempting to draw their country into a "web" of multilateral involvements that would hamper China's international diplomacy. In their view, U.S. encouragement was mainly designed to strengthen American dominance in East Asia and elsewhere.

After China greatly increased regional multilateral activities and expanded trade relations with developing countries in the early 2000s, China hawks began to see a new version of the "China threat." They argued that China was using its soft power as part of a comprehensive strategy to diminish U.S. influence in key regions. By offering attractive trade incentives, investing in local industries, encouraging cultural exchanges, and concluding high-level "partnership" agreements, China was rapidly expanding its political influence at U.S. expense, the hawks contended.

These critics frequently stress that China has adopted several approaches that harm U.S. interests:

Portraying China's own authoritarian political system as a better "model" for developing countries

Chinese diplomats allegedly tell their colleagues in developing states that they cannot afford the "luxury" of democracy and an unfettered free-market economy. They hold out China's mixed system—which relies on market reforms and high-level economic guidance from an elite central government—as a far better model for less developed countries.

Offering "no strings attached" trade and aid

Virtually all U.S. and Western trade, investment, and humanitarian aid agreements with developing countries require compliance with important norms of conduct. As noted earlier, among these conditions are human rights principles, effective accounting rules, transparency practices for "good governance," labor standards to protect workers, and rules that prevent environmental violations. China's agreements with developing countries have been silent on all these points.

Allowing state-owned enterprises to take the lead

American and Western companies that invest in developing countries are accountable to their shareholders, who typically do not have strong interests in advancing U.S. government policy for its own sake. U.S. companies are also subject to numerous regulatory requirements and must frequently file public reports about their activities. However, the state-owned enterprises in China that invest overseas have no such disclosure obligations. Nor are they responsible to private shareholders who normally seek profitable short to medium term investments. Because these Chinese companies are government-controlled, backed by considerable state assets, and benefit directly from official diplomacy, critics believe they possess an advantage in negotiating trade and investment deals with developing countries. The state-owned enterprises, as Kerry Dumbaugh of the Congressional Research Service observes, "have the luxury of being able to take a longer-term, strategic view—one more closely integrated with national priorities—without having to demonstrate immediate profits."[36]

Correcting the record

The Center for Strategic and International Studies in Washington, DC, in its March 2009 "Smart Power Initiative," co-chaired by former Deputy Secretary of State Richard Armitage and Professor Joseph Nye of Harvard University, laid to rest key arguments advanced by critics. CSIS' detailed study of Chinese decision-making rejects the notion that China has adopted a comprehensive strategy for asserting soft power. It also underscores the limitations on China's soft power and refutes the view that China's growing influence comes at U.S. expense.

Entitled "Chinese Soft Power and Its Implications for the United States," the CSIS report affirms that China has increased its soft power for largely defensive reasons.[37] As discussed earlier, China has utilized trade and investment agreements, concessionary loans, cultural programs, and exchanges with other countries to portray itself as a friend and partner that can assist other countries in their own economic development. From a diplomatic standpoint, China has sought to improve its image and reputation, especially among developing countries, as a means of fending off allegations that it seeks regional dominance and poses a security or economic threat.

In the concluding section of its report, CSIS finds that

> China has yet to develop a comprehensive, coherent, national soft power strategy, although there are disparate policies toward this end. There has been no coordination among ministries or agencies that would carry out a soft-power policy, and no central leading group or leader has been assigned to oversee soft-power promotion.

Thus, "in the short run, China's soft-power policy will likely remain largely *ad hoc* and primarily reactive, aimed at combating the China-threat theory and focused on promoting cultural soft power."[38]

As the CSIS report implies, the most important questions, looking to the future, are whether China's growing soft power will present a challenge to the soft power of the United States—and what the U.S. can do to head off that possibility. America's soft power has long exceeded China's on a global basis, despite the negative attitudes toward the U.S., especially in Muslim countries, which have been generated by the long wars in Iraq and Afghanistan. A study by the Pew Global Attitudes Project of public opinion released in July 2011 found that in 23 countries surveyed, 60 percent of people gave a positive assessment of the U.S. compared to 52 percent for China.[39]

An earlier 2008 survey of select East Asian countries and the United States, conducted by the Chicago Council on Global Affairs, concluded that a majority of people (outside of China) regarded the United States as the most influential country with respect to economy, political values, diplomacy and culture—the factors most closely identified with soft power. However, the survey also revealed a positive view of China's rising influence among developing countries, indicating that China's effort to improve relations in the developing world has met with some degree of success.[40]

Beyond the lead that the United States holds over China with respect to soft power, the CSIS Smart Power Initiative points to another reassuring factor: while China's soft power is likely to increase,

> this does not necessarily mean that Washington and Beijing are on a collision course, fighting for global influence .... A number of factors ultimately will limit China's soft power, including its own domestic political, socioeconomic and environmental challenges. [Also] there

are a number of critical areas of mutual interest between the United States and China on which the two powers can work together—and in some cases already are. Energy security and environmental stewardship top that list, along with transnational issues such as public health and nonproliferation ... [Global] leadership does not have to be a zero-sum game. China can only become preeminent if the United States continues to allow its own powers of attraction to atrophy.[41]

Limitations on China's soft power

China's leaders have put particular emphasis on promoting the country's "spiritual civilization" and culture as a way of increasing China's attractiveness overseas. They have offered their own national goal of making China a "harmonious society"—based on traditional Confucian ethics and Socialist ideals—as a model for other developing countries.[42] (As President Hu Jintao described in 2006, a harmonious society not only seeks to increase its material wealth and level of technological prowess, but also addresses the social problems which accompany rapid economic growth, such as income inequality and environmental damage.) For the purpose of cultural outreach, as noted earlier, China has established "Confucius Institutes" in many countries, including more than 40 in the United States.

The fear of some U.S. critics that Chinese culture, language and political concepts will make China more attractive than America to developing countries does not appear well founded. American movies, music and other fruits of U.S. popular culture have penetrated virtually all societies in Southeast Asia, Latin America, Africa and the Middle East. This has created broad familiarity with the "American way of life" even though some people (including many Americans) find aspects of U.S. pop culture objectionable. While support for U.S. government policy declined in numerous countries and regions during the Bush administration-led "War on Terror," this change did not weaken the hold that American culture had on the views and aspirations of people around the world. From a cultural standpoint, the United States has little to fear from the expansion of China's soft power.

China has also sought to establish partnerships and cooperative economic relations with many developing countries, both to strengthen its own development and expand its influence, as discussed previously. Its "win-win" approach to diplomatic negotiations is symbolized by the "no strings attached" aid and economic development agreements it frequently offers. An absence of bureaucratic red tape, labor standards, human rights conditions and environmental requirements has eased the way for developing countries to enter into these agreements. But the shallow nature of these compacts—including their lack of transparency, relative simplicity and avoidance of complex issues—will not suit China well in the long term.

While Beijing appears on the surface to be establishing valuable relationships, these ties lack the depth that comes with deep discussion, negotiation
and agreement on the most effective terms and conditions for trade and aid.

In the field of humanitarian assistance, moreover, which adds greatly
to a country's reputation, the United States dwarfs China. The U.S. fits
the characterization offered by former British Prime Minister Tony Blair
of a country willing to shoulder its international responsibilities: "to be
the recipient of every demand, to be called upon in every crisis, to be
expected always and everywhere to do what needs to be done."[43] Despite
its pretensions, China is currently incapable of competing with the United
States in the field of humanitarian aid. After the Christmas 2004 tsunami
hit Indonesia, for example, the U.S. pledged $405 million while China
offered $63 million. It was later reported China ultimately gave assistance
amounting to only $22.6 million.[44]

While critics often say China derives a competitive advantage from
state-owned enterprises that invest overseas and follow government policy,
this argument is shortsighted. The large overseas presence and activities
of U.S. multinational corporations and NGOs that act independently of
government policy are far more beneficial to America's image. With a few
glaring exceptions, these companies and non-governmental organizations
contribute to foreign economies, advance American values and conduct
programs that improve the well-being of many societies. When it comes
to furthering soft power, these diverse and dynamic American organizations leave China's state-owned enterprises in the dust. One good example
is the Carter Center in Atlanta, an NGO that seeks to eliminate needless
suffering among the world's poorest people through its health programs
to eradicate preventable diseases—such as Guinea worm, river blindness
and malaria — by using health education and simple, low-cost methods.
An example from the private sector is the Disney Worldwide Conservation
Fund which supports global nonprofit organizations that protect wildlife
and the ecosystems closely linked to their survival.

Perhaps the greatest limitations on China's ability to project soft power
overseas arise from its own domestic problems and constraints. Consider
the following:

> Contrary to the view most Americans hold of China as an unstop-
> pable economic powerhouse, China is still an impoverished,
> developing country.[45] According to 2010 data from the World
> Bank, China's per capita gross national income (GNI) was $7,570,
> approximately 32 percent below the world average of $11,058.
> China's per capita GNI contrasts unfavorably with $29,010 for
> South Korea, $15,010 for Mexico, $47,020 for the United States
> and $10,760 for Kazakhstan.

The public health care system in China is in what is best described as a "precarious" state.[46] One survey indicated that because of excessive costs, 49 percent of sick Chinese people do not seek the care of a doctor and 30 percent reject hospitalization. The decline in infant mortality since 1990 was greater in India than China, although China's wealth increased at a significantly faster rate during this period.

Of the 20 cities in the world with the worst air pollution, 16 of them are in China. According to the World Health Organization, two-thirds of 300 Chinese cities do not meet acknowledged standards of acceptable air quality.[47]

China's planned national spending for education of about 4 percent of GDP for 2012 is far less than the average of about 13 percent among developed countries. The fees charged by many Chinese schools put education beyond the reach of poor children who live in rural areas. In the field of education, "enormous problems persist, and inequities and inequalities are growing."[48]

As a result of fast economic growth and long-time neglect of environmental problems, pollution afflicts more than 70 percent of China's rivers and lakes, 25 percent of Chinese people cannot obtain acceptable drinking water, a third of Chinese people inhale polluted air, more than 80 percent of waste in Chinese cities is not treated according to environmental standards, and one-third of the country is subject to acid rain.[49]

Inequality of wealth has greatly increased during the period China has adopted market reforms. Forty-five percent of national wealth is owned by 10 percent of Chinese. Urban residents have per capita incomes three times more than that of people living in rural areas. Urban incomes have been growing at twice the rate of rural incomes.[50]

Facing these major social problems, China's leaders realize they must concentrate scarce resources on resolving domestic issues that accompany the country's fast economic development. Unless they do so, they risk creating a level of serious social instability that could drive the Communist Party from power.

China's dire internal needs and structural weaknesses clearly limit the extent to which its leaders can project the country's soft power overseas. The highest government priority is addressing major domestic weaknesses. Public funds must be prudently allocated to improving health care, cleaning up air and water pollution, increasing the quality of education, and responding to other pressing social issues, rather than enhancing China's international image. At the same time, the very existence of these serious domestic problems diminishes China's attractiveness as a model for developing countries—especially when compared to the United States and Western Europe where educational standards are high, income inequality is far less, environmental regulations are strictly implemented, health care is relatively good, and per capita income is many times higher.

How the U.S. should respond

The growth in China's soft power through its expanding ties with developing countries nonetheless presents a challenge to the United States. How the U.S. responds to this new competition will affect not just the extent of American influence in the developing world during coming decades, but also the quality and stability of the U.S.-China relationship itself. The U.S. should seek to shape China's foreign policy and take advantage of China's energetic outreach to developing countries. By "leveraging" the increase in China's soft power—drawing on the large number of common and complementary interests between the two countries—the U.S. will better be able to achieve its own foreign policy goals.

Professor David M. Lampton of Johns Hopkins University puts it this way:

China needs technology, capital, markets, and a sufficiently peaceful international environment that permits minimal diversion of resources to defense for at least the next decade, and probably considerably longer. America needs to sell its technology, import comparatively inexpensive goods, productively employ its capital, foster peace and stability in Asia (Korea, the Taiwan Strait, and the subcontinent), and effectively address a plethora of global issues, ranging from the spread of HIV to the proliferation of weapons of mass destruction to the need for peacekeeping operations .... The United States also increasingly needs China to be a responsible macroeconomic manager and engine of regional economic growth.[51]

Cooperation on aid and assistance to developing countries

Consistent with Lampton's analysis, the U.S. should:

Press China to adhere to good governance as well as incorporate labor and environmental standards into its trade and investment agreements

Like other major powers, China has an important stake in supporting international norms that protect the environment, conserve energy, uphold labor rights, ensure transparency in business contracts and safeguard investments.

Confer closely with China in bilateral and multilateral settings to optimize the foreign aid and humanitarian assistance each country provides to developing countries

This would increase the impact of their aid programs, prevent duplication of efforts, identify synergies and build on each country's relative strengths while minimizing their weaknesses.

Join China in pursuing a dialogue with multilateral economic organizations in East Asia, Latin America, Southeast Asia and Africa to advance mutual interests in developing countries

Based on their common objectives, the two countries could strive to greatly increase efficiency and reduce bureaucratic obstacles within the international organizations that channel economic assistance and investment programs to various regions.

Collaborate closely with China on increasing the efficiency and effectiveness of its new institutions that implement foreign aid and humanitarian assistance programs

China could benefit greatly from extensive U.S. experience in this field, going back many years, by acquiring the expertise to better monitor delivery of aid, synchronize national aid programs with the efforts of other governments and ensure the highest standards of internal transparency and accountability.[52]

Cooperation to meet transnational threats

To turn the perceived danger posed by China's increasing soft power into an opportunity and benefit for the United States, the U.S. should also strengthen cooperation with China for addressing common transnational threats. China's cooperation is essential, in fact, for the U.S. and the international community to deal with these problems, ranging from epidemic disease, poor health care, energy insecurity to climate change, cross-border environmental pollution, inadequate education and natural disasters.

China would likely be receptive to cooperation in these areas, as Cui Liru, a senior research official, indicates:

As mankind enters the 21st century, nontraditional issues stand out, natural disasters like earthquake, tsunami, hurricane, epidemic disease[s] like SARS, mad cow, [and] bird flu, and negative consequences of industrialization like environmental pollution [and the] greenhouse effect, to name just a few. In face of them, not a single country can stand aloof.[53]

Of course, many transnational problems directly afflict China and pose obstacles to its future economic development. If China encounters shortages of energy and water, remains vulnerable to epidemic diseases, fails to overcome environmental pollution and does not improve its health and educational infrastructure, it will not achieve the essential goal of both its domestic and foreign policy—becoming a developed country. By virtue of its own self-interest, therefore, China is likely to increasingly join with other countries in common efforts to address transnational problems.

The benefits to the U.S. from collaborating with China on these issues are manifest. Cooperation strengthens China's commitment to pursuing responsible international leadership, rather than narrower national interests. Accepting American assistance undercuts the nationalist view in China that the two countries are locked in a zero-sum game for international influence. Obtaining China's support for addressing common transnational challenges is a way of leveraging China's strength in pursuit of U.S. policy goals.

There is another dimension as well. Helping China overcome the obstacles to its economic and social development advances American interests because "the consequences of failure in China will not remain confined within its borders," as Lampton writes:

> If China's leaders cannot effectively deal with the [social and economic problems they face], a toxic combination of popular nationalism, domestic frustration, and elite desperation to divert attention from domestic failings will spill into the international system. The environmental and refugee implications of Chinese failure are self-evident. There also is the ever-present danger that if the Chinese feel threatened, incipient Chinese nationalism will be harnessed to assertive, perhaps aggressive, purposes abroad.[54]

Because of China's interdependence and critical role in the international economy, China's domestic failures can have severely negative *global* effects. It is in the interest of the United States to prevent any "spillover" from occurring.

Reinvigorating America's global engagement

Around the world, America has a more positive image than China, according to the 2011 survey of the Pew Global Attitudes Projects. Despite the damage that the image of the United States has suffered, mainly among

Muslim countries, as a result of the wars in Afghanistan and Iraq as well as from U.S. efforts to combat terrorism through measures such as drone strikes, the United States can enhance its soft power considerably by once again adopting policies that increase its international stature. Upholding the tenets of the Bill of Rights, avoiding foreign military interventions that do not have UN approval, providing humanitarian aid, disavowing torture, pursuing mutually beneficial trade agreements, building diplomatic coalitions and working collaboratively with other countries rather than pursuing unilateral measures—would all go a long way to raising U.S. popularity.[55]

Strengthening U.S. public diplomacy so it focuses more specifically on the problems faced by developing countries and has greater sensitivity for cultural differences, would likely do wonders for the American image abroad. To the extent that U.S. diplomats can take a problem-solving approach by showing how American aid, humanitarian assistance, technical support, trade, and investment helps relieve a country's problems, it would go far to strengthening the United States' image.

Focusing on overcoming adverse material conditions in the developing world is normally a better approach than heavily promoting U.S. political principles abroad. While standing up for American values is essential, U.S. efforts to improve the practical lives of ordinary people—by eradicating disease, strengthening the local economy, fending off the effects of natural disasters and building local infrastructure—are the best way to demonstrate the worth of political principles that Americans hold dear. People who benefit from clean water, greatly improved health care, better roads, new communication technologies and a more comfortable life that they attribute to American assistance and investment will certainly be more supportive of American democracy and political values in the long term.

Showing greater sensitivity to foreign cultures is also critical. People who live in developing countries are well aware of numerous aspects of American life through the movies, pop music and television programs that are disseminated worldwide. What they want and need to hear, however, is far greater U.S. appreciation for their own culture and traditions. This means much more than encouraging American diplomats to participate frequently in local cultural events, which they already do. It requires a coordinated effort by all U.S. officials stationed overseas to explain American policy in ways specific to the language and culture of each country, taking into account local attitudes and values. Most important, it also means highlighting how the traditions and values of the country are respected in the United States. One example is conveying to Middle Eastern people the freedom of worship and vibrant community life experienced by American Muslims, as well as realistically portraying the obstacles those U.S. Muslims have overcome and continue to face. Another example is highlighting concrete cases where the tradition or cultural achievement of a country has been adopted or become highly respected in the United States.

To best improve America's image and soft power, the core principles that should infuse U.S. public diplomacy are clear: true respect for a foreign country's religious and cultural traditions while showing how the United States is significantly helping to better the material standards of living in that country. An America that respects and cares as well as an America that brings material improvements to the lives of ordinary people will surely prove attractive and increase its soft power in the decades to come.

CHAPTER SEVEN

Getting it right: a new framework for U.S.-China relations

Much of U.S. policy toward China is driven by fear—fear of a future military challenge to American dominance in the Asia Pacific and fear of a Chinese economic juggernaut that could harm the United States in coming years. Despite these anxieties, the United States today holds an immense military and strategic advantage over China in both nuclear and conventional forces. The U.S. economy is larger and more developed than China's economy even while the U.S. maintains a substantial lead over China in technology and manufacturing expertise in numerous fields.

Out of concern for China's rise as a major power, China hawks advocate strengthening the status quo in U.S.-China strategic relations by relying on a containment strategy to limit China's military activities. Protectionists consistently push for trade measures that put obstacles in the way of Chinese goods, services and investment entering the U.S. market. Both factions tend to regard the lack of human rights and democracy in China as inalterable facts.

The risks of serious conflict between the United States and China are masked by the desire of both governments to maintain a strong semblance of stability in their security and economic relations. Occasionally, the possibility of military confrontation raises its ugly head—as it did in the March 2009 clash of U.S. and Chinese vessels in the South China Sea or the June 2010 surprise and simultaneous surfacing of three of America's most powerful submarines, capable of launching nuclear missiles, in close proximity to China. Conflicts over trade also sometimes break into the open, as we saw in the September 2009 imposition of harsh U.S. tariffs against Chinese tire exports which sparked speculation about a "trade war." Serious concern about a trade war also arose in October 2011 after the Senate passed a sweeping measure to impose high punitive tariffs on Chinese imports for manipulating the value of its currency. Whenever it appears that a serious confrontation could occur, concerned U.S. diplomats and officials jump into action, trying to mitigate the problem and preserve the status quo. To date, they have fortunately been successful, even though their very success tends to make them all the more reluctant to address fundamental problems in the U.S.-China relationship.

To overcome the structural weaknesses in U.S.-China relations—which could lead to a major military or economic conflict between the two countries—it is in America's best interests to seek a new paradigm for relations with China. A paradigm shift that leads the two countries to deal with each other on an intrinsically friendly basis would enhance U.S. security, strengthen the U.S. economy and encourage the expansion of democracy and human rights practices in China. Achieving this new paradigm is possible through a Framework Agreement which addresses outstanding disputes between the U.S. and China on security, economic and political issues.

In the context of U.S.-China relations, a Framework Agreement is best considered a joint declaration of principles and goals—a conceptual expression of diplomatic architecture—rather than a "grand bargain" in the sense of an all-or-nothing solution. Critics may find fault with some elements of the Framework Agreement proposed here, and surely it can be improved through scrutiny and reflection by many good minds. The most important thing is for the proponents of peaceful coexistence between the U.S. and China to undertake a serious ongoing exercise in conflict resolution and "win-win" thinking that leads to rapprochement and mutual accommodation. Doing so makes it far more likely that the two countries will resolve their major outstanding security, economic and political disputes—an objective that is in the best interests of both China and the United States at a time when the status quo is becoming progressively more risky and untenable.

The U.S. and China are not doomed to confront each other in a terribly destructive war any more than the U.S. and Soviet Union were destined to do so. But to prevent the occurrence of worst-case scenarios, American and Chinese leaders must exhibit a strong desire to achieve a stable peace through the exercise of reciprocal restraint. Such leadership would make a Framework Agreement both politically feasible and allow for the step-by-step implementation of its agreed principles and goals over time. This leadership would be founded on a precept that is recognized and esteemed in both Chinese and American political culture—that achieving most of a nation's core objectives through prudent compromise is far better than risking a mutually destructive war to achieve maximalist national goals.

Before laying out critical elements of a Framework Agreement, it is worthwhile summarizing the weaknesses in current U.S. policy and the benefits of improved relations with China.

Security policy

The foremost shortcoming in U.S. security policy toward China is its uncritical embrace of the view that the only way to protect the United States against a future threat from China is to maintain military dominance in the Asia Pacific. As noted in Chapter Two, for more than a hundred years, U.S. strategic doctrine called for "preventing the hegemony of a hostile power in any of the three regions outside of North America with major industrial or energy resources—Europe, Asia, and the Middle East," in the words of historian and policy expert Michael Lind of the New America Foundation.[1]

Since the demise of the Soviet Union, the U.S. has become the dominant worldwide power and currently seeks to maintain its superiority in Asia through measures aimed at containing China. The pursuit of U.S. domination represents, as Lind puts it, "a radical departure from America's previous policy of seeking to preserve rather than prevent a diversity of power in the world, while sharing the burdens of preserving the peace with other rich and militarily powerful states."[2] From a pragmatic standpoint, this policy is costly, risky, and above all, unnecessary for achieving the core goals of U.S.-Asia policy: regional stability, security and prosperity. Moreover, it continues to stoke resentment and spur nationalism in China. A policy of strong U.S. deterrence and engaging China through closer security cooperation against common threats will be more than adequate to prevent China from seeking regional dominance.

Another major weakness in American security policy is its unstated premise that China inevitably poses a decisive military threat to the United States. To justify this premise, China hawks regularly hype China's future and potential capabilities, while obscuring the current reality that the U.S. dwarfs China in both nuclear and conventional military capabilities. They almost always fail to note the United States is highly likely to strengthen its military superiority to China over time, and the U.S. spends more than three times as much as China on defense.

As a means of deterring or defeating China in the most likely worst-case scenario—a Chinese attack on Taiwan—the U.S. has pursued what it officially terms a "hedging" strategy to counter China's future military capability. This strategy couples intensive intelligence gathering off China's coast and a major buildup of U.S. military forces in the Pacific with a determined effort to create stronger alliances with India and Japan as well as closer ties with other countries in East Asia. The Obama Administration has

accelerated the strategic encirclement of China through a series of coordinated military measures it initiated in November 2011. This U.S. strategy
deepened anxiety in China about a potential "U.S. threat" and strengthened
the position of hardliners calling for the modernization of China's armed
forces to prepare for an expected U.S. attack. Building up U.S. forces to
threaten China has thus increased the likelihood of a self-fulfilling prophecy
of war between the two countries. The more the U.S. seeks to hedge against
the "China threat," the more intensively China prepares for conflict with its
most likely adversary. Justifying new U.S. military pressure as a response
to perceived Chinese "assertiveness" obscures the reality of a U.S.-China
action-reaction dynamic that entails more aggressive military measures by
both sides.

The greatest security benefit to the United States of improving relations
with China would be ending the likely prospect of a future military
conflict if the Taiwan standoff precipitously deteriorates. On a structural
level, China and the U.S. remain on a collision course over Taiwan. The
U.S. is committed to defending the island and preserving the status quo
in the Taiwan Strait.[3] China is equally determined to reunite Taiwan
with the "motherland" and redress the legacy of its "century of humiliation" when foreign powers carved up China into colonial fiefdoms. A
peaceful resolution of the Taiwan conflict would remove the major irritant
in U.S.-China security relations and replace the current impasse with far
greater stability. It would protect Taiwan's democracy against the threat
from China's communist regime, thus achieving a long-standing U.S. policy
objective in Asia.

Improved relations with China would also allow the U.S. to more easily
shape the direction and extent of China's military modernization as well
as its over-arching security goals. If the "U.S. threat" to China ends and
America is perceived as a friendly country, China would very probably
reduce its defense expenditures, which are now preeminently aimed at
defeating U.S. forces in a future confrontation. China would be far more
amenable to reaching mutual arms control and threat reduction agreements
that significantly increase strategic stability between the two countries.

A Framework Agreement between the U.S. and China, moreover, would
provide guidance for resolving maritime disputes in the South and East
China Seas that have previously led to confrontations between the United
States and Chinese forces (as well as a security crisis between China and
Japan). A Framework Agreement would limit and scale back U.S. military
activities off the coast of China and Chinese military activities off the
coast of Japan. By establishing new coastal buffer zones that reflect each
country's legitimate desire for protection against attacks from the sea or
air, the Agreement would sharply reduce the chance of conflict. Through
facilitating legal settlement of disputed maritime claims with the assistance
of a recognized international legal tribunal, it would end hostile encounters

by a number of East Asian countries over islands and surrounding maritime areas rich in oil and gas.

Another further security benefit of improved U.S.-China relations is that it would allow the United States to leverage Chinese capabilities in meeting transnational security threats far more than the U.S. can do now. Mutually beneficial security cooperation would include much more effective joint measures to combat terrorism, proliferation of weapons of mass destruction, piracy, pandemic disease, environmental degradation and human trafficking. It would also be conducive to conducting military-to-military discussions in an atmosphere of mutual trust (which currently does not exist) to de-conflict U.S. and Chinese military operations and avoid accidental confrontations.

Economic policy

During both the Bush and Obama Administrations, U.S. economic policy has been heavily influenced by the views of protectionists who condemn the large U.S. trade deficit with China. The trade measures they have supported—in the form of quotas, taxes, tariffs or non-tariff barriers imposed on Chinese imports—seek to punish China for practices that have allegedly led to the loss of American jobs to China. Yet the arguments advanced by protectionists frequently do not withstand scrutiny. The increase in the U.S. trade deficit with China, often cited as justification for punitive measures, as we saw in Chapter Four, is largely due to the shift of manufacturing and assembly operations to China from other Asian countries such as Japan and South Korea. When critics point to the increase in China's trade deficit, they typically fail to note that the U.S. deficit with the rest of East Asia has significantly declined. Moreover, nearly 60 percent of exports to the United States that are categorized as Chinese for purposes of calculating the deficit come from companies owned by foreign investors, many of the them American. Perhaps most importantly, protectionist efforts to blame China for causing U.S. job losses—due in large part to factors entirely *unrelated* to China—will not bring back those jobs and risk triggering a trade war that could have a major negative effect on both the U.S. and Chinese economies. U.S. manufacturing jobs have mainly been lost because of the productivity gains by American workers and not as a result of the U.S. deficit with China.

On the question of China's undervalued currency, Beijing's decision to allow the RMB to appreciate to its actual market value would certainly advance economic relations between the United States and China. But as numerous economists point out, appreciation of the RMB will not reduce the U.S. trade deficit or bring jobs back. Exaggerating the impact of China's undervalued currency and attacking China for "gaming the system" through its monetary practices will strengthen neither the U.S. economy, nor U.S.-China economic relations.

High tariffs, surcharges, quotas and "Buy American" laws that partially or completely close America's domestic market to various Chinese products also inevitably trigger a nationalist backlash in China. For decades, the U.S. has touted the benefits of free trade and urged Chinese officials to both adopt market reforms and eliminate trade barriers. When the U.S. takes a contrary position by imposing its own protectionist measures, as the Obama Administration did on Chinese-made tires, solar panels and wind-energy towers, it appears hypocritical and shows a willingness to penalize China for its success in the highly competitive international marketplace.

In the largest sense, protectionism damages American national security as well as the American economy. The decades-long policy of seeking to integrate China into the international economy has had the specific security objective of cementing China's support for the U.S.-led international system as a whole. This policy was founded on the historically documented view that countries with a real stake in an open and fair trading system also become major proponents of the stability and peace that makes normal commerce possible. By frustrating China's legitimate business activities, the U.S. weakens China's overall commitment to existing security and economic arrangements.

Improving U.S. relations with China would significantly benefit the American economy over the long term. China's requirements for social and economic development provide large opportunities for American firms that can obtain broad access to the Chinese market and operate success-fully there. China needs American capital, experience, technology, products and services. U.S. firms that are not restricted by Chinese tariffs, taxes, so-called "indigenous innovation" policies and other regulatory measures can harness the skills of China's talented people as well as the country's natural resources and economic dynamism as a means of strengthening U.S. competitiveness in such key industrial areas as electronics, industrial machinery and chemicals. Their business activities will generate new jobs, revenue and expansion of manufacturing plants in the United States. As China's economy expands, the United States will benefit, in turn, from a flow of Chinese capital invested in new U.S. plants and infrastructure, leading to more technological innovation, new products and new jobs that improve America's economic well-being. Over time, the U.S. will also likely accrue an overall surplus in services trade with China, through the services U.S. companies provide in the fields of banking, computers, engineering and insurance, among others.

It is important to recall the favorable trends in U.S.-China trade over the last several years and keep in mind the realistic projections for future positive developments:

China is now the third-largest export market of the United States and U.S. firms have invested approximately $50 billion there.

U.S. exports to China increased by approximately 640 percent from $16 billion to $104 billion during the 2000 to 2011 period.

Up to 240,000 American jobs will be created by 2015 through the projected growth in services that U.S. companies supply in China, if current trade barriers are eliminated.

China is the largest export market for American agricultural products, with U.S. exports totaling $17.5 billion in 2010.[4]

Democracy and human rights

Beyond publishing annual assessments of human rights conditions, focusing public attention on individual cases of concern and making periodic statements about the importance of democracy and human rights, the U.S. actually does little to actively promote internal political reform in China. This is so for two major reasons.

First, critics of China, on both the right and the left, are often largely indifferent to China's domestic political conditions. China hawks warn regularly about the future Chinese military threat and call for greater U.S. defense preparedness to deal with that danger. Protectionists often demand stronger trade measures to safeguard American jobs from the impact of Chinese imports. Yet both groups accept the rule of China's Communist Party as a given, immutable fact. Expressing concern about China's authoritarian practices would distract from the central agenda of each side—be it on security or economic issues.

Second, U.S. administrations have been reluctant to unduly pressure China over its internal political practices for fear of a backlash by the Chinese government. They understandably worry that "publicly shaming" or sanctioning China would be portrayed as American interference in China's internal affairs and be used as justification for a further crackdown on dissident groups. Although these fears are entirely legitimate, they often block necessary discussion of what the United States *can* do to strengthen internal Chinese groups seeking democracy and human rights. No doubt political reform in China must come *from within*—such as through the Charter 08 dissident movement—and cannot be forced from the outside by foreign powers.

For both these reasons, U.S. hawks and protectionists have effectively reached a consensus view: it is not worthwhile for the American government to spend significant political capital on advancing political reform within China. Each U.S. faction is so concerned with its own specific issues that it does little more than lament China's internal political shortcomings.

Improving relations with China, on the other hand, would enable the U.S. to further a core objective of engendering major political liberalization. As we know, China's leaders legitimize one-party authoritarian rule as necessary to protect against foreign countries that are bent on trampling China's national interests. Chinese nationalists bristle at the thought of Taiwan becoming an independent country, with U.S. support, and perpetuating the tragic history of China's dismemberment by foreign powers. If China's leaders are no longer able to cite a "U.S. threat" to the country's integrity and well-being, they will lose their ability to use internal repression as a response to that threat. China's dissident movement, which is striving to achieve significant political reform, would be able to more effectively organize itself as a legitimate alternative to the Communist Party and achieve broad popular support. For the first time since China's communist revolution, it would be able to publicly advocate Taiwan, the United States, other foreign countries and Hong Kong, as political models for China's future internal political development.

Improving U.S.-China relations would strengthen China's political evolution toward greater democracy and human rights for other reasons as well. With the drastic reduction of restrictive trade measures by both countries, a more open and mature Chinese economy would include: 1) a newly powerful private sector that would act as a counter-weight to central government authority; 2) more extensive reliance on rule of law and public accountability; and 3) accelerated development of economic and political pluralism which is ultimately necessary for the economic system to work efficiently.

Key elements of a framework agreement

The potential benefits that the United States would obtain through improved relations with China will require a paradigm shift in relations between the two countries. Achieving this new paradigm is possible through a Framework Agreement—a declaration of principles and goals – which addresses outstanding disputes between the U.S. and China on major security, economic, and political issues. As strategic trust develops between the two countries, the mutually agreed goals would be realized in stages over time through step-by-step negotiations.

Security measures

The security elements of a Framework Agreement would include the following measures.

China would agree to:

Permanently eliminate the short-range ballistic missiles it has emplaced in the vicinity of Taiwan, and suspend their future production;

Significantly reduce and redeploy the naval and air forces it now maintains near Taiwan, while ending all military exercises to prepare for an attack on Taiwan;

Substantially increase military transparency, especially regarding China's development of new weapons systems;

Enter into a binding treaty commitment not to use force against Taiwan, the United States or its allies;

Pull back, permanently and verifiably, all forces now engaged in surveillance and patrolling of Japanese territory from a defined coastal security zone surrounding Japan;

Consent to submit its maritime disputes in the South and East China Seas for adjudication to the International Tribunal for the Law of the Sea, an independent judicial body established by the 1982 Convention on the Law of the Sea; and

Increase security cooperation with the United States both in the Asia Pacific and on common global issues.

By virtue of these measures, the U.S. would greatly strengthen the security of Taiwan, Japan, South Korea and the United States; create true stability in the Cross-Strait region for the first time in more than 60 years; improve Taiwan's position in political negotiations with China about future relations; effectively eliminate the possibility of a major military conflict between the United States and China; and facilitate the settlement of maritime disputes in the South and East China Seas (either through judicial decision or settlement negotiations directly between the parties under supervision of the court).

In exchange for the significant foregoing commitments by China, the United States would agree to:

Pull back, permanently and verifiably, all forces now engaged in surveillance, reconnaissance and patrolling of Chinese territory from a defined coastal security zone surrounding China;

Reduce overall U.S. forces in the Asia Pacific to a level consistent with normal peacetime needs, including protecting sea lines of communication, while retaining a sufficient military presence to deter the threat from North Korea;

Significantly scale down arms sales to Taiwan; and

Enter into a binding treaty commitment not to use force against China.

These measures would significantly improve China's security; protect Taiwan's democratic political system; effectively eliminate the possibility that aggressive U.S. intelligence activity near China's coasts could lead to a major military conflict between the United States and China; facilitate the settlement of maritime disputes in the South and East China Seas; allow some U.S. forces to be deployed away from the Asia Pacific to other regions; and engender greater cooperation with China on security-related issues.[5]

Impact of security measures in a framework agreement

Taiwan

Taiwan currently faces an overwhelming military threat from China, which uses its forces to pressure and intimidate the island's government. China's buildup of missiles along its coast across from Taiwan has continued over the past decade despite periodic improvements in cross-Strait relations. The number of China's deployed short-range ballistic missiles has now reached somewhere between approximately 1,000 and 1,200 according to the U.S. Defense Department.[6] In 1995 and 1996, missiles were the weapon of choice China wielded to threaten imminent attack by conducting "tests" in the vicinity of Taiwan.

As noted earlier, beyond missile deployments, China has concentrated air and naval assets, especially submarines, near Taiwan. One objective of these Chinese forces, in the event of conflict, is to significantly degrade Taiwan's defenses so the island becomes vulnerable to a full-scale amphibious assault. Professor Robert Sutter of George Washington University makes the compelling point that "the military balance in the Taiwan Strait is no longer 'healthy' for Taiwan" and that "annual reports by the U.S. Defense Department now testify to the growing imbalance in military capabilities."[7]

Professor Lyle Goldstein, former director of the China Maritime Institute at the U.S. Naval War College, argues that the easing of tensions between Taiwan and China as well as a military balance where China holds the upper hand create a "window of opportunity … in U.S-China relations that has not been adequately exploited."

> With respect to the sensitive [Taiwan] arms-sales issue, a new US approach is now warranted. Stark geographic reality, combined with the radically altered military balance in China's favour, suggest that continued arms sales are, to a very large extent, symbolic in nature. For example, more advanced F-16s could be purchased by Taipei, but in an actual conflict with China, these aircraft would almost surely never leave the ground, as their bases would likely be quickly obliterated by Chinese missile strikes. Thus, it will make little or no practical difference to the military balance if such arms sales are made or not. Arms sales could safely be reduced gradually over time in both volume and scope, consistent with the 1982 communiqué between Washington and Beijing. Diplomacy should also yield local confidence-building measures, such as the withdrawal of some Chinese strike platforms to locations at greater distance from Taiwan, a proposal that Jiang Zemin himself put on the table back in 2002.[8]

If China were to permanently eliminate the missiles facing Taiwan, while significantly and verifiably reducing and redeploying the air and naval forces currently threatening the island, Taiwan's security would be markedly improved. This outcome can be achieved through mutual threat reduction measures that reduce, eliminate and redeploy advanced weapons and military equipment that either Taiwan or China could employ in the event of conflict. Such measures would make it far more difficult for either side to threaten or intimidate the other for political purposes, in addition to significantly lowering their capacity to wreak destruction during an actual war.

Because Taiwan is now militarily inferior to China with regard to missiles, naval vessels and air force assets, it lacks the diplomatic leverage to eliminate the security threat that China poses. Short of agreeing to reunification—which is currently opposed by a majority of Taiwan's citizens—there are no measures Taiwan can offer as a sufficient *quid pro quo* to secure significant Chinese arms reductions. And, without reciprocal security measures, China refuses to engage in what it considers "unilateral disarmament."[9]

By contrast, the U.S. is capable of securing a drastic reduction in China's military threat to Taiwan by offering reciprocal military measures that would lead to far greater stability in the region, creating a transformed regional security environment. China is highly likely to reduce, redeploy and eliminate its missile, naval and air forces now threatening the island, in exchange for the U.S. pulling back forces now engaged in surveillance and patrolling of Chinese territory, significantly reducing U.S. military deployments in the Asia Pacific, and scaling down major arms sales to Taiwan.

It is also important to recall that Taiwan's prior negotiations with China on long-term political issues reflect the profound difficulty the two sides face in reaching an agreement that could truly stabilize their relations for the foreseeable future. Taiwan understandably fears being absorbed by China, knowing full well that Beijing's foremost objective is national reunification at the earliest possible time. A large majority of Taiwan's people reject Beijing's promise to guarantee the island's autonomy and democratic political system through a so-called "one country, two systems" formula. For its part, China worries that Taiwan's Democratic Progressive Party (DPP), though currently out of power, could strongly re-emerge in the future, and once again lead a drive for political independence which effectively thwarts national reunification.

A Framework Agreement would strengthen the security of Taiwan and the preservation of its democratic political system without requiring it to agree to eventual reunification with China. It would be entirely up to the Taiwanese government and people whether to conduct bilateral negotiations on political reunification at some future time. The two sides would be able to carry out their negotiations in a largely non-threatening and stable security environment, which would help support, in and of itself, a successful agreement on difficult political issues.

Eliminating the Risk of a U.S.-China military conflict

The proposed security measures in a Framework Agreement would end the current military standoff over Taiwan as well as the broader friction arising from aggressive U.S. air and sea surveillance along China's coast. Whenever China-Taiwan relations become acrimonious—as they typically do when the Taiwanese political party favoring independence is in power or when Chinese leaders play to nationalist public opinion and threaten a future attack on the island—it greatly heightens the security risks that the U.S. faces in Asia. In the event of an imminent or actual attack on Taiwan, the U.S. would almost certainly send military forces to the island's aid, with proponents of intervention citing U.S. obligations under the Taiwan Relations Act.[10] National security strategists would argue that a military response is essential to ensure the credibility of the overall U.S. security posture in Asia, particularly the defense commitments to Japan and South Korea.

The current standoff over Taiwan effectively puts the U.S. at the mercy of political elements in China *and* Taiwan that seek to achieve their goals without regard for U.S. interests. Those interests include both protecting Taiwan and avoiding a war with China that could conceivably escalate to a nuclear exchange. By realizing a Framework Agreement with China that protects Taiwan's democracy, stabilizes the region and eliminates the risk of a U.S.-China conflict over Taiwan, the U.S. would greatly advance its core policy objectives.

Once China significantly reduces, eliminates and redeploys the missile, air and naval forces currently threatening Taiwan, the U.S. would no longer need to carry out close surveillance and intrusive reconnaissance of China's coast, whose essential purpose is to probe and evaluate China's military capabilities. As discussed in Chapter Two, there is a history of small-scale confrontations between U.S. and Chinese military forces, especially in the region of the South China Sea, that could blow up into a major conflict. More dangerous encounters can be expected to occur in the future, as Mark Valencia, a maritime expert at the Nautilus Institute, points out:

> Military and intelligence gathering activities in [coastal areas] are likely to become more controversial and more dangerous. In Asia, this disturbing prospect reflects the increasing and changing demands for technical intelligence; robust weapons acquisition programs of the littoral states, especially increasing electronic warfare capabilities; and the widespread development of information warfare capabilities. Further, the scale and scope of U.S. maritime and airborne intelligence collection activities are likely to expand rapidly over the next decade, involving levels and sorts of activities quite unprecedented in peacetime. They will not only become more intensive; they will produce defensive reactions and escalatory dynamics; and they will lead to less stability in the most affected regions, especially in Asia.[11]

A U.S.-China Framework Agreement that strengthens Taiwan's security by significantly reducing China's capability to threaten it would make the current level of U.S. reconnaissance unnecessary. By agreeing to curtail American coastal surveillance in exchange for China's arms reductions, the U.S. would also go far toward ending the ongoing military friction with China that could potentially escalate to a major military confrontation.

Strengthening Japanese security

Feuding over the Senkaku/Diaoyu Islands and clashes in their vicinity have sharply heightened Tokyo's concerns about the presence of Chinese forces near Japan.[12] Following the September 2010 crisis when a Chinese fishing trawler rammed a Japanese patrol vessel, Japan announced it would build up its military capabilities to defend the islands. Under new defense guidelines, Japan is shifting ground forces once intended to counter the Soviet Union to the south and acquiring new submarines, fighter jets and destroyers. It is also forming new ground units that can be transported by air to defend the disputed territory in the event of another crisis.

Under a Framework Agreement between China and the United States, Beijing would agree to pull back all its forces, permanently and verifiably, from a coastal security zone around Japan, including the Senkaku/Diaoyu

Islands. This measure would significantly reduce the Chinese military threat to Japan as well as the need for Tokyo to build up its forces in the region. The new zone would strengthen Japan's security by providing more warning time as well as more freedom of action for Japan's air and naval self-defense forces to conduct operations in the area of the East China Sea.

It is very much in China's interest to recognize a coastal security zone around Japan in the context of a Framework Agreement. The new security zone would relieve pressure on Japan's leaders to pursue a buildup aimed at preparing for a possible military conflict with China. More broadly, it would undercut the right-wing political figures in Japan who advocate developing a nuclear deterrent force. According to one informed estimate, Japan has already stockpiled enough plutonium to build a thousand nuclear bombs, should it choose to do so.[13] China is deeply concerned about the prospect of a nuclear-armed Japan and surely recognizes that Tokyo's deep-seated fear of Chinese forces operating near the Japanese islands increases the risk of a Japanese nuclear break-out.

By agreeing to a coastal zone that strengthens Japan's security, China would also facilitate joint development of the maritime resources in the vicinity of the Senkaku/Diaoyu Islands, especially oil and gas deposits, and lay the basis for settling competing territorial claims. Although the two countries reached a "political agreement" on resource sharing and exploration in 2008, it has never been implemented because of deep suspicion on both sides. Much of that suspicion stems from Tokyo's fear of China using its claims to the Senkaku/Diaoyu to allow for a greater military presence near Japan. On China's part, suspicion is compounded by fear of aggressive Japanese intentions in light of the "history" issue—Japan's oppressive occupation of China from 1931 to 1945. The increased presence of Chinese vessels and aircraft near the islands and resulting security tensions makes it extremely difficult to resolve legal disputes over land and resources—even though both countries would clearly benefit from settling the issue to spur joint development. A coastal security zone that protects Japan, recognized by China under a new Framework Agreement, would foster resolution of the Senkaku/Diaoyo conflict and lead to broader cooperation between the two countries.

Ending the U.S. military containment of China

The buildup of U.S. forces in the Pacific today continues apace in the name of "hedging" against the possibility of a future war with China. The United States conducts intensive reconnaissance and intelligence gathering along China's coast while continuing to deploy extensive military assets to the region—particularly long-range bombers, aircraft carriers and submarines. Steps taken by the Obama Administration in November 2011 accelerated deployments in the name of "rebalancing," a term as benign as "hedging," which largely disguises the serious nature of the military preparations taking place. A Framework Agreement would bring about an end to the effective U.S. policy of containing China for an overriding reason: following resolution of major security disputes between the two countries, there would no longer be any rationale for pursuing a containment strategy.

At its base, containment aims to maintain U.S. military dominance in East Asia and discourage Chinese military activity in the Western Pacific, including in the South China and East China Seas. If the U.S. successfully uses diplomatic means to end the Chinese threat to Taiwan, secure Taiwan's democratic system for the long term and halt dangerous military encounters along China's coast, a Cold War-style containment policy would not find significant mainstream support in the United States. The U.S. could return to its traditional strategic doctrine of preventing any other power, including China, from dominating the Asia Pacific.

Abandoning containment would have several other important consequences from the standpoint of the United States. A major reduction in the "U.S. threat" would eliminate the primary factor driving China's military modernization program. The U.S. would be in a better position to shape the scope of China's military development in the future. In addition, sharply lowering military tensions in the South China and East China Seas would encourage the peaceful settlement of the competing claims to islands and maritime resources in that region. Territorial disputes could then be considered on their own legal merits, apart from considerations of power politics and military strategy. A recognized institution with deep expertise in maritime affairs—the International Tribunal for the Law of the Sea— would be able, for the first time, to fairly resolve those controversies. The parties could also pursue settlement negotiations in the context of a legal proceeding to resolve the issues between themselves and avoid risking an adverse judicial decision. Finally, since China would no longer be regarded as a potential major security threat, the U.S. would be able to scale down its forces in the Asia Pacific. A reduced but still strong U.S. military presence coupled with greater security cooperation would be more than sufficient to deter and dissuade China from seeking regional dominance.

Nuclear weapons

While a Framework Agreement would considerably stabilize the region and allow the U.S. to revert to a peacetime military posture in the Asia Pacific, it would not resolve all security issues between the two countries. Among the most serious remaining security problems are the threat posed to the United States and its allies by China's relatively small nuclear force and the threat to China from a much larger U.S. nuclear force as well as advanced U.S. missile defense systems. The relationship between these two nuclear forces will become more destabilizing in the future if the U.S. acquires a "first-strike capability" that substantially diminishes China's ability to retaliate.

Though the nuclear balance would be outside the scope of a Framework Agreement, it would provide a strong foundation for negotiating future strategic arms control accords between the United States and China. If the major security disputes in U.S.-China relations are eliminated and the U.S. ends its effective containment policy toward China, the two countries would have major incentives to more completely stabilize their relations by radically reducing the strategic nuclear threat that each country poses to the other.

Economic measures

The economic elements of a Framework Agreement would include American and Chinese commitments to:

> Negotiate a bilateral free trade agreement that eliminates protectionist measures and trade barriers on both sides as a means of maximizing mutual trade and investment; and

> Achieve Asia Pacific regional economic integration through a Trans-Pacific Partnership agreement which includes China.

Taken together, these measures would strengthen the United States by: 1) further opening China's market to more U.S. exports of goods and services; 2) helping American manufacturers become more globally competitive; 3) creating thousands of new U.S. jobs by allowing American companies to invest more extensively in China's economic development; 4) assisting U.S. companies in harnessing China's economic strengths; 5) encouraging major capital flows from China to the United States, which will foster technological innovation and job creation in the U.S.; and 6) preventing the rise of trade arrangements in Asia that discriminate against American firms.

Impact of economic measures in a framework agreement

A U.S.-China free trade agreement

Despite the potentially large economic benefits offered by a bilateral free trade agreement (FTA), the United States and China have thus far not attempted to negotiate an agreement of this kind. As we know, China has focused mainly on reaching free trade agreements with Asian countries to expand regional economic opportunities and improve relations with its neighbors. The U.S. has not yet seriously contemplated negotiating an FTA with China, in part because it would be perceived as downgrading the U.S. relationship with Taiwan and further complicate the United States' regional security posture.

A U.S.-China FTA would achieve a major net increase in trade and investment for both countries. From a U.S. standpoint, it would lower the prices of consumer goods in the United States as well as the costs that U.S. businesses pay for imported goods. It would spur market reform in China, increase the transparency of regulatory activities there, encourage Chinese direct investment in the United States and stimulate greater innovation in both countries.

Most importantly, an FTA would significantly reduce protectionist measures on both sides and in so doing, eliminate the possibility of a U.S.-China trade war. Without a comprehensive bilateral agreement that effectively tears down existing tariff and non-tariff barriers, the U.S. and Chinese governments remain vulnerable to pressure from domestic groups that seek protection for parochial economic interests. The Obama Administration's imposition of tariff surcharges on U.S. imports of tires from China, at the behest of the United Steelworkers union, is a case in point. Without an FTA in place, domestic vested interests inevitably use the political process to seek their own narrow advantage at the expense of the nation as a whole. After an FTA drastically scales down protectionist regulations, these domestic interests would have far less ability to impose economic restrictions that could trigger retaliatory measures and potentially spark a trade war.

A trans-Pacific partnership that includes China

To revitalize the American economy and ensure its future competitiveness, the U.S. needs to benefit from the economic dynamism of Asia, the new "engine" for global growth. By exercising leadership in realizing an inclusive free trade bloc in the Asia Pacific through the Trans-Pacific Partnership (TPP), the U.S. will enhance its international stature and greatly contribute to both regional prosperity and stability.

At the highest levels of the U.S. government, it is common knowledge that the "huge and growing markets of the Asia-Pacific already are key destinations for U.S. manufactured goods, agricultural products and service suppliers."[14] U.S. exports of goods to the Asia Pacific in 2010 totaled about $775 billion. That amounted to an astonishing 61 percent of all goods exports globally, and represented a more than 25 percent increase over similar exports a single year earlier. Seventy-two percent of all U.S. agricultural exports in 2010 went to Asia, totaling approximately $83 billion. U.S. agricultural exports to China alone nearly tripled in five years from about $6.7 billion in 2005 to approximately $17.5 billion in 2010.[15] China is now the number one export market for U.S. agricultural products and the second largest export market for U.S. agricultural, fisheries, and forest products, just behind Canada. According to the latest available data, U.S. private services exports to Asia in 2009 were 37 percent of all U.S. service exports globally, amounting to about $177 billion.

From an economic standpoint, an inclusive Trans-Pacific Partnership would do more than just reduce tariffs in creating a new free trade bloc in the Asia-Pacific. It would eliminate a variety of trade barriers in this rapidly growing region and widely expand access for U.S. goods and services. It would help protect intellectual property, harmonize different national regulations governing trade, enable global supply chains to operate more efficiently, encourage investment in the United States and prevent government subsidies from distorting trade relationships. In an overall sense, it would enhance U.S. competitiveness, while creating thousands of new American jobs. The United States Chamber of Commerce aptly sums up the excitement of the U.S. business community about such an agreement in its December 2011 testimony to Congress that American business

> wants and needs an ambitious TPP agreement completed as soon as possible—an agreement with high standards that will create jobs, spur growth and raise living standards and strengthen our nation's commercial, strategic, and geopolitical ties across the most dynamic and economically vibrant region in the world.[16]

Unlike the Obama Administration's current policy of seeking to build a Trans-Pacific Partnership that excludes China—once again, the world's second-largest economy and America's second-largest trading partner for merchandise—the Framework Agreement would recognize the reality of China's important economic role in Asia.

Critically, an inclusive Trans-Pacific Partnership would deepen regional economic integration in a way that does not require Asian countries to choose between China and the United States in pursuing international trade and investment. America's friends and allies—Japan, South Korea and the Philippines among them—have made it clear that while they welcome a robust U.S. economic role in Asia, they do not want to be caught up in a U.S.-China conflict over trade and investment issues. Quite understandably, they want to benefit economically from trade and investment with both the U.S. and China, and do not see any contradiction in doing business with the two countries simultaneously. Doug Bandow, Senior Fellow of the Cato Institute, seriously questions the Obama Administration's strategy of excluding China from the TPP negotiations:

> China's growth is explosive. By not including China in the TPP, we're taking our competition with them to the economic realm, which is not

at all a strong point for the U.S. I can't imagine our friends and allies in Asia wanting to choose between the U.S. and China on this issue, or creating a trade agreement that the most important economic power in the region can't be part of. The administration's approach communicates to the Chinese that they're involved in a long term and hostile competition with the U.S.[17]

By negotiating a Trans-Pacific Partnership that includes China, the U.S. will exercise leadership in creating an unprecedented regional trade area that confers the numerous economic advantages on the United States which were noted previously. The TPP will allow the U.S. to better leverage China's economic strengths and bring about far greater regional prosperity than an agreement which excludes China. This broader U.S. approach to the TPP will also reinforce political stability and strengthen regional cooperation for resolving common economic and security problems. Instead of attempting unrealistically to isolate China and seeking to limit that country's trade and investment in the region, this U.S. initiative would keep faith with both America's longstanding commitment to the principles of free trade as well as to promoting international institutions that advance the interests of all member states.

Political measures

The United States and China would agree in a Framework Agreement on a set of overriding political principles and international norms to guide their future relationship. These principles and norms would be drawn from the Helsinki Final Act, which was reached between the United States, the Soviet Union and other countries in 1975. As discussed earlier, that accord provided for sovereign equality and respect for the rights inherent in sovereignty; refraining from the threat or use of force; the inviolability of frontiers and the territorial integrity of states; a commitment to peaceful resolution of disputes and non-intervention in the internal affairs of other states; a respect for human rights and fundamental freedoms, including the freedom of thought, conscience, religion or belief; equal rights and self-determination of peoples; engendering cooperation between states; and the fulfillment in good faith of each state's obligations under international law. This political component of a Framework Agreement would affirm principles of great importance to China's government while also legitimizing and institutionalizing human rights and precepts of democracy. And as previously suggested, in so doing it would significantly strengthen the domestic forces in China that are seeking to build a democratic political system that upholds human rights.

Background on the Helsinki agreement

The Helsinki Final Act of 1975 on security and cooperation in Europe proved critical in bringing human rights and fundamental freedoms to the people of Russia and Eastern Europe. It did so by formally accepting the legitimate security concerns of the Soviet Union and setting forth comprehensive political-military principles that intertwined sovereign equality, the inviolability of frontiers, non-interference in the internal affairs of other states and respect for human rights.

In exchange for endorsing the Soviet Union's post-World War II territorial gains, American negotiators effectively obtained Soviet agreement to respect the legitimacy of dissident movements throughout the Soviet bloc. The famous Article 7 and Basket III of the Helsinki Final Act formally committed the signatories to uphold human rights, the free exchange of peoples, open borders, freedom of information and family reunifications. After the accord was concluded, human rights organizations in the Soviet Union and Eastern Europe established monitoring groups that focused international attention on violations. As an eminent group of U.S. experts wrote in 2003,

> [T]he animating insight of Helsinki was that by publicly raising human rights issues to high priority levels, the U.S. would set forces in motion that would undermine the legitimacy of the communist empire. And so it turned out to be.[18]

The Helsinki agreement specifically strengthened several dissident organizations—the "Charter 77" movement in Czechoslovakia, "Solidarity" in Poland and the "Helsinki Monitors" in Russia. After the Helsinki Final Act was concluded, these groups increasingly held their governments accountable for human rights violations by citing the standards in the Act. In the words of former Secretary of State Henry Kissinger,

> Basket III was destined to play a major role in the disintegration of the Soviet satellite orbit, and become a testimonial to all human rights advocates in NATO countries .... Basket III obligated all signatories to practice and foster certain enumerated basic human rights. Its Western drafters hoped that the provisions would create an international standard that would inhibit repression of dissidents and revolutionaries. As it turned out, heroic reformers in Eastern Europe used Basket III as a rallying point in their fights to free their countries from Soviet domination.[19]

Agreement to the Helsinki principles in the political section of a Framework Agreement would be feasible for the reasons noted in Chapter

Five. China is profoundly interested in improving its security through a sharp reduction of both intensive U.S. military pressure along its coast and U.S. arms sales to Taiwan. To achieve a new security relationship with the United States, China would reason that affirming principles of international relations it highly values—such as sovereign equality, territorial integrity of states and non-intervention in internal affairs—is an acceptable price to pay, despite the accompanying commitments it would have to make toward respecting human rights and fundamental freedoms. A faction in China's leadership that is open to and indeed seeks political reform would also support the Helsinki principles just as a progressive leadership faction previously pushed for Beijing's entry to the World Trade Organization in the late 1990s, precisely for the purpose of hastening internal reforms in China.

Impact of political measures in the framework agreement

Supporting human rights and democracy in China

The most effective way for the United States to strengthen the movement among Chinese people for democracy and human rights is by reaching a Framework Agreement with China that re-sets security and economic relations as well as legitimates political principles modeled on the Helsinki Final Act. Both the security and political provisions of a Framework Agreement would significantly bolster the proponents of peaceful political change in China, who continue to challenge the authoritarian practices of the country's one-party regime. Just as Helsinki gave international legitimacy to the struggles of human rights advocates in Russia, Czechoslovakia, Poland and other Eastern European countries during the Cold War, a comparable agreement will help to peacefully transform China's political system.

To understand why this is so, it is valuable to examine China's prosecution of writer and activist Liu Xiaobo, who helped draft Charter 08, the seminal document calling for greater human rights and democracy in China that ultimately obtained more than 10,000 signatures during the fall of 2008. Following Liu's conviction and sentence to eleven years in prison for "inciting subversion of state power" in December 2009, a middle-level diplomat at the U.S. Embassy in Beijing protested the decision, arguing that "persecution of individuals for the peaceful expression of political views is inconsistent with internationally recognized norms of human rights."[20] Earlier, U.S. officials included Liu on a list of "cases of concern" they gave to Chinese leaders.[21] When President Obama visited China in November 2009, he publicly and privately asserted the importance of human rights, saying

I spoke to President Hu about America's bedrock beliefs that all men and women possess certain fundamental human rights.[22] We do not believe these principles are unique to America, but rather they are universal rights and that they should be available to all peoples, to all ethnic and religious minorities.

In the Liu case, the assertion of important principles of human rights and democracy by both the U.S. president and the U.S. Embassy in China had no discernible impact on the Chinese government's decision to prosecute a major dissident. Nor did the U.S. government's effort to underscore his importance in a list they passed to Chinese officials.

Another prominent Chinese dissident, Wei Jingsheng, who is now living in the United States and spent 18 years in Chinese prisons, explains why the U.S. statements in support of Liu Xiaobo and human rights did not keep him out of prison:

> As under Mao and Deng, standing up to the American superpower is meant to stem growing internal opposition and cow China's restless people into subservience under a one-party dictatorship. This is particularly critical as greater democracy in China would expose its own economic problems.[23]

China's leaders use fear of the "American superpower" to legitimate their harsh repression of the country's human rights and democracy movement. By standing up to the United States on human rights issues, the Chinese government invokes powerful nationalist feelings and portrays itself as preserving domestic stability against foreigners who seek to interfere in China's internal affairs. Characterizing the United States as a major security threat is premised, of course, on the effective U.S. containment policy toward China, U.S. arms sales to Taiwan, and broad suspicion of American intentions as the dominant power in the Asia Pacific.

So long as the United States pursues aggressive measures to prepare for a military conflict with China, Beijing will continue to invoke the "U.S. threat" to justify its repression of dissidents who seek greater human rights and democracy. Railing against the United States, whenever the political need arises, suits China's authoritarian leaders well. It enables them to stir up Chinese nationalism as a means of legitimizing continued one-party rule and helps them to underscore the importance of "domestic stability" for China's well-being in the face of a foreign security threat. It allows these leaders to portray China as a "developing country" that cannot afford the luxury of Western-style human rights and full-blown democracy as long as it has to confront a potentially hostile American military power in Asia. In the words of former Soviet dissident Natan Sharansky, an authoritarian state like China utilizes an external threat to "unify the people and justify draconian security measures at home."

A good illustration of the current weakness of U.S. policy toward human rights and democracy in China is found in the "U.S.-China Joint Statement," released in November 2009 during President Obama's visit. As a way of showing progress on human rights, President Obama and Chinese President Hu agreed to schedule a meeting of the U.S.-China "human rights dialogue":

> The United States and China underlined that each country and its people have the right to choose their own path, and all countries should respect each other's choice of a development model. Both sides recognized that the United States and China have differences on the issue of human rights. Addressing these differences in the spirit of equality and mutual respect, as well as promoting and protecting human rights consistent with international human rights instruments, the two sides agreed to hold the next round of the official human rights dialogue in Washington D.C..... [24]

In this Joint Statement, the U.S. and China effectively "agreed to disagree" about the controversial issue of human rights. By noting that "all countries should respect each other's choice of a development model," the statement put the Chinese conception of human rights—which emphasizes conferring "economic and social rights" that guarantee material well-being—on par with the fundamental political and individual freedoms found in Western countries. At the planned follow-up meeting on human rights, held in Washington during May 2010, U.S. and Chinese representatives "had a variety of discussions on a variety of topics, including religious freedom, labor rights, freedom of expression, rule of law, racial discrimination, and multilateral cooperation." According to a U.S. diplomat who participated, "The discussions ... were candid and constructive, including a range areas where we disagree." [25]

The United States can far more effectively promote democracy and human rights in China through a Framework Agreement that improves U.S.-China security relations. A new security relationship would decisively reduce the "U.S. threat" that China's leaders repeatedly invoke to justify their repression of political dissidents. China's leaders would no longer be able tap into deep nationalist resentment of foreign powers as a means of legitimating their harsh "domestic stability" measures. An end to the U.S. policy seeking to contain China, in the context of a Framework Agreement that stabilizes China's security relations with Taiwan, would also open China to the powerful and positive influence of Taiwan's and Hong Kong's political systems. The United States itself, no longer perceived within China as a foreign country seeking to undermine China's emergence as a world power, could instead be emulated for its constitutional commitment to fundamental political freedoms and democracy.

Finally, it is worthwhile pointing out how the economic provisions of a Framework Agreement could promote democracy and human rights in China on a longer term basis. As previously noted, China's market reforms and economic growth have led to a relaxation of some political controls, a richer flow of information through the internet, greater rule of law and the development of non-governmental organizations for advancing various social and economic interests. U.S. economic engagement with China has likely had some positive impact in promoting these changes, although "many of the factors that have contributed to human rights gains are not products of U.S. policy," as Professor Jacques deLisle of the University of Pennsylvania points out. Nevertheless, China's market reforms, economic expansion, economic engagement with the United States, growing middle class, development of NGOs and widespread use of the internet have not prevented China's leaders from repressing political dissidents, journalists, religious groups and ethnic minorities. The eleven year prison sentence meted out to reform leader Liu Xiaobo is manifest evidence of this fact.

A U.S.-China free trade agreement that drastically reduces trade barriers and fully opens China to foreign investment while fostering the flow of Chinese capital overseas, could have a more decisive impact on domestic political conditions than any other internal economic reforms that have thus far occurred. China's reforms to date have not likely been sufficiently robust to instigate the democratic political changes that some Western theorists and officials have expected or predicted. China's middle class may simply not have reached enough critical mass or become cognizant enough of its potential political power to demand rights and legal protections that would safeguard its economic and social gains. China's private sector as a whole may not have grown sufficiently large or strong enough to counter-balance the authority of a central government that is highly skilled in applying the tools of political repression. Economic activity may not have increased to a sufficient extent to foster widespread demand for the rule of law and public institutions that are free from Communist Party influence. A U.S.-China Free Trade Agreement and China's membership in a Trans-Pacific Partnership that brings about far deeper market reforms and a significant loosening of government control over the economy, however, could well have a decisive effect in increasing democracy, the rule of law and public accountability in China.

The advent of real constitutional government, the rule of law, human rights protections, an independent judiciary, a multiparty political system and freedom of expression will no doubt bring major domestic benefits to the Chinese people. These changes would also have great significance for

U.S.-China relations. By establishing a commonality of political values and norms between the two countries, they would lay the soundest basis for friendly relations between the United States and China for the indefinite future.

CHAPTER EIGHT

Realizing Japan's foreign policy goals

Ensuring the security of Japan is a central objective of American policy in the Asia Pacific. For more than half a century, U.S. troops, air and naval forces have protected Japan against foreign aggression. During the Cold War, the United States stood side by side with Japan in facing down the Soviet Union, which posed a major threat to the Japanese islands. Following the demise of the Soviet empire, the U.S.-Japan alliance continues to deter both China and North Korea from taking actions that could harm Japan's national security.

American military support has played an especially critical role because of the unique requirements of Japan's constitution, which the United States effectively dictated after the country's surrender in World War II. Under Article 9, Japan renounced "war as a sovereign right" as well as "the threat or use of force as means of settling international disputes."[1] The constitution allows Japan only to form "Self-Defense Forces," which cannot legally be used to carry out aggressive military actions overseas.

Until the mid-1990s, Japan's reliance on the United States enabled it to minimize defense expenditures and focus heavily on expanding economic activities. Japan's policy, set forth in the famous "Yoshida doctrine," defined the country as a preeminently civilian power that would channel its national ambitions into international commerce. Japan prospered during the postwar period with this foreign policy approach, which helped it become one of the largest global economic powers.

In the past 15 years, however, at the urging of the United States, Japan has significantly built up its military forces and loosened the constraints of its postwar constitution in order to become what is often termed a "normal nation." U.S. national strategy, since the Clinton administration, has regarded the U.S.-Japan alliance as the "lynchpin" of American power in the Asia Pacific. Japan has now acquired impressive power projection capabilities for deploying forces from the Asia Pacific to the Middle East. It has also endorsed new defense guidelines that give it an important operational role in support of U.S. forces in Asia and elsewhere.

With Japan's military buildup and China's concurrent military modernization, the tensions between Japan and China have noticeably increased since the mid-1990s. As discussed previously, Japan's military planners have devised a series of worst-case scenarios for confronting China over competing territorial claims to the uninhabited Senkaku/Diaoyu Islands in the East China Sea. More broadly, Japan's defense establishment worries about the growing power of China's navy, which could pose a future threat to the sea-borne commerce on which Japan depends for vital energy imports.

Despite friction over security and political issues, Japan's economic relations with China have boomed during the past decade.[2] Total Japan-China trade increased virtually every year and in 2011 reached a record high of $345 billion—an approximately 14 percent increase over 2010. Japan's imports from China in 2011 rose 20 percent to $183 billion, also setting a record. In 2009, China became the largest global export market for Japan, exceeding the United States for the first time.

Among the core issues now facing the Democratic Party of Japan (DPJ) which came to power in August 2009, are addressing Japan's strategic rivalry with China without harming economic relations, and defining Japan's optimal role in Asia. The DPJ victory ended the 50-year reign of Japan's Liberal Democratic Party (LDP) and initially signaled a strong desire to engage China in building a new "East Asian Community" modeled, in part, on the European Community, to increase regional prosperity. Newly elected Prime Minister Yukio Hatoyama declared that new frameworks for economic and security cooperation in Asia would be premised on the ongoing existence of the U.S.-Japan alliance, which would remain the "cornerstone of Japanese diplomatic policy."[3]

In spite of the DPJ's professed desire for Japan to conduct a more "autonomous foreign policy," the tenor of U.S.-China relations has a profound impact on Japan's ability to assert leadership in Asia or mitigate friction with its powerful neighbor. As Japan expert Mike Mochizuki of George Washington University notes, the U.S. plays the "central role" in shaping alliance relations with China, though Japanese policy toward China is also a "significant variable in the Sino-U.S. relationship."[4] The ability of Japan to alter its relations with China depends significantly on whether U.S.-China relations are conflictual, cooperative or somewhere in-between. Given the strength of the U.S.-Japan alliance, China largely regards Japan as a country that acts on behalf of the United States in strategic contexts, even though Japanese policy and diplomacy may proceed on a separate track.

Achieving an improvement in U.S.-China relations would greatly benefit Japan, in the years ahead. An easing of U.S. and Japanese tensions with China—brought about by a U.S.-China Framework Agreement—would help Japan realize a *modus vivendi* with China that lessens Sino-Japanese rivalry, increases Japan's security and enhances Tokyo's regional and global prominence. It would reinforce the value and benefits of the U.S.-Japan alliance while engendering greater U.S. support for Japan's efforts to create an East Asian Community (that includes the United States) and to establish a multilateral security mechanism in the region. A more prominent Japanese role in Asia, including its leadership in security and economic organizations, would significantly decrease the possibility that a rising China could seek to dominate the region. Japan could take additional comfort from the fact that its military buildup since the mid-1990s, undertaken with the ongoing assistance of the United States, would allow it to remain "far ahead" of China militarily for the foreseeable future, as Professor Richard Samuels of MIT suggests.[5]

The evolution of Japan's policy toward China

During the 1980s and early 1990s, Japan pursued a comprehensive engagement strategy toward China and provided considerable amounts of development assistance, largely for building infrastructure projects with the assistance of Japanese firms. These projects proved beneficial to China and profitable to Japan, drawing the countries closer together while also helping integrate China into the global economy.[6]

Engaging China through economic aid had the political goals of nurturing peaceful relations and encouraging China to participate in a stable regional order.[7] Japan aimed to advance its own interests by becoming China's leading trade partner and simultaneously obtaining diplomatic leverage it could use in bilateral negotiations. In the 1990s, Japan increasingly directed its assistance to energy and environmental projects. It mainly sought to develop China's indigenous sources of energy and help China remedy severe environmental degradation.

Japan's comprehensive engagement strategy with China was fully consistent with the Yoshida Doctrine of "mercantile realism" that Japan embraced in the postwar period, which called for Japan to adopt a low-cost military posture and pursue overseas commercial activities while relying heavily on the U.S. to guarantee Japan's security. China, South Korea and countries in Southeast Asia that suffered from Japanese wartime aggression were comfortable with this strategic approach. It seemed to ensure Japan would never again become a major military power that could threaten their own national security. In the words of an anonymous pundit, the

United States served as the "cork in the bottle" that would restrain Japan's rearmament.

With the collapse of the Soviet Union at the end of the Cold War, new tensions arose in the Japan-China relationship. When China conducted nuclear weapons tests in 1995 despite Japanese warnings, Japan suspended $75 million in development assistance. In 1996, after China sought to intimidate Taiwan with a series of missile tests near the island, negative attitudes toward China in Japanese public opinion mounted. Conflict between Japan and China over competing claims to ownership of the Senkaku/Diaoyu Islands and their surrounding seabed only reinforced these critical Japanese views. The consequence was, as Professor Michael Green of Georgetown University observes, "[I]n the space of only a few years, Japan's fundamental thinking on China shifted from a faith in economic interdependence to a reluctant realism." Japanese disappointment led to a realistic assessment that the strategy of economic engagement would have to be "tempered by a suspicion of Chinese motives, doubts about Japanese capabilities to effect change in China, and a desire to use multilateral and bilateral security networks to balance, and even contain, Chinese influence."[8]

Combining economic engagement, military hedging and support for regional organizations

Since the mid-1990s, Japanese policy toward China has been characterized by a mixture of economic engagement and military hedging as well as efforts to build economic and security structures for the region as a whole.

Security

With the encouragement of the United States, Japan has strengthened its military capabilities and more effectively integrated its forces within the U.S.-Japan alliance. Japan's policy shift, which accelerated during the administration of Prime Minister Junichiro Koizumi between 2001 and 2006, had several features:[9]

> *Narrowly interpreting the restrictions of Japan's Constitution to allow Japan's Self-Defense Forces to play a more robust role within the alliance*
>
> After the 9/11 attacks, Japan's national legislature (the Diet) approved deploying the country's forces to support the United States on a case-by-case basis. Legislative actions included sending

ships of the Maritime Self-Defense Force in November 2001 to the Indian Ocean to provide logistical support for the U.S. Navy as part of *Operation Enduring Freedom* (the war in Afghanistan); authorizing army troops and elements of the Air Self-Defense Force to participate in non-combat reconstruction missions in Iraq; and initiating a series of measures to provide the Self-Defense Forces with more mobility so they could be utilized both regionally and globally to assist U.S. military operations.

New interest in developing power projection capabilities

Among the items of military equipment that Japan purchased or plans to acquire are Boeing 767 tankers for in-flight refueling, helicopter carriers, precision-guided munitions and long-range transport aircraft.

Ending the prohibition in the Yoshida Doctrine against dispatching Japanese troops overseas

Since 1992, when Japan first sent troops in a non-combatant and logistical capacity to support a United Nations peacekeeping mission in Cambodia, Japan has joined a number of UN peace-keeping operations that required its forces to undertake dangerous duties.

A new willingness to consider the option of developing nuclear weapons in response to the nuclear threat from both North Korea and China, if Japan comes to doubt the credibility of the U.S. nuclear umbrella

A leader of Japan's Democratic Party, Ichiro Ozawa, told Chinese leaders during a 2002 visit to China that "[I]f Japan desires, it can possess thousands of nuclear warheads. Japan has enough plutonium in use at its nuclear power plants for three to four thousand .... If that should happen, we would not lose [to China] in terms of military strength."[10]

Ending the 1976 ban on sharing military technology

Beginning in 2003, Japan decided to acquire a ballistic missile defense system (BMD) from the United States and participate in joint-development of new BMD technology. According to the director of the U.S. Missile Defense Agency, the most important partner of the United States in BMD development has been Japan.[11]

Economy

While building up its Self-Defense Forces in response to China's increasing military capabilities, Japan has nevertheless pursued a policy of strong economic engagement with China over the last 15 years. Japanese businesses trade and invest extensively in China to reap the commercial advantages of China's rapid economic development. In many respects, the Japanese and Chinese economies are now complementary and interdependent. China's highest priority is economic modernization and this policy requires both Japanese capital and expertise. For its part, Japan needs markets for its manufactured goods and benefits greatly from establishing factories in China that produce goods for export and employ relatively low-cost Chinese labor. While Japan no longer provides China with government-to-government development aid in the form of low-interest loans and grants, its companies supply China with investment funds, capital equipment and cutting-edge commercial technology as well as education and training for Chinese workers. Japanese exports to China bolster Japan's economic growth while imports of industrial inputs from China make Japan's manufactured products more competitive internationally.

The importance of the China market to Japan is underscored by economic data. In 2009, as noted earlier, China became Japan's largest export market, surpassing the United States for the first time. Japan's imports from the U.S. have fallen by approximately 50 percent in the last ten years while its share of imports from China has effectively doubled.[12]

More broadly, many major economic interests of China and Japan today overlap. Both countries import large amounts of energy and both benefit from policies that promote resource development, encourage energy efficiency, identify new alternative energy sources and ensure the safety of international shipping routes. Both countries have an interest in ensuring a vibrant regional and global economy that will further their national economic prosperity.

The increasingly popular view in Japan that trade and investment in China creates a "win-win" situation for both countries was not evident ten to fifteen years ago. Especially in the late 1990s, many Japanese saw China as a major economic threat to their country. They feared a process of "hollowing," by which workers would lose their jobs to cheaper Chinese labor and, in turn, small and medium-sized Japanese firms would be destroyed by lower-priced Chinese imports.[13] When a number of Japanese firms moved their production operations to China, concerns about the hollowing of Japan's economy only mounted.

In recent years, however, Japan's business community has increasingly regarded China as an excellent economic opportunity rather than a burden or a threat. The rapidly growing importance of China as a market for Japanese exports, as well as the considerable profits made by Japanese firms in China that manufacture goods for export, have strengthened this view. To benefit as much as possible from the complementary nature of the two countries' economies, Japanese firms have taken a more strategic approach, as Naoko Munakata, a Senior Fellow at the Research Institute of Economy, Trade and Industry, explains:

> Japanese manufacturers have avoided head-to-head price competition with producers in China and shifted domestic production to higher value-added devices and materials. Successful companies have been able to compensate for hollowing-out of lower added operations and to boost overall sales through strong exports.[14]

In December 2011, the recently installed prime minister, Yoshihiko Noda, reached agreement with his Chinese counterpart, Premier Wen Jiabao, on beginning formal talks on a new free trade pact among China, Japan and South Korea.[15] Following their summit meeting, Premier Wen reaffirmed China's interest in closely coordinating with Japan to achieve "a new free trade zone and East Asian financial cooperation," including measures to issue bonds denominated in Japanese currency in mainland China.

Japan's decision to proceed with creating a new China-Japan-South Korea free trade zone balanced its earlier move to join the negotiations on a Trans-Pacific Partnership, which Prime Minister Noda announced in November 2011, just before attending the APEC summit in Honolulu. The Japanese approach stood in stark contrast to the policy of the U.S. administration to exclude China from the current TPP negotiations. A *Yomiuri Shimbun* editorial reflects the overall thinking behind Tokyo's decision-making:

> Japan's announcement of its intention to join the TPP negotiations is likely to make more countries interested in the pact and encourage them to ask to be part of it. The expansion of the European sovereign debt crisis has left the future of the global economy shrouded in uncertainty. There are growing hopes that the Asia-Pacific region, seen as a growth center, will strengthen economic cooperation and serve as a locomotive for the world economy .... *In light of this, it is indispensable for Japan, which stands with the United States, to also advance strategic trade policy with China.*[16]

Regional multilateral diplomacy

Japan has made concerted efforts in the last fifteen years to build regional economic and security structures in Asia. These multilateral organizations, involving a number of other Asian countries, have two overall aims:

fostering economic prosperity by increasing trade and investment on a regional basis; and addressing disputes concerning political, economic and security issues.

Japan's efforts have special significance as a response to the rise of China. Japan has worked to strengthen regional organizations that can influence Chinese policy by imposing international norms of conduct on Beijing and by increasing the political leverage Japan exercises over China and North Korea.[17] Leading Chinese scholars credit Japan with overcoming China's resistance to becoming involved in regional multilateral organizations in the late 1990s and persuading China to actively embrace these organizations as an effective means of advancing Chinese interests.

In a larger sense, Japan's multilateralism has entailed a constructive, low-key approach, which helped restore its prestige and legitimacy in Asia as a means of overcoming the legacy of aggression during World War II. This approach also counters the criticism, heard frequently in the past, that Japan is so self-absorbed with internal issues that it cares little for regional concerns. Engagement of this kind has enabled Japan's leaders to reduce political opposition at home to the country taking a more prominent role in international affairs.

The future direction of Japanese foreign policy

Largely in response to the rise of China, Japan today faces a series of critical choices about how best to achieve its core foreign policy goals of maintaining regional stability; enhancing Japanese and Asian economic prosperity; continuing the U.S.-Japan alliance as the cornerstone of Japan's security posture; and asserting greater Japanese leadership within new multilateral frameworks in East Asia.

Some Japanese politicians who are closely aligned with the Liberal Democratic Party (LDP) that ruled Japan for more than 50 years until its defeat in August 2009, have focused heavily on accelerating Japan's military buildup. One LDP faction sees a more muscular Japan as an instrument of American military power. It seeks to do everything possible to strengthen Japan's operational capabilities to carry out alliance objectives in Asia and beyond. Another LDP faction favors a greater buildup of Japan's military forces to achieve a more traditional goal—enabling Japan to obtain great power status. This group would like to acquire American technology, equipment and training, but objects to Japan remaining operationally subordinate to the United States. It believes that once Japan obtains the military wherewithal, the country should assert Japan's autonomy as a major independent power, both regionally and globally.

The current government which is led by the Democratic Party of

Japan (DPJ) has pursued a more balanced approach toward achieving the country's foreign policy goals. The DPJ strongly supports the modernization of Japan's military forces. But it has placed far more emphasis than the LDP on Japan obtaining greater "political and economic independence" by leading East Asia toward "regional integration." It advocates a new regional security framework as a means of significantly improving Japan's relations with China and South Korea. It aims to reduce and, if possible, end the strategic rivalry between China and Japan.

While the DPJ has endorsed the U.S.-Japan alliance as the basis for "Japanese diplomatic policy," it moved quickly after the August 2009 election to curtail several unpopular military commitments that prior LDP governments made to the United States.[18] In mid-October 2009, for instance, then Prime Minister Hatoyama ended an eight-year mission of Japan's Maritime Self-Defense Force for refueling U.S. Navy vessels in the Indian Ocean, in support of military operations in Afghanistan. Shortly thereafter, Japan provided a $5 billion package of aid for Afghanistan to strengthen education, vocational training and infrastructure throughout the country.

In late October 2009, Hatoyama announced that Japan would reassess a 2006 agreement on the basing of U.S. forces on the island of Okinawa, a Japanese territory. This decision was part of a larger effort by the Democratic Party to bring greater "equality" to the U.S.-Japan alliance. The prime minister called for a "comprehensive review" of prior alliance agreements, including those requiring Japan to pay billions of dollars to the United States in "host nation support," and those limiting legal jurisdiction over U.S. troops that commit crimes on Japanese territory.

Overall, the DPJ government has adopted a different strategy for achieving Japan's major foreign policy goals than its LDP predecessors. That strategy entails strong endorsement of the U.S.-Japan alliance but is less concerned with playing a global support role for American military operations. It places greater emphasis on diplomatically engaging China through regional multilateral frameworks. Finally, it seeks to assert greater Japanese leadership and autonomy by realizing the vision of an East Asian Community.

Reducing Sino-Japanese rivalry

Under the DPJ-led government, Japan regards adjusting to the rise of China by bolstering multilateral structures in East Asia as a critical means of advancing the country's national interests. To succeed, however, Japan must overcome several major challenges and obtain the support of the United States.

The issue of history

For decades, Japan's wartime history of invading and occupying China has figured as a divisive factor in Sino-Japanese relations. The political issue has been whether Japan sufficiently acknowledged and expressed contrition for aggression and atrocities committed by its armed forces during World War II and the earlier colonial period. In the eyes of many Chinese, Japan's repeated and carefully negotiated official apologies have been insincere. They believe Japan still has not taken responsibility for the historic crimes it committed and suppresses information about its military occupation in school textbooks and other official publications.

Former Chinese president Jiang Zemin expressed China's view of the history issue and its larger significance during a state visit to South Korea in 1995, when he said, "[W]e must be vigilant against a Japanese militarist minority. Although a half century has passed since the end of a war between China and Japan, some Japanese politicians still have a wrong historical view."[19]

As China's potential threat to Japan began to appear more dangerous, since the mid-1990s, there has also been growing Japanese impatience and anger with China for frequently demanding apologies and condemning Japan's wartime conduct. The insistence by former Japanese Prime Minister Koizumi on making annual visits between 2001 and 2006 to the Yasukuni Shrine—which honors Japan's war dead including more than 1,000 convicted war criminals and 14 so-called "Class A" war criminals—inflamed Chinese public opinion. Koizumi's actions seriously disrupted the normal exchange of visits by leaders of the two countries, including the commemoration of two important events marking Sino-Japanese reconciliation—the twenty-fifth anniversary of the 1978 bilateral Peace and Friendship Treaty and the thirtieth anniversary of 1972 Sino-Japanese normalization of diplomatic relations. Following Koizumi's visits to Yasukuni shrine, Chinese commentators frequently underscored the danger that "militaristic elements" could emerge in Japan and lead the country toward new aggression in Asia.[20]

Public animosity toward Beijing spiked in 2005 when widespread anti-Japanese riots broke out in China over the "history issue," following reports of new Japanese textbooks minimizing the country's wartime atrocities.[21] Shortly thereafter, less than 40 percent of Japanese people expressed a positive view of China in public opinion polls, compared to more than 80 percent who viewed China favorably during the 1980s.

When Prime Minister Koizumi's successor, Shinzo Abe, took power in 2006, he attempted once again to address differences with China during an early visit to Beijing. Chinese Premier Wen Jiabao reciprocated in 2007 with a state visit and a well-received address to the Japanese Diet.[22] Abe was successful in establishing a "joint history project," co-led by Japanese and Chinese scholars, to investigate painful events during Japan's occupation of China, as a means of laying the groundwork for reconciliation.

Energy and territorial disputes

The ongoing dispute over sovereignty of the Senkaku/Diaoyu Islands in the East China Sea as well as the surrounding energy-rich seabed continues to complicate Sino-Japanese relations. After World War II, the U.S. administered the islands as part of the territory of Okinawa, which reverted to Japan in 1972. China argues, however, that until 1945, Taiwan administered the islands and they are historically part of China, dating back to the fifteenth-century Ming Dynasty. Chinese leader Deng Xiaoping sought to defer the issue when he declared in 1978 that "the next generation" should solve the problem. But under pressure to exploit untapped oil deposits near the islands, Beijing announced in 1992 that the islands were Chinese territory.

Japanese rightists subsequently carried out a series of unauthorized landings on the islands to claim them for Japan. In 2004, Japan demanded an apology from China after a nuclear-powered submarine entered the area and China diplomatically acknowledged its error. In 2005, the *Asahi Shimbun* reported that Japan's Self-Defense Forces were carrying out a highly classified study of how to respond to further Chinese incursions.[23] The study hypothesized that if Chinese forces landed on the islands, Japan would respond with an air and naval operation leading up to a counter-attack by ground forces to retake the territory.

After considerable difficulty, China and Japan finally reached a cooperation and joint exploration agreement in June 2008 on the status of the islands and the 200-mile exclusive economic zone surrounding them.[24] The agreement called for the East China Sea to be a "sea of peace, cooperation and friendship" and described procedures for pursuing joint energy exploration through "mutual agreement." An expert with the Chinese Academy of Social Sciences, Liu Nanlai, commented at the time that "[T]he agreement [between the two countries] is flexible and pragmatic without prejudicing their respective legal positions."

Less than two years after the signing of this pact, however, Japan's foreign minister issued a warning in January 2010 that Japan might take undefined "measures" if China proceeded with development of a gas field within the joint exploration area around the islands. According to news accounts, Japan feared China would illicitly siphon off gas from the Japanese side.[25] An exchange of diplomatic notes calmed tensions for a time by affirming that the dispute should be handled through consultations on joint exploration under the June 2008 agreement.

Conflict again erupted over the Senkaku/Diaoyu Islands in September 2010, when the Japanese Coast Guard arrested a Chinese trawler captain intruding into claimed Japanese territory and the encounter escalated to a major diplomatic crisis.[26] The deeply seated fears on both sides are revealed in the increasingly harsh official statements and actions as well as public expressions of anger that occurred.

Following the arrest of the Chinese captain for "obstructing officers on duty," China announced that Japan had "seriously damaged Sino-Japan bilateral relations." China then suspended all high-level exchanges with Japan and a Foreign Ministry spokesperson ominously threatened unspecified future action: "We demand the Japanese side immediately release the Chinese captain unconditionally. If the Japanese side clings obstinately to its course, making mistake upon mistake, then China will take strong countermeasures and Japan will bear the consequences." China backed up its rhetoric with what appeared to be an officially sanctioned embargo on the export to Japan of "rare earths," metals crucial to Japan's electronics and automobile industries.

Japan's initial arrest of the trawler captain showed how seriously it objected to the incursion of Chinese vessels into claimed Japanese territory. On the Japanese side, one leading newspaper warned that "if China thinks that by taking a strong stance that Japan will just roll over, then it is mistaken." In China, nationalists demonstrated in front of Japanese schools and diplomatic missions, and there were mass cancellations of trips to Japan by Chinese tourists. As the political furor in both countries mounted, Japanese diplomats wisely sought to contain the crisis. Prosecutors in charge of the case suspended their investigation and released the trawler captain, citing diplomatic considerations.

In the aftermath, however, Japan's foreign minister, Seiji Maehara, reasserted Japan's right to bring the captain to trial because the disputed islands were an "integral part of Japanese territory." He denied the validity of competing Chinese claims in bluntly declaring that "[T]erritorial issues do not exist in this region." Not surprisingly, Chinese analysts saw the situation differently. The director of the Center for Security Strategy at Beijing University of Aeronautics and Astronautics, Wang Xiangsu, commented that, "Japan is trying to get China to eat the bitter fruit .... They want China to accept the fact that they control the islands."

Far from achieving a resolution of the territorial conflict over the Senkaku/Diaoyu Islands, the September 2010 incident revealed just how determined both governments are to assert their overlapping claims, the cooperation and joint exploration agreement of two years earlier notwithstanding. Just below the surface of this dispute, of course, are Japan's fears of China's growing naval power and China's fears of containment by U.S. and Japanese military forces. To drive home the reality of their overwhelming superiority, the United States and Japan conducted a joint military exercise in the East China Sea in early December 2010 involving about 60 vessels including the nuclear-powered aircraft carrier *George Washington*, 400 planes and 44,000 troops. The exercise featured a simulated retaking of one of the Senkaku/Diaoyu Islands that had been "seized by hostile forces."

A year after the divisive trawler incident, encounters between Chinese and Japanese vessels continued to occur, though none of them fortunately triggered a new crisis.[27] A brief review of the record reveals the following:

> August 2011: Two Chinese Maritime Enforcement Agency ships enter claimed Japanese waters near the Senkaku/Diaoyu Islands, leading to a protest by Japan's foreign minister.

> September 2011: A Japanese Coast Guard aircraft identifies a Chinese maritime research ship in Japan's "exclusive economic zone" near the Senkaku/Diaoyu, leading to a warning that the Chinese vessel is operating in an unauthorized area.

> October 2011: Two Chinese Fisheries Patrol ships maneuver in the "contiguous zone" near the Senkaku/Diaoyu but do not enter Japanese waters after being challenged by a Japanese patrol boat.

> November 2011: A Japanese Coast Guard vessel inspects a Chinese fishing boat operating in claimed Japanese waters. The Coast Guard arrests the captain and releases him three days later, after the captain pays a hefty fine. China terms the matter a "regular fisheries case."

> December 2011: Japanese Coast Guard aircraft identify a Chinese maritime research ship in an unauthorized area and issue two warnings before the Chinese vessel responds appropriately.

The continuing encounters between China and Japan in the East China Sea one year or more after the September 2010 crisis demonstrate the issue remains unresolved and is capable of escalating quickly to a level that could draw Japan and the United States into a serious military confrontation with China.

Sino-Japanese naval competition

Over the last decade, Japan and China have strengthened their naval capabilities. Their efforts to modernize naval weapons systems as well as enlarge the size and versatility of their fleets could potentially stoke a serious naval rivalry in the future. Not surprisingly, pressure for naval expansion arises from the desire of both countries to protect vital sea lanes through which they receive critical energy supplies. Both are heavily dependent on oil and gas that arrive by ocean-going tankers from the Middle East. Japan-based scholar Leszek Buszynski describes the Chinese perspective:

> China's escalating dependence upon oil imports has created an obsession with the security of its sea lanes, particularly the Malacca Straits through

which an estimated 80 percent of its oil is shipped. China currently imports around 47 percent of its oil ... ; by 2020, imports are expected to increase by 63 percent. As the Chinese economy grows, it becomes more vulnerable to external disruption, particularly in Southeast Asia and the Indian Ocean. For this reason, extended sea lane protection is likely to become a major priority for the Chinese navy in the future.[28]

Despite China's dependence on overseas energy, it now has a relatively limited ability to protect the sea lanes it relies on for vital energy shipments. While China has purchased a number of Russian submarines and developed new submarine classes of its own, it would need much more robust long-range power projection capabilities to protect oil shipments moving from the Indian Ocean through the Malacca straits. To date, China has hesitated to build a "blue water" fleet of this kind, both for reasons of cost and to avoid stimulating a naval arms race with Japan.

The pressing reality for Japan is that it is dependent on Middle East sources for 87 percent of its energy needs and understandably fears a more powerful Chinese Navy could threaten the sea lanes through which vital energy shipments pass. Japan has expanded its own naval capabilities to defend these sea lanes, alongside the United States, as well as to develop a sea-based capability for countering North Korean missiles. Japan currently possesses a fleet of six Aegis anti-ballistic missile-equipped destroyers, more than three dozen guided-missile destroyers, 16 conventional submarines and a helicopter carrier. Following the September 2010 crisis with China, Japan approved plans to increase the current number of submarines from 16 to 22 and strengthen its Aegis destroyer fleet.

Nevertheless, like China, Japan has been reluctant to broadly expand its maritime force and develop a blue water navy with long-range capability.[29] Doing so would both create a highly contentious domestic political issue by potentially violating the constitutional limit on Japan's Self-Defense Forces while aggravating the naval rivalry with China.

Currently, Japan's "superior naval and air capabilities" give it sufficient capability to deter any conventional military threats from China, as Professor Mike Mochizuki of George Washington University points out, while the U.S. nuclear umbrella protects Japan against nuclear threats.[30] But there is a real risk that China and Japan will come to see expanding their naval forces as a normal and necessary response to the problem of sea lane insecurity due to both countries' heavy dependence on overseas energy imports. In the words of Leszek Buszynski,

[A]s both countries develop their [naval] capabilities to achieve what they both consider to be a normal defense posture for their security, an action-reaction effect is accentuated. The action of one becomes a reason and a justification for the further expansion of capabilities of the other .... Sino-Japanese naval rivalry would indeed be an unsettling factor for the region with the potential to derail the impressive regional integration that has taken place in East Asia over the past decade. [31]

The thinking behind Japan's current policy toward China

Leading Japanese diplomatic strategists, including former Deputy Foreign Minister Hitoshi Tanaka and Keio University Professor Yoshihide Soeya, have laid out policy proposals that underlie much of the DPJ's views of Japan's future role in Asia. To understand the government's interest in improving relations with Japan's neighbors, especially China, and in promoting regional cooperation, it is valuable to understand the visions offered by these experts.

Beginning in March 2006, when Japan-China relations hit a postwar low, Tanaka called for a "grand bargain" between the two countries:

> The single most important and urgent objective of Japanese policy-makers should be to achieve a 'grand bargain' with China that places existing issues between the two nations in the context of a mutually acknowledged need to build healthier bilateral ties. The goal would be to create a win-win framework for future relations that constructively addresses existing issues between the two countries .... A grand bargain between China and Japan, the two most powerful nations in East Asia, is a prerequisite for creating healthy bilateral ties and consolidating long-term peace and stability in the region. Nevertheless, policymakers must also acknowledge that Japan and China are very different countries with different political systems, cultures, values, and visions for the region. Consequently, Japan must proactively engage China through multilateral frameworks as much as possible.[32]

In several noteworthy articles, Tanaka outlined the major elements of a "grand bargain."[33] First, Japan should encourage China to take a more active role in international institutions while obtaining its support for permanent Japanese membership on the UN Security Council in a "mutual acknowledgement of the positive contributions that both nations can make to global governance." Second, China and Japan should develop much deeper bilateral cooperation on the critical issues of energy security and energy efficiency, building on Japan's considerable experience with severe energy shortages (such as the "oil shock" of the 1970s) as well as environmental protection. And lastly, the two countries should work together to build a "regional architecture" with economic and security dimensions "that will be integral to ensuring long-term peace and prosperity in East Asia."

The new regional framework would have several overall components, according to Tanaka: a strategic dialogue among Japan, China and the United States to promote confidence-building and transparency on military activities; an economic partnership within a new "East Asian Community" to further regional economic development and prosperity; and a multilateral security forum that would promote cooperation in East Asia by addressing non-traditional security issues of concern to all countries – such as infectious diseases, natural disasters, nuclear proliferation, environmental degradation, maritime piracy and human trafficking. The greater stability created through "cooperative countermeasures" to eliminate broad security threats would support continued economic growth.

Tanaka makes it clear that while Japan asserts leadership to strengthen Asian stability, it should rely on the U.S.-Japan alliance as a "hedge against uncertainty" and as a "security guarantee." He also underscores that the new regional security framework Japan seeks should complement, not supplant, the ongoing military alliance with the United States. Finally, he points out that China's active involvement in building new regional security and economic institutions will help ensure its strong support for East Asian stability and prosperity in the future.

Professor Yoshihide Soeya, another leading diplomatic strategist, lays out his vision of Japan as a more autonomous "middle power" in Asia based on the continuation of the U.S.-Japan alliance:

> To me, the important task for Japan is to construct its own 'autonomous' strategy, not in the traditional sense expected from an independent strategic player, but an independent, autonomous strategy premised on the alliance with the U.S. To me, this is a typical middle power strategy, like Australia, like Canada or like South Korea .... Diplomatically speaking, the central focus of such middle power strategy should be geared toward cultivating a middle ground between the U.S. and China, two truly strategic players in the region and the world. The task for Japan, to me, is to create a solid infrastructure, so to speak, of an East Asian regional order between the U.S. and China.[34]

By embracing its status as a "middle power" and acting more independently in Asia, Soeya believes Japan can effectively focus its energies on creating a new East Asian order. Making common cause with other middle powers like Australia, South Korea and the Association of Southeast Asian Nations (ASEAN), while treating China as a partner and not a rival, would allow Japan to lead in constructing economic and security frameworks that bring greater regional stability and economic growth. Japan's continuing alliance with the U.S. would assure other Asian countries that Japan does not seek the military capabilities of a great power under the guise of becoming a "normal nation."

Soeya's arguments reflect an underlying premise that Japan's future well-being depends heavily on playing a leading diplomatic leadership role within an economically dynamic Asia that is stable and at peace. In keeping with this vision, Japan's hard military power should and will remain limited for the foreseeable future, consistent with Japan's constitutional restraints.

Also essential for Japan is "avoiding political rivalry [with China] in the course of Asia's growth and concentrating limited diplomatic resources on Asia's integration and development," as Professor Ryo Sahashi of Kanagawa University observes.[35] By successfully integrating China into the regional and international economic order, Japan will become a "stabilizer" between the U.S. and China. In this situation, Japan would also feel less threatened by closer U.S.-China relations.

Japan's current foreign policy shows the additional influence of Dr. Yoichi Funabashi, a respected diplomatic thinker and former editor-in-chief of *Asahi Shimbun*, who stresses that the U.S.-Japan alliance should acquire new mutual goals beyond deterring and countering possible aggression by China or North Korea. Such aims should include "securing a stable Japan-China relationship, encouraging policy dialogue among Japan, the United States, and China, and constructing 'maritime peace' centered on those same three nations" to create stable relations with China and in the region as a whole. Funabashi's emphasis on "maritime peace" underscores Japan's security concern about potential vulnerability to a future Chinese naval threat and the desire to avoid a conflict over the Senkaku/Diaoyu Islands along with the energy-rich seabed surrounding them. He suggests that a U.S.-China-Japan dialogue could lead these countries to cooperate in jointly policing East Asia's sea lanes through which vital energy supplies are transported.

Dr. Funabashi also highlights the importance that the alliance should give to Japan's inherent strength as a "global civilian power."[37] In this view, Japan's greatest asset is not its military prowess, but rather the economic and technological capabilities which have propelled it, in past decades, to become a leading global economy. Japan can best support the U.S.-Japan alliance and play an international leadership role by emphasizing "humanitarian and disaster relief assistance; peace-building and peacekeeping; economic development for nation-building; nuclear nonproliferation and nuclear disarmament ... and global environment protection with an eye toward creating a low-carbon society."[36]

Assessing Japan's foreign policy

Japan's foreign policy under a government led by the Democratic Party is best understood as a politically centrist response to the security and economic challenges that Japan now faces. Among Japan's greatest assets, on the security side, are the alliance with the United States, highly capable Self-Defense Forces which have been extensively modernized over the past 15 years, and increasing mastery of cutting-edge defense technologies. Japan now seeks to leverage all these assets to strengthen the country's security for the foreseeable future. As indicated, it does not believe that relying exclusively on an accelerated military buildup—enabling Japan to acquire "great power" status—is the best way to assert Japanese leadership, deal with China, or create greater stability in East Asia. These three goals are best achieved, as Dr. Funabashi described, on the foundation of the U.S.-Japan alliance and Japan's own self-defense capabilities by ensuring Japan takes a leading role in establishing new economic and security organizations in Asia while strengthening cooperation with China.

The regional organizations are a means of "taming" China's growing power in a non-confrontational way.[38] They aim to encourage China to act responsibly in international affairs and abide by norms of conduct that are acceptable to other countries in the region. A China that works within accepted norms and institutional structures to advance its interests will be a far better neighbor than a China that believes it must act unilaterally to achieve its national objectives.

The benefits from bilateral cooperation are self-evident. If Japan and China effectively reduce energy insecurity and prevent environmental degradation for mutual benefit, it will significantly help to reduce their rivalry. Achieving concrete "win-win" solutions will reinforce their policies of cooperation and create a "virtuous cycle." Moreover, the ongoing practice of regular trilateral consultations among China, Japan and the United States that Japan now seeks will prove these countries can work together successfully for the greater good of the region.

To reiterate an important point, Japan's current foreign policy reflects the considered view that incessantly building up Japan's military forces in an arms race with China, and perpetuating a long-lasting rivalry is not good for Japan. A far better approach is to work to shape China's development in ways conducive to regional stability because this will best advance Japan's security and prosperity. With the ongoing support of the U.S.-Japan alliance, Japan can retain the confidence that it will have the wherewithal to defend itself, should that ever become necessary.

Writing in 2007, well before the Democratic Party took power, Professor Richard Samuels of MIT made this prescient observation on the advent of Japan's "middle power" strategy:

No significant party in the Japanese security discourse refuses to accept the legitimacy of the [Japanese Self Defense Forces]. All agree, moreover, that China, with its great power ambitions, needs to be integrated peacefully and that a non-democratic China is inimical to Japanese interests. Thus, it seems at least plausible that the 'middle power' road—amended to allow a fuller hedge against Chinese power and U.S. decline—will be an attractive successor to the Yoshida Doctrine. This new consensus is likely to resemble Goldilocks' preferences: Japan's relationships with the United States and China will be neither too hot nor too cold, and its posture in the region will be neither too big, nor too small.[39]

U.S. responses

Harsh U.S. criticism of Japan

After taking office in 2009, Prime Minister Hatoyama initially made good on his campaign promises to reduce the "unequal" burden that Japan shoulders in its military alliance with the United States. As noted earlier, he ended the Maritime Self-Defense Force mission of refueling U.S. Navy vessels to support U.S. forces in Afghanistan, while balancing this with a $5 billion contribution of aid for Afghan development, and most significantly, proposed a "comprehensive review" of basing arrangements for U.S. forces in Japan and Okinawa in particular. The extent of U.S. deployments in Okinawa and the issue of Japan's "host nation support" are well described by George Packard, former dean of the Johns Hopkins' School of Advanced International Studies:

> The size and impact of the U.S. military footprint in Japan today is almost surely going to be a bone of contention in the months and years ahead. There are still some 85 facilities housing 44,850 U.S. military personnel and 44,289 dependents. Close to 75 percent of the troops are based in Okinawa, an island a little less than one-third the size of Long Island.[40]

The U.S. response to Hatoyama's early proposals was not long in coming. In late October 2009, Secretary of Defense Robert Gates made a two-day visit to Japan and demanded the new government follow through quickly on the Bush-era deal for moving the Marine air base at Futenma to a less densely populated location on the island. He reportedly gave a near-term deadline for Prime Minister Hatoyama to make a public commitment, prior to President Obama's scheduled visit. Gates' bluntness extended to protocol—he rejected the usual informal dinner with top Japanese defense officials and even turned down a ceremonial salute by honor guards of the Self-Defense Forces. According to the Washington-based journalist Ayako Doi, "[A]ll that stunned the Japanese, and blew away any warm and fuzzy feelings they had about the Obama administration."[41]

In the following months, U.S. officials and former officials with close ties to the Pentagon continued to pressure Japan over Futenma. U.S. Ambassador to Japan John Roos upped the ante by declaring in late January 2010 that "Okinawa is becoming not less but more important for [the] defense of Japan and maintaining peace in this region."[42] Richard Lawless, former Bush administration deputy under-secretary of defense for Asian and Pacific security affairs, publicly floated the threat of curtailing the U.S. commitment to Japan's defense:

> This point cannot be stressed enough. From the U.S. perspective, Japan's inability and unwillingness to execute the keystone element of the realignment—the agreed upon Futenma relocation—will unavoidably compel Washington to re-examine our entire forward basing strategy in the Pacific writ large .... This re-examination will necessarily include our force posture in Japan, which could very well have an impact on our ability to sustain our commitments to the alliance.[43]

Michael Finnegan, a former Department of Defense military planner and senior research associate at the National Bureau of Asian Research, reinforced Lawless's comments:

> Crisis is too strong a word at this time. However, Japan's inability to carry out the realignment will likely cause a significant and perhaps fundamental shift in the U.S. approach to Japan and the alliance relationship. Japan should bear in mind the important reality that the alliance—particularly the role played by U.S. forces stationed in Japan and in the region—deters aggression against Japan. Japan's failure to meet its basing commitments will naturally have a detrimental effect on the relationship, hurting the interests of both nations.[44]

United States pressure on Japan over a period of several months had a significant political impact. In late May 2010, Prime Minister Hatoyama reversed his campaign pledge on Okinawa and, at U.S. insistence, agreed to uphold the 2006 pact regarding Futenma. This decision ignited angry feelings of betrayal in Okinawa and after Hatoyama's popularity throughout Japan plummeted below 20 percent (from an earlier high of 75 percent when he took office), the prime minister resigned.

The Futenma issue remained unmitigated through April 2012, when the U.S. and Japan announced an interim agreement that did not directly address the relocation of the Marine air base. Under the agreement, the

U.S. indicated it would move 9,000 marines from Okinawa to Guam and other U.S. bases by 2014, while keeping intact the earlier plan to build a new base on another part of the island. The new agreement "decoupled" the question of reducing the U.S. troop presence in Okinawa from the issue of base relocation. It helped the Japanese government show progress in alleviating the military burden on local residents. U.S. officials called the agreement "a resounding victory for our bilateral alliance" and emphasized that "the ability to rotate forces along a wider belt in the Pacific would give the [U.S.] military greater agility *in countering potential Chinese expansion* while not diminishing deterrence on the Korean peninsula."[45]

Looking back to the confrontations between U.S. and Japanese officials in 2009 and 2010 that led to Hatoyama's resignation, it is to some extent understandable that Secretary of Defense Gates, Ambassador Roos, and some former senior Pentagon officials felt offended by a possible revision of the realignment of forces agreement on Okinawa. After all, the two governments carefully negotiated and approved this agreement just a few years earlier, during the Bush administration. U.S. frustration with Japan's policy shift reflects, in part, the difficulty and awkwardness of revamping complicated military deployments in the Asia Pacific and is exacerbated by American inter-service rivalries.[46] In the view of Dr. George Packard, the U.S. Marine Corps has a particularly strong "proprietary attitude" toward the Futenma base, after suffering terrible losses in the battle for Okinawa during World War II.

On another level, however, it was ill-advised for current and former U.S. officials to effectively accuse Japan of undermining the alliance because Tokyo exhibited sensitivity to domestic opinion over a controversial deployment. The American accusation, coupled with implied and explicit threats to pull back its forces now defending Japan, shows deep disrespect for that nation's democratic system. It also ignores the views of Japan's ruling party and serious Japanese strategic thinkers who seek to advance their country's security and prosperity at a time of profound historic change in the region. Japan's vision of its future regional and global role is clearly built on the foundation of the ongoing U.S.-Japan alliance. If the United States intends to preserve and revitalize this alliance, it should accept and implement Japanese preferences rather than risk a schism based on narrowly conceived views of American interests.

In July 2010, following Hatoyama's resignation, Japan experts Sheila Smith of the Council on Foreign Relations and Yuki Tatsumi of the Stimson Center in Washington offered these observations on the Okinawa controversy that remain true today:

> It is time to end the corrosive effect this haggling over Futenma has had on our alliance. Fourteen years ago, [U.S. and Japanese leaders] made a promise to the people of Okinawa to close Futenma; ten prime ministers

and three presidents later, that promise remains unfulfilled. Our publics
are increasingly frustrated with a lack of resolution, and until Futenma
is closed, the alliance risks being held hostage to the inequity of concentrating so many U.S. military bases on Okinawa. (Sheila Smith)

[Futenma] keeps the [Japanese and American] governments from
discussing a broader range of common security concerns ... [T]he world
needs an economically and politically strong Japan to work with the
United States to address a wide range of global challenges .... (Yuki
Tatsumi)[47]

A better U.S. approach

The United States should support Japan's evolving foreign policy under the
DPJ government for two reasons – it is good for Japan and it is good for
America. As Japan's longstanding and closest partner, the U.S. should be
enlightened enough to accept the greater autonomy and independence of
Japan, both regionally and globally.

There are some Americans, of course, who feel uncomfortable unless
Japan acquiesces to the decisions of its more powerful partner. They tend
to believe that a Japan which does America's bidding is the essence of the
U.S.-Japan alliance. A far better view is that the U.S. should appreciate
a more independent Japanese foreign policy as the sign of a mature ally
that understands its identity, takes pride in its national values and strives
to make major contributions to peace and prosperity, both regionally and
globally.

There is another, more self-interested reason to support Japan's foreign
policy – a more autonomous, independent Japan that pursues a middle
power strategy built on the U.S.-Japan alliance will strengthen and revitalize
its relationship with the United States. But greater U.S.-Japan cooperation
can only proceed apace if the U.S. relieves some burdens imposed by the
security alliance.

Dr. George Packard has called for the U.S. to relieve these burdens as a
means of shoring up the overall relationship:

The U.S. government should respect Japan's desire to reduce the U.S.
military presence on its territory, as it has respected the same desire on
the part of Germany, South Korea, and the Philippines. It should be
willing to renegotiate the agreement that governs the presence of U.S.
troops in Japan, which to some is redolent of nineteenth-century asser-
tions of extraterritoriality. It should be aware that, at the end of the day,
Japanese voters will determine the future course of the alliance. Above
all, U.S. negotiators should start with the premise that the security treaty

with Japan, important as it is, is only part of a larger partnership between two of the world's greatest democracies and economies. Washington stands to gain far more by working with Tokyo on the environment, health issues, human rights, the nonproliferation of nuclear weapons, and counterterrorism.[48]

Fully settling the dispute over the relocation of the U.S. Marines base to the satisfaction of Japan also strengthens Japan's commitment to its military obligations under the alliance. An agreement of this kind would demonstrate America's respect for Japanese public opinion and the citizens of Okinawa, who daily bear the serious inconvenience of living next door to an active air base. It is shortsighted for the U.S. to push hard for basing rights that run up against the Japanese government's policy of creating greater equality in the alliance and more effectively asserting Japanese views.

In the same vein, the United States should strongly support Japan's policy of exerting leadership in Asia through fostering new regional frameworks. This policy is deeply rooted in a longstanding Japanese interest in multilateralism as a means of shaping China's development while exerting Japan's own foreign policy independence. As Japan expert Michael Green of Georgetown University notes:

[Multilateralism] remains at the center of Japan's diplomacy—as it should. Regional and global institutions are becoming important components of Japan's China policy, because these institutions shape Chinese norms of international behavior and increase Tokyo's leverage on Beijing .... In addition, declining expectations of Japanese economic power are giving way to new calls for Japan to compensate by demonstrating more political initiative in multilateral institutions .... The United States should support Japan's aspirations to play a larger role in multilateral organizations and forums .... Encouraging and supporting Japan's initiative in multilateral institutions can contribute to a more balanced, and therefore healthier and more sustainable U.S.-Japan security alliance.[49]

It is highly likely that more effective regional frameworks in Asia will help manage and resolve disputes between Japan and China in the future. Preventing these disputes from getting out of hand and becoming a major source of regional instability is very much in the interest of the United States. As a democracy, market economy and country that prizes the rule of law, Japan's ability to shape the norms of new regional security and economic frameworks will create structures that are congruent with American norms and values.

Japan and improved U.S.-China relations

There are some in Japan who fear an improvement in U.S.-China relations. They believe that reconciliation between the United States and China would downgrade the importance of Japan in American eyes and occur at Japan's expense. People who think this way argue that Japan's importance and prestige in Asia is based on its role as the leading U.S. ally in deterring Chinese aggression. From their standpoint, a resolution of U.S. strategic differences with China would sharply diminish the importance of Japan since it would markedly reduce the likelihood of a future military confrontation between the U.S. and China.

The government of Japan is unlikely to give in to these fears, however, because an improvement in U.S.-China relations is fully consistent with the vision set forth by the current government and leading Japanese diplomatic strategists. A U.S.-China Framework Agreement that helps to resolve fundamental and long-standing disputes would strengthen Japanese security, ensure regional stability and advance Japanese prosperity.

American efforts to improve relations with China must no doubt have the blessing of Japan and be coordinated closely with its government. Japan must be confident that U.S.-China reconciliation would not lead to joint Sino-American dominance in the region, to the detriment of Japan. Japan must be a full partner in the U.S. policy of improving relations with China, precisely because this policy would advance Japan's interests in realizing a more prosperous and more stable Asia.

If Japan were to become alarmed that improved U.S. relations with China were occurring at Japan's expense by effectively undermining its security, Japan could obtain "compensation," as Michael Green observes, by undertaking a large-scale military buildup or becoming a nuclear weapons state (drawing on existing stocks of plutonium to manufacture nuclear bombs).[50] The prospect of Japan seeking "great power" status by military means—although entirely contrary to current Japanese policy—would deeply unsettle the region and lead to serious instability rather than an outcome that is mutually beneficial to both the U.S. and Japan.

U.S.-China relations and Japan's Asia policy

Japan's ability to shape its own relations with China or exercise regional leadership depends considerably on the tenor of U.S.-China relations, as noted earlier. Given the strength of the U.S.-Japan alliance, Japan is not now a fully independent actor since its strategic options are heavily influenced by the nature of U.S. policy toward China.

It is therefore important to ask whether Japan can likely achieve its current foreign policy goals *without* an improvement in U.S.-China relations. An honest assessment leads to the conclusion that Japan will encounter a number of obstacles so long as the U.S.-China standoff on core security issues continues.

Obstacles to Japanese policy

Under existing circumstances, Japan's effort to reduce and reposition American forces will likely be resisted by the United States government. The U.S. Department of Defense will argue, as it has in the case of the Futenma controversy, that an ongoing buildup of both U.S. and Japanese forces in the Pacific is required to deter a rising China as well as a nuclear North Korea. Should deterrence fail, Japanese forces and bases will be crucial to defeating either of these two potential adversaries. The U.S. will stress that the defense of Japan depends on the strength of the U.S.-Japan security partnership—and that any perceived weakening of Japan's commitment would be a boon to China which "regularly seeks to marginalize the efficacy and relevance of the alliance," in the words of a special report from the National Bureau of Asian Research.[51] Even a Japanese government that is committed to developing greater autonomy within the alliance will be hard-pressed to find sources of leverage for alleviating U.S. pressure. As U.S. patience wears thin, the Pentagon would likely move from veiled threats of removing American forces in Japan to more explicit measures. Japan would almost certainly be forced to yield because its foreign policy fundamentally assumes and depends on the ongoing U.S. security alliance.

While the U.S. may tolerate some increased Japanese activity toward strengthening regional frameworks in Asia, there is also a clear limit to how much multilateralism the U.S. will now accept, most notably on security issues. The traditional Pentagon view is that new regional frameworks undermine the "hub-and-spokes" alliance structure that the United States has maintained for more than 50 years in the Asia Pacific. The U.S. is the hub of a number of military alliances and partnerships there, of which the two most important "spokes" are the U.S. alliances with Japan and South Korea. As is well known, these security relationships allow the U.S. to operate numerous military facilities in the region where troops are stationed, naval battle groups are forward-deployed and various strike aircraft are based. Most Pentagon strategists see the competition between regional structures and the U.S. network of bilateral alliances as a zero-sum game: the more that countries in Asia rely on multilateral organizations for their security, the less they rely on the United States and its military prowess. From this standpoint, as the prestige of regional structures rises because of their perceived efficacy, the prominence of the United States as a "protector" falls.

A more moderate and balanced U.S. view grants that regional structures have utility but insists they are inherently weak and cannot be relied upon to address fundamental security issues. Alan Romberg, Director of the East Asia Program at the Stimson Center in Washington, states:

> I share the view that an East Asia regional security structure is not likely to prosper. I think that a lot of things are happening in the region in terms of regionalism, but I do not think even if the nuclear negotiations in Korea were satisfactorily resolved and as a result of that you were able to form some peace and security mechanism as has been talked about, I do not see that as maintaining the essential peace on the hard security issues. I can see it playing all sorts of useful roles, but it is not going to solve the Taiwan issue, it is not going to solve the Korean issue, it is not going to solve the disputes between China and Japan over resources in the arena of the East China Sea and so on. It will do a lot of other good things but it is not going to do that, so I would not see that as a key factor, if you will, as a substitute for alliances.[52]

Because skepticism about the Japanese approach to regional frameworks abounds in the United States security community, American push-back against Japanese efforts to trim the U.S. military presence is likely to be strong and unforgiving.

A third obstacle to Japan's foreign policy will be U.S. resistance to the principle of creating a "win-win framework" for future relations between China and Japan (as an element of the "grand bargain" proposed by former Deputy Foreign Minister Hitoshi Tanaka). As we know, the purpose of this framework would be to help overcome divisive issues concerning history, disputed territories and energy security while strengthening bilateral relations and building confidence on military matters. But so long as the U.S. diligently prepares for a Chinese attack and maintains a heavy forward deployment of forces to contain China, the U.S. will inevitably regard a "win-win framework" of this kind as a way for China to weaken the U.S.-Japan alliance. From the standpoint of China hawks in the United States, a Japanese policy of building healthy bilateral ties with China is a threat to U.S. military superiority in the Asia Pacific. It calls into question the reliability of Japan in the event of conflict with China and casts doubt on Japan's strategic commitment to support American forces.

A U.S. policy that facilitates Japan's foreign policy goals

U.S. resistance to Japanese foreign policy—reflected in the obstacles cited above—largely follows from the current American standoff with China on overriding security issues. The alliance structure that the United States has built in the Asia Pacific since World War II is now effectively focused on containing China. This status quo spurs American strategic planners to do all they can to improve military preparedness, preserve the existing security system and ensure that Japan will be at the side of the U.S. in case of war with China.

While it is possible Japan could make minor, incremental improvements in its relations with China during the years ahead, American sensitivities will grow increasingly difficult for Japan to surmount if current trends continue. Clearly, the "realignment" of U.S. forces on Okinawa is the most sensitive issue at the present time. The initial vehement U.S. response to Tokyo's efforts to alter basing arrangements there reveals the depth of American opposition that Japan can expect to other changes it may propose in U.S. military deployments.

The best way for Japan to achieve its foreign policy goals is therefore to diplomatically help the United States transform its relations with China. A major improvement in U.S.-China relations would eliminate a number of obstacles Japan now faces in pursuing its foreign policy. This improvement would facilitate a "grand bargain" between China and Japan, as outlined by former Deputy Foreign Minister Tanaka, which remains a major component of Japanese strategic thinking.

Resolution of outstanding security issues with China would in turn allow the U.S. to reduce its military "footprint" in Japan. While some American deployments would remain necessary to ensure deterrence, hedge against uncertainty and uphold security, the burden on Japan would be far less. The United States would find it considerably easier to shift American forces away from populated areas and reduce the number of deployed personnel, when the "China threat" is significantly diminished.

Second, American enthusiasm for the regional security and economic frameworks favored by Japan would become far greater when the United States no longer finds it necessary to rely heavily on the existing hub-and-spokes security system to contain China. At such a point, U.S. strategic planners would more deeply appreciate the role of multilateral structures for managing, preventing and resolving security conflicts. These organizations would embody the commitment of the United States and Japan to maintaining regional stability. A major focus would be on countering transnational security threats (such as piracy, infectious disease, international crime, human trafficking, terrorism and environmental degradation) rather than the military threat from China. On the economic side, so long as a new East Asian Community welcomes the membership of the United States, as the DPJ insists, the U.S. would be much more inclined to view it as a useful means for advancing regional prosperity rather than as an instrument for China to assert economic domination in East Asia.

Third, in the context of improved American relations with China, the U.S. would not view a new "win-win framework" for resolving Sino-Japanese disputes with deep skepticism, as some American officials do now. China and Japan's efforts to overcome divisive issues of history, cooperate on critical energy and environmental issues, and jointly support new regional frameworks would be seen as immeasurably reinforcing regional stability. U.S. security planners would not resist reconciliation between Japan and China because it would be consistent with the rapprochement the United States had achieved with China through a Framework Agreement of its own.

Japan's fear of abandonment by the United States

American strategists seeking to strengthen Japanese support for the U.S.-Japan alliance occasionally invoke the specter of a U.S. "accommodation" with China. Their not-so-subtle message is that unless Japan assumes a greater military burden and plays a larger role supporting U.S. overseas deployments, the United States will cut a separate deal with China and essentially abandon Japan. They suggest that resolution of major security disputes between the U.S. and China would clear the way for Washington and Beijing to exercise joint domination in Asia and beyond, a situation known as "condominium" in the jargon of international relations theory. Their argument invokes real fear among some Japanese politicians and diplomats who worry about the U.S. abruptly withdrawing the security umbrella it has placed over Japan for more than half a century.

The dirty little secret, of course, is that the last thing the purveyors of this argument want to do is weaken the ties between the United States and Japan. Their major purpose is to spur a greater Japanese commitment to the alliance and a further military buildup by threatening abandonment. It is not a nice tactic, but has proven to be an effective one. The knee-jerk reaction of some Japanese politicians that Tokyo should assume a greater alliance burden to prevent U.S.-China rapprochement is an understandable but deeply mistaken response to this fallacious argument.

In fact, improved U.S.-China relations are essential to the ultimate success of the foreign policy that Japan has now embraced. For the sake of advancing its own national security, Japan should help the United States reach a resolution of outstanding disputes with China, while putting aside far-fetched fears of abandonment that are disingenuously spawned by some American strategists and threaten to harm Japan's vital national interests.

CHAPTER NINE

Achieving Korean reunification

Since the 1953 Korean War Armistice, a simple truce suspending military operations, South and North Korea have co-existed for more than 50 years in a technical state of war. Though inter-Korean relations have waxed and waned during this time, the two Koreas have never been able to sign a peace agreement ending their profound enmity and laying the basis for national reunification. This tragedy continues to the present day.

Thanks in large part to the U.S.-Korea alliance, South Korea has successfully deterred a threatened North Korean attack for over half a century, and has risen from one of the world's poorest countries to the thriving and prosperous democratic country it is today. Yet the primary goal of U.S. policy in Korea remains the same as it was 50 years ago—protecting South Korea, Japan and the United States from the ongoing North Korean security threat. With Pyongyang's development of nuclear weapons, military provocations and inflammatory rhetoric, that threat remains as serious as ever.

The division of Korea is one of the last vestiges of the Cold War. The Demilitarized Zone and the "military demarcation line" running through it along the 38th parallel symbolize a still continuing ideological confrontation. That confrontation retains the power to destabilize the Korean peninsula and spark a new Korean war. Following a North Korean artillery attack on a small South Korean island in late November 2010, rhetorical threats and military countermeasures mounted so high, that it appeared a new civil war in Korea could break out at any time.

South Korea's policy objectives

Like the United States, a primary aim of South Korea's foreign policy is to deter, protect against and reduce the military threat from North Korea. Under more conservative governments like the one led by President

Myung-bak Lee beginning in February 2008, South Korea often takes the truculent approach of sternly warning Pyongyang of disastrous consequences, should it pursue aggression against the South. Under the more liberal preceding administrations of Presidents Roh Moo-hyun and Kim Dae Jung, South Korea strived more actively to maintain stability and lower tensions with North Korea through its so-called "Sunshine Policy." This policy also sought to strengthen South Korea's economy, which still suffers from the international perception of impending war on the Korean peninsula.

The security goal of deterring North Korea is a means toward achieving Seoul's most important foreign policy objective: national reunification. The great majority of South Korea's people yearn for reunification of the Korean nation, which achieved independence from Japan at the end of World War II. Despite the stark political differences in their two governments, Koreans who live north and south of the Demilitarized Zone (DMZ) form a single ethnic group and share the same culture and history. During the Korean War, many families became divided, as refugees streamed south and chaos engulfed the country. To bring quick reunification, many political conservatives in South Korea would like to see the collapse of North Korea's regime, which would allow South Korea to forcefully unify the country. For their part, South Korean liberals skeptically reject the imminence of North Korea's collapse and support peaceful reconciliation with Pyongyang as the best way of achieving reunification. Some common ground between these factions can be found in the proposal for a "National Commonwealth" which South Korean President Roh Tae Woo announced in late 1989. Roh believed that such a Commonwealth—an interim structure allowing peaceful co-existence between the two Koreas—would be a major step toward "democratic unification" in which South Korea would play the dominant role."[1]

As another significant foreign policy objective, South Korea has worked during the last decade to play a leading role in achieving greater regional cooperation in Northeast Asia. A major architect of this policy, under the administration of President Roh Moo-hyun, was Ambassador Chung-in Moon, now a professor at Yonsei University, who argued that

> as a peace-loving nation that has never invaded a neighboring country and serves as a bridge situated in the geopolitical center of Northeast Asia, [South Korea] is in a better position than any other country in Northeast Asia to selflessly and fairly initiate and play the leading role in promoting reconciliation and cooperative efforts region-wide.

These cooperative efforts would build "mutual trust throughout the region" and assure "a lasting peace in Northeast Asia."[2]

More recently, Deputy Foreign Minister Hyun Cho emphasized that

South Korea seeks a "regional security architecture" in Northeast Asia. In Cho's view, regional security cooperation is best achieved by first focusing on non-traditional and transnational threats, including piracy, cyber-crimes and terrorism as well as by working to strengthen energy security. He recommends a step-by-step approach that builds on past successes as the optimal means of making substantial progress towards a full-blown multi-lateral security forum.[3]

President Myung-bak Lee has established an additional and important South Korean foreign policy objective—playing a major global economic role as a leader of the G-20 group of nations, reinvigorated in response to the global financial crisis. Lee stresses his country's unique history. Once one of the world's most impoverished countries, South Korea has now become a significant donor of development aid as the world's fifteenth largest economy, contributing approximately $1.2 billion in assistance to developing countries in 2010 alone.[4] Lee argues that hosting the G-20 meeting in Seoul in November 2010 enabled South Korea to "move toward center stage from the periphery of the international arena. Until now, Korea just followed others and was passive in international society and did not have a say. Now ... the world will treat us differently." Lee further empha-sizes that the "Korea model" of economic development has inspired many developing countries, and believes South Korea can play a "bridging role" between developed and developing economies.

Relations with China as a means of achieving South Korea's foreign policy goals

In the late 1980s, South Korea realized it could advance its core foreign policy goals of reducing the North Korean threat and moving towards national reunification by establishing diplomatic relations with China, a long-time adversary. South Korea also sought to benefit from the growth of China's economy, a factor that has become more important over time.

Though American and South Korean troops fought bloody battles against Chinese forces that intervened on behalf of North Korea during the Korean War, the U.S. did not let that inconvenient truth stand in the way of agreeing to formal relations with China in 1972. When South Korea successfully established diplomatic ties with China in 1992, it had to overcome a problem that the U.S. did not directly face—China's formal alliance with North Korea, obligating it to come to Pyongyang's defense in the event of attack. North Korea strongly resisted Beijing's decision to recognize South Korea, which China took both to increase its influence on the Korean peninsula and to benefit from South Korea's economic development.

South Korea's strategic thinking postulated that if China came to highly value its political and economic relations with South Korea, then Beijing would be far less likely to intervene on North Korea's side in the event of a new Korean conflict. China's foremost objective would be to promote stability and likely encourage Pyongyang to take a more moderate approach toward the South. Equally important, South Korean strategists calculated that China would be more willing to accept Korean reunification if it regarded Seoul as a friendly government that would not be hostile to China in the future. These strategists also believed that the growth of trade between the two countries would prove mutually profitable and help anchor the political-diplomatic relationship.

Since establishing formal relations in 1992, South Korea has closely cooperated with China on diplomacy toward North Korea. At first in the "Four Party talks" (involving the United States, China, South Korea and North Korea) during the late 1990s and then in the "Six Party talks" (with the addition of Japan and Russia) beginning in 2003, South Korea urged China to use its leverage to negotiate an end to Pyongyang's nuclear weapons program. During the so-called "second nuclear crisis" from 2002 to 2004, following revelation of Pyongyang's efforts to acquire uranium enrichment technology for building nuclear weapons, South Korea began to fear the U.S. would preemptively attack North Korea, triggering a new war on the Peninsula. Seoul soon aligned its positions on North Korea more closely with Beijing, believing China's and South Korea's interests in preserving stability could balance the United States.

David Kang, professor of international relations and director of the Korean Studies Institute at the University of Southern California, explains South Korea's policy toward China at the time in this way:

> South Korea's identity ... has two fundamental strands. Most important is an intense desire for the unification of the peninsula, which is South Korea's overriding foreign policy goal. Second, Korea has a long history of stable relations with China, and a much more recent and conflicted history with Japan and the United States. This identity, long masked by the Cold War and a succession of military governments, is increasingly asserting itself in South Korea.

> The ultimate goals of [the U.S. and South Korea] are also different. The United States has consistently made eliminating North Korea's nuclear and missile programs its primary goal on the peninsula, while many in South Korea view their primary goal as unification with the North, whether or not it has nuclear weapons. China shares this goal of peaceful change in North Korea. Perhaps because of these shared goals, the current interactions between South Korea and China have been largely

positive, from cooperation over the North Korean issue to expanding economic and cultural ties between the South and China.[5]

South Korea's diplomacy toward China has furthered two additional goals of Seoul's foreign policy: realizing a "regional and broader global role that reflects South Korea's demonstrable political, military, and diplomatic success"; and breaking out "of its perceived position as a junior partner" in the U.S.-Korea alliance. In both respects, South Korea has sought "to become more of an actor—rather than simply being acted upon—that can play a useful role building bridges in Asia and beyond," as a RAND report has noted.[6]

South Korea is no longer content to play a subordinate role in the U.S.-Korea alliance and intends to achieve greater equality. This sentiment lay behind President Lee's call in 2009 to transform the alliance into something much larger:

> This alliance will no longer just be about ensuring security, but much more. It will continue to carry out its purpose of securing peace, but at the same time, it will be a comprehensive strategic alliance for the 21st century that encompasses economic, social, cultural, educational, scientific and technological cooperation.[7]

In the economic sphere, South Korea-China trade relations have exceeded all expectations during the last two decades.[8] Trade increased from approximately $2.5 billion in 1990 to beyond $100 billion in 2005, when China became South Korea's largest trading partner. After China joined the World Trade Organization (WTO) in late 2001 and significantly reduced its tariff barriers, South Korean conglomerates poured unprecedented investments into large-scale, technology-intensive projects in major industrial sectors, including computers, electronics, automobiles, and steel. Large Korean firms also concentrated on manufacturing intermediate goods as inputs to "assembly operations" for products that were then exported by China to global markets. Since this wave of South Korean investment began, South Korea's foreign investments in China have expanded by more than 10 percent each year with the result that South Korea-China trade reached approximately $250 billion in 2011. The two countries aim to increase their trade to $300 billion by 2015.

It is fair to say that South Korea now heavily depends on China from an economic standpoint.[9] Many of the leading South Korean conglomerates such as Samsung Electronics and Hyundai Motors—major pillars of the country's economy—have shifted manufacturing and assembly operations to China to take advantage of the lower cost structure and cheaper wages. Many medium and small South Korean businesses have relocated significant parts of their operations to China simply to remain competitive and survive. In tandem with the growth in South Korea-China economic ties, powerful domestic constituencies in South Korea, ranging from the largest conglomerates to small business owners, have developed a strong stake in ensuring that political issues, including sometimes tempestuous South-North relations, do not disrupt relations with China. In May 2012, South Korea and China decided to begin formal discussions on a bilateral free trade agreement, which will markedly lower tariff and non-tariff barriers to mutual trade and investment.[10]

South Korea's fears of China

While Seoul's ties with Beijing have grown increasingly close during the last two decades, several significant differences emerged in the 2003 to 2006 period that revealed structural weaknesses in the relationship. In 2004, South Koreans began to worry that a rising China might seek regional dominance and attempt to impose its will on their country. This concern peaked when China seemed to claim lands occupied by the historic "Koguryo" kingdom, an ethnic Korean territory on the border of North Korea and China, which China argued actually belonged to the Chinese empire. Public anger in South Korea rose to a high level, as many people took deep personal offense that China was trying to "engineer ... historical distortions" to ensure a future unified Korea could not claim territory in Northeast China where millions of ethnic Koreans continue to live. A compromise emerged when China agreed to publicly withdraw its claims and proposed academic exchanges to resolve the dispute.[11]

A second major issue centers on China's harsh treatment of North Korean refugees who often seek legal protection in embassies, international schools and other places of sanctuary after their escape.[12] China officially classifies the refugees as "illegal economic immigrants" and insists on forcibly returning them to North Korea. China also considers the fate of the refugees to be a matter of "national sovereignty" that can only be discussed bilaterally between China and North Korea. South Korea has strongly protested the Chinese view and called for China to treat the plight of refugees as a "humanitarian issue," allowing them to be repatriated to South Korea.[13]

South Korea has also become increasingly anxious that China's concern for "stability" on the Korean peninsula will undercut its support for Korean reunification. Conservative diplomatic theorists like Professor Taeho Kim of South Korea's Hallym University question the meaning of China's formal position that it favors the "peaceful, independent and gradual unification of the Korean peninsula." Kim assesses that China "prefers stability to unification" and gives "de facto support for the North Korean regime," thus furthering the division of Korea. China provides this "de facto support," in large part, through its considerable economic assistance to Pyongyang, including the 500,000 tons of food and 300,000 to one million tons of oil it supplies on an annual basis.[14] In 2006, China and North Korea reportedly negotiated a five-year economic aid and development package worth about $2 billion to Pyongyang. During the first seven months of 2011, trade between the two countries totaled approximately $3.1 billion, an increase of about 85 percent over the previous year. On an overall basis, China has accounted for an estimated 70 percent of North Korea's trade.

China's economic activity in North Korea has been so extensive that one South Korean writer refers to North Korea as China's "fourth northeastern province" while many worry that North Korea's rapidly increasing dependence on China, together with Beijing's rising influence over Pyongyang, could create additional obstacles to future Korean reunification.[15]

China's policy objectives

China has several overall policy goals for the Korean peninsula that include utilizing North Korea as a "strategic buffer" to keep the United States and South Korean forces at a distance from China's border; maintaining stability and preventing the collapse of North Korea's regime; denuclearizing North Korea so the entire Peninsula becomes a "nuclear-free zone"; and strengthening economic ties with both South and North Korea to further China's economic growth and development.

Professor Shen Dingli, a leading Chinese foreign policy expert at Fudan University in Shanghai, succinctly sums up China's view of North Korea's strategic role:

> North Korea ... serves as China's strategic buffer zone in Northeast Asia. With a shared border of 1,400 kilometers, North Korea acts as a guard post for China, keeping at bay the tens of thousands of U.S. troops stationed in South Korea. This allows China to reduce its military deployments in Northeast China and focus more directly on the issue of Taiwanese independence.[16]

China's assessment of North Korea's strategic value, as Shen emphasizes, is premised on a possible future military confrontation with the United States over Taiwan.[17] In the event of a conflict, U.S. forces could not easily open a second front against China in Northeast Asia because North Korea's 1.2 million-strong standing army would block the way to the Chinese border. Moreover, North Korea provides China with "strategic depth." If a conflict broke out on the peninsula, actual military engagements would likely take place in North Korea rather than in Chinese territory.

Shen's analysis clarifies that the value to China of preserving North Korea as a buffer zone is tied directly to the ongoing standoff between the U.S. and China over Taiwan. China is not primarily interested in the division of Korea for its own sake, but because this division potentially helps China achieve its foremost foreign policy objective—reunifying Taiwan with the mainland. The converse is also true. Shen acknowledges that "following the resolution of the Taiwan question, the possible strategic value that China held with North Korea and its nuclear arms would disappear."[18] At that point, China would no longer need North Korea as a buffer zone in Northeast Asia.

A second overall policy objective of China on the Korean Peninsula is maintaining ongoing stability. In practical terms, stability translates into preventing the collapse of North Korea's regime. The adverse consequences to China of such a collapse would be severe. Massive flows of North Korean refugees, like those that occurred during the North Korean famine of the mid-1990s, could destabilize the Yanbian Korean autonomous region in Northeast China. A regime collapse would likely traumatize the region's economy, leading to large fall-offs in foreign direct investment, trade, liquidity and production. In the event of a crisis, it is quite possible that China could intervene militarily along the full-length of the North Korean frontier in order to establish control and prevent the flow of refugees. One Pentagon estimate suggests that China would seek to establish a zone of control at a depth of approximately 40 kilometers inside North Korea during a period of instability.[19]

A third Chinese policy goal is to denuclearize North Korea. After Pyongyang's nuclear tests in October 2006 and May 2009, China took a leading role at the United Nations Security Council to sanction North Korea for the tests. China's foremost concern is that Pyongyang's drive to accumulate a nuclear arsenal will trigger an arms race and destabilize Northeast Asia. China fears that Japan could deploy nuclear weapons in a several month period, should it choose to do so. South Korea could eventually follow suit, not willing to be the odd-man out in a China-North Korea-Japan nuclear triangle. On nuclear issues, China is also anxious that an accident at North Korea's nuclear test sites near the Chinese border could have severe environmental and economic consequences in China and that nuclear weapons technologies could fall into the hands of hostile states or terrorist groups.

Another of China's overall policy objectives is to strengthen economic relations with both South Korea and North Korea to further China's economic growth and development. As already noted, China has been South Korea's largest trading partner since 2005. Over the years, China has benefited considerably from the investment, technology and experience of the South Korean companies that have increasingly moved manufacturing and assembly operations there.

China's economic involvement with North Korea has a much different complexion, with the investment and trade flow going mainly in the opposite direction. A Council of Foreign Relations report has documented China's role as the primary provider of aid, trade and investment to North Korea, describing its activities in several key areas as follows: China supplies approximately 45 percent of North Korea's food; almost 90 percent of its energy imports; and about 80 percent of its consumer goods. During the period 2005 to 2007, China moved aggressively to gain greater control of North Korea's valuable mineral resources, acquiring a 50-year contract right for mining gold, zinc, copper, coal and iron. China has been especially interested in obtaining rights of use at the North Korean port of Rajin-Sonbong, which could give its northeast provinces physical access to the East Sea/Sea of Japan. With its ten-year lease of Rajin port in March 2010, China plans to use new rail links to transport goods manufactured in its northeast provinces to Rajin for shipment to overseas destinations.[20]

South Korea's strategic dilemma

China's major policy objectives on the Korean peninsula and the core foreign policy goals of South Korea overlap in many respects. Deterring and reducing the military threat from North Korea is the highest immediate South Korean concern, as it has been for decades. China similarly seeks to head off a North Korean confrontation with South Korea and, for this reason, has made maintaining stability its foremost policy goal for the Korean peninsula. A new war in Korea would put China's long-term economic development at risk and possibly trigger a much-unwanted military confrontation with the United States.

South Korea has increasingly relied on Beijing's influence to restrain Pyongyang and to lead the diplomatic effort to roll back North Korea's nuclear weapons program in the Six Party talks, which made halting progress for several years. Both South Korea and China seek a diplomatic solution for eliminating Pyongyang's nuclear capability and both countries support a nuclear-free Korean peninsula.

South Korea and China also have in common the important objective of pursing rapid economic development. Their mutual trade and investment has exceeded all expectations and will almost certainly intensify in the years ahead. Numerous business leaders and politicians in South Korea recognize that China is now so important to the profitability of South Korea's firms—small, medium and large—that a rupture in relations would be devastating to the country's economy.

Because South Korea has become increasingly dependent on China for achieving its security, diplomatic and economic goals, observers worry the country faces a strategic dilemma in the years ahead. The essence of this dilemma is South Korea's need and desire to maintain good relations with both China and the United States, without deeply offending either partner.

If South Korea is too deferential toward China, this could cause great concern in the United States, which has had a security alliance with South Korea for more than half a century. U.S. officials would worry publicly (as they have occasionally done in the past) about South Korea's "reliability" in meeting its alliance obligations. They would raise the especially sensitive question of whether South Korea would allow the U.S. to use forces based on the Korean Peninsula for combat against China in the event of a "Taiwan contingency"—a Chinese attack on Taiwan. The bottom line issue for many U.S. officials is whether the rise of China—and China's growing importance to South Korea—could lead South Korea to someday downgrade or even abandon its long-standing security alliance with the United States.

If South Korea, on the other hand, aligns too closely with the United States in a way that China perceives as threatening its fundamental interests, then China could begin to regard South Korea as a potential adversary. It could take actions that undermine South Korea's political position vis-à-vis North Korea, penalize South Korean businesses that trade and invest in China, or otherwise harm South Korea's national interests. China currently accepts the reality of the U.S.-South Korea alliance, but does not want to see a greatly expanded South Korean security role within it. China would be particularly concerned about a reunified Korea that is allied with the United States and allows American forces to occupy areas near the Chinese border.

Professor Jae Ho Chung of Seoul National University, a scholar who has analyzed South Korea's strategic dilemma of being caught "between dragon and eagle," as he puts it, sums up the future problem for his country this way:

> How to find a suitable middle ground while maximizing the benefits of maintaining good relations with both the United States and China therefore is the key to South Korea's principal foreign policy goals—namely, survival, development and unification .... [N]ot only will America's support be indispensable for reunification and post-reunification reconstruction, but South Korea's economic relationship with the United States is also much too intimately intertwined with its strategic ties ... Nor can China be dispensed with ... The bottom line for Seoul, therefore, is not to antagonize China and, in this regard ... being sucked into a U.S.-China conflict over Taiwan or elsewhere in the region must be avoided under all circumstances.[21]

A strategic "middle ground" allows South Korea to avoid having to choose between China and the United States. It permits South Korea to obtain economic benefits from trade and investment with both China and the U.S., while enjoying the protection of the American forces stationed on the Korean peninsula as well as the U.S. nuclear umbrella.

Maintaining this "best of all possible worlds," however, is heavily dependent on the existence of ongoing, generally amicable U.S.-China relations. If relations between the United States and China severely deteriorate, or in the worst case, a military confrontation occurs, South Korea would quickly lose the luxury of its middle ground, as noted previously. If it sides with the U.S., China could regard South Korea as a hostile state. If it fails to support American interests, the United States would see South Korea as a weak and unreliable ally.

The impact of strategic competition and distrust between the United States and China

Most Americans are convinced that tensions on the Korean peninsula have a single cause—North Korea. Pyongyang's rhetorical threats against South Korea, the United Nations and the United States are frequently inflammatory and always offensive. In 2009 and 2010 alone, North Korea threatened to "turn Seoul into a sea of fire," treat UN Security Council sanctions as a "declaration of war," and "wipe out the aggressors" if "the U.S. imperialists start another war" in Korea. Pyongyang's tests of nuclear devices in October 2006 and May 2009 confirmed popular suspicion that North Korea was bent on becoming a nuclear weapons state and developing a military capability to launch long-range ICBMs against U.S. targets. Because North Korea's leadership is ruthless and erratic, and its regime imprisons hundreds of thousands of people in numerous *gulags*, the country has understandably become Foreign Public Enemy #1 (alongside Iran) to many Americans.

Events leading to the edge of war

Over a period of ten months, extending from March through December 2010, U.S. and South Korean animosity toward Pyongyang mounted to a level not seen since the 1994 crisis when North Korea threatened to produce nuclear weapons and nearly triggered a war.[22] It appeared to many observers that a new Korean war could break out at any time, following the sinking on March 26, 2010 of a South Korean Navy ship, the *Cheonan*, and North Korea's artillery attack in late November on a small South Korean island.

While engaging in anti-submarine operations close to the maritime border with North Korea, the South Korean Navy vessel exploded and split in half with a loss of 46 lives. Although an investigation conducted by the U.S., United Kingdom, Sweden and Australia blamed a North Korean torpedo for the sinking, Pyongyang rejected all responsibility.

Much to the frustration of the United States, the UN Security Council did not condemn North Korea by name for the attack in its July statement on the issue.[23] During Council deliberations, China insisted that the cause of the disaster was uncertain and effectively protected Pyongyang against any UN sanctions. China called for "calm" in the interest of "maintaining stability" on the Korean peninsula throughout the Security Council debate. President Obama was so incensed with China's position that he accused it of "willful blindness" for refusing to hold North Korea accountable.

China's reaction to the *Cheonan* disaster and its support for North Korea at the United Nations had the effect of mollifying Pyongyang. But the weak UN statement only increased U.S. resolve to engage in joint naval exercises with South Korea to warn North Korea and strengthen deterrence. Through September 2010, the two countries conducted exercises off the east, south and west coasts of South Korea. Plans for operations off the west coast (in the Yellow Sea) drew sharp criticism from the deputy chief of staff of China's People's Liberation Army (PLA) who asserted that China "strongly opposes the drill in the Yellow Sea because of its close proximity to Chinese territorial waters." Another senior PLA officer argued that

> The drill area selected by the United States and South Korea is only [about 300 miles] away from Beijing. China will be aware of the security pressure from military exercises conducted by any country in an area that is so close to China's heartland.

The officer emphasized that portions of the drill would be conducted in an area which is "a gateway to China's capital region." In history, he continued, "foreign invaders repeatedly took the Yellow Sea as an entrance to enter the heartland of Beijing and Tianjin."[24]

The event that brought South and North Korea closest to the edge of war was an artillery barrage that North Korea unleashed on Yeonpyeong, a small island in the Yellow Sea just south of the maritime border between the two countries.[25] The toll from the North Korean attack on November 23, 2010 included the deaths of two South Korean marines and two civilians, 19 injuries and the destruction of many houses as well as serious damage to infrastructure. South Korea returned artillery fire and deployed fighter jets in response to the artillery barrage, which Pyongyang claimed was provoked by a South Korean military exercise. According to South Korean news accounts, more than 40 North Korean soldiers were killed or wounded by the South Korean counterstrike. The incident took on symbolic significance because it was the first time since the Korean War that North Korea had launched a direct attack on South Korean territory, causing civilian casualties.

Following the Yeonpyeong assault, the U.S. and South Korea held a joint military exercise in the Yellow Sea involving the aircraft carrier *George Washington*, and together with Japan called for North Korea to cease provocations. President Lee of South Korea announced a policy of meeting future North Korean provocations with "actions" instead of "words" and ordered a "live-fire exercise" on Yeonpyeong Island for mid-December. North Korea threatened to respond fiercely with "second and third self-defensive blows that cannot be predicted" if the exercise went ahead as planned. At the United Nations, the Security Council could not agree on the wording of a statement to calm the situation, with Russia and China objecting to U.S. insistence on singling out North Korea for criticism. China separately called for restraint, saying it opposed any acts that could "sabotage regional peace and stability."[26]

In Washington, the American government spoke with two voices on the impending South Korean live-fire exercise.[27] General James Cartwright, Vice Chairman of the Joint Chiefs of Staff, expressed deep concern that an uncontrollable clash could occur:

What we worry about, obviously, is if [South Korea's live-fire exercise] is misunderstood or if it's taken advantage of as an opportunity. If North Korea were to react to that in a negative way and fire back at those firing positions on the islands, that would start potentially a chain reaction of firing and counter-firing .... What you don't want to have happen out of that is ... for us to lose control of the escalation. That's the concern.

The State Department, however, signaled U.S. support for Seoul's military exercise through a statement of its spokesman, P. J. Crowley:

South Korea is entitled to take appropriate steps in its self-defense. Making sure that its military is prepared in the event of further provocations is a perfectly legitimate step for South Korea to take. North Korea should not see these South Korean actions as a provocation. These are routine exercises. There's nothing, you know, provocative or unusual or threatening about these exercises. There's no need for it to increase tensions in the area. This is a pre-announced live-fire exercise. The North Koreans clearly should know what is going to happen. It is not directed against North Korea.

Of course, South Korea's live-fire exercise *was* clearly directed at North Korea and anything but routine. General Cartwright's fears were well founded, with South Korea's military placed on highest alert and fully prepared to send F-15K fighter-bombers against North Korean targets if so ordered.

On the afternoon of Monday, December 20, South Korean marine units on Yeonpyeong Island fired artillery barrages at hypothetical targets for approximately one and a half hours, while F-15s flew overhead. North Korea did not respond with any military actions. A day later, North Korea's official news agency quoted the country's army supreme command as saying it was "not worth reacting" to the exercise. According to newspaper reports, China's high-ranking State Councilor Dai Bingguo was so worried about the outbreak of war that he drew on China's considerable influence in North Korea and personally urged high-ranking officials not to retaliate for the South Korean exercise.[28]

U.S.-China strategic competition as a source of tensions in Korea

China's support for North Korea at the United Nations as well as its opposition to joint U.S.-South Korean military exercises near the Chinese coast reveal the tensions that arise in Korea from U.S.-China strategic competition, separate and apart from Pyongyang's provocations. China feels compelled to support North Korea and maintain the status quo on the Peninsula because of its deep-seated fear of the United States and the current U.S. policy of effectively containing China. So long as strategic competition between the United States and China remains strong and the dispute over Taiwan continues, China will regard the North Korean "strategic buffer" as militarily essential.

China is driven to reinforce the existing power structure on the Korean Peninsula—and the ongoing division of the Korean nation—because this alignment of forces takes considerable military pressure off Beijing. Without North Korean troops "standing guard," as Professor Shen Dingli of Fudan University puts it, Beijing would face a much greater military threat in northeast China that the U.S. could exploit if a conflict over Taiwan occurs off China's southeast coast. That is why in December 2010, China's paramount concern for maintaining stability in Korea led it to persuade Pyongyang not to respond to Seoul's live-fire exercise on Yeonpyeong Island.

China's desire for stability on the Korean Peninsula is closely related to its need to preserve a strategic buffer. Stability, in this case, signifies China's strong preference to maintain the Kim Jong-un regime in power, following the death of his father, Kim Jong Il, in December 2011. Despite the disdain that many in Beijing feel for the government in Pyongyang, China's leaders would rather live with serious tensions on the Korean Peninsula than face the chaos likely to result from the collapse of North Korea's regime. A sudden breakdown of the Kim Jong-un government could lead to a quick loss of Chinese influence in North Korea and possible intervention by combined South Korean and U.S. forces to stem a humanitarian disaster and maintain order. As previously noted, massive flows of North Korean refugees to China's northeastern provinces could stir upheaval in China. This is Beijing's "nightmare scenario" and it is bent on doing everything possible to prevent a precipitous collapse in North Korea from occurring. In part, China's policy goal of stability aims at preventing the expansion of American influence and the weakening of China's authority on the Korean peninsula. This objective is directly tied to Beijing's strategic competition with Washington and China's efforts to reduce the pressure it feels from the presence of U.S. forces in the region.

U.S.-China strategic distrust sustains tensions in Korea in an additional way. Since the mid-1990s, the United States and South Korea have diligently sought to end Pyongyang's nuclear weapons program through diplomatic means. The nuclear negotiations, carried on since 2003 in the Six Party Talks, have thus far proven incapable of reaching their intended goal despite periodic breakthroughs. Throughout the history of the talks, North Korea has relied on Beijing's support to resist the pressure of the other parties. To achieve a successful outcome, U.S. negotiators have sought to persuade China to use its influence in a concerted way to press North Korea to give up the nuclear program. But because of its competitive security relationship with the United States, China has often been unwilling to push North Korea too hard for fear of destabilizing and undermining the regime. This dynamic has been a major obstacle to attaining the diplomatic goal of the Six Party talks—denuclearization of the Korean Peninsula.

More broadly, it is clear that strategic competition and mistrust between the U.S. and China are major obstacles to Korean reunification. China's fear of U.S. strategic encirclement has led it to adopt a policy of preserving North Korea as a strategic buffer, upholding North Korea's regime as a means of maintaining stability, and frequently supporting Pyongyang's position in the Six Party negotiations. These policies sustain structural tensions on the peninsula and severely hamper a resolution of differences that could eventually lead to peaceful reunification of the two Koreas. Thus, South Korea's foremost national objective of achieving reunification has effectively become a casualty of the strategic competition between the U.S. and China.

This situation also adversely affects Seoul's ability to achieve other important foreign policy goals. So long as serious tensions on the Peninsula continue, foreign investors will limit their trade and investment in South Korea, based on fears of a future military conflict. The effect of a tense security climate on South Korea's economy is widely known as the "Korea discount" and interferes with the country's ability to maintain and increase economic growth.

Moreover, as long as the Korean Peninsula remains a possible "global hot spot," South Korea will find it difficult to achieve its ambitions of exercising leadership in achieving greater regional security cooperation in Northeast Asia or becoming a global economic leader. The frequently virulent rhetorical exchanges between Seoul and Pyongyang have the effect of lowering South Korea's international prestige as a leader on economic and political issues. Other nations tend to draw the conclusion that if South Korea is unable to resolve its differences with its fraternal neighbor on the other side of the 38th parallel, it does not have the intrinsic capabilities or qualities necessary to exercise regional or global leadership. This judgment may be unfair and unwarranted, but it is a judgment that nonetheless occurs and has an adverse impact on South Korea's international prospects.

Risks of future military conflict

The ongoing strategic competition between the United States and China has other equally profound and long-lasting implications for South Korea's national security. One immediate danger is that South Korea could be drawn into a U.S.-China military conflict against its will. This situation could result from a U.S. decision to transfer American troops and aircraft on the Korean peninsula to the vicinity of Taiwan, if a shooting war appears on the verge of breaking out between Taiwan and China. Despite South Korea's trepidations about allowing the United States to move any of its troops off the Peninsula to meet regional military contingencies, Seoul accepted the principle of so-called "strategic flexibility," in a 2006 agreement with the United States, that could allow for such a transfer. Four years later, Admiral Michael Mullen, chairman of the Joint Chiefs of Staff, underscored U.S. intentions to invoke this principle when he publicly noted the discussions he was then having with South Korea's military leadership on "what we will be able to do in the next several years in support for deployments, literally, off the Peninsula ... [This is a] very important part of a strategic concept for security both for the region and globally."[29]

The real danger for Seoul, of course, is that if it is "sucked into a U.S.-China conflict" over Taiwan on the side of the United States, it would antagonize China, in the view of Korean scholar Jae Ho Chung.[30] This could easily put South Korea's core policy goals of economic development and reunification at risk, given China's role as South Korea's leading trade partner and the highly influential role it plays in shaping geopolitical outcomes on the Korean Peninsula.

The potential use of U.S. forces based in Korea to meet a Taiwan contingency highlights Seoul's strategic dilemma and its need to maintain friendly relations with both China and the United States. Ongoing security competition between the U.S. and China creates an ever-present risk that South Korea could rapidly lose its ability to keep a balance in relations with the two countries. A serious U.S.-China military conflict, which forces a choice and likely turns one of these two great powers into an enemy, is an outcome to be avoided at all costs.

It may be that the greatest risk inherent in Seoul's strategic dilemma lies much closer to home than a conflict between the United States and China over Taiwan. The potential collapse of North Korea's regime could also trigger a confrontation between the U.S. and China, and force South Korea to make difficult strategic decisions. While it is highly likely Seoul would ally itself with Washington in the event of a collapse, as previously suggested, Beijing's probable response of moving troops across the border to restore order and prevent major refugee flows could severely complicate South Korea's goal of achieving Korean reunification. In a worst case, American and South Korean forces would confront Chinese troops occupying portions of North Korea in the aftermath of a regime breakdown.

In May 2010, a leading U.S. think-tank in Washington, the Center for Strategic and International Studies (CSIS), recommended the United States, South Korea and China cooperate closely to prepare for "North Korean contingencies" and specifically, the collapse of the North Korean regime.[31] The main proposal of a report authored by Asia experts Bonnie Glaser of CSIS and Scott Snyder of the Council on Foreign Relations, was that "all three nations should discuss the circumstances under which foreign military intervention would be necessary and agree that international coordination is desirable prior to deployment of any forces into North Korea." CSIS advised the U.S. and South Korea to "mitigate Chinese suspicions" by providing reassurances to China about the joint U.S.-South Korean military planning effort actively underway to prepare for Pyongyang's collapse. Overall, CSIS argued that "a process of providing mutual reassurances will enhance the sense of shared interests and concerns about the situation in North Korea as well as the future of the peninsula and Northeast Asia."

Despite the positive thrust of the CSIS report, it failed to point out that the strategic competition between the United States and China makes it highly unlikely that China would agree to cooperate with the U.S. regarding future North Korean instability. Beijing fears that American and South Korean forces entering North Korea would seek to implement the effective U.S. strategy of militarily containing China. Although the CSIS report recommends that, "U.S. policymakers should make greater efforts to assuage Chinese concerns about U.S. strategic encirclement" as a way of furthering cooperation on North Korea, the stark reality is that containment and encirclement remain core objectives of current United States policy. Under these circumstances, it is unrealistic to suggest the U.S. could engage in a process of providing "mutual reassurance" on a subject as sensitive as military planning for regime breakdown in North Korea.

Clearly, strategic competition between the U.S. and China is the primary, oftentimes unspoken, obstacle to achieving the kind of cooperation on North Korea that the CSIS report rightly recommends. This situation is extremely unfortunate because close coordination between the U.S. and China will be necessary if the regime in Pyongyang collapses or becomes so weakened that social chaos threatens to overwhelm the country. The alternative to cooperation, as already noted, is a possible confrontation between U.S. and South Korean troops, on one side, and Chinese forces on the other side, as each country rushes in to provide humanitarian aid, take control of nuclear weapons sites, prevent massive refugee flows and restore order. U.S.-China strategic mistrust thus carries the serious risk of escalating to a crisis and confrontation in Korea in the future.

The beneficial impact in Korea of a U.S.-China framework agreement

Because the underlying security competition between the United States and China is a major cause of structural tensions on the Korean Peninsula, an improvement in U.S.-China relations would greatly help South Korea achieve its leading foreign policy goals. Advancing the security and well-being of a close and long-standing U.S. ally, consistent with American interests, provides an important additional rationale for the United States to pursue a Framework Agreement with China.

Once the U.S. and China have resolved their outstanding disputes on major security issues—especially the status of Taiwan and the close-in U.S. military deployments along China's coast—China would no longer regard North Korea as an essential strategic buffer. As Professor Shen of Fudan University acknowledges, "[F]ollowing the resolution of the Taiwan question, the possible strategic value that China held with North Korea and its nuclear arms would disappear."[32] China would no longer require a strategic buffer on the Korean peninsula when the chance of a military conflict with the U.S. over Taiwan was virtually non-existent.

The same logic applies to China's goal of maintaining stability on the Korean Peninsula. As long as strategic competition with the United States continues, China realistically fears the collapse of North Korea's regime could trigger a joint U.S.-South Korean intervention into North Korea. In China's view, the overall aim of such an incursion would be to forcibly reunify the country under South Korean rule. Quick reunification of this kind would mean the presence of U.S. forces on a Chinese land border for the first time since the Korean War, putting significant military pressure on China and furthering the effective American policy of containment.

After the United States and China resolve their outstanding differences on security issues, however, China would realize that North Korea's regime poses a greater security threat to China than the instability that would follow its collapse. The skepticism and disdain that Chinese leaders already hold toward Pyongyang (but rarely express) would likely come to play a major role in its foreign policy. China would far more readily acknowledge that a nuclear-armed North Korea, which pursues failed economic policies and treats its citizens harshly is much more of a risk to China's future well-being than a reunified Korea that embraces South Korea's democratic political system.

Instead of planning unilateral military measures to stabilize North Korea, take control of nuclear weapons sites and prevent large-scale refugee flows across the border, China would likely be eager to engage in full-scale military planning with the United States and South Korea. The value of cooperation and coordination with the U.S., at this point, would clearly outweigh Beijing's several fears of offending North Korea's leaders, weakening the regime in Pyongyang merely by discussing a collapse scenario with the U.S. and South Korea, or disclosing secret information about China's military strategy that the U.S. could use against Beijing.

Joint planning for a potential collapse would include a division of roles and responsibilities for de-conflicting forces, providing humanitarian aid, restoring public order and securing North Korea's nuclear facilities. On a political level, it could entail laying the groundwork for the reunification of Korea, including the role of the United Nations in supervising and providing a legitimate, interim political structure leading to the formation of a new government.

At a point when China no longer highly values North Korea as a strategic buffer and no longer prizes stability in North Korea above all else, conditions will become far more favorable for Seoul's pursuit of its critical foreign policy goals. Beijing's support for Pyongyang in the talks on North Korea's nuclear weapons program currently ensures that the other four parties—the U.S., South Korea, Japan and Russia—cannot use concerted pressure to isolate North Korea diplomatically and potentially destabilize the regime. By contrast, Beijing's far less concern for stability in Pyongyang, after reaching a Framework Agreement with the United States, would for the first time permit an effective coordinated effort to compel North Korea to denuclearize. China would be much more willing to join in putting pressure on Pyongyang to achieve a successful outcome in the nuclear negotiations.

More broadly, the beneficial effect of a U.S.-China Framework Agreement, over the long term, would be to end South Korea's strategic dilemma—whether to side more closely with China or the United States, the two nations on which it critically depends. As previously noted, given the current strategic competition between Washington and Beijing, Seoul's approach has been to cultivate good relations with both countries and avoid choosing between them. Seoul has thus deepened the U.S.-South Korea alliance on security issues, while strengthening its economic ties with China. This approach is only possible, however, so long as U.S.-China relations do not become openly antagonistic. If the United States and China enter a prolonged period of mutual hostility—a new Cold War with sharply increased suspicion of the other's aggressive intentions—South Korea could no longer retain the luxury of avoiding a strategic choice.

Following the resolution of major U.S.-China security issues, such a choice by South Korea would not be necessary. South Korea could more easily deepen ties with the United States without offending China. Conversely, it could strengthen political and security relations with China without arousing the significant suspicions and anxieties of its close American ally. Henceforth, South Korea could build its regional and global role on the foundation of good relations between the two great powers on which it most heavily depends.

Most importantly for South Korea, Beijing would also take a far more positive view of the leading Korean foreign policy goal—national reunification—after resolving critical security disputes with the United States. China would reason that a friendly, unified Korea on its border would not be an instrument of American containment and therefore would not pose a threat to China's security. Beijing would not need the insurance of a strategic buffer adjoining its Northeastern provinces because it would no longer fear an imminent American attack or regard the presence of South Korean troops along the Chinese border as highly risky. At this point, preserving the ongoing division of Korea and upholding the North Korean regime (under the pretext of "maintaining stability") would provide no major security benefits to China. Beijing would be inclined to acquiesce in Korean reunification, so long as it occurred in a manner that avoided social chaos, disruptive flows of North Korean refugees into China, and loss of control over nuclear weapon sites.

Achieving U.S. objectives in Korea

A U.S.-China Framework Agreement would create conditions that are conducive to the continuation of the U.S. alliance with South Korea, an important objective of U.S. policy in the region. Admiral Michael McDevitt, a leading strategist of U.S.-Asia relations at the Center for Naval Analyses, has described why a U.S. presence over the long-term would be "sensible" for South Korea:

> From Seoul's perspective, a [U.S.-South Korea] alliance keeps its options open for both the present and the future. It gives Seoul leverage and something to bargain over with the North, and eases pressure from

the [South Korean] military for increased defense budgets. Moreover, rapprochement with Japan would be easier if the United States remains a common ally of both Korea and Japan. Finally, of course, sustaining a [U.S.-South Korea] relationship guarantees help from the only nation in the world that could help Korea successfully resist Chinese military intimidation and pressure.[33]

Even though the United States and China may settle their major differences on security issues, Seoul will always have a prudent concern about China seeking to dominate the Korean peninsula, by virtue its proximity, size and power. The optimal counter-balance for either South Korea or a reunified Korea is its alliance with a "distant superpower" that could provide diplomatic, material and military support, if necessary, to help strengthen South Korea's autonomy and freedom of action. So long as strategic competition between the U.S. and China remains at a high level, one of China's security objectives will remain to minimize the combined U.S.-South Korean threat to China through the reduction of the United States military presence on the peninsula. In the context of improved U.S.-China relations, however, China would likely perceive the basing of American forces in South Korea as a way for Seoul to hedge against future uncertainty rather than directly threaten Beijing.

Finally, resolution of major outstanding disputes with China through a Framework Agreement would directly assist the United States in reaching its overriding security objective for the Korean Peninsula—causing Pyongyang to give up its stockpile of nuclear weapons as well as all the plutonium and enriched uranium it has produced to build new weapons. Eliminating North Korea's nuclear weapons capability would remove a major threat to South Korea, Japan and the United States by preventing Pyongyang from utilizing these weapons and by ending the risk of North Korea transferring its nuclear weapons or materials to terrorist groups and rogue states.

The United States and Korean reunification

While the United States has long given official support to the goal of Korean reunification, it has never been a high American policy priority. To the extent the U.S. continues to publicly endorse this goal, it does so largely at the urging of its South Korean ally, for whom reunification is the foremost national aspiration. A U.S.-China Framework Agreement would underscore U.S. support for Korean reunification—and thereby provide major benefits to the United States on the Korean Peninsula.

A reunified, democratic Korea that comes into existence through the manifest support and assistance of the United States would be inclined to be a U.S. ally for the foreseeable future. Much of the domestic South

Korean opposition to the alliance arises from claims of the political left that America played a major role in dividing Korea and therefore bears responsibility for this national tragedy. By acting as a "midwife" for Korean reunification, the United States would solidify support across the political spectrum, which is essential to the ongoing existence of the alliance. The continued presence of U.S. forces, following reunification, would contribute to regional stability and provide reassurance to both Korea and Japan against any future possibility that China could seek to dominate the region.[34]

Reunification under South Korea's democratic political system would also be a triumph for the American values of democracy, rule of law and protection of human rights. Extending South Korea's democracy to North Korea would show the superiority of this system of governance, which supplanted South Korea's own authoritarian regime in the late 1980s. Even more importantly, reunification led by South Korea would free North Korea's long-suffering people from the despotic regime that has ruled the country for more than 60 years. Today, there are at least six political prisons in North Korea holding more than 175,000 inmates.[35] The horrific conditions inside these camps have come to light through reports of refugees who were former prisoners and managed to flee the country. According to recent surveys analyzed by Professor Stephan Haggard of the University of California and Marcus Noland, Deputy Director of the Peterson Institute for International Economics, 90 percent of refugees held in political prisons "reported witnessing forced starvation, 60 percent reported witnessing deaths due to beating or torture, and 27 percent reported witnessing executions."[36]

By entering into a Framework Agreement with China that fosters reunification under South Korean auspices and frees North Korea's people from the repressive conditions in which they live, the United States would contribute greatly to achieving a historic vindication of human rights, as an element of realizing its policy goals on the Korean Peninsula.

CHAPTER TEN

Conclusion: the China fallacy

In February 1972, President Richard Nixon traveled to Beijing and achieved a fundamental shift in relations between the United States and China. During his week-long visit, the U.S. and China ended more than two decades of hostility and laid the basis for normal diplomatic relations that continue to the present day. The wisdom of the diplomatic strategy that Nixon and Secretary of State Henry Kissinger devised and implemented has become evident in many ways over the forty years since their historic 1972 trip. Cooperation between the two nations helped bring about the demise of the Soviet Union during the last years of the Cold War. Good U.S.-China relations facilitated the remarkable economic transformation of China since Deng Xiaoping's embrace of market economy principles in 1978. In the words of former U.S. Deputy Secretary of State Robert Zoellick, diplomatic ties have fostered China's emergence as a "responsible stakeholder" that strengthens many regional and global institutions.[1]

No less than in 1972, it is once again in the best interests of the United States to embrace and pursue a new strategy that improves America's relations with China. By achieving a rapprochement with China, the U.S. would conserve American power and invest in international stability for the long term. Realizing a new paradigm for U.S.-China relations would confer numerous security, economic and political benefits on the United States over the coming decades. By failing to act boldly and by accepting the "tyranny of the status quo," however, the U.S. risks moving down a path that could lead to military confrontation or a serious deterioration in relations with China during the foreseeable future.

In recent years, the status quo of U.S. relations with China has increasingly been shaped by the fear-mongering of China hawks and protectionists in the United States. It is not the threat China currently poses which primarily gives force to the views of these critics. Their political strength—and the resonance they find among the American public—derives largely from widespread fears of what the future may bring. In the face of their pessimism, it is all the more important to recognize the reality of current security and economic conditions regarding China.

America is still without question the world's only superpower and possesses the military prowess to invade and destroy any other country. American forces now dominate the vast maritime area in the Asia Pacific. The overall military balance remains highly skewed in favor of the United States, measured by both quantitative and qualitative comparisons of strategic nuclear forces and conventional weapons systems.

On the economic front, China is now the third-largest export market for the United States and the U.S. is China's largest single country trading partner. American exports to China reached about $104 billion in 2011, a new record, and now exceed U.S. exports to every country in the world except for Canada and Mexico.[2] Forty-eight of America's 50 states have achieved triple-digit growth in exports to China since 2000, far more than their exports to any other country. U.S. companies have invested approximately $50 billion in China and the United States stands to benefit greatly from billions of dollars in direct investments by Chinese companies over the next decade.

Sustaining America's greatness in the decades ahead will require some hard choices, but there are many reasons for optimism, as *New York Times* columnist Thomas Friedman and Johns Hopkins University Professor Michael Mandelbaum remind us in *That Used to Be Us*. Friedman and Mandelbaum point out that U.S. society retains the special characteristics that justify a sense of American exceptionalism among nations.

> [If] you were to design a country ideally suited to flourish in the world we are living in, it would look more like the United States than any other. In a world in which individual creativity is becoming ever more important, America supports individual achievement and celebrates the quirky. In a world in which technological change and creative destruction take place at warp speed, requiring maximal economic flexibility, the American economy is as flexible as any on the planet. In a world in which transparent, reliable institutions, and especially the rule of law, are more important than ever for risk-taking and innovation, the United States has an outstanding legal environment. In an age in which even the cleverest inventors and entrepreneurs have to try and fail, sometimes repeatedly, before finding the business equivalent of a mother lode, the American business culture understands that failure is often the necessary condition for success.[3]

Optimism about America's future, however, does not mean we can afford to pursue foreign policy goals which are not grounded in reality. That is why it is so important for U.S. leaders to pay heed to the wisdom of the National Intelligence Council, the center for strategic thinking in the United

States "intelligence community" which brings together representatives of 17 intelligence agencies and organizations within the Executive branch. The National Intelligence Council tells us that by 2025, "the unprecedented shift in relative wealth and economic power roughly from West to East now under way will continue" and "the international system will be a global multipolar one."[4] The United States "will remain the single most powerful country but will be less dominant" as emerging market economies like China, India, Brazil and Russia exercise greater international influence. Among those four nations, "China is poised to have more impact on the world over the next 20 years than any other country."

In thinking about the future in Asia, the United States has a fundamental choice. It can continue to accelerate the strategic containment of China to preserve U.S. dominance, and in so doing, burden the American economy with excessive defense expenditures while heightening the risk of a devastating war. Or it can prudently conserve American power by seeking a stable peace through rapprochement with China, while rebuilding America's economy to cope with the challenges of the twenty-first century. Diplomatically resolving the outstanding security and economic conflicts with China would allow the U.S. to return to the traditional strategic doctrine that guided America for a century and helped underwrite American prosperity—preventing any other country from exercising dominance in the Asia Pacific.

Risks to the United States from maintaining the status quo of U.S.-China relations

Although China has not yet become the mortal security and economic threat that critics portray, fears of China's future dominance have already foreclosed consideration of alternative options for U.S. policy. Only one approach today has broad legitimacy within the American foreign policy community—the ongoing effort to improve U.S. security and economic standing vis-à-vis China within the constraints of the existing power structure in the Asia Pacific.

Despite the acknowledged importance of U.S.-China relations, their current structure and character are accepted as immutable givens by most American politicians, diplomats and policymakers. This widespread acceptance of the status quo creates a rigidity that carries with it very serious risks for the United States. Among these risks are the following:

> The current U.S. policy of seeking to contain China—often officially termed a strategy of pure "hedging"—is likely to become unstable over time. China's resistance to close-in surveillance of

its coast by the U.S. Navy and Air Force will continue to grow and result in more "accidental" military confrontations that could easily spiral out of control. Up to now, these encounters have markedly ratcheted up bilateral tensions but were contained through crisis consultations among American and Chinese diplomats. It is highly improbable the U.S. can continue to "bat one thousand percent" and prevent military escalation when similar events occur in the future. Risks of conflict are particularly high in the regions of the South and East China seas. Since July 2010, the U.S. regards the South China Sea as a "national interest," and has indicated it is prepared to intervene in disputes over competing claims by China, Taiwan, Vietnam and several other Southeast Asian countries to small island territories and undersea petroleum resources. The U.S. considers Japan's claim to the Senkaku/Diaoyu Islands in the East China Sea to fall under the U.S.-Japan Security Treaty and would almost certainly come to Japan's defense in a clash with Chinese forces. In both regions, the scope and scale of intrusive intelligence activities by the U.S. Navy and Air Force against Chinese targets are expected to increase rapidly over the next decade, heightening the risks of confrontation.

While relations between Taiwan and China are at an historic high point as a result of Taiwanese President Ma Ying-jeou's conciliatory policy, the opposition Democratic Progressive Party (DPP) could return to power in 2016. If and when the DPP once again shapes Taiwan's foreign policy, it could well carry out its pledge to declare Taiwan's independence, triggering a harsh nationalist reaction from Beijing, which considers reunification with Taiwan a leading security policy goal. The United States would likely intervene to defend Taiwan from any military threats, in part to uphold the credibility of its commitments to protect Japan and South Korea. The result might well be a full-scale conflict between the United States and China which could escalate to a nuclear confrontation.

If the transition to North Korea's young and inexperienced leader, Kim Jong-un, does not go smoothly and a power struggle occurs, there could be a breakdown of public order in North Korea, leading to the collapse of the Kim regime. Following a collapse, South Korea, the United States and China would likely send forces into the North, as noted earlier. Given the current strategic competition between China and the United States, there exists a real danger that the two countries will not "de-conflict" their forces either prior to a North Korea crisis or in the immediate period after a breakdown occurs. Consequently, South Korean troops, with the support of

U.S. military components, will more than likely encounter Chinese forces moving across the North Korea-China frontier to create a new security zone extending inside North Korea. Other Chinese forces may head for Pyongyang or provincial capitals to establish a political and military presence. As in the case of a Taiwan conflict, the chances of a U.S.-China military confrontation are high.

Rather than face severe regional tension caused by ongoing strategic competition between the U.S. and China, Japan and South Korea may seek to loosen their alliance commitments to the United States at some point in the future. They could reason that it is easier to play a significantly more autonomous political role without a security treaty binding them to the United States. By establishing true political and diplomatic independence, while leveraging their ties with both the U.S. and China, Japan and South Korea could effectively dismantle the American "hub and spokes" alliance system, because it no longer provides them with sufficient security and stability in the Asia Pacific.

Although U.S. forces responding to a crisis in the Taiwan Strait would surely have qualitative superiority, it is likely China would employ a so-called "asymmetric strategy" relying on a relatively inexpensive weapon (known colloquially as an "assassin's mace") to temporarily neutralize U.S. military advantage.[5] American military professionals believe China could conceivably prevent U.S. aircraft from destroying China's surface-to-air missile sites and thus keep the United States from quickly establishing air superiority. If China achieves some military success in a Taiwan crisis, it would harm the credibility of American military deterrence in the Asia Pacific, even if U.S. forces prevail in the end. The Japanese and South Korean governments and publics would seriously question the value of the U.S. commitment to their security. The rationale for the ongoing American military presence in Asia would be deeply compromised.

On more than one occasion, protectionist measures the U.S. imposed on China during the Obama Administration appeared likely to trigger strong retaliatory measures from Beijing that could have led to a trade war. China's ultimately cautious responses to a punitive U.S. tariff on tire imports in 2009 and aggressive American trade investigations in 2010, together with the judicious reluctance in 2011 of Treasury Secretary Timothy Geithner and Republican congressional leaders to declare China a "currency manipulator," prevented events from getting out of control. So long as protectionists hold sway in the United States Congress, however, there is the ever-present danger of a trade war, which could cause major losses of American jobs and great damage to U.S. businesses. The United States and China could find themselves drawn into an antagonistic rivalry between competing trade blocs in the Asia Pacific—one dominated by the U.S. and the other by China—which would seriously inhibit international commerce rather than stimulate it. This risk became more acute in November 2011 when the Obama Administration sought to exclude China from its initiative to build a free trade bloc in Asia known as the Trans-Pacific Partnership.

The ongoing strategic competition between the United States and China strengthens China's Communist Party and helps ensure it will remain in power for the foreseeable future. Whenever the need arises, the Chinese Communist Party justifies its repression of dissidents and its reluctance to adopt human rights practices as necessary for maintaining public order. Party officials frequently cite the security threat from the United States, and the acute danger of a U.S. attack during a crisis over Taiwan, to give legitimacy to harsh measures they take against individual human rights activists and democracy movements like Charter 08. The Party aligns itself closely with China's broadly felt nationalist desire to stand up to all foreign threats so as to redeem the country from the "century of humiliation" it endured at the hands of colonial powers. One of the greatest risks the U.S. faces is that an increasingly confrontational posture toward China will shore up a regime whose precepts are contrary to core American political principles. The soundest basis for stable long-term U.S.-China relations—a commonality of democratic political values—will be that much harder to achieve.

Moving to a new paradigm for U.S.-China relations

The risks faced by the United States in pursuing its current policy toward China make it clear that reinforcing the status quo of U.S.-China relations is fraught with serious dangers. This is not a strategic approach that will optimize U.S. interests and could lead, in fact, to a number of dire outcomes. The United States would be well-advised to seek a new paradigm for U.S.-China relations by pursuing rapprochement with China through a process of reciprocal restraint, where each country practices accommodation and expects reciprocity. The principles and goals to guide this process are best expressed through a Framework Agreement which addresses outstanding disputes between the U.S. and China on security, economic and political issues. This agreement would create a new diplomatic architecture between the two countries, strengthening stability in the Asia Pacific for decades to come.

Before embarking on this new course, however, Americans will understandably ask a logical question: why will adopting a new paradigm for U.S.-China relations enable the United States to advance its national interests and "win" in a historical context? What major security, economic and political benefits will improved relations with China confer on the United States? In these concluding pages, it is valuable to underscore what those benefits will be.

Security benefits

The American people have proven time and again during the last two hundred years they are not afraid to go to war for the sake of a just cause. But their willingness to fight for the interests and values of their country and its allies does not mean they intrinsically prefer military over diplomatic means for resolving complex international problems. It is fair to say an overwhelming majority of Americans seek to avoid war in the nuclear age, if security disputes can be resolved through an equitable settlement of differences. Thus, the greatest benefit of significantly improving relations with China is that the United States would avoid a military conflict for the foreseeable future with a country it now considers a major potential adversary. But other security benefits of rapprochement are also tangible and important:

> *The U.S. would be in a far better position to help shape the direction of China's military modernization*

> A large-scale reduction in the "U.S. threat" would allow China to considerably ratchet down the scope, scale and tempo of its military modernization programs as well as the portion of the national defense budget devoted to modernization. China's leaders would no longer perceive an urgent need to engage in a broad military buildup to give them the capability to counter an expected U.S. attack in the immediate future.

> *Taiwan's democratic political system and national security would be protected for the long term*

> Instead of negotiating under severe threat of missile attack and invasion, Taiwan could deal with China in a stable and non-threatening security environment following the elimination, reduction and redeployment of Chinese forces. As it chooses,

Taipei could seek to settle sensitive political issues with Beijing regarding national reconciliation. Or it could refrain from negotiating a permanent settlement and retain *de facto* independence.

Rather than preparing to confront China militarily, the U.S. could leverage China's capabilities much more effectively to meet transnational security challenges of concern to the United States as well as America's allies and friends in East Asia

These challenges include preventing the proliferation of nuclear weapons and materials, halting terrorism, ensuring energy security, assuring the safety of maritime commerce and severely restricting the trafficking of arms, narcotics and people. U.S.-China cooperation within existing and new regional security structures in East Asia will no doubt strengthen multilateral approaches to transnational problems.

The government of Japan, led by the country's Democratic Party since August 2009, acknowledges that an arms race and confrontational approach to China is not in its national best interests

Tokyo has chosen to reaffirm the importance of the U.S.-Japan alliance and bolster its armed forces at the same time as it pursues greater autonomy through a "middle power" strategy. This strategy calls for Japan to assert a significant leadership role in East Asia, while making a concerted effort to strengthen regional and global institutions that will shape China's behavior and increase Tokyo's leverage over Beijing. An improvement in U.S.-China relations will eliminate difficult obstacles Japan faces in pursuing its foreign policy goals and facilitate a "grand bargain" between Japan and China that strengthens regional security and cooperation.

By eliminating China's need to preserve North Korea as a strategic buffer and keep the Kim Jong-un regime in power, improved U.S.-China relations would encourage Beijing to work much more closely with the United States to denuclearize North Korea

Better relations would also greatly reduce the possibility that U.S. and Chinese military forces could confront each other in North Korea if the regime in Pyongyang collapses. Beijing and Washington would far more easily be able to coordinate their planning for a "North Korea contingency" to ensure that troops crossing into North Korea from China and South Korea would not regard each other as hostile forces.

*An improvement in U.S.-China relations would provide strong
American support for Seoul's most important long-term foreign
policy goal—achieving the reunification of the Korean nation*

> Because China would no longer prize North Korea as a strategic
> buffer or regard a regime in Pyongyang as an essential ally, Beijing
> would support a friendly, democratic reunified Korea that is
> conducive to regional stability in Northeast Asia and poses no threat
> to China's security. By facilitating Korean reunification in this way,
> the U.S. would solidify strong support in South Korea for continuing
> the U.S.-Korea alliance over the long term. Following reunification,
> Koreans, north and south, would favor their country's alliance with
> a "distant superpower" as a prudent hedge against any possible
> effort by China to dominate the Korean peninsula.

Economic benefits

China's rapidly growing economy provides many benefits to the United
States—to consumers who buy low-priced Chinese goods, American
companies that use Chinese inputs for their manufacturing operations,
exporters who sell large quantities of products and services to China, and
U.S. firms that operate profitable businesses in China or receive infusions of
Chinese investment. But Washington's economic relations with Beijing are
far more fragile than generally recognized due to strong political pressure
from U.S. protectionists. In September 2009, the Obama Administration
gave in to arm-twisting by the United Steelworkers union and imposed
a high punitive tariff on Chinese tires. This action came close to starting
a trade war when China threatened to retaliate against U.S. imports. A
year later, under pressure from the Steelworkers and other protectionists,
Democratic Party leaders encouraged candidates to scapegoat China for
high unemployment during the global financial crisis. In October 2011, the
Senate passed legislation to impose yet more tariffs on Chinese products
because of "currency manipulation," despite data showing that market
forces pushed up the value of China's currency by nearly 7 percent over
the prior year. And in his 2012 State of the Union address, kicking off an
election year, President Obama appealed to protectionists by emphasizing his
administration "brought trade cases against China at nearly twice the rate
as the last administration."[6] Neither were Republican presidential candidates immune to the political attractions of "China bashing." Governor
Mitt Romney, in particular, called in fall 2011 for "confronting China"
on trade by threatening to brand it a "currency manipulator" and impose
new tariff duties.[7] The *Wall Street Journal* cautioned that "once a President
unleashes protectionist furies, they are hard to contain" and suggested

Romney's position was "a political maneuver to blunt the criticism he'll receive because some of [his former private equity firm's] companies sent jobs overseas or ... to win over working-class precincts in Pennsylvania and Ohio." The *Journal* astutely observed that "[G]iving Americans the impression that a trade war will bring those jobs back to the U.S. is offering false hope. It also distracts from the other fiscal and regulatory reforms that are needed to attract capital and create jobs."

Allegations of unfair trade practices resonate especially deeply with the U.S. electorate because China has a communist government and is viewed by many Americans as a potential security threat. Protectionists can multiply public fears of the economic threat that China poses to U.S. jobs and workers because the country's general reputation is so poor. These critics ignore the truth that the United States cannot expect to rapidly grow its economy—providing opportunities and jobs for American workers—if it undermines and attempts to block international trade by China. Nationalist measures such as "Buy American" laws as well as oppressive tariff and non-tariff barriers directed against China invite retaliation and, in the worst case, can trigger a trade war with highly negative effects on both countries and the global economy.

By resolving outstanding security disputes with China, the U.S. would lay the basis for a broad bilateral free trade agreement, which markedly lowers tariff and non-tariff barriers. An FTA would maximize mutual trade and investment by significantly scaling down protectionist measures and opening each country's market to a far greater extent than now. It would encourage Chinese companies and entrepreneurs to make major capital investments in the United States, especially in new plants and infrastructure, within an American legal framework that effectively screens out any threats to U.S. national security from foreign direct investment. Large capital flows would move in the other direction as well, as U.S. investors considerably increase their participation in China's historic process of economic development.

In the largest sense, improved relations with China would allow the United States to leverage China's expected economic growth and, in so doing, immeasurably strengthen America's economy and create new jobs, new technologies and new products that raise the U.S. standard of living. China is already the biggest growth market for U.S. goods and services. It is still a developing country whose immense social and economic needs will not be fulfilled for decades. These needs create opportunities for U.S. companies and workers to reap major economic rewards and create thousands of new jobs by investing capital, technology, skills and know-how to help China reduce environmental pollution, provide world-class health services, and construct major infrastructure facilities, to mention only several sectors. But these opportunities will only come to fruition if a Free Trade Agreement eliminates the burden of tariffs, non-tariff barriers, excessive taxes, and other restraints on foreign trade.

Equally important for U.S. companies doing business in Asia is that improved relations would end the worrisome possibility that China and the United States could support rival trading blocs in East Asia, or that the current movement toward economic integration in the region could lead to a new economic organization that excludes the United States. Once they no longer view each other as strategic competitors, the U.S. and China will have every reason to work together to achieve a free trade area of the Asia Pacific, which is built in part on their bilateral FTA. A Trans-Pacific Partnership that includes China would advance crucial objectives of American economic policy—liberalizing U.S.-China trade, obtaining greater access to the Chinese market for U.S. goods and services, preventing government subsidies that distort trade relationships, protecting intellectual property and fostering both greater Chinese investment in the United States and greater U.S. investment in China. An inclusive Trans-Pacific Partnership would avoid forcing Asian countries to choose between the United States and China, and in particular, help mitigate the latent rivalry between Japan and China. U.S. involvement would ensure that Japan's economic interests are fully protected and that Tokyo obtains large rewards from expanded trade.

Political benefits

Strategic competition between the U.S. and China is a major factor that allows China's communist regime to justify internal repression, infringe human rights and curb the growth of democracy. By settling outstanding security disputes and improving relations with Beijing, the United States would do far more to advance human rights and democratic practices in China than the U.S. has been able to do through any other policy measures to date.

This is because improving relations will remove the Communist Party's primary means of legitimizing repression—its argument that foreign countries, particularly the United States and its allies, use domestic political dissent to destabilize the country. China's leaders often seize on the desire of outside powers to exploit China's ethnic differences and exacerbate internal disputes to keep the country weak. Exhibit A, in Communist Party propaganda, is the alleged U.S. aim of preventing China from completing its historic process of reunification through America's military support for Taiwan. China portrays human rights and democracy activists as either foreign agents or unwitting dupes who allow the United States to interfere in China's internal affairs and damage its national sovereignty. Once the "U.S. threat" to China is effectively removed, China's leaders would no longer be able to characterize the repression of dissidents as a form of national defense. They could no longer stir strong nationalist public opinion against political activists, such as the supporters of Charter 08, by claiming they are "traitors" who have allied themselves with a foreign power that is a serious external threat to China.

Following resolution of the Taiwan issue, including guarantees for the island's autonomy and democratic political system, China would also be able to look explicitly to Taiwan and Hong Kong for political practices that would benefit China as a whole. The Taiwan model would have more influence on China's future political development than purely Western political systems precisely because Taiwan represents homegrown "Chinese democracy" that emerged through internal reform.

The China fallacy

China hawks and protectionists alike regularly convey dire warnings to the American people about the "China threat." Gripped by fears of China's ascendance, and aware that China is still ruled by a communist regime, it is all too easy to succumb to the conventional wisdom that accelerating the strategic containment of China and taking protectionist measures to block China's trade and investment is in the U.S. best interests. The better course for fair-minded Americans is to debunk the fallacy that the U.S. and China will inevitably go to war or that China's rise is occurring at the expense of the United States. We need to ask ourselves whether the U.S. can achieve more optimal relations with China that would lead to far greater benefits for the American people. We need to weigh deeply the alternative approach of improving ties with China as a means of best advancing our own security, economic and political interests as well as the interests of our allies in Asia and elsewhere. America's future depends on it.

Fortunately, how the United States deals with China's rise is not fixed for all time by existing policy. It is entirely realistic for the United States to settle its outstanding security disputes with China. It is eminently feasible for the U.S. to reach an agreement with China that drastically lowers trade barriers, unleashes unprecedented capital flows between the two countries, creates thousands of new American jobs and fosters the creation of an Asia economic bloc that is fully inclusive of the United States, China, Japan and South Korea as well as other countries in the region. By effectively ending the strategic competition with China and eliminating the "U.S. threat" to its security, the U.S. will greatly strengthen the forces of democracy and human rights within China.

At this historic juncture, the United States faces a crucial strategic choice in the Asia Pacific. It can continue its major military buildup to prepare for war with China while continuing to erect trade barriers that protect the American market against Chinese products. Or it can strive to achieve a new paradigm for improved U.S.-China relations, drawing on America's superior military, economic and political power.

The best way of overcoming the "China threat" and advancing U.S. interests in the Asia Pacific is by achieving a stable peace with China through the resolution of outstanding security and economic disputes between the two countries. The means to this goal is rapprochement based on the practice of reciprocal restraint. A Framework Agreement of the kind described in Chapter Seven would provide the diplomatic architecture for rapprochement by allowing the United States to move away from its risky and unnecessary strategy of preserving American dominance in East Asia and return to its traditional strategy of preventing any other country from dominating the region. It would enable the United States to leverage China's economic growth and secure Taiwan's democracy.

In the broadest sense, this approach would ensure long-term stability and security in the Asia Pacific, promote U.S. economic prosperity, keep faith with America's closest Asian allies and underscore America's profound commitment to democracy and human rights. It would end the "China threat" for generations to come.

EPILOGUE

To fully appreciate the importance to the United States of good relations with China, it is worth recalling the wise words spoken by American presidents and senior foreign policy officials during the last 40 years.

President Richard M. Nixon

February 1972

The Chinese people are a great people, the American people are a great people. If our two peoples are enemies, the future of this world we share together is dark indeed. But if we can find common ground to work together, the chance for world peace is immeasurably increased .... So let us ... start a long march together, not in lockstep, but on different roads leading to the same goal, the goal of building a world structure of peace and justice in which all may stand together with equal dignity and in which each nation, large or small, has a right to determine its own form of government, free of outside interference or domination. The world watches. The world listens. The world waits to see what we will do .... There is no reason for us to be enemies. Neither of us seeks the territory of the other; neither of us seeks domination over the other; neither of us seeks to stretch out our hands and rule the world.[1]

President Jimmy Carter

December 1978

The United States of America and the People's Republic of China have agreed to recognize each other and to establish diplomatic relations as of January 1, 1979 .... As a nation of gifted people who comprise about one-fourth of the total population of the Earth, China plays, already, an important role in world affairs, a role that can only grow more important in the years ahead .... The change that I'm announcing tonight will be of great long-term benefit to the peoples of both our country and China—and, I believe, to all the peoples of the world. Normalization—and the expanded commercial and cultural relations that it will bring—will contribute to the well-being of our own Nation, to our own national interest, and it will also enhance the stability of Asia .... These events are the final result of long and serious negotiations begun by President Nixon in 1972, and continued under the leadership of President Ford. The results bear witness to the steady, determined, bipartisan effort of our country to build a world in which peace will be the goal and the responsibility of all nations.[2]

President Ronald Reagan

April 1984

We have begun to write a new chapter for peace and progress in our histories with America and China going forward hand in hand .... We must always be realistic about our relationship, frankly acknowledging the fundamental differences in ideology and institutions between our two societies. Yes, let us acknowledge those differences. Let us never minimize them. But let us not be dominated by them. I have not come to China to hold forth on what divides us, but to build on what binds us. I have not come to dwell on a closed-door past, but to urge that Americans and Chinese look to the future, because together we can and will make tomorrow a better day .... We can work together as equals in a spirit of mutual respect and mutual benefit .... America and China are both great nations. And we have a special responsibility to preserve world peace.[3]

President William J. Clinton

June 1998

Some Americans believe we should try to isolate and contain China because of its undemocratic system and human rights violations, and in order to retard its capacity to become America's next great enemy ....

Seeking to isolate China is clearly unworkable .... [Choosing] isolation over engagement would not make the world safer. It would make it more dangerous. It would undermine rather than strengthen our efforts to foster stability in Asia. It would eliminate, not facilitate cooperation on issues relating to weapons of mass destruction. It would hinder, not help the cause of democracy and human rights in China. It would set back, not step up worldwide efforts to protect the environment. It would cut off, not open up one of the world's most important markets. It would encourage the Chinese to turn inward and to act in opposition to our interests and values.[4]

Former National Security Advisor Samuel R. Berger

January 2001

[A] principle that guides our foreign policy in a global age is that peace and security for America depends on building principled, constructive relations with our former great power adversaries, Russia and China .... With China, our challenge has been to steer between the extremes of uncritical engagement and untenable confrontation. That balance has helped maintain peace in the Taiwan Straits, secured China's help in maintaining stability on the Korean Peninsula, and allowed us to negotiate an historic agreement to bring it into the World Trade Organization. [The WTO Agreement] ... represents the most constructive breakthrough in U.S.-China relations since normalization in 1979. For China, it is a declaration of interdependence, and a commitment to start dismantling the command and control economy through which the Communist Party exercises much of its power.[5]

Former National Security Advisor Brent Scowcroft

September 2006

[W]e've had seven presidents reaffirm the general direction of our relations with China, but they didn't all start out that way .... [Tiananmen Square] was a serious crisis in the relationship. We had to respond. It was an outrageous act .... President [George H. W.] Bush felt he had to respond but he did not want to sever this relationship which had been gradually built up and gradually deepened .... [T]here have been some really, really rough spots in this relationship. But I think the fact that it has endured shows that it is deeply important both to the United States and China, and it will not survive any blows that either side can strike at it but it's strong enough to endure most of them. So I'm proudly optimistic for the future.[6]

Former Secretary of State
James Baker

March 2011

Allow me to be blunt. Some in the United States—not a majority by any means, but certainly a vocal minority—see China's rise as a threat somehow to America's international status. They believe that conflict between our two countries is inevitable as Chinese ambitions clash with American position and power. Ladies and gentlemen, these observers are wrong. And they are not only wrong, they are dangerously wrong. And the reason is very simple—their analyses grossly underestimate the broad areas where Chinese and American interests converge.[7]

Former Secretary of the Treasury
Henry Paulson, Jr.

April 2011

There's no doubt in my mind that ... the more cross border investment we have, the more US investment in China and the more Chinese investment in US, the stronger the relations will be between the two countries .... And as I look at fundamental problems [the United States is] dealing with, whether they are the economic problem globally, whether they're national security, whether the environment, [I believe] that these issues will be easier to solve if you get the biggest developed nation and the biggest developing nation working well together and with others, and [those problems will] be impossible to solve if we don't work together .... [W]hat we're going to find is that a prosperous growing Asia is going to be very good for the US, and a prosperous US is going to be good for Asia .... [T]he more engagement you have, the more investment you have ... [and] then when the inevitable difficulties take place, or [political conflicts occur], in Washington or Beijing, it would be easier to bridge those, the more ties we have between our two countries.[8]

Former Secretary of State Henry Kissinger

May 2011

In his essay 'Perpetual Peace,' the philosopher Immanuel Kant argued that perpetual peace would eventually come to the world in one of two ways: by human insight or by conflicts and catastrophes of a magnitude that left humanity no other choice. We are at such a juncture. When Premier Zhou Enlai and I agreed on the communiqué that announced the secret visit, he said: "This will shake the world." What a culmination if, forty years later, the United States and China could merge their efforts not to shake the world, but to build it.[9]

Former National Security Advisor Zbigniew Brzezinski

January 2012

The United States' central challenge over the next several decades is to revitalize itself, while promoting a larger West and buttressing a complex balance in the East that can accommodate China's rising global status .... If the United States and China can accommodate each other on a broad range of issues, the prospects for stability in Asia will be greatly increased .... [The] United States must recognize that stability in Asia can no longer be imposed by a non-Asian power, least of all by the direct application of U.S. military power. Indeed, U.S. efforts to buttress Asian stability could prove self-defeating, propelling Washington into a costly repeat of its recent wars, potentially even resulting in a replay of the tragic events of Europe in the twentieth century.[10]

ACKNOWLEDGMENTS

I would first like to express deep gratitude to the teachers, mentors, and colleagues who helped shape my views and approach to the issues discussed in this book, dating from my days as a student of political theory, law, and international relations at Cornell University and the University of Chicago; through my service at the National Security Council, the U.S. Arms Control and Disarmament Agency, and the State Department; and in my work since that time as a policy advisor and international business strategist: Peter Almquist, Samuel R. Berger, Gerhard Casper, Jong-hyun Choi, Jean-Marc Coicaud, Pierce Corden, Ralph Cossa, Joseph Cropsey, Kenneth W. Dam, Robert Einhorn, Eldon Eisenach, Leon Fuerth, Banning Garrett, Bonnie Glaser, James E. Goodby, Gidon Gottlieb, John D. Holum, Hong-choo Hyun, Hyung-taek Hong, Morris Janowitz, Jungsoo Jang, Byung-ki Kim, Won Kim, Woosang Kim, Isaac Kramnick, Alan Kreczko, Tae Sun Kwon, Dong Hwi Lee, Hye Min Lee, John Mearsheimer, Jack N. Merritt, Jongryn Mo, Chung-in Moon, Paul Moore, Shinil Park, Alan Romberg, Todd Rosenblum, Barbara F. Starr, Maiky Tran, Tang Tsou, Paul Warnke, Joel Wit, and Young-kwan Yoon. I am particularly indebted to Sandy Berger, Joe Cropsey, Jim Goodby, John Holum, Chung-in Moon and Paul Warnke.

I am very lucky to have good friends and family who have believed in me and sustained me over the years: Bruce Fredrickson, Joy and Stanley Gaines, Anna and George M. Gross, Florence and Alfred Gross, Gerald Gross, Jane Gross, Jeffrey M. Gross, Kenneth W. Gross, Lisa Gross, Peter Gross, Sue Gross, Hannah Hammer, Alex Copson, Betsy Hurowitz, Donald Hurowitz, Christopher Keats, SY Kim, Fredric J. Klink, Judy Levine, Noah Levine, Eileen Lipson, Sandra Lipson, Theresa Lipson, Alice and Norman Newhouse, David Newhouse, Jonathan Newhouse, Mark Newhouse, Peter Newhouse, Robyn Newhouse, Young Ae Oh, YM Park, Walter Philbin, Jonathan Puth, Andrew Racine, Esteban Rosas, Jack Scovil, Temoor Sidiqi, Daniel Sobo, Lanny Thomas, Ellen Wang and John Zuckerman. I am especially indebted to Jeff Gross, Ken Gross, Jonny Newhouse, Mark Newhouse and Andy Racine.

Susan Leon offered excellent editorial advice that improved the manuscript in numerous ways. Doug Bandow, Jean-Marc Coicaud and Jim Goodby provided invaluable comments, drawing on their deep policy expertise. Michael Hagan and Benjamin Landy were my companions on the journey of researching the book and made major contributions. My editor at Bloomsbury, Marie-Claire Antoine, decided to publish my manuscript and superbly shaped the book. John Mark Boling, Kara Zavada, Tanya Leet and assistant editor Ally Jane Grossan of Bloomsbury admirably handled marketing and publicity with wise counsel from Kate Pinnick, Ellin Sanger, Keith Blackman, Meg Walker and Dan Sobo. Kim Storry, Jennifer Laing, Nicholas Church and Jeremy Complin did a superlative job of preparing the book for publication. My agent, Jason Allen Ashlock, guided me throughout and taught me a great deal about the publishing process.

I am grateful for more than I can say to Lisa Gross and Sue Gross. This book is dedicated to my beloved parents, Gloria and Robert Gross.

ABOUT THE AUTHOR

Donald Gross is a policy expert, strategist and lawyer with many years of experience in government, public affairs, diplomacy and international business. He is also an Adjunct Fellow of Pacific Forum CSIS, a non-profit foreign policy research institute affiliated with the Center for Strategic and International Studies. Mr. Gross held several U.S. government positions before returning to the private sector in 2000. From 1997 until 2000, he was senior advisor to the Under Secretary for Arms Control and International Security Affairs in the Department of State, where he developed diplomatic strategy toward East Asia and served in senior positions on U.S. delegations negotiating sensitive issues with China, Japan, South Korea and North Korea. Prior to joining the State Department, he was counselor and senior policy advisor of the U.S. Arms Control and Disarmament Agency from 1994 to 1997 and director of legislative affairs at the National Security Council in the White House from 1993 to 1994. Before and immediately after his government service, Mr. Gross practiced law in New York, Washington, DC and Seoul, Korea. Mr. Gross graduated *magna cum laude* from Cornell University and earned his law degree at the University of Chicago, where he also pursued doctoral studies in political science. He is a graduate of the program for senior executives in national and international security at Harvard University's Kennedy School of Government.

NOTES

Chapter One

1 Robert E. Scott, "Growing Trade Deficit with China Cost 2.8 Million Jobs Between 2001 and 2010," EPI Briefing Paper, Economic Policy Institute, September 20, 2011, http://www.epi.org/files/2011/BriefingPaper323.pdf.

2 U.S. Census Bureau, "Trade in Goods with China," 2011, http://www.census.gov/foreign-trade/balance/c5700.html.

3 U.S. Trade Representative, "U.S.-China Trade Relations Entering a New Phase of Greater Accountability and Enforcement," February 2006, http://www.ustr.gov/sites/default/files/Top-to-Bottom%20Review%20FINAL.pdf.

4 An historically significant example of U.S. diplomacy regarding an individual human rights case in China is that of blind dissident Chen Guangcheng, who escaped from security forces keeping him under house arrest and sought refuge at the U.S. Embassy in Beijing. Assistant Secretary of State for East Asian and Pacific Affairs Kurt Campbell and State Department Legal Adviser Harold Koh led intense negotiations concerning Chen with Chinese officials in late April and early May 2012, prior to a meeting of the U.S.-China "Strategic and Economic Dialogue" in Beijing.

   Commenting on the outcome of the negotiations, Secretary of State Hillary Clinton said she was "pleased that we were able to facilitate Chen Guangcheng's stay and departure from the U.S. Embassy in a way that reflected his choices and our values. I was glad to have the chance to speak with him today and to congratulate him on being reunited with his wife and children. Mr. Chen has a number of understandings with the Chinese government about his future, including the opportunity to pursue higher education in a safe environment. Making these commitments a reality is the next crucial task." According to the *New York Times*, American officials "were satisfied with the pledges from the Chinese authorities that Mr. Chen, 40, would be allowed to live a normal life." They described Chinese negotiators as working "intensely and with humanity."

   See Jane Perlez, "Blind Chinese Dissident Leaves U.S. Embassy for Medical Treatment," *New York Times*, May 2, 2012.

5 Natan Sharansky, "A Dissident Defends Us All," *New York Times*, October 15, 2010.

6 Henry Kissinger, *On China*, (New York: The Penguin Press, 2011), p.522.

Chapter Two

1   PBS, *Frontline: The War Behind Closed Doors*, excerpts from 1992 Wolfowitz draft, http://www.pbs.org/wgbh/pages/frontline/shows/iraq/etc/wolf.html.

2   See Nina Hachigian and Mona Sutphen, *The Next American Century*, (New York: Simon & Schuster, 2008) pp.167–9.

3   Michael Lind, *The American Way of Strategy*, (New York: Oxford University Press, 2006), pp.151–2 (emphasis added).

4   Richard Bernstein and Ross H. Munro, *The Coming Conflict with China*, (New York: Vintage Books 1997), pp.4 and 11.

5   Bill Gertz, *The China Threat: How the People's Republic Targets America*, (Washington: Regnery Publishing Inc., 2000), p.199.

6   Steven W. Mosher, *Hegemon, China's Plan to Dominate Asia and the World*, (San Francisco: Encounter Books, 2000), p.99.

7   Edward Timperlake and William C. Triplett II, *Red Dragon Rising*, (Washington, DC: Regnery Publishing 2002), p.197.

8   John J. Mearsheimer, "Better to be Godzilla than Bambi," *Foreign Policy*, January/February 2005.

9   Robert Kagan, "The Illusion of Managing China," *Washington Post*, May 15, 2005.

10 Testimony of the Honorable Rob Simmons, U.S.-China Economic and Security Review Commission, September 15, 2005.

11 See Zbigniew Brzezinski, "Clash of the Titans: Make Money, Not War," *Foreign Policy*, January 5, 2005, http://www.foreignpolicy.com/articles/2005/01/05/clash_of_the_titans. See also an excellent analysis of international relations theory on power transition as applied to U.S.-China relations in Zhiqun Zhu, *U.S.-China Relations in the 21st Century*, (London and New York: Routledge, 2006). Professor Zhu, MacArthur Chair in East Asian Politics at Bucknell University, concludes: "There are basically two ways to prevent war: by eliminating the source of conflict that would lead a nation to resort to the use of arms, and by rendering the use of arms so unattractive that a nation would rather not start a war. Britain and Germany failed to achieve either a century ago. Today globalization and deepening interdependence have linked China and the United States inextricably together .... Great powers are increasingly united by common interests, instead of being divided by conflicting ideologies. The twenty-first century holds extraordinary opportunities for the United States and China to form coalitions against new global challenges such as terrorism and environmental degradation .... If both the United States and China take on the historic challenge and exercise statesmanship and creativity, the two powers can not only cooperate well in global and regional issues, but also manage a potential power transition peacefully in the future."

12 Brzezinski, "Clash of the Titans: Make Money, Not War."

13 G. John Ikenberry, "The Rise of China and the Future of the West," *Foreign Affairs*, January/February 2008, p.31.

14 Ibid.

15 Ding Xinghao and Yu Bin, "Hu's Not Coming to Dinner, but ... ," PacNet #4, Honolulu: Pacific Forum CSIS, April 13, 2006.

16 Hillary Clinton, "America's Pacific Century," *Foreign Policy*, November 2011, http://www.foreignpolicy.com/articles/2011/10/11/americas_pacific_century, pp.1, 3 and 10.

17 Jackie Calmes, "U.S. Expands Military Ties to Australia, Irritating China," *New York Times*, November 16, 2011.

18 "Remarks by President Obama to the Australian Parliament," The White House, Office of the Press Secretary, November 27, 2011, p.4.

19 Floyd Whaley, "Clinton Reaffirms Military Ties with the Philippines," *New York Times*, November 16, 2011.

20 Jane Perlez, "Panetta Outlines New Weaponry for the Pacific," *New York Times*, June 1, 2012; Craig Whitlock, "U.S. Eyes Return to Some Southeast Asia Military Bases," *Washington Post*, June 22, 2012; William Wan, "Defense Secretary Leon Panetta Highlights U.S. Ties to Vietnam During Visit," *Washington Post*, June 3, 2012. (Panetta's remarks were especially striking since Vietnam is a communist country which bears responsibility for the deaths of nearly 60,000 American soldiers, sailors, airmen and marines during the Vietnam war, and has failed to account for approximately 1,700 MIAs. "Vietnam War Casualties," *Wikipedia,* http://en.wikipedia.org/wiki/Vietnam_War_casualties.)

21 "Vietnam War Casualties," *Wikipedia*, http://en.wikipedia.org/wiki/Vietnam_War_casualties.

22 Bill Gertz, "Pentagon Battle Concept Has Cold War Posture on China," *Washington Times*, November 9, 2011.

23 Jose Carreno, Thomas Culora, Captain George Galdorisi, U.S. Navy (retired), and Thomas Hone, *Proceedings* (Vol. 136/8/1,290, U.S. Naval Institute, August 2010), pp.5–6.

24 J. Noel Williams, "Air-Sea Battle, An Operational Concept Looking for a Strategy," *Armed Forces Journal*, September 2011, pp.2–3.

25 Ben Feller, "Countering China, Obama Asserts U.S. a Pacific Power," *Associated Press*, November 17, 2011.

26 Hugh White, "Competing for Primacy in Asia," *New York Times*, November 21, 2011.

27 Stephen Glain, "By Choosing Arms Over Diplomacy, America Errs in Asia," *New York Times*, December 15, 2011.

28 Michael Green, "Examining Washington's 'Pivot'," *Joong Ang Daily*, December 5, 2011.

29 Wikipedia, "Hainan Island Incident," http://en.wikipedia.org/wiki/Hainan_Island_incident.

30 Wikipedia, "USNS Impeccable," http://en.wikipedia.org/wiki/USNS_Impeccable_(T-AGOS-23); Mark J. Valencia, "Foreign Military Activities in Asian EEZs: Conflict Ahead?," (Washington: The National Bureau of Asian Research, May 2011).

31 Lyle Goldstein, "The South China Sea's Georgia Scenario," *Foreign Policy*, July 11, 2011, p.2.

32 Ibid.

33 Valencia, "Foreign Military Activities in Asian EEZs: Conflict Ahead?," p.8.

34 Goldstein, "The South China Sea's Georgia Scenario," p 3; Lyle Goldstein, "Resetting the U.S.-China Security Relationship," *Survival*, Vol. 53 No. 2, April-May 2011, pp.98–9.

35 Michael D. Swaine and M. Taylor Fravel, *China's Assertive Behavior, Part Two: The Maritime Periphery*, China Leadership Monitor, No. 35, Summer 2011, p.11.

36 Mark Valencia, "Intelligence Gathering, the South China Sea, and the Law of the Sea," Nautilus Institute, August 30, 2011, http://www.nautilus.org/publications/essays/napsnet/forum/summaries/2011/Valencia_SCS, p.2.

37 Steven Lee Myers and Choe Sang-hun, "North Koreans Agree to Freeze Nuclear Work; U.S. to Give Aid," *New York Times*, February 29, 2012.

38 Choe Sang-hun, "UN Council to Expand North Korea Sanctions," *New York Times*, April 16, 2012; Joshua Altman, "Amb. Rice: China essential in passing UN resolution condemning North Korean missile test," *The Hill*, April 16, 2012, http://thehill.com/video/administration/221705-un-ambassador-security-council-resolution-is-a-way-to-up-the-pressure-on-north-korea; Louis Charbonneau, "UN condemns N. Korea launch, warns on nuclear test," *Reuters*, April 16, 2012.

39 Avery Goldstein, *Rising to the Challenge*, (Stanford: Stanford University Press, 2005), p.12.

40 Michael D. Swaine and Ashley J. Tellis, *Interpreting China's Grand Strategy: Past, Present, and Future* (Santa Monica, CA: RAND, 2000), p.65.

41 See Bates Gill, *Rising Star,* (Washington: Brookings Institution Press, 2007), p.10; Michael D. Swaine, "China's Regional Military Posture," p.272, in David Shambaugh, ed., *Power Shift*, (Berkeley: University of California Press, 2005); and Robert Sutter, "China's Regional Strategy and Why It May Not Be Good for America," in *Power Shift*, p.296.

42 Henry A. Kissinger, "The Future of U.S.-Chinese Relations," *Foreign Affairs*, Volume 91, Number 2, March/April 2012, p.50.

43 Hans M. Kristensen, Robert S. Norris and Matthew G. McKinzie, "Chinese Nuclear Forces and U.S. Nuclear War Planning," Natural Resources Defense Council, (Washington: November 2006), p.1.

44 "Nuclear Weapons: Who Has What at a Glance," (Washington: Arms Control Association, updated: August 2012, http://www.armscontrol.org/factsheets/Nuclearweaponswhohaswhat).

Under the New Strategic Arms Limitation Treaty (New START) that became effective on February 5, 2011 and "was negotiated on the basis of

George W. Bush-era nuclear targeting plans," the United States and Russia will have 7 years to reduce their arsenals to a level where "each still will be allowed to deploy 1,550 strategic nuclear weapons on as many as 700 missiles and bombers until 2021 or beyond. Thousands of additional warheads are held in reserve. Unless they adjust their thinking, both countries will spend hundreds of billions of dollars to modernize and maintain similar nuclear force levels for decades to come." See Daryl G. Kimball, "Ending Cold War Nuclear Thinking," *Arms Control Today*, (Washington: Arms Control Association, March 2012, http://www.armscontrol.org/act/2012_03/Focus).

45 "Fact Sheet: U.S. Nuclear Modernization Programs," Arms Control Association, August 2012, pp.2–3, http://www.armscontrol.org/factsheets/ USNuclearModernization. For the estimate on numbers of Chinese ICBMs, see Office of the Secretary of Defense, *Military and Security Developments Involving the People's Republic of China, 2011*, (Washington: U.S. Department of Defense, 2011), p.34.

46 "Fact Sheet: U.S. Nuclear Modernization Programs," p.3.

47 Office of the Secretary of Defense, "Military and Security Developments Involving the People's Republic of China 2011," August 2011, p.32.

48 "Fact Sheet: U.S. Nuclear Modernization Programs," p.4; Federation of American Scientists, WMD, B-2 Spirit, http://www.fas.org/nuke/guide/usa/ bomber/b-2.htm; David Axe, "U.S. Getting a New Bomber," *The Diplomat*, February 27, 2012, www.the-diplomat.com/flashpoints-blog/2012/02/27/u-s-getting-a-new-bomber; Kristensen, Hans M., Norris, Robert S. and McKinzie, Matthew G., "Chinese Nuclear Forces and U.S. Nuclear War Planning," pp.2–3.

49 It is valuable to keep in mind the important assessment by Professor Sidney D. Drell and Ambassador James E. Goodby of Stanford University, two leading American thinkers in the field of arms control and nonproliferation, that "[b]ased on an analysis of the present and prospective threats that define missions for U.S. nuclear weapons,... the strategic arsenal required by the United States can be reduced to considerably lower numbers." In their 2007 report entitled "What Are Nuclear Weapons For? Recommendations for Restructuring U.S. Strategic Nuclear Forces," Drell and Goodby recommend a "U.S. force structure of 500 operationally deployed nuclear warheads, plus 500 in a responsive force." The "operationally deployed force" would consist of "three Trident submarines on station at sea, each loaded with 24 missiles and 96 warheads (a mix of low-yield W76s and high-yield W88s) ... 100 Minuteman III ICBMs in hardened silos, each with a single W87 ... [and] 20–25 B2 and B52H bombers configured for gravity bombs or air-launched cruise missiles." Moreover, "reducing the D5 missiles from their full complement of eight warheads to four per missile will substantially increase their maximum operating areas. The same total numbers of missiles and warheads could be distributed on a larger number of Trident submarines in the interest of greater operational flexibility and survivability, albeit at higher operational costs."

For the "responsive force," Drell and Goodby propose "three Trident submarines, each loaded with 96 warheads, in transit or being replenished in port for their next missions as part of a Ready Responsive Force for a rapidly building crisis, plus two or three unarmed boats in overhaul ... [and] 50–100 additional Minuteman III missiles taken off alert and without warheads, and 20–25 bombers, unarmed, in maintenance and training, all of which would comprise a Strategic Responsive Force, for a more slowly building confrontation."

Importantly, Drell and Goodby point out that their proposed responsive force "is composed of existing warheads and delivery systems and requires no new nuclear weapons. It retains the current diversity of systems as a hedge against common failure modes. We believe that, if other nuclear-armed nations cooperate, nuclear deterrence might be maintained entirely with a responsive force, with the responsive force consisting of no more than the 500 warheads that are initially postulated for the operationally deployed force. A world without nuclear weapons should be the ultimate goal."

See Sidney D. Drell and James E. Goodby, "What are Nuclear Weapons For? Recommendations for Restructuring U.S. Strategic Nuclear Forces," An Arms Control Association Report, Washington: Arms Control Association, Revised and updated October 2007, http://www.armscontrol. org/pdf/20071104_Drell_Goodby_07_new.pdf.

50   *The Military Balance 2011*, International Institute for Strategic Studies (IISS), (London: Routledge, 2011); Michael Swaine, *America's Challenge, Engaging a Rising China in the Twenty-First Century,* (Washington: Carnegie Endowment for International Peace, 2011), p.152.

51   Gordon Lubold, "US needs more F-22 fighters than Gates wants, says an Air Force commander," *Christian Science Monitor*, June 18, 2009; "Air Force grounds F-22 fleet yet again," *RT*, http://rt.com/usa/news/air-force/f-22-fleet-549; "F-22 Raptor," U.S. Air Force Fact Sheet, posted November 25, 2009, http://www.af.mil/information/factstheets.

52   China tested a prototype of a stealth fighter, the J-20, in January 2011. According to U.S. defense expert Richard Aboulafia, a modern fighter "requires at least 11 supporting systems to be effective." Of these, the Chinese prototype showed a mastery of "just one." See David Axe, "China's Over-hyped stealth jet," *The Diplomat*, 7 January 2011. Deputy Chief of Naval Operations for information dominance Vice Adm. David J. "Jack" Dorsett indicated "it would be years before the [J-20] jet could be deployed." See Ken Dilanian, "China's development of stealth fighter takes U.S. by surprise," *Los Angeles Times*, January 7, 2011. The Pentagon's 2011 report on Chinese military capabilities characterized the prototype as "highlight[ing] China's ambition to produce a fighter aircraft that incorporates stealth attributes ..." See Office of the Secretary of Defense, *Military and Security Developments Involving the People's Republic of China, 2011*, p.4.

53   Robert F. Dorr, "U.S. Air Force Improving AWACS Capabilities," January 27, 2011, http://www.defensemedianetwork.com/stories/u-s-air-force-improving-awacs-capabilities; Federation of American Scientists, Military Analysis Network, http://www.fas.org/man/dod-101/sys/ac/e-3.htm.

54   "The Pentagon Budget: Myth vs. Reality, Cato Institute, February 29, 2012, http://www.cato-at-liberty.org/the-pentagon-budge-myth-vs-reality.

55 Keith B. Richburg, "China military spending to top $100 billion in 2012, alarming neighbors," *Washington Post*, March 4, 2012, http://www. washingtonpost.com/world/china-military-spending-to-top-100-billion-this-year/2012/03/04/gIQAJRnypR_story.html.

56 Dennis J. Blasko, "An Analysis of China's 2011 Defense Budget and Total Military Spending—The Great Unknown," *China Brief*, Jamestown Foundation, Volume XI, Issue 4, March 10, 2011.

57 *The Military Balance 2011*, pp.104, 111, 119, 130 and 157.

58 Goldstein, *Rising to the Challenge*, p.211.

59 C. Fred Bergsten et al., *China's Rise: Challenges and Opportunities*, (Washington, DC: Peterson Institute for International Economics and Center for Strategic and International Studies, 2008), p.203.

60 Ibid.

61 Bernard D. Cole, *The Great Wall at Sea, China's Navy in the Twenty-First Century* (Annapolis: Naval Institute Press, 2010), p.43.

62 Ibid.

63 Michael McDevitt, *China's Naval Modernization: Cause for Storm Warnings?*, paper presented at the 2010 Pacific Symposium, The Institute for National Strategic Studies of The National Defense University, June 16, 2010, p.11.

64 Cole, *The Great Wall at Sea*, p.202.

65 Ibid., p.170 and McDevitt, *China's Naval Modernization*, p.3.

66 McDevitt, *China's Naval Modernization*, p.27.

67 Cole, *The Great Wall at Sea*, p.198.

68 Seth Cropsey, "Keeping the Pacific Pacific," *Foreign Affairs*, September 27, 2010.

69 McDevitt, *China's Naval Modernization*, p.29.

70 William Wan, "China test-drives first aircraft carrier," *Washington Post*, August 10, 2011.

71 Brad Glosserman, "China Policy: Avoiding a Cold War Redux," *PacNet #31*, Honolulu: Pacific Forum CSIS, June 2, 2011.

72 Cole, *The Great Wall at Sea*, p.56.

73 Ibid., pp.113 and 150.

74 McDevitt, *China's Naval Modernization*, p.27.

75 Ibid., p.29.

76 M. Taylor Fravel and Evan S. Medeiros, "China's Search for Assured Retaliation," *International Security*, Vol. 75, No. 2 (Fall 2010), p.81.

77 Ibid., p.83.

78 Ibid., pp.82 and 84.

79 U.S. Department of Defense, Annual Report to Congress, *Military and Security Developments Involving the People's Republic of China 2011*, p.35.

80 Fravel and Medeiros, "China's Search for Assured Retaliation," p.87.

81 David M. Lampton, "Power Constrained: Sources of Mutual Strategic Suspicion in U.S.-China Relations," (Washington: The National Bureau of Asian Research, June 2010), pp.11, 15 and 20.

82 Charles Glaser, "Will China's Rise Lead to War?," *Foreign Affairs*, Volume 90, Number 2 (March/April 2011), pp.90–1.

83 Ted Galen Carpenter, *America's Coming War with China*, (New York: Palgrave MacMillan 2005), p.5.

84 Susan Shirk, *China: Fragile Superpower* (New York: Oxford University Press, 2007), p.186.

85 Michael D. Swaine, "Trouble in Taiwan," *Foreign Affairs* 83, No. 2 (March-April 2004), p.42.

86 Taiwan Relations Act, http://usinfo.org/docs/basic/tra_e.html.

87 C. Fred Bergsten et al., *China's Rise: Challenges and Opportunities* (Washington: Peterson Institute for International Studies and Center for Strategic and International Studies, 2008), p.175.

88 Shirk, *China: Fragile Superpower*, pp.2–3.

89 David Shambaugh, "Return to the Middle Kingdom," in *Power Shift* (Los Angeles: University of California Press 2005), p.39. See also Alan D. Romberg, *Cross-Strait Relations: Weathering the Storm*, China Leadership Monitor, No. 30, November 2009, p.18.

90 Shirk, *China: Fragile Superpower*, p.205.

91 Andrew Jacobs, "President of Taiwan is Re-elected, a Result That is Likely to Please China," *New York Times*, January 14, 2012.

92 Jacques deLisle, "Taiwan's 2012 Presidential and Legislative Elections: Winners, Losers, and Implications," Philadelphia: Foreign Policy Research Institute, January 2012, p.7.

93 "China's Cyberwar," *Washington Post,* December 15, 2011.

94 William J. Lynn III, "Defending a New Domain," *Foreign Affairs*, September/October 2010, pp.2–4.

95 Graham Webster, "Cyber Cold War Haunts the U.S. and China," Aljazeera.net, December 22, 2011.

96 Michael Joseph Gross, "Enter the Cyber-dragon," *Vanity Fair*, September 2011, pp.1–2.

97 Adam Segal, "Chinese Computer Games: Keeping Safe in Cyberspace," *Foreign Affairs*, Volume 91, Number 2, March/April 2012, p.16.

98 Ibid., pp.16–17.

99 Ibid, p.15; Adam Segal, "The Role of Cyber Security in U.S.-China Relations," *East West Forum*, June 21, 2011.

100 William J. Lynn III, "The Pentagon's Cyberstrategy, One Year Later," *Foreign Affairs*, September 28, 2011; http://www.foreignaffairs.com/articles/68305/william-j-lynn-iii/the-pentagons-cyberstrategy-one-year-later?page=show; Segal, "Chinese Computer Games: Keeping Safe in Cyberspace," p.18.

101 Ibid.

102 Adam Segal and Matthew Waxman, "Why a Cybersecurity Treaty is a Pipe Dream," October 27, 2011; http://globalpublicsquare.blogs.cnn.com/2011/10/27/why-a-cybersecurity-treaty-is-a-pipe-dream; Segal, "Chinese Computer Games: Keeping Safe in Cyberspace," pp.18–19.

103 Helene Cooper, "U.S. Arms for Taiwan Send Beijing a Message," *New York Times,* February 1, 2010.

104 Ibid.

105 Helene Cooper, "U.S. Approval of Taiwan Arms Sales Angers China," *New York Times*, January 30, 2010; Keith Bradsher, "U.S. Deal with Taiwan Has China Retaliating," *New York Times*, January 31, 2010.

106 James B. Steinberg, U.S. Deputy Secretary of State, "U.S.-China Cooperation on Global Issues," speech at the Brooking Institution, Washington, D.C., May 11, 2010.

107 Neil MacFarquhar, "UN Approves New Sanctions to Deter Iran," *New York Times,* June 9, 2010.

108 Bonnie Glaser and Brittany Billingsley, "Friction and Cooperation in Run-up to Hu's US Visit," *Comparative Connections*, Pacific Forum CSIS, January 2011.

109 Elisabeth Bumiller and Edward Wong, "China Warily Eyes U.S.-Korea Drills," *New York Times*, July 20, 2010.

110 Mark Landler, "Offering to Aid Talks, U.S. Challenges China on Disputed Islands," *New York Times*, July 23, 2010.

111 Thomas J. Christensen, "The Advantages of an Assertive China: Responding to Beijing's Abrasive Diplomacy," *Foreign Policy*, March/April 2011.

112 Joseph S. Nye, Jr., "China's Bad Bet Against America," *PacNet,* # 14, Pacific Forum CSIS, March 25, 2010.

113 Ralph Cossa, "U.S.-China Relations on a Downward Slide," *PacNet*, # 4A, Pacific Forum CSIS, February 10, 2010.

114 Denny Roy, "China in 2010: The Perils of Impatience," *PacNet* # 52, Pacific Forum CSIS, November 4, 2010.

115 Helene Cooper, "Asking China to Act Like the U.S.," *New York Times*, November 27, 2010.

116 Mark Landler and Sewell Chan, "Taking Harder Stance Toward China, Obama Lines up Allies," *New York Times*, October 25, 2010.

Chapter Three

1   "A Date Which Will Live in Infamy": FDR Asks for a Declaration of War, December 8, 1941, http://historymatters.gmu.edu/d/5166.

2   David Greenberg, "Beware the Military-Industrial Complex," *Slate*, January 14, 2011.

3 John F. Kennedy Inaugural Address, January 20, 1961, http://www.bartleby. com/124/pres56.html.

4 The views of Kupchan and Ikenberry are rooted in a tradition that extends back in the United States to Karl Deutsch, a Harvard political scientist, and Kenneth Boulding, an economist at the University of Colorado. See Karl W. Deutsch, *Political Community and the North Atlantic Area,* (Princeton: Princeton University Press, 1957) and Kenneth Boulding, *Stable Peace,* (Austin: University of Texas Press, 1978). For other major contributions to this field, see Emanuel Adler and Michael Barnett, eds, *Security Communities,* (Cambridge: Cambridge University Press, 1998); Jean-Marc Coicaud, Charles A. Kupchan, Emanuel Adler, and Yuen Foong Khong, *The Peaceful Change of International Order,* (New York: United Nations University Press, 2001), and James E. Goodby, Petrus Buwalda and Dmitri Trenin, *A Strategy for Stable Peace,* (Washington: United States Institute of Peace Press, 2002).

5 G. John Ikenberry and Charles A. Kupchan, "Liberal Realism, The Foundations of a Democratic Foreign Policy," *The National Interest,* Fall 2004, p.40.

6 Charles A. Kupchan, *How Enemies Become Friends, The Sources of Stable Peace*, (Princeton: Princeton University Press, 2010), p.30.

7 Kissinger, *On China*, p.526.

8 Kupchan, *How Enemies Become Friends*, pp.41 and 394.

9 G. John Ikenberry, *Liberal Order and Imperial Ambition* (Cambridge: Polity Press 2007), pp.263 and 117.

10 Kupchan, *How Enemies Become Friends*, p.43.

11 U.S. National Intelligence Council, *Global Trends 2025: A Transformed World,* (Washington: Office of the Director of National Intelligence, November 2008), pp.iv and vi.

12 Lampton, "Power Constrained: Sources of Mutual Strategic Suspicion in U.S.-China Relations," (Seattle: The National Bureau of Asian Research, June 2010), pp.11, 15 and 20.

13 http://www.globalsecurity.org/military/systems/ship/ssgn-726.htm; Mark Thompson, "U.S. Missiles Deployed Near China Send a Message," *Time,* July 8, 2010, http://www.time.com/time/printout/0,8816,2002378,00.html.

14 Paul C. Warnke, "Apes on a Treadmill," *Foreign Policy,* No. 18 (Spring, 1975).

15 Fred C. Bergsten, et al., *China's Rise: Challenges and Opportunities* (Washington: Peterson Institute for International Studies and Center for Strategic and International Studies, 2008), p.198 (emphasis added).

16 Ibid., p.202.

17 U.S. Department of Defense, Annual Report to Congress, *The Military Power of the People's Republic of China 2005.*

18 George P. Shultz, William J. Perry. Henry A. Kissinger, and Sam Nunn, "A World Free of Nuclear Weapons," *The Wall Street Journal,* January 4, 2007.

19   James Goodby, "A World Without Nuclear Weapons is a Joint Enterprise," *Arms Control Today*, Washington: Arms Control Association, May 2011, pp.6–7, http://www.armscontrol.org/act/2011_05/Goodby.

20   Michael Wines, "South China Sea Dispute Flares Up," *New York Times*, June 10, 2011; Michael Swaine and M. Taylor Fravel, "China's Assertive Behavior, Part Two: the Maritime Periphery," *China Leadership Monitor*, No. 35, Summer 2011, p.6.

21   Mark Landler, "A New Era of Gunboat Diplomacy," *New York Times*, November 12, 2011.

22   Till Papenfuss, "Risk of Accidental Escalation in the South China Sea," International Peace Institute, July 6, 2011.

23   Ibid.

24   Richard Bush, *The Perils of Proximity, China-Japan Security Relations*, (Washington: Brookings Institution Press, 2010), pp.70–1.

25   Ibid., pp.73–4.

26   "China, Japan and the Sea," *New York Times*, September 24, 2010.

27   Associated Press, "Clinton Tells Maehara Senkakus Subject to Japan-U.S. Security Treaty," September 23, 2010; Treaty of Mutual Cooperation and Security Between Japan and the United States of America, Article V, http://www.mofa.go.jp/region/n-america/us/q&a/ref/1.html.

28   Bush, *The Perils of Proximity, China-Japan Security Relations*, p.224.

29   Ibid., pp.54 and 80; Swaine and Fravel, "China's Assertive Behavior, Part Two," p.8.

30   Josh Rogin, "Is the Obama administration getting tough on China?," *Foreign Policy*, August 6, 2010, http://thecable.foreignpolicy.com/posts/2010/08/06/is_the_obama_administration_getting_tough_on_china.

31   M. Taylor Fravel, *Strong Borders, Secure Nation, Cooperation and Conflict in China's Territorial Disputes*, (Princeton: Princeton University press, 2008), p.300.

32   Ibid., pp.316–17.

33   Bush, *The Perils of Proximity, China-Japan Security Relations*, p.86.

34   Ibid., pp.85–6; Richard Bush, "China-Japan Security Relations," Policy Brief #177, (Washington: Brookings Institution October 2010), pp.3–4.

35   Clive Schofield et al., "From Disputed Waters to Seas of Opportunity, Overcoming Barriers to Maritime Cooperation in East and Southeast Asia," Washington: National Bureau of Asian Research, NBR Special Report #30, July 2011, pp.27–8.

36   Mark Valencia, "A Code of Conduct for the South China Sea: What Should It Contain?," Nautilus Institute, December 8, 2011, www.nautilus.org.

37   Bush, *The Perils of Proximity, China-Japan Security Relations*, pp.292–300.

38   "From Disputed Waters to Seas of Opportunity," p.25.

39   Lyle J. Goldstein, "Resetting the US-China Security Relationship," *Survival*, Vol. 53, No. 2, April–May 2011, p.94.

40   Fukuda Yasuo, "Forging the Future Together," speech at Peking University, December 28, 2007, www.mofa.go.jp/region/asia-paci/China/speech0712. html.

41   Mark J. Valencia, "The South China Sea: Back to the Future," *Global Asia*, Vol. 5, No. 4, Winter 2010, p.9.

42   Shirk, *China: Fragile Superpower*, p.194; Michael Pillsbury, ed., *Chinese Views of Future Warfare* (Washington, D.C.: National Defense University Press, 1997).

43   Hachigian and Sutphen, *The Next American Century*, p.179–80.

44   Bates Gill, *Rising Star* (Washington: Brookings Institution Press, 2007), p.172.

45   Ezra Vogel, ed., *Living with China* (New York: WW Norton, 1997), p.2.

46   Douglas Paal, "China and the East Asian Security Environment: Complementarity and Competition," in Vogel, ed., *Living with China*.

47   *"China's Regional Military Posture,"* p.247–5.

48   Jonathan Pollack, "The Transformation of the Asian Security Order," in Shambaugh, ed., *Power Shift*, p.343.

49   David M. Lampton, "Power Constrained: Sources of Mutual Strategic Suspicion in U.S.-China Relations," (Washington: The National Bureau of Asian Research, June 2010), p.11.

50   "Resetting the U.S.-China Security Relationship," p.92.

51   Gill, *Rising Star*, p.181.

52   Ibid.

53   See David C. Kang, *China Rising*, (New York: Columbia University Press, 2007), p.186.

54   Stephanie Kleine-Ahlbrandt and Andrew Small, "China's New Dictatorship Diplomacy," *Foreign Affairs*, Vol. 87, No. 1, January/February 2008, p.38.

55   Ibid., p.56.

56   See Robert G. Sutter, *China's Rise in Asia*, (Oxford: Rowman and Littlefield, 2005) p.13 and sources cited therein.

Chapter Four

1   "List of Countries by GDP," *Wikipedia* (citing 2011 data from the International Monetary Fund), http://en.wikipedia.org/wiki/List_of_countries_ by_GDP_(nominal); "List of Countries by GDP Per Capita," *Wikipedia* (citing 2011 data from the International Monetary Fund), http://en.wikipedia. org/wiki/List_of_countries_by_GDP_(PPP)_per_capita.

2   *China's Economy: Retrospect and Prospect*, Asia Program Special Report No. 129, (Washington: Woodrow Wilson International Center for Scholars, July 2005), p.1.

3   Jeffrey Hays, "*Deng's Economic Reforms—Facts and Details*," www.facts
     anddetails.com/china, p.2.

4   Ibid., p.4.

5   Jeffrey Sachs, cited in Fareed Zakaria, *The Post-American World*, (New York:
     W.W. Norton & Company, 2009), p.89.

6   Ibid., pp.91–2.

7   Supachai Panitchpakdi and Mark L. Clifford, *China and the WTO*, (New
     York: John Wiley & Sons 2002), p.3.

8   Ibid., p.33.

9   Testimony of Calman J. Cohen, President, Emergency Committee for
     American Trade (ECAT) before the U.S.-China Economic and Security Review
     Commission, "Hearing on Evaluating China's Past and Future Role in the
     World Trade Organization," June 9, 2010, p.1

10   Emergency Committee on International Trade, *ECAT 2011Agenda*, prepared
     for the ECAT Annual Meeting on June 14, 2011, pp.248–9.

11   Ibid., p.244.

12   U.S. Trade Representative, "*U.S.-China Trade Relations: Entering a New
     Phase of Accountability and Enforcement,*" February 2006, p.5.

13   Steven Mufson and Peter Whoriskey, "Threat of Trade War with China
     Sparks Worries in a Debtor U.S.," *Washington Post*, September 15, 2009.

14   David W. Chen, "China Emerges as a Scapegoat in Campaign Ads," *New
     York Times*, October 9, 2010.

15   Ibid.

16   Ibid.

17   Swaine, *America's Challenge, Engaging a Rising China in the Twenty-First
     Century,* pp.210–11.

18   Secretary Geithner's Remarks on "The Path Ahead for the U.S.-China
     Economic Relationship," delivered at Johns Hopkins University, School
     of Advanced International Studies, January 12, 2011, http://china.usc.edu/
     ShowArticle.aspx?articleID=2340.

19   Jennifer Steinhauer, "Senate Jabs China Over Its Currency," *New York Times*,
     October 11, 2011.

20   Ibid.

21   Chris Marshall, "Desperate US Protectionism Against China Will Backfire,"
     www.citywire.co.uk/money/article/a531795, October 19, 2011.

22   The White House, Office of the Press Secretary, Remarks by the President in
     the Meeting with Trans-Pacific Partnership, November 12, 2011.

23   Kenneth G. Lieberthal and Jonathan Pollack, "Establishing Credibility
     and Trust: The Next President Must Manage America's Most Important
     Relationship," Campaign 2012 Papers, No. 6, Washington: Brookings, March
     16, 2012. Lieberthal and Pollack note that "President Obama's advocacy of
     the Trans-Pacific Partnership (TPP) at the Asia-Pacific Economic Cooperation

summit in Honolulu did not preclude Chinese membership in this regional grouping, but it highlighted requirements for a level of transparency, reciprocity, and attentiveness to environmental and labor standards well beyond China's present practices."

24 David Nakamura, "Obama at APEC summit: China must 'play by the rules'," *The Washington Post,* November 12, 2012.

25 The White House, Office of the Press Secretary, Press Gaggle by Deputy National Security Advisor for International Economic Affairs Mike Froman, November 12, 2011.

26 David Pilling, "Trans-Pacific Partnership: Far-reaching agreement could form powerful new trade bloc," *Financial Times*, November 8, 2011.

27 The China Business Forum, *The China Effect: Assessing the Impact on the US Economy of Trade and Investment with China*, Oxford Economics and The Signal Group, January 2006, p.i.

28 See Mathew J. Slaughter and Robert Z. Lawrence, "More Trade and More Aid," *New York Times*, June 8, 2011, where the authors write: "[T]rade is indeed worth it for America. Annual national income today is at least $1 trillion higher than it would have been absent decades of trade and investment liberalization .... [Yet trade] is not worth it for every individual American. Trade creates unemployment for some and wage losses for others; its gains do not directly accrue to every worker and community." Slaughter and Lawrence therefore recommend "more trade and more aid"—passage of free trade agreements that "create jobs linked to exports and international investment" as well as a "broader safety net that helps workers regardless of why they lost their jobs." Key elements of Slaughter and Lawrence's proposal were included in Trade Adjustment Assistance legislation passed by the Congress in late September 2011. See "Baucus Hails Passage of Worker Training, Job Opportunities Bill to Lower Costs for U.S. Businesses," September 22, 2011, http://finance.senate.gov/newsroom/chairman/release/?id=59561d8c-ca1a-44c1-9898-809691521b63.

29 Hachigian and Sutphen, *The Next American Century*, p.234.

30 Barry Eichengreen and Douglas Irwin, "The Protectionist Temptation: Lessons from the Great Depression for Today," March 17, 2009, http://www.voxeu.org/index.php?q=node/3280.

31 Thomas Lum and Dick K. Nanto, *China's Trade with the United States and the World*, (Washington: Congressional Research Service, January 4, 2007), p.2.

32 Kenneth Lieberthal, Brookings Institution, Washington, DC, communication with author, June 2007.

33 *China and the US Economy*, (Washington: the U.S.-China Business Council, January 2009).

34 US-China Business Council, *U.S.-China Trade in Context* (Washington: US-China Business Council, 2008).

35   Daniel Ikenson, "China Currency Bill Will Destroy U.S. Jobs, Not Create Them," *Forbes*, October 5, 2011.

36   Dong Tao, a UBS economist, as quoted in Susan Shirk, *China: Fragile Superpower* (New York: Oxford University Press, 2007), p.26; Hachigian, *The Next American Century*, p.108.

37   *Reestablishing a Consensus on US-China Trade* (Washington: Business Roundtable 2006), p.12.

38   Lael Brainard and Robert E. Litan, "Services Off-shoring, American Jobs and the Global Economy," *Perspectives on Work*, Winter 2005, p.9.

39   *ECAT 2011 Agenda*, p.246; *China and the US Economy*, p.12.

40   Alan Wheatley, "Punishing China no boon for U.S. manufacturing jobs," *Reuters*, October 12, 2011.

41   Peterson Institute for International Economics, *The Dollar and the Renminbi*, Statement by C. Fred Bergsten at a hearing on U.S. Economic Relations with China, before the Banking Committee's Subcommittee on Security and International Trade and Finance, May 23, 2007.

42   Morris Goldstein and Nicholas R. Lardy, "China's Currency Needs to Rise Further," *Financial Times*, July 22, 2008.

43   Mark Landler and Steven Lee Myers, "U.S. is Seeing Positive Signs From China," *New York Times*, April 26, 2012; Ian Katz, "Geithner Calls China's Changes on Yuan Very Significant," *Business Week*, April 18, 2012, http://www.business-week.com/news/2012-04-18/geithner-calls-china-s-yuan-band-widening-very-significant.

44   The China Business Forum, *The China Effect*, p.7.

45   Daniel J. Ikenson, "Appreciate This: Chinese Currency Rise Will Have a Negligible Effect on the Trade Deficit," (Washington: Center for Trade Policy Studies, Cato Institute, March 24, 2010).

46   The China Business Forum, *The China Effect*, p.8.

47   U.S.-China Business Council, USCBC Report: "Total Yearly US State Exports to China Pass $100 Billion for the First Time," March 28, 2012, https://www.uschina.org/public/documents/2012/03/yearly-us-exports.html.

48   Swaine, *America's Challenge*, p.214; Euromonitor International, "Chinese Consumers in 2020: A Look into the Future," March 11, 2009, www.euromontor.com/Chinese_Consumers_in 2020_A_look_into_the_future.

49   Report of the National Intelligence Council's 2020 Project (Washington: National Intelligence Council, 2004).

50   Robert J. Samuelson, "Our one-sided trade war with China," *Washington Post,* October 7, 2011.

51   "China's Forex Reserves Show First Decline in Three Months," Bloomberg News, April 24, 2012, http://www.bloomberg.com/news/2012-04-24/china-s-forex-reserves-show-first-decline-in-three-months-1-.html.

52   "China Increases its US Debt Holding for Second Month," *BBC News Business*, April 26, 2012, http://www.bbc.co.uk/news/business-17737572.

53 Fred C. Bergsten, et al., *China's Rise: Challenges and Opportunities*, (Washington: Peterson Institute for International Studies and Center for Strategic and International Studies, 2008), pp.18–19.

54 Rupert Cornwell, "London Debut for China's New Chief," The *Independent*, April 1, 1998.

55 Bergsten, *China's Rise*, p.18.

56 Fareed Zakaria, "China's Not Doing Us a Favor," CNN, August 14, 2011, http://globalpublicsquare.blogs.cnn.com/2011/08/14/why-china-needs-u-s.

57 Bergsten, *China's Rise*, p.80.

58 *ECAT 2011 Agenda*, p.252.

59 Wayne Morrison, *China-U.S. Trade Issues*, (Washington: CRS Report to Congress, Updated March 7, 2008), pp. 8–11.

60 Bergsten, *China's Rise*, pp.81–7.

61 *ECAT 2011 Agenda*, p.252.

62 Office of the United States Trade Representative, "22nd U.S.-China Joint Commission on Commerce and Trade Outcomes," November 20–21, 2011; http://www.ustr.gov/about-us/press-office/fact-sheets/2011/november/2011-us-china-joint-commission-commerce-and-trade-ou.

63 Bergsten, *China's Rise*, p.85.

64 Dexter Roberts, "China: Closing for Business?," *Business Week*, March 25, 2010.

65 Ibid.

66 "Remarks by Ambassador Gary Locke to the American Chamber of Commerce in China and the U.S.-China Business Council," Embassy of the United States, Beijing, China, September 20, 2011.

67 Joe McDonald, "U.S. envoy says China pledges access to clean energy suppliers; China urges efforts for Growth," *Associated Press*, November 24, 2011, http://www.csmonitor.com/Business/Latest-News-Wires/2011/1124/Clean-energy-market-China-promises-open-access.

68 "Remarks by Ambassador Gary Locke to the American Chamber of Commerce in China and the U.S.-China Business Council," Embassy of the United States, Beijing, China, September 20, 2011.

69 James Kynge, *China Shakes the World*, (Boston: Houghton Mifflin Company, 2006), p.223.

70 USCBC Report: "Total Yearly US State Exports to China Pass $100 Billion for the First Time," The US-China Business Council, Washington, DC, March 28, 2012, https://www.uschina.org/public/documents/2012/03/yearly-us-exports.html; U.S. Department of Commerce, Trade Stats Express (tse.export.gov); *China: The Case for Engagement*, (Washington: Engage China Coalition, 2011), www.EngageChina.com, p.4.

71 *China and the U.S. Economy*, p.12.

72 *China: The Case for Engagement*, p.6

73   *China and the U.S. Economy*, p.8.; Daniel H. Rosen and Thilo Hanemann, *An American Open Door? Maximizing the Benefits of Chinese Foreign Direct Investment*, New York: Asia Society et al., (May 2011), p.26.

74   Secretary Geithner's Remarks on "The Path Ahead for the U.S.-China Economic Relationship."

75   *ECAT 2011 Agenda*, p.245.

76   *An American Open Door?* pp.8 and 29.

77   Ibid., p.34.

78   Ibid., p.22.

79   Ibid., pp.20–2; James Flanigan, "A Wave of Chinese Money Gives a Lift to Companies Struggling in Tough Times," *New York Times*, July 6, 2011.

80   Asia Society, "An American Open Door?," www.asiasociety.org, May 7, 2011.

81   Ibid., pp.42–4.

82   Ibid., p.44.

83   Ibid., p.48.

84   Ibid., p.52.

85   Ibid., p.51.

86   "USW Calls EPI Job Loss Study an 'Alarm' for Trade Enforcement," *Sacramento Bee*, September 20, 2011.

87   Matthew Daly, "US Again Imposes Clean-Energy Tariffs on China," *Associated Press*, May 30, 2012, http://www.google.com/hostednews/ap/article/ALeqM5jT2pUzL7KmlXObbZDs57uztGkWEQ?docId=09c84b8a31bf46528eafd7f5f01180b6; Matthew L. Wald, "U.S. Imposes Duties on Chinese Wind Tower Makers," *New York Times*, May 30, 2012.

88   Chris Marshall, "Desperate U.S. Protectionism against China will Backfire," www.citywire.co.uk, October 12, 2011.

89   *An American Open Door? Maximizing the Benefits of Chinese Foreign Direct Investment*, p.62.

90   *New York Times*, July 7, 2005.

91   "Comments of the Emergency Committee for American Trade on the Development of a National Export Initiative Plan," *Emergency Committee for International Trade* (July 26, 2010), pp.7–8.

92   Statement of the U.S. Chamber of Commerce on the Trans-Pacific Partnership, *Hearing of the U.S. House of Representatives Committee on Ways and Means*, December 14, 2011, p.6.

93   Hachigian and Sutphen, *The Next American Century*, pp.85–98.

94   "Testimony of Calman J. Cohen Before the U.S.-China Economic and Security Review Commission," *Hearing on Evaluating China's Past and Future Role in the World Trade Organization*, Emergency Committee for American Trade, June 9, 2010, p.15.

95   Cordell Hull, *The Memoirs of Cordell Hull*, Volume 1, (New York: Macmillan Publishers, 1948), p.84.

96   Johan Norberg, "China Paranoia Derails Free Trade," *Far Eastern Economic Review*, Jan/Feb 2006, Vol 169, p.48.

97   "Vietnam War Casualties," *Wikipedia*, http://en.wikipedia.org/wiki/Vietnam_War_casualties.

98   "Malaysian Tribunal Finds Bush and Blair Guilty of War Crimes," *Salon*, November 23, 2011; http://www.salon.com/2011/11/23/bush_and_blair_found_guilty_of_war_crimes_for_iraq_attack/.

99   Derek Scissors, " 'Rebalancing' Chinese Investment in the U.S.," *Web Memo published by the Heritage Foundation*, No. 2956, July 13, 2010, p.3.

100 *An American Open Door?* pp.70–1.

101 Swaine, *America's Challenge*, p.207.

102 G. John Ikenberry, "The Rise of China and the Future of the West," *Foreign Affairs*, January/February 2008, p.37.

103 Harry Harding, testimony before the Senate Foreign Relations Committee, Washington, May 15, 2008.

Chapter Five

1   Edward S. Steinfeld, *Playing Our Game, Why China's Economic Rise Doesn't Threaten the West*, (New York: Oxford University Press, 2010), p.231.

2   Susan Shirk, *China: Fragile Superpower*, (New York: Oxford University Press, 2007), p.7.

3   David M. Lampton, *The Three Faces of Chinese Power*, (Berkeley: University of California Press, 2008), p.248.

4   Tom Orlik, "Unrest Grows as Economy Booms," *Wall Street Journal*, September 26, 2011; http://online.wsj.com/article/SB10001424053111903703604576587070600504108.html.

5   Lampton, *The Three Faces of Chinese Power*, p.247; "China, Beware: The Party Congress in China," *Economist*, October 13, 2007.

6   Shirk, *China: Fragile Superpower*, p.10.

7   Lampton, *The Three Faces of Chinese Power*, pp.247–9.

8   Like previous five-year plans, the most recent one is both a policy directive from China's leadership and roadmap for government officials and regulators who are responsible for its implementation.

9   Didi Kirsten Tatlow, "The Twists and Turns of Chinese Political Reform," *New York Times*, March 21, 2012; Peter Ford, "China PM Wen Jiabao Says Political Reform 'Urgent,' *Christian Science Monitor*, March 14, 2012.

10   Sharon Hom, "Has U.S. Engagement with China Produced a Significant Improvement in Human Rights?" *Framing China Policy: The Carnegie*

Debate, March 5, 2007, p.3; Edward Wong, "Human Rights Advocates Vanish as China Intensifies Crackdown," *New York Times*, March 11, 2011; Andrew Jacobs and Jonathan Ansfield, "Well-Oiled Security Apparatus in China Stifles Calls for Change," *New York Times*, February 28, 2011.

11 U.S. Department of State, 2010 Human Rights Report: China (includes Tibet, Hong Kong, and Macau), April 8, 2011, http://www.state.gov/j/drl/rls/hrrpt/2010/eap/154382.htm.

12 Barry Naughton, "China's Left Tilt," in Cheng Li, ed., *China's Changing Political Landscape,* (Washington: Brookings Institution Press, 2008), p.157.

13 "China Vows to Continue Crackdown on Tibetan Unrest," *Associated Press*, February 7, 2012.

14 *China's Forbidden Zones*, Human Rights Watch, July 6, 2008, pp.9–10.

15 Jacques deLisle, *Pressing Engagement: Uneven Human Rights Progress in China, Modest Successes of American Policy, and the Absence of Better Options,* (Washington: Carnegie Endowment, Fall 2008), p.1.

16 Cheng Li, "Assessing China's Political Development" in Cheng Li, ed., *China's Changing Political Landscape,* p.10.

17 Ibid., pp.10–11.

18 Richard Baum, "China's Information Revolution," in *China's Changing Political Landscape*; 2011 CIA World Factbook, "China Communications 2011," www.theodora.com/wfbcurrent/china/china_communications.html.

19 Henry S. Rowen, "The Short March: China's Road to Democracy," *National Interest* (Fall 1996), pp.68–9.

20 "The Other Moore's Law," *Economist*, February 14, 2009.

21 Cheng Li, "Will China's 'Lost Generation' Find a Path to Democracy," in Cheng Li, ed., *China's Changing Political Landscape,* p.108.

22 Cheng Li, "China's Midterm Jockeying: Gearing Up for 2012 (Part 1: Provincial Chiefs)," *China Leadership Monitor*, No. 31, Winter 2010, p.1.

23 Michael Wines, "China Premier Calls for End to Corruption," *New York Times*, April 16, 2012; Michael Wines, "A Populist's Downfall Exposes Ideological Divisions in China's Ruling Party," *New York Times*, April 6, 2012.

24 Michael Wines, "China Premier Calls for End to Corruption."

25 Michael Wines and Sharon LaFraniere, "Party May Be Long-Term Loser in Chinese Scandal," *New York Times*, April 13, 2012; Anton Wishik, "An Interview with Cheng Li: The Bo Xilai Crisis: A Curse or a Blessing for China," Washington: The National Bureau of Asian Research, April 18, 2012, http://www.nbr.org/research/activity.aspx?id=236.

26 Richard Baum, "China's Information Revolution," in Cheng Li, ed., *China's Changing Political Landscape* (Washington: Brookings Institution Press, 2008) at pp.180–1.

27 Guobin Yang, "The Co-Evolution of the Internet and Civil Society in China," *Asian Survey*, Vol. 43, No. 3, May–June, 2003, p.406.

28 "Apple Takes Heat from Chinese NGOs of Supply Chain Pollution," Business Green, January 24, 2011, http://www.greenbiz.com/print/41525; Charles Duhigg and Nick Wingfield, "BITS; Apple in Shift, Pushes An Audit of Sites in China," *New York Times*, February 14, 2012.

29 "Has U.S. Engagement with China Produced a Significant Improvement in Human Rights?," pp.4–5.

30 "Charter 08" (translated by Perry Link), *New York Review of Books*, Volume 56, Number 1, January 15, 2009.

31 "'Charter' Democrats in China," *Wall Street Journal*, March 31, 2009.

32 "A Time for Muscle Flexing," *Economist*, March 19, 2009, p.4, http://www.economist.com/node/13326082.

33 Andrew Jacobs and Jonathan Ansfield, "Nobel Peace Prize Given to Jailed Chinese Dissident," *New York Times*, October 8, 2010; Andrew Jacobs, "Beijing Calls Nobel Insult to People of China," *New York Times*, October 12, 2010; Michael Wines, "China Assails Nobel Peace Prize as 'Card' of West," *New York Times*, November 5, 2010.

34 Edward Wong, "Chinese Defend Detention of Artist on Grounds of 'Economic Crimes,'" *New York Times*, April 7, 2011; Edward Wong, "Dissident Chinese Artist is Released," *New York Times*, June 22, 2011; "Ai Weiwei," Times Topics, *New York Times*, November 15, 2011.

35 Will Hutton, *The Writing on the Wall*, (New York: Free Press, 2006), pp.2, 302 and 317.

36 A poem entitled simply "Tiananmen" by the British poet and journalist James Fenton captures the feelings many Americans harbor toward the massacre of demonstrators in 1989:

Tiananmen
Is broad and clean
And you can't tell
Where the dead have been
And you can't tell
What happened then
And you can't speak
Of Tiananmen.

You must not speak.
You must not think.
You must not dip
Your brush in ink.
You must not say
What happened then,
What happened there.
What happened there
In Tiananmen.

The cruel men
Are old and deaf
Ready to kill

But short of breath
And they will die
Like other men
And they'll lie in state
In Tiananmen.

They lie in state.
They lie in style.
Another lie's
Thrown on the pile,
Thrown on the pile
By the cruel men
To cleanse the blood
From Tiananmen.

Truth is a secret.
Keep it dark.
Keep it dark.
In our heart of hearts.
Keep it dark
Till you know when
Truth may return
To Tiananmen.

Tiananmen
Is broad and clean
And you can't tell
Where the dead have been
And you can't tell
When they'll come again.
They'll come again
To Tiananmen.

James Fenton, *Out of Danger: Poems* (New York: Farrar, Straus and Giroux, 1995).

37   deLisle, *Pressing Engagement*, pp.3–4.

38   Paul Richter, "Hillary Clinton to table Human Rights Issues in China Talks," *Los Angeles Times*, February 21, 2009.

39   Bonnie Glaser and David Szerlip, "U.S.-China Relations: The Honeymoon Ends," *Comparative Connections*, Honolulu: Pacific Forum CSIS (March 2010); Douglas Paal, "China and the United States—A Difficult Year Ahead," Carnegie-Tsinghua Center for Global Policy, February 9, 2010; http://carnegietsinghua.org/publications/?fa=24819.

40   David Barboza, "Departing U.S. Envoy Criticizes China on Human Rights," *New York Times*, April 6, 2011.

41   Shirk, *China: Fragile Superpower*, p.262.

42   Natan Sharansky, "A Dissident Defends Us All," *New York Times*, October 15, 2010 (emphasis added).

43   Henry Kissinger, *Diplomacy,* (New York: Simon & Schuster, 1994), p.759.

44 The one-China policy was first stated in the Shanghai Communiqué of 1972: "the United States acknowledges that Chinese on either side of the Taiwan Strait maintain there is but one China and that Taiwan is a part of China." President Obama endorsed this view during his November 2009 visit to China when he said "I have been clear in the past that my administration fully supports a one-China policy ... We don't want to change that policy and that approach." "Obama Affirms 'One-China' Policy," *Washington Times*, November 17, 2009.

Chapter Six

1 Zheng Bijian, "China's 'Peaceful Rise' to Great-Power Status," *Foreign Affairs*, September/October 2005, pp.18–20.

2 Wu Baiji, "The Chinese Security Concept and Its Historical Evolution," *Journal of Contemporary China* 14, No. 44 (August 2005), p.413.

3 Avery Goldstein, *Rising to the Challenge*, (Stanford: Stanford University, 2005), p.12.

4 Lampton, *The Three Faces of Chinese Power*, (Berkeley: University of California Press, 2008), p.30.

5 See Bates Gill, "China's Evolving Regional Security Strategy," in David Shambaugh, ed., *Power Shift*, (Berkeley: University of California Press, 2005), pp.248–52 and Robert Sutter, "China's Regional Strategy and Why It May Not Be Good for America," in Shambaugh, ed., *Power Shift*, (Berkeley: University of California Press, 2005), pp.290–2.

6 Elizabeth Economy, "China's Rise in Southeast Asia: implications for the United States," *Journal of Contemporary China*, August 2005, p.412.

7 Zheng, "China's 'Peaceful Rise' to Great-Power Status," pp.18–20.

8 Ibid., p.24.

9 Joseph S. Nye, Jr., "Soft Power: The Means to Success in World Politics," *Public Affairs* (2004), p.xi.

10 Nargiza Salidjanova, U.S.-China Economic & Security Review Commission, "Going Out: An Overview of China's Outward Foreign Direct Investment," March 30, 2011, pp.7–10.

11 Derek Scissors, "Chinese Outward Investment: More Opportunity than Danger," Washington: The Heritage Foundation, Backgrounder, July 13, 2011, p.2; Derek Scissors, "Chinese Outward Investment: Slower Growth in 2011," Washington: The Heritage Foundation, January 9, 2012, p.3. For U.S. data, see "Foreign Direct Investment (FDI) Statistics – OECD Data, Analysis and Forecasts," OECD, 2012; http://stats.oecd.org/Index.aspx?DatasetCode=FDI_FLOW_PARTNER.

12 Scissors, "Chinese Outward Investment: Slower Growth in 2011."

13 Jamil Anderlini, "China Insists on 'Tied Aid' in Africa," *Financial Times*, June 25, 2007; Deborah Brautigam, "The Chinese in Africa: The Economist

Gets Some Things Right, Some Wrong," May 20, 2011; http://www.chinaafricarealstory.com/2011/05/chinese-in-africa-economist-gets-some.html.

14 China Briefing, "China-Costa Rica FTA Comes Into Effect," August 2, 2011, http://www.china-briefing.com/news/2011/08/02/china-costa-rica-fta-comes-into-effect.html; Barbara Kotschwar et al., "Chinese Investment in Latin American Resources: The Good, the Bad, and the Ugly," (Washington: Peterson Institute for International Economics, February 2012), pp.2–3; Joel Epstein, "China, Fast Forward," City Watch, January 27, 2012, http://www.citywatchla.com/in-case-you-missed-it/2752-china-fast-forward.

15 Kotschwar, "Chinese Investment in Latin American Resources: The Good, the Bad, and the Ugly," p.19.

16 Sarah Y. Tong and Catherine Chong Siew Keng, "China-ASEAN Free Trade Area in 2010: A Regional Perspective," (Singapore: National University of Singapore, East Asia Institute, April 10, 2010), p.8, http://www.eai.nus.edu.sg/BB519.pdf.

17 China's Foreign Policy and "Soft Power" in South America, Asia and Africa, A Study Prepared for the Committee on Foreign Relations, United States Senate, by the Congressional Research Service, April 2008.

18 Ibid.

19 Jian-ye Wang, "What Drives China's Growing Role in Africa?," IMF Working Paper, (Washington: International Monetary Fund, October 2007), p.5; Thomas Lum et al., "China's Foreign Aid Activities in Africa, Latin America, and Southeast Asia," (Washington: Congressional Research Service, February 25, 2009), p.10; "The Chinese in Africa: Trying to Pull Together," The Economist, April 20, 2011; Christopher Alessi and Stephanie Hanson, "Expanding China-Africa Oil Ties," New York Council on Foreign Relations, updated February 8, 2012.

20 China's Foreign Policy and "Soft Power" in South America, Asia and Africa, p.113; "The Chinese in Africa: Trying to Pull Together"; Wang, "What Drives China's Growing Role in Africa?"

21 Susan Shirk, China: Fragile Superpower, (New York: Oxford University Press, 2007), p.131.

22 Michael Yahuda, "The Evolving Asian Order" in Shambaugh, ed., Power Shift, pp.347–9.

23 "China Now Member of Inter-American Development Bank," China Daily, January 13, 2009.

24 "Main Points of Wen's Speech at ASEAN+3 Summit," Xinhua, November 29, 2004.

25 Chinese Premier Wen Jiabao's speech at the China-ASEAN summit, "Join Hands to Create A Better Future for China-ASEAN Relations," October 30, 2006, http://asean-chinasummit.fmprc.gov.cn/eng/fhhd/t278048. html.

26 Kerry Dumbaugh, "China's Foreign Policy and 'Soft Power' in South America, Asia, and Africa," Committee on Foreign Relations, United States Senate, April 2008, p.110.

27 "Expanding China-Africa Oil Ties."

28 Dumbaugh, "China's Foreign Policy and 'Soft Power' in South America, Asia, and Africa," p.68.

29 Abdoulaye Wade, "Time for the West to Practice What It Preaches," *Financial Times*, January 24, 2008, p.6.

30 Bates Gill, *Rising Star, China's New Security Diplomacy*, (Washington: Brookings Institution Press 2007), p.165.

31 Neil MacFarquhar, "UN Approves New Sanctions to Deter Iran," *New York Times*, June 9, 2010; Rick Gladstone and William J. Broad, "Iran is Pressed to Give Nuclear Inspectors Full Access to Sites," *New York Times*, M8, 2012.

32 Mark Landler and Steven Lee Myers, "U.S. is Seeing Positive Signs from China," *New York Times*, April 26, 2012.

33 Tim Johnston and Ben Bland, "Myanmar Suspends $3.6 bn China Dam Project," *Financial Times*, September 30, 2011.

34 "China's CNPC, Sudan Sign Deal for New Offshore Oil Block," *Sudan Tribune*, July 2, 2007; "China Wins $1.15 bln Sudan Railways Construction Contract," *Sudan Tribune*, March 5, 2007.

35 Joshua Eisenman, "Zimbabwe: China's African Ally," *China Brief 5*, No. 15 (2005), pp.9–11.

36 Kerry Dumbaugh, "China's Foreign Policy: What Does it Mean for U.S. Global Interests?," Washington: Congressional Research Service (July 18, 2008), p.13.

37 "Chinese Soft Power and Its Implications for the United States," A Report of the CSIS Smart Power Initiative, McGiffert, Carola, ed., (Washington, DC: Center for Strategic and International Studies, March 2009), p.v.

38 Ibid., p.25.

39 Pew Research Center, Pew Global Attitudes Project, July 13, 2011, http://www.pewglobal.org/2011/07/13.

40 CSIS, "Chinese Soft Power and Its Implications for the United States," p.8.

41 Richard L. Armitage and Joseph L. Nye, Co-Chairs, "CSIS Commission on Smart Power," Washington: Center for Strategic and International Studies, (November 2007), p.26.

42 "China's Party Leadership Declares New Priority: 'Harmonious Society'," *Washington Post*, October 12, 2006, p.A18.

43 Tony Blair, "Doctrine of the International Community," speech to the Chicago Economic Club, April 22, 1999.

44 Xing Zhigang, "China Pledges to Increase Humanitarian Aid," *China Daily*, January 19, 2006.

45 World Development Indicators database, World Bank, July 1, 2011.

46 Lampton, *The Three Faces of Chinese Power*, p.223.

47 Ibid., p.33.

48 "Government to Increase Spending on Education," *China Daily*, March 1,

2010, http://www.chinadaily.com.cn/china/2010-03/01/content_9515384.
html; OECD public expenditures on education, http://www.oecd.org/
dataoecd/61/14/48630949.pdf.; Lampton, *The Three Faces of Chinese Power,*
p.228.

49 *The Independent,* October 19, 2005; *China Daily,* February 12, 2006.

50 *China Daily,* June 19, 2005; *Xinhua News Service,* July 7, 2005; *China
Daily,* August 22, 2005.

51 Lampton, *Same Bed, Different Dreams,* (Los Angeles: University of California
Press, 2001), p.11.

52 Kerry Dumbaugh, "China's Foreign Policy and 'Soft Power' in South
America, Asia, and Africa," Committee on Foreign Relations, United States
Senate, April 2008, p.15.

53 Cui Liru, "Thoughts on the Evolving World Order," *Contemporary
International Relations* 15, October 2005, pp.4–5.

54 Lampton, *The Three Faces of Chinese Power,* p.251.

55 On the importance of the United States being seen as a strong proponent
of human rights and a beacon of hope to the oppressed, President Jimmy
Carter eloquently writes: "The United States is abandoning its role as the
global champion of human rights. Revelations that top officials are targeting
people to be assassinated abroad, including American citizens, are only the
most recent, disturbing proof of how far our nation's violation of human
rights has extended. This development began after the terrorist attacks
of Sept. 11, 2001, and has been sanctioned and escalated by bipartisan
executive and legislative actions, without dissent from the general public.
As a result, our country can no longer speak with moral authority on these
critical issues.... At a time when popular revolutions are sweeping the globe,
the United States should be strengthening, not weakening, basic rules of
law and principles of justice enumerated in the Universal Declaration of
Human Rights. But instead of making the world safer, America's violation
of international human rights abets our enemies and alienates our friends.
As concerned citizens, we must persuade Washington to reverse course and
regain moral leadership according to international human rights norms that
we had officially adopted as our own and cherished throughout the years."
Jimmy Carter, "A Cruel and Unusual Record," *New York Times,* June 24,
2012.

Chapter Seven

1 Michael Lind, *The American Way of Strategy,* (New York: Oxford University
Press, 2006), p.151.

2 Ibid., p.152.

3 See Taiwan Relations Act, United States Code, Title 22, Chapter 48, Sections
3301–16

4   Office of the U.S. Trade Representative, http://www.ustr.gov/countries-regions/china.

5   For alternative formulations of possible reciprocal security measures between the U.S. and China, see Lyle Goldstein, "Resetting the U.S.-China Security Relationship," *Survival*, Vol. 53, No. 2, April-May 2011, pp.98–9, and Michael Swaine, *America's Challenge, Engaging a Rising China in the Twenty-First Century* (Washington: Carnegie Endowment for International Peace, 2011), p.360 and footnote 31, p.619.

6   Office of the Secretary of Defense, "Military and Security Developments Involving the People's Republic of China 2011," August 2011, p.2; Jonathan Adams, "Why US Ignores China and Sells Arms to Taiwan," *Christian Science Monitor*, February 18, 2010.

7   Robert Sutter, "Taiwan's Future: Narrowing Straits," (Washington: The National Bureau of Asian Research, May 2011), pp.16 and 5.

8   Lyle Goldstein, "Resetting the U.S.-China Security Relationship," *Survival*, Vol. 53, No. 2, April-May 2011, pp.108–9.

9   Under current circumstances, the best bilateral political agreement with China that Taiwan can hope for is commonly termed a "peace agreement"— essentially a promise by China not to use force against Taiwan in exchange for Taiwan's promise not to seek political independence. Such an agreement, however, would not allay the deep suspicion existing on both sides: Taiwan would still fear a change in China's stated intention not to attack the island while China would retain deep anxiety about the emergence of new political leadership that seeks juridical independence for Taiwan at some future time. As one example of such fears on the Taiwanese side, the island's military currently resists even the discussion with China of "confidence building measures"—which typically fall far short of actual arms reductions. See Alan D. Romberg, "Cross-Strait Relations: Weathering the Storm," *China Leadership Monitor*, No. 30, November 2009, pp.14–15.

10   See Taiwan Relations Act, United States Code, Title 22, Chapter 48, Sections 3301–16.

11   Mark Valencia, "Tempting the Dragon," *Far Eastern Economic Review*, March 11, 2009.

12   Martin Fackler, "Japan Plans Military Shift to Focus More on China," *New York Times*, December 12, 2010; Rahul Prakash, "Japan's New Defence Policy: A Shift from the Past?," Observer Research Foundation, December 28, 2010, www.orfonline.com/cms/sites/orfonline/modules/analysis; "Summary of National Defense Program Guidelines for FY 2011 and beyond," Japan Ministry of Defense, approved by the Security Council and the Cabinet on December 17, 2010, http://www.mod.go.jp/e/d_act/d_policy/pdf/summaryFY2011.pdf.

13   "Japan's MOX Program and Nuclear Proliferation," Tokyo: Citizens Nuclear Information Center, May 15, 2009, http://cnic.jp/english/topics/cycle/MOX/moxprolif.html.

14   The White House, Office of the Press Secretary, "FACT SHEET: The United States in the Trans-Pacific Partnership," November 12, 2011.

15 U.S. Department of Agriculture, "Selected Success Stories on U.S. Exports to China in 2010," April 15, 2011, http://gain.fas.usda.gov/Recent%20 GAIN%20Publications/Selected%20Success%20Stories%20on%20U.S.%20 Exports%20to%20China%20in%202010_Beijing_China%20-%20 Peoples%20Republic%20of_4-15-2011.pdf.

16 Statement of the U.S. Chamber of Commerce on the Trans-Pacific Partnership, (Hearing of the U.S. House of Representatives Committee on Ways and Means, December 14, 2011), p.5.

17 Doug Bandow, Senior Fellow, Cato Institute, Washington, DC, private communication with author, December 2011.

18 Leith Anderson et al., "From Helsinki to Pyongyang; How to deal with North Korea? Nixon showed the way," *Wall Street Journal*, January 18, 2003.

19 Henry Kissinger, *Diplomacy*, (New York: Simon & Schuster, 1994), p.759.

20 Andrew Jacobs, "Leading China Dissident Gets 11-Year Term for Subversion," *New York Times*, December 25, 2009.

21 Sharon LaFraniere, "China Indicts Prominent Dissident," *New York Times*, December 12, 2009.

22 Andrew Higgins and Anne E. Kornblut, "Obama Pushes China on Currency, Human Rights," *Washington Post*, November 17, 2009.

23 Wei Jingsheng, "President Obama, Push Back on China," *New York Times*, December 30, 2009.

24 Edward Cody, "U.S. Reopens Talks with Chinese on Rights," *Washington Post*, May 28, 2008; The White House, Office of the Press Secretary, *U.S.-China Joint Statement*, Beijing: November 17, 2009, p.3.

25 U.S. Department of State, "Briefing on the U.S.-China Human Rights Dialogue," May 14, 2010, http://www.state.gov/r/pa/prs/ps/2010/05/141899. html.

Chapter Eight

1 The Constitution of Japan, Article 9, *National Diet Library*, http://www.ndl. go.jp/constitution/e/etc/c01.html#s2

2 Japan External Trade Organization (JETRO), "Analysis of Japan-China Trade for 2011 and Outlook for 2012," Press Release, February 23, 2012, http:// www.jetro.go.jp/en/news/releases/20120223142-news.

3 Yukio Hatoyama, "A New Path for Japan," *New York Times*, August 27, 2009.

4 Mike M. Mochizuki, "Dealing with a Rising China," in Thomas U. Berger, Mike M. Mochizuki and Jitsuo Tsuchiyama, eds, *"Japan in International Politics,"* (Boulder: Lynne Rienner Publishers, 2007), p.229.

5 Richard J. Samuels, *Securing Japan*, (Ithaca: Cornell University Press 2007), p.269

6 Kenneth B. Pyle, *Japan Rising*, (New York: Public Affairs 2007), p.327.

7 Ibid., p.326.

8   Michael J. Green, *Japan's Reluctant Realism,* (New York: Palgrave 2003), pp.78–9.

9   Christopher W. Hughes, *Japan's Re-emergence as a "Normal" Military Power,* Adelphi Paper 368 (New York: Oxford University Press; London: International Institute for Strategic Studies 2004), p.93.

10 Pyle, *Japan Rising,* pp.366–7; Hughes, *Japan's Re-emergence as a "Normal" Military Power,* pp.11–12.

11 Testimony of Air Force Lt. Gen. Henry Oberding III, House Armed Services subcommittee hearing, March 9, 2006.

12 Samuels, *Securing Japan,* p.136.

13 Ibid., p.144.

14 Naoko Munakata, "China's Impact and Regional Economic Integration – A Japanese Perspective," *Statement before the U.S.-China Economic and Security Review Commission,* December 4, 2003. Following the March 2011 disaster at the Fukushima-Daiichi nuclear plant, fears of "hollowing" have re-emerged in some regions where manufacturing industries have declined due to competition from South Korea, China and Taiwan. See Martin Fackler, "Declining as a Manufacturer, Japan Weighs Reinvention," *New York Times,* April 15, 2012.

15 Kiyoshi Takenaka, "Japan, China Look to Trade Talks, Debt Buys," *Reuters,* December 25, 2011.

16 "Japan's TPP Participation Key to Asia-Pacific Economic Integration," *Yomiuri Shimbun,* November 15, 2011 (emphasis added).

17 Green, *Japan's Reluctant Realism,* pp, 194–195; Lu Zhongwei, "Sino-Japanese Relations: Understanding and Promoting," in *Contemporary International Relations* 12, No. 10, October 2003, p.506.

18 Michael J. Green, *Adjusting to Untested Political Terrain,* Comparative Connections, (Honolulu: Pacific Forum CSIS, January 2010), pp.2–3.

19 Michael H. Armacost and Kenneth B. Pyle, "Japan and the Unification of Korea: Challenges for American Policy Coordination," in Nicholas Eberstadt and Richard J. Ellings, eds, *Korea's Future and the Great Powers* (Seattle: University of Washington Press, 2001), p.134.

20 Mike M. Mochizuki, *China-Japan Relations: Downward Spiral or a New Equilibrium,* in David Shambaugh, ed., "Power Shift," (Berkeley: University of California Press, 2005), p.147.

21 Samuels, *Securing Japan,* p.139.

22 Peter Van Ness, "Japan, the Indispensable Power in Northeast Asia," *Global Asia,* Vol. 5, No. 1, Spring 2010, p.92.

23 "Chugoku no shinko mo sotei" [Hypothesizing Even a 'Chinese Attack']," *Asahi Shimbun,* September 26, 2006; cited in Mochizuki, *Dealing with a Rising China,* p.248.

24 "China, Japan Reach Principled Consensus on East China Sea Issue," *Xinhua,* June 18, 2008; "Expert: Agreement on East China Sea Development 'Flexible and Pragmatic,' *Xinhua,* June 18, 2008.

25 "Choppy Waters," *The Economist*, January 21, 2010.

26 Ian Johnson, "China and Japan Bristle Over Disputed Chain of Islands," *New York Times*, September 8, 2010; Martin Fackler and Ian Johnson, "Arrest in Disputed Seas Riles China and Japan," *New York Times*, September 19, 2010; Martin Fackler, "Japan Retreats with Release of Chinese Boat Captain," *New York Times*, September 24, 2010; "Japan, U.S. to Begin Biggest-Ever Military Exercises on Friday," *The Hindu*, December 2, 2010; Todd Crowell, "US Sails with Japan to Flashpoint Channel," *Asia Times*, December 3, 2010.

27 James J. Przystup, "Japan China Relations: Another New Start," *Comparative Connections*, Honolulu: Pacific Forum CSIS, January 2012.

28 Buszynski, *Sino-Japanese Relations: Interdependence, Rivalry and Regional Security*, p.159.

29 Ibid., p.161; Rahul Prakash, "Japan's New Defence Policy: A Shift from the Past?," Observer Research Foundation, December, 28, 2010, www.orfonline. com/cms/sites/orfonline/modules/analysis.

30 Mochizuki, *China-Japan Relations: Downward Spiral or a New Equilibrium*, p.144; see also Samuels, *Securing Japan*, p.169.

31 Buszynski, *Sino-Japanese Relations: Interdependence, Rivalry and Regional Security*, pp.155 and 161.

32 Hitoshi Tanaka, *A Japanese Perspective on the China Question*, East Asia Insights, Vol. 3, No. 2 (Tokyo: Japan Center for International Exchange, May 2008), p.4.

33 Hitoshi Tanaka, *Getting China Policy Right*, East Asia Insights, Vol. 3, No. 6, Tokyo: Japan Center for International Exchange, December 2008, p.2; Hitoshi Tanaka, *Asia Uniting: Many Tiers, One Goal*, Global Asia, Vol. 5, No. 1, Spring 2010, pp.17 and 21; Ibid., pp.18 and 21, and Tanaka, *A Japanese Perspective on the China Question*, p.4.

34 Yoshihide Soeya, *Speech to the Sasakawa Peace Foundation*, November 20, 2008, p.4.

35 Ryo Sahashi, *New Thinking About Foreign Policy Strategy in Japan*, East Asia Forum, www.eastasiaforum.org, January 27, 2010, p.2.

36 Yoichi Funabashi, *A 21st Century Vision for the Alliance*, Honolulu: Pacific Forum CSIS, PacNet#7, February 18, 2010; See Susan Shirk, "American Hopes: An Agenda for Cooperation that Serves US Interests," *Global Asia*, Vol. 5, No. 1, Spring 2010, p.31.

37 Yoichi Funabashi, *A 21st Century Vision for the Alliance*, Pacific Forum CSIS, PacNet #7, February 18, 2010.

38 Shirk, "American Hopes: An Agenda for Cooperation that Serves US Interests," p.28.

39 Richard J. Samuels, *Securing Japan*, (Ithaca: Cornell University Press 2007), p.132.

40 George R. Packard, *The United States-Japan Security Treaty at 50*, Foreign Affairs, Vol. 89, Number 2, March/April 2010, pp.99–100.

41 Ayako Doi, *Risky Business: U.S. Pressure Over Okinawa Base Could Poison the Alliance*, PacNet #71A, Honolulu: Pacific Forum CSIS, November 4, 2009.

42 Yuka Hayashi, "U.S. Pushes for New Okinawa Site," *The Wall Street Journal*, January 29, 2010.

43 *Updating the U.S.-Japan Alliance: An Interview with Mike Finnegan, Richard Lawless, and Jim Thomas*, Washington: National Bureau of Asian Research, April 2, 2010, p.2.

44 Ibid., p.2.

45 Thom Shanker, "U.S. Agrees to Reduce Size of Force on Okinawa," *New York Times*, April 26, 2012 (emphasis added).

46 Packard, *The United States-Japan Security Treaty at 50*, p.101.

47 Sheila Smith, "Time for Leadership for the US-Japan Relationship," PacNet #35, Honolulu: Pacific Forum CSIS, July 29, 2010; Yuki Tatsumi, "Japan's Drift and its Implications for the US-Japan Alliance," PacNet #34, Honolulu: Pacific Forum CSIS, July 23, 2010.

48 Packard, *The United States-Japan Security Treaty at 50*, p.102.

49 Michael J. Green, *Japan's Reluctant Realism*, (New York: Palgrave 2003), pp.194–5.

50 Green, *Japan's Reluctant Realism*, p.108.

51 National Bureau of Asian Research, *Managing Unmet Expectations in the U.S.-Japan Alliance*, NBR Special Report #17, November 2009, p.25.

52 Alan Romberg, Comments on Soeya, *Speech to the Sasakawa Peace Foundation*, p.13.

Chapter Nine

1 Cheon Seong-chang, "Establishing Supranational Institutions: European Lessons for a Unified Korea," East Asian Review, Vol. 16, No. 1, Spring 2004, pp.73–4; Bonnie S. Glaser and Scott Snyder, *Responding to Change on the Korean Peninsula*, Washington: Center for Strategic and International Studies, May 2010, p.9.

2 Chung-in Moon, "An Unavoidable Choice," *Chosun Ilbo*, April 12, 2005.

3 Cho Hyun, "Complex Legacies: Bridge-Building in Northeast Asia," *Global Asia*, Vol. 5, No. 1 (Spring 2010), pp.22–6.

4 *A New Era of Leadership*, www.Korea.net (November 2009), p.9; Scott A. Snyder and Seukhoon Paul Choi, "From Aid to Development Partnership," Working Paper, (Washington: Council on Foreign Relations February 2012), p.3.

5 David C. Kang, *China Rising*, (New York: Columbia University Press, 2007), p.105.

6 "The Responses of U.S. Allies and Security Partners in East Asia to China's Rise," *Pacific Currents*, Santa Monica: RAND (2008), p.82.

7   Meeting with President Lee Myung-bak, Council on Foreign Relations, September 21, 2009, http://www.cfr.org/africa/meeting-his-excellency-lee-myung-bak-video/p20246.

8   U.S.-China Business Council, *Foreign Direct Investment in China*, 2009, www.uschina.org/statistics/fdi_cumulative.html; Scott A. Snyder, "China-Korea Relations: New Challenges in the Post Kim Jong Il Era."

9   Scott A. Snyder, *China's Rise and the Two Koreas*, (Boulder: Lynne Rienner Publishers, 2009), p.47; Jae Ho Chung, *Between Ally and Partner*, (New York: Columbia University Press, 2007), p.94; "China, South Korea to Negotiate toward FTA: Communique," *China Post*, January 12, 2012; "China, Japan, China to Pursue Trilateral Free Trade Agreement," Dong-A Ilbo, December 17, 2011, http://www.truthabouttrade.org/2011/12/17/korea-china-japan-to-pursue-trilateral-free-trade-agreement; Scott A. Snyder and See-won Byun, "China-Korea Relations: New Challenges in the Post Kim Jong Il Era," *Comparative Connections*, Honolulu: Pacific Forum CSIS, January 2012.

10 "China, South Korea Start Talks on Free-Trade Pact, *Bloomberg News*, May 2, 2012, http://www.bloomberg.com/news/print/2012-05-02/china-south-korea-start-talks-on-free-trade-pact.html.

11 Taeho Kim, "Sino-ROK relations at 15: An Overview and Assessment," (Hong Kong: Centre for Asian Pacific Studies, Lingnan University, August 2007), p.19.

12 David Hundt, *The Rise of China and South Korea: Sunshine and Beyond*, (Melbourne: Deakin University, April 2010); see www.scientificcommons.org.

13 Taeho Kim, "Sino-ROK relations at 15: An Overview and Assessment," pp.18–19.

14 Snyder, *China's Rise and the Two Koreas*, pp.112 and 114; Sang-Hun Choe, *China Gains Influence in Korean Affairs as North and South Warily Seek Its Help, New York Times*, April 2010; Snyder and Byun, "China-Korea Relations: New Challenges in the Post Kim Jong Il Era."

15 Han Ki-heung, "China's Next Province?," *Dong-A Ilbo*, March 23, 2006.

16 Shen Dingli, "North Korea's Strategic Significance to China," *China Security*, (Washington: World Security Institute, Autumn 2006), p.20.

17 Ibid., p.21.

18 Ibid., p.22.

19 Interview with former U.S. Department of Defense official who served on the joint planning staff, January 2009.

20 Jashree Bajoria, *The China-North Korea Relationship,* (New York: Council on Foreign Relations, July 2009), p.2; Glaser and Snyder, *Responding to Change on the Korean Peninsula*, p.22; Scott Snyder, China-Korea Relations: "Fire Sale, Hot Money, and Anxieties about Investment," *Comparative Connections*, Honolulu: Pacific Forum CSIS, April 2010, pp.3–4; "China leases Rajin Port in North Korea's East Coast," *Reuters*, March 14, 2010.

21 Jae Ho Chung, *Between Ally and Partner*, pp.108–9 and 119.

22 Frank James, *U.S., N. Korea Claim Win as UN Condemns Ship Sinking*, National Public Radio, July 9, 2010, www.npr.org.

23 Na Jeong-ju, "Obama Criticizes China for 'Willful Blindness' to NK Provocation," *Korea Times*, June 28, 2010; Victor Cha, "U.S.-Korea Relations: The Sinking of the Cheonan," *Comparative Connections*, (Honolulu: Pacific Forum CSIS, July 2010); Victor Cha, "U.S.-Korea Relations: Smooth Sailing in the Wake of the Cheonan," *Comparative Connections*, (Honolulu: Pacific Forum CSIS, October, 2010).

24 Elizabeth Bumiller and Edward Wong, "China Warily Eyes U.S.-Korea Drills," *The New York Times*, July 20, 2010; Cha, "U.S.-Korea Relations: Smooth Sailing in the Wake of the Cheonan"; Bonnie Glaser, "U.S.-China Relations: Tensions Rise and Fall Once Again," *Comparative Connections*, (Honolulu: Pacific Forum CSIS, October, 2010).

25 "More than 40 N. Korean Soldiers Killed or Injured During Yeonpyeong Battle: Report," *Yonhap News Agency*, March 2, 2012; "10 NK Deaths in Yeonpyeong Response," *The Daily NK*, March 2, 2012; Victor Cha, "U.S.-Korea Relations: A Tumultuous Ending of Year 2010," *Comparative Connections*, (Honolulu: Pacific Forum CSIS, January 2011).

26 Steve Herman, "N. Korea Says Live-Fire Drill Will Prompt Another Attack," *VOA News.com*, December 17, 2010; John M. Glionna, "Seoul Unfazed by North Korea's Threats Over Military Drills," *Los Angeles Times*, December 19, 2010.

27 Charles Keyes, "General: South Korea Drill Could Cause 'Chain Reaction," CNN, December 16, 2010; http://articles.cnn.com/2010-12-16/us/korea. military.exercise_1_military-exercises-live-fire-pyongyang?_s=PM:US; U.S. Department of State, Daily Press Briefing, December 16, 2010, http://www. state.gov/r/pa/prs/dpb/2010/12/153016. html.

28 Mark McDonald and Martin Fackler, "North Korea Says It Will Not Retaliate After South's Drills," *New York Times*, December 20, 2010; Victor Cha, "U.S.-Korea Relations: A Tumultuous Ending of Year 2010," *Comparative Connections*, (Honolulu: Pacific Forum CSIS, January 2011).

29 Young-jin Kim, "US Troops in Korea to be Deployed to Conflict Areas," *Korea Times*, July 23, 2010.

30 Chung, *Between Ally and Partner*, pp.108–9 and 119.

31 Glaser and Snyder, *Responding to Change on the Korean Peninsula*, pp.31–2.

32 Shen, "North Korea's Strategic Significance to China," p.22.

33 Michael McDevitt, "The Post-Korean Unification Security Landscape and U.S. Security Policy in Northeast Asia," in *Korea's Future and the Great Powers*, Nicholas Eberstadt and Richard J. Ellings, eds, (Seattle: University of Washington Press, 2001), pp.264–5.

34 Michael McDevitt, "The Post-Korean Unification Security Landscape and U.S. Security Policy in Northeast Asia," in *Korea's Future and the Great Powers*, Nicholas Eberstadt and Richard J. Ellings, eds, pp.264–5.

35   "Human Rights in North Korea," *Wikipedia*, http://en.wikipedia.org/wiki/
     Human_rights_in_North_Korea.

36   Stephan Haggard and Marcus Noland, "Economic Crime and Punishment in
     North Korea," (Washington: Peterson Institute of International Economics,
     March 2010), pp.11–12.

Chapter Ten

1   Robert B. Zoellick, Deputy Secretary of State, "Whither China: From
     Membership to Responsibility?," Remarks to National Committee
     on U.S.-China Relations, September 21, 2005; http://www.ncuscr.org/
     files/2005Gala_RobertZoellick_Whither_China1.pdf.

2   USCBC Report: Total Yearly US State Exports to China Pass $100 Billion for the
     First Time," The US-China Business Council, Washington, DC, March 28, 2012,
     https://www.uschina.org/public/documents/2012/03/yearly-us-exports.html.

3   Thomas L. Friedman and Michael Mandelbaum, *That Used to Be Us*, (New
     York: Farrar, Straus and Giroux, 2011), pp.351–2.

4   U.S. National Intelligence Council, *Global Trends 2025: A Transformed
     World*, (Washington: Office of the Director of National Intelligence,
     November 2008).

5   David Hambling, "China Looks to Undermine U.S. Power, With 'Assassin's
     Mace'," July 2, 2009, www.wired.com/danger_room.

6   The White House, Office of the Press Secretary, Remarks of President Barack
     Obama, State of the Union Address, "An America Built to Last," January 24,
     2012.

7   "Mitt Romney's 59 Economic Flavors," *Wall Street Journal*, September 7, 2011.

Epilogue

1   U.S. Embassy Beijing, "China: Toast of the President at a Banquet Honoring
     Premier Chou En-Lai of the People's Republic of China at a Banquet
     Honoring the President in Peking, February 21, 1972; http://beijing.
     usembassy-china.org.cn/uploads/images/KSGdr5mRZX9WHAA2cyiw4Q/
     Toasts_of_the_President_and_Premier_Chou_En-lai_of_the_Peoples_
     Republic_of_China_at_a_Banquet_Honoring_the_President_in_Peking.pdf.

2   President Jimmy Carter, Address to the Nation on Diplomatic
     Relations Between the United States and the People's Republic of
     China, December 15, 1978; http://www.presidency.ucsb.edu/ws/index.
     php?pid=30308#axzz1ovsXSHyx.

3   U.S Embassy Beijing, "Remarks [of President Ronald Reagan] to Chinese
     Community Leaders in Beijing, China," April 27, 1984; http://beijing.

usembassy-china.org.cn/uploads/images/kXU4O4MWEdt5j2u8SVEFhQ/
Remarks_to_Chinese_Community_Leaders_in_Beijing.pdf

4   The White House, Office of the Press Secretary, "Remarks by the President on U.S.-China Relations in the 21st Century," June 11, 1998; http://clinton4. nara.gov/textonly/WH/New/html/19980611-18132.html.

5   "Remarks by Samuel R. Berger Assistant to the President for National Security Affairs," January 11, 2001; http://www.cfr.org/us-strategy-and-politics/remarks-samuel-r-berger-assistant-president-national-security-affairs/ p3870.

6   Q & A with Lt General Brent Scowcroft, U.S. Department of State, Office of the Historian, Conference on "Transforming the Cold War: The United States and China, 1969–1980," September 25, 2006, http://history.state.gov/ conferences/2006-china-cold-war.

7   James Baker: "Those Who View China as Threat 'Dangerously Wrong'," Asia Society, March 29, 2011; http://asiasociety.org/blog/asia/ james-baker-those-who-view-china-threat-dangerously-wrong.

8   Henry Paulson, Jr., Speech in Hong Kong, April 11, 2011, http://www. chinausfocus.com/finance-economy/increase-of-mutual-investments-will-strengthen-the-relations-between-us-and-china.

9   Kissinger, *On China*, (New York: The Penguin Press, 2011), p.530.

10 Zbigniew Brzezinski, "Balancing the East, Upgrading the West," *Foreign Affairs*, January/February 2012, pp.97 and 101.

INDEX